Jack Thomson

# AN Understanding Teenagers' Reading

## READING PROCESSES
## AND THE TEACHING OF LITERATURE

Jack Thomson

# Understanding Teenagers' Reading

## READING PROCESSES AND THE TEACHING OF LITERATURE

**NP**
NEW YORK

**CROOM HELM**
LONDON

methuen
AUSTRALIA

METHUEN AUSTRALIA PTY LTD
44 Waterloo Road, North Ryde, N.S.W. 2113
Melbourne     Adelaide     Brisbane     Perth

First published 1987

Set in 10/12 point Roman
by Midland Typesetters


National Library of Australia

Cataloguing-in-Publication Data
Thomson, Jack.

   Understanding teenagers' reading

   Bibliography.
   Includes index.
   ISBN 0 454 01443 0.

   1. Literature - Study and teaching (Secondary). 2.
   Creative writing (Secondary education). 3. Youth -
   Books and reading. I. Title.

807'.12


First published in the United States of America in 1987 by
Nichols Publishing Company, Post Office Box 96, New
York, NY 10024

Library of Congress

Cataloguing-in-Publication Data
Thomson, Jack.

   Understanding teenagers reading.

   Bibliography: p.
   1. Literature - Study and teaching (Secondary) -
   Australia. 2. Developmental reading. I. Title.

PN71.A8T46 1987   807'.1294
87-18585
ISBN 0 89397 289 4

# 1 TEACHING LITERATURE: MORE QUESTIONS THAN ANSWERS

> We had the experience but missed the meaning.
> T.S. Eliot, 'The Dry Salvages', *Four Quartets*.

## LITERATURE IN SOCIETY AND SCHOOL

You don't have to be a research investigator of reading habits in our society to know that the reading of literature is not central to the lives of most people. Few people read much either at school or when they have left, and of those few who do see reading as an important leisure activity, only a minority read what school syllabuses have tried to make them value as good literature. Mills and Boon sell better than Patrick White and Martin Boyd despite the fact that Mills and Boon don't get the large captive readership that being prescribed on school and university reading lists ensures.

Who or what is to blame, then, for this failure of literary education? Is it some aspect of the education 'system' whose hierarchical structures and bureaucratic malaise have produced authoritarian schools, imposed syllabuses and pliant teachers? Is it the universities, as the institutions responsible for the academic education of teachers and the major influences on the selection of texts set for study in the public examinations? Is it the Colleges of Advanced Education, as the institutions responsible for the professional training of teachers? Is it permissive parents, the television and home video industries, the community at large and its values? Is it that reading literature is not a worthwhile activity anyway; or that we don't know enough about the productive strategies to pass them on to others? Perhaps reading literature is, after all, merely the cultivated and bizarre taste of a well-to-do, eccentric and impractical elite, something akin to eating caviar and artichokes, for example? It is about time we tried to find out these things.

I find my own history as a reader, at least until the age of about 27, more representative then exemplary. At that age I was just beginning to learn how to read from the work I was doing for a Masters degree in English Literature. I had also been teaching English in secondary schools for seven years, without knowing much about why I was doing it or how to go about it.

As a high-school pupil, I read pretty well nothing beyond set texts, very quickly picking up the message of the hidden curriculum at my selective high school that reading books had little relevance to academic success. Besides, not one English teacher ever suggested the title of a book worth reading outside school, or conveyed the impression by word or example that reading might be an enjoyable or valuable experience.

Having performed creditably in English at school, without ever doing much reading, I went on to study English at university where the lecturers assumed that all the students were committed, sophisticated and voracious readers either of the 'great tradition' of English literature or of works of historical significance in the development of literary genres and forms. They never attempted to test that assumption despite clear prima facie evidence that it was nonsense. We were all too busy playing the academic games of pseudo-literary criticism and presumptuously ranking the world's great writers on a league table of merit, their positions on the table depending on how 'life promoting' they were, to use an expression we all picked up and never understood. Without knowing why, we also got the feeling we were terribly virtuous for studying English. There was an idea about the place that doing English was morally fine and made you a better person. Again, there was no evidence whatsoever that English lecturers and students were better or more civilised than others, but it was reassuring to feel superior to those taking utilitarian courses in things like how to build bridges or heal the sick. It was comforting to be a member of an elite preserving civilising values during the dark ages of post-industrial capitalism, and if you felt guilty about your ignorance of current affairs and your political naïveté , it was particularly consoling to know that 'the poem itself' with its organic unity was of eternal value while McCarthyism, the Suez crisis and the Budapest uprising were merely trivial temporal disturbances to a system that would soon right itself if it could only attain the perfection of art and balance and reconcile its opposite and discordant impulses.

I felt that I, in particular, needed all this security because, behind the self-righteous glow, I had increasingly uneasy feelings that I didn't understand the literature any more than the politics, and that while others managed to get worked up about the 'simple, sensuous and passionate' nature of poetry, it left me alarmingly cold. The more

I listened to the lectures, the more I realised that it would be unwise to try to do any thinking for myself or to record my own honest responses in essays or examinations. Like many others, I read the set books dutifully and then found out what was important to know about them by reading and making extensive notes from books of literary criticism. It was digests of these notes that I swotted for the examinations, which I duly passed.

The notion that there might be a range of theories of literary criticism, each with different answers to questions about what reading literature entailed or was useful for; that each of these theories of literature enshrined a particular ideology; that one of these theories was held by my lecturers (and others rejected); that I was being culturally shaped by unwittingly and covertly absorbing the theory in vogue at my university at that time: all this was, in the 1950s, as remote from my imagination as hitchhiking in the galaxy was from my vacation pursuits.

Now, as an English teacher of nearly 30 years' experience, I find that school students of the 1980s are confronting the same sorts of difficulties I had in the 1950s. We invite them to participate in an activity, a game — reading literature — which we regard as enjoyable, valuable and useful in various ways, but we don't pass on the rules of the game or the strategies for playing it well. We simply point out how certain masterplayers have performed in specific instances, how eminent critics have read and interpreted individual books. We have not systematically identified and passed on the rules and strategies that make for what Johnathan Culler calls 'literary competence'[1].

## PRECEPT AND PRACTICE IN THE TEACHING OF LITERATURE

Between what we claim to be teaching in literature and what most of our students are actually experiencing and learning there lies a gigantic chasm:

1. We claim we are trying to develop a love of reading but our practices prohibit pleasure. Most students can read, but very few choose to do so for enjoyment.
2. We claim we are extending students' understanding of life and enhancing their personal development, but we often choose books that don't speak to our students about the issues that concern them most. Particularly is this true of many of the literary texts set for the Higher School Certificate examination.

3. We claim we are 'fostering enjoyment and the encouragement of reading interests, insight into human nature and the relationship of language and literature to it' (NSW Syllabus in English, Years 7 to 10, Objectives), but we set examinations that test knowledge about literary methods rather than the quality of literary experience. The responses we claim we want to develop (sensitivity, discrimination, taste) are the ones most difficult to assess by written examination, so we test the most easily testable things: the factual, so-called 'objective' analysis rather than the subjective, honest, felt response; knowledge of literary forms, conventions and techniques rather than an understanding of how they work.

Where, then, can we look for guidance? What might be done to improve matters?

## STARTING POINTS

A logical procedure would be to begin by finding out what students' reading habits are and examining current theory, research and teaching practice to see what help they might offer in answering questions such as: Why read literature? How do good readers read? How do school students at different levels of literary development read? What satisfactions do they seek and attain from reading, and from which books? What bores them, and what does boredom mean? What activities in class do they find productive/unproductive/ destructive to their reading development?

The unanswered questions might then become the starting points for further investigations. This is the procedure adopted for this research project, and it provides the rationale of this book and the form of its organisation.

Contemporary reader-response literary criticism tells us that literature should be conceived of as an activity, and experience rather than as an object of study; and reading and responding to literature should be conceived of as processes of making and sharing meanings, as ways of exploring and understanding what it means to live, as well as ways of understanding one's own and authors' meaning-making processes. The problem is how to teach literature so that it is seen, read and responded to in these ways by our students. What is needed is a deeper understanding of exactly how we and our students read literature, what kinds of things we actually do when we read well, and what kinds of things we do or don't do when we read badly. If we knew more about our own reading processes and those of our students (both productive and unproductive strategies), as well as the stages in the growth of mature literary judgment, from what Margaret Early has called 'unconscious enjoyment' to 'conscious delight'[2], we might be able to create more appropriate contexts and situations in our classrooms within which our students might read more literature with more enjoyment at the same time as learning to read and respond progressively more deeply.

## THE RESEARCH PROJECT

This book, then, is about the theory and practice of reading and teaching literature. It examines critical theory for any insights that might be used to improve the practices of reading and teaching, and it reports the discoveries of a research project devised to investigate what secondary school students read, why they read or don't read, and how they go about reading. It is the last aspect of the investigation that proved to be the most illuminating; that is, the students' reading-learning processes — the developmental stages involved and the strategies they use — and the implications of both process-stages and process-strategies for the teaching of literature.

The research data consists of the written questionnaires completed by all the students in Year 8 (13 to 14 year-olds) and Year 10 (15 to 16 year-olds) attending the two State high schools in Bathurst, NSW, in both 1978 and 1984, transcripts of individual interviews with five per cent of these students and written questionnaires completed by their English teachers. The students' written questionnaires provided information about what they read (and view) and why; the interviews provided information about how they read (process-strategies) and what progress looks like, in terms of identifiable developmental levels (process-stages); while the teachers' questionnaires provided information about their purposes and methods in the teaching of literature — the attitudes, values and organised classroom activities that would be influencing the attitudes and reading habits of the students surveyed.

The major aim of the investigation was to formulate both a process model and a developmental model of literary response and to relate them to one another so as to reach some understanding not only of what progress in literary learning might look like (what staging points or levels can be identified to mark progress) but also, and more significantly, what strategies students use at each particular staging point or level.

Knowing where their students are at (stages) and exactly how they read (strategies) would be of tremendous help to teachers in developing reading programmes for both whole classes, groups within classes and individual students. Such knowledge, or the power to find it readily, would be of crucial importance in helping teachers make more reliable decisions about:

- selecting or negotiating class texts for shared reading and response-developing activities;

- selecting/negotiating a range of texts for group work in class (with group selection being based, at least some of the time, on clearly identified developmental levels of response shared by members);

- matching individual pupils with individual books in a wide-reading programme; and

- planning developmental reading programmes for individuals and groups within classes, so that each student progresses in manageable stages to higher levels of response through being taught the strategies needed, at the time he or she is ready and able to master them.

In his book *Developing Response to Fiction*, Robert Protherough articulated the kinds of uncertainty experienced by English teachers when we try to be explicit about what it is that novels do to and for our pupils:

. . . they [English teachers] are suspicious of a gulf between the actual responses of children and what as teachers they *feel* should be made of the stories read. Most of all, they are uncertain of what their own role should be in "teaching" a novel. They are uncomfortably aware that there are no clear links between teaching and pupil response, no secure models of how that response develops, and not even any consensus about the kind of language in which to explore these processes.[3]

This book is addressed primarily to English teachers. I hope it will prove to be of practical use in helping you to clarify for yourselves 'what (your) role should be in teaching a novel'. To that end it provides:

1. a model of how pupil response develops;
2. ideas about ways you might connect your teaching with the way pupils respond, ways of identifying exactly what skills the students have and building on them so they might be helped to develop their responsiveness through increasing mastery of a set of strategies of increasing sophistication and power; and
3. suggestions about the kinds of language appropriate (for students, if not for teachers) for exploring and communicating response, from tentative first thoughts to highly ordered and explicit final drafts.

## REFERENCES

1. Johnathan Culler, *Structuralist Poetics*, Routledge and Kegan Paul, London, 1975.

2. Margaret Early, 'Stages of Growth in Literary Appreciation', *English Journal*, vol. XLIV, March 1960, pp.161-67.

3. Robert Protherough, *Developing Response to Fiction*, Open University Press, Milton Keynes, 1983, p.4.

# 2  STUDENTS' READING AND VIEWING HABITS

This chapter summarises and explores the main implications of the written questionnaire completed by all the students in Years 8 and 10 of the two Bathurst secondary schools in 1978 and 1984. The information collected includes the students' reading and television/video viewing habits and attitudes. There were 1007 students involved in the survey, 541 in Year 8 (250 in 1978 and 291 in 1984) and 466 in Year 10 (213 in 1978 and 253 in 1984).

## THE RESEARCH FINDINGS

The message of a great mass of statistics is stark and clear: teenagers spend a lot of time watching television and video, and very little time reading. The majority watches television for more than three hours a night; over 30 per cent read no books outside school set texts; only 20 per cent read books regularly, and of these only a small minority reads what teachers would regard as good children's and adolescent literature. Mental passivity is the characteristic feature of all the leisure pursuits of the majority.

## *THE AMOUNT OF READING*

The Bathurst findings are comparable with those of other surveys conducted in Australia and overseas. Table 1 compares the amount of book reading by the Bathurst students in 1978 and 1984 with that of students in two other major surveys: the massive English Schools Council project, 'Children's Reading Habits 10-15', carried out between 1969 and 1974 under the direction of Frank Whitehead at the University of Sheffield Institute of Education[1], and the 1977 Australian survey of eight Sydney secondary schools and one country secondary school carried out by Ken Watson of Sydney University[2].

Table 1: Comparison of the average number of books read
in one month

| Group | Year 8 (aged 13-14) | Year 10 aged (15-16) |
|---|---|---|
| Whitehead's English students | (aged 12-13) 2.2 | (aged 14-15) 1.9 |
| Bathurst students — 1978 | 1.9 | 1.7 |
| — 1984 | 1.4 | 1.5 |
| Watson's Sydney students | 3.2 | 3.0 |

## Comments

1.  The Schools Council survey showed that English students did less voluntary reading as they grew older. The older ages of the Bathurst groups relative to their compared English groups suggests that the differences in amount of reading between the English and the Bathurst students is not very significant. The figures for the two groups would certainly be closer if the ages were the same.

2.  Ken Watson's sample excluded students who 'were experiencing considerable difficulty in the act of reading', and his figures include texts read for English classes as well as those read outside of school. Both the Schools Council and Bathurst samples include backward readers and the figures exclude class texts.

3.  The 1984 Bathurst students, while appearing to read less than their 1978 counterparts, were actually reading more, as more texts were being read in English classes in 1984 than in 1978. Whereas a class text generally occupied a whole term in 1978, in 1984 all but bottom stream classes were averaging about one novel a month, or three to four each term.

4.  There were very few students in the Bathurst survey who read any poetry outside school. 'I hate poetry' was a frequently offered unsolicited comment. The only poetry that was popular with any group was the poetry in *Dolly* magazine, mentioned by 18 per cent of Year 10 girls in 1984.

## TELEVISION VIEWING AND NOVEL READING

A colossal amount of time is spent watching television and considerably less time reading literature. The average number of programmes watched each night by the Bathurst Year 8 students was 6.4 in 1978 and 5.1 in 1984; Year 10 students averaged 5.1 in 1978 and 4.1 in 1984. These figures compare with the findings of other surveys. Tindall and Reid in 1974 and 1975, and Tindall, Reid and Goodwin in 1976 found that the average viewing of Sydney school children was approximately three hours a day, and that 20 per cent watched far more than four and a half hours a day.[3] Ken Watson in 1977 found that 45 per cent of Year 8 students in his New South Wales survey watched more than 20 hours a week and only 27 per cent watched twelve hours or less, while 48 per cent of Year 10 students watched more than 16 hours a week and only 22 per cent watched eight hours or less.[4] The Schools Council study in England found that the average viewing of English students aged 10 to 15 was two and a half hours a day.[5]

The main attitudes are clear in the following representative comments by Bathurst students. In answer to the question, 'How many programmes do you watch each night?' many replied, 'As many as what's on'. In many of the homes, television is on continuously from the time the students arrive home from school until they go to bed after 11 o'clock. The attitude of a generation of children familiar with media noise from birth is summed up by a Year 8 girl who said, 'I watch four to six programmes a night. When I'm doing homework I can't concentrate with dead silence.' A top-stream Year 8 girl who watches 'as many as are on', said, 'I haven't really got a favourite programme. I like a mixture and if I don't like a film I do knitting or something.' This comment reflects the attitude and behaviour of many. There is little thought given to selecting a programme for viewing and no thought of turning off a programme which is not being enjoyed. Many students react to television boredom merely by doing something else as well as watching it. Television is the main foreground noise in the lives of the majority of these students. When it isn't the foreground noise, it is often the background noise. Rarely is it shut out during the evening hours of transmission.

In addition to television viewing, over one third of the Bathurst students in the 1984 survey watched two or more films a week on home video. The average number of films viewed each week in 1984 was 1.5 for both Year 8 and Year 10 students. The amount of home video viewing explains the diminution of television viewing in 1984 as compared with 1978. The following is a representative student comment on video viewing: 'I used to read a couple of books every week but when we got video I quit reading.' (Year 10 boy).

In their television viewing preferences boys and girls shared a liking for comedy ('Happy Days', 'Fawlty Towers') but differed in other respects. Boys favoured sport, violent action and science fiction (Rugby League, 'The A Team', 'Magnum', 'The Fall Guy', 'Dr Who'), while girls preferred romance, soap opera and pop music ('Dynasty', 'Dallas', 'The Restless Years', 'A Country Practice', 'Countdown'). Sex differences were also apparent in magazine reading. In the magazines they prefer (*Dolly*, *Women's Weekly*, *New Idea*, *Cleo*, *Cosmopolitan*, *TV Week*, *Woman's Day*, *Seventeen*, *Girl*), girls avidly read articles on romance, fashion, teenage problems ('What should I do to be popular'), advice on health, make-up, relationships, and the lives of pop-stars and movie stars. Reading magazines was not nearly as popular with boys. The most popular boys' magazines were those about cars, motor-bikes and trucks, and most readers were in lower stream classes. The danger is that the magazines which girls read, and which are written for their age and sex, might give them stereotyped attitudes about the role of women in society.

The following are representative comments describing the kinds of television programmes most liked by boys and girls.

**Action/suspense:** boys comments:

'an action-packed adventure, murder, thriller, mystery series'

'a kung-fu action-packed adventure with martial arts and weapons'

'an adventure programme with police and gangsters and plenty of shoot-outs'

'I would like to see good fights, car chases and smashes, sex, bikes, bike fights and disco music'

'I would ask for an exciting cop show full of action with some laughs in it. I think a cross between "Starsky and Hutch" and "Mash".'

'thrillers — a real suspense thriller with a hero that nearly dies, plus sex'

'action-packed violence, sex and fights with tough guys'

'sex, blood, vilens, horra, excitement, lots of laughs, drugs, boose, all in Spase'

**Romance and teenage problems:** girls comments:

'a programme that has everything – romance, action, a good story line, sad and happy parts and is suitable for my age group.'

'I would like a television show just like the novels called *Sweet Dreams.*'

'a drama and adventure show with a lot of romance and an occasional murder'

'something to do with children from 13 to 16 about school life and the problems of boy friends, over-protecting parents and drugs'

'"Sons and Daughters" because it's about people and the real things that really happen in their lives'

Perhaps the sentimental and romantic yearnings of many of the girls are encapsulated in the following comment: 'I like "The Love Boat" because everything's nice on a boat and I want to go on a cruise when I get older.'

The boy who wrote the following, represents many of the boys who want non-stop action and excitement in an extensive and incongruous range of forms: 'The programme I would like to watch most would be a mix of horror, gore, mystery, bike riding, car chases, very funny with lots of sex.'

The major reading preferences of boys and girls were very similar to their film and television viewing preferences. The differences were as follows:

1. Humour was not mentioned as a reading preference anywhere near to the same extent that comedy was as a television/movie choice. This seems to be a function of expectation, as few of the students were aware of the availability of comic novels.

2. Romantic novels and novels about adolescents facing the problems of personal relationships, sexuality, identity, drugs, etc. were even more popular with girls than films and television programmes on these issues. This also seems to be a function of the greater availability of the literature. There are numerous novels readily available to teenagers about these problems of their lives, which tend to be focussed on more directly and explored

more deeply than in film and television where the romantic relationships are more often between adults.

The following are representative comments describing the kinds of books most liked by boys and girls.

**Boys comments:** summarising representative boys' preferences for exciting action uncluttered with description, analysis and reflection:

'Novels that don't rave on in the first chapter, that get into the action and have lots of climaxes.'

'Characters who are killers, spies and double-crossers, in places that are exciting and mysterious.'

'about a person in charge that's tough'

'fugitives, robots, aliens and investigators'

'rough people ard troublemakers'

'Goodies and badies who are all scared by threatening creatures.'

'Cool, smooth-talking people who joke a lot and get into lots of fights.'

**Girls' comments:** summarising representative girls' preferences for stories of romance, mystery, adventure and teenage problems:

'novels with excitement and danger with sad and love scenes here and there'

'Adventurous people who are apt to fall in love.'

'mysterious, exciting, romantic people and lonely, scared people'

'Issues which concern teenagers — drugs, parents, friends, sex and jobs.'

'kids about our age who are pregnant and don't know what to do'

'handsome, strong and daring men, and beautiful and shy women'

'spunky guys and beautiful, helpless women'

The comments, as well as the categorisations and preferences, seem to reflect a desire or need to project images that are stereotypes of sex roles.

By far the most popular category of fiction was that of teenage romance, mentioned by the majority of girls in both the 1978 and

1984 surveys. Titles in the *Sweet Dreams* and Mills and Boon series were extremely popular with girls in both Year 8 and Year 10. However, the most popular books, mentioned mainly by Year 10 girls in 1984, were the trilogy by Virginia Andrews — *Flowers in the Attic, Petals in the Wind* and *If There Be Thorns* — and another novel by her, *My Sweet Audrina.* Because Virginia Andrews' work is so popular, an analysis of the appeal and effects of her novels is included in the final part of this chapter.

## STUDENTS' OPEN COMMENTS ON READING AND THEIR IMPLICATIONS FOR TEACHING

On the last page of the questionnaire the students were invited to make any comments they liked about their reading in or out of school. (The page was left blank to encourage commentary.) About half of the students made comments varying from one or two sentences to a full page of constructive reflection.

The comments fall into four main categories:

1. Negative criticism, in the form of dogmatic assertion, from students who dislike reading, who associate all reading with boredom and who are highly critical of the books they are asked to read in English and/or the teaching methods employed in English classes.

2. Expressions of the status of literature in life, ranging from those by students who see reading literature as central to education and life (very few) to those who see literature as something to do when there is nothing else at all available (very many).

3. Pleas for assistance (both overt and covert), from those who feel guilty for not reading, who see themselves as inadequate as learners and incompetent as readers, and who would genuinely appreciate some help. They are not all from low-stream classes, as some are at the lower end of top-stream classes.

4. Constructive suggestions, from those across the whole reading range who offer interesting and constructive suggestions for improving the teaching of literature.

### Negative criticism

*Boredom:* There were many comments from students of all ability levels which emphasised the boredom of reading and strong antagonism towards it:

'Reading, it's not very good.'

'I hate reading.'

'The only time I read books from the school is when I have to.'

'I don't like reading at school. And I don't like reading at home either. I don't like reading.'

'I am a sporting person and I don't read much. The only sort of reading I do is magazines, sporting papers and newspapers. I would rather see a movie or watch television.'

'The standard of school novels is really pathetic. They are totally boring and unreadable.'

'All the books in school that I have read are boring and too hard to understand. And some aren't even written in English (e.g., *Romeo and Juliet*).'

*Lack of choice of class texts:*

'We should read more books we enjoy instead of the books our English teacher gives us to read in English.'

'I reckon we should be able to choose our own novels.'

These kinds of comments suggest the need for teachers to consider negotiating the curriculum with their pupils, and to make their purposes in teaching specific books more explicit to them. Many students have no inkling of why they are being asked to read the texts selected for them or what they are expected to gain from reading them:

'I don't like love or mushy stories.' (Year 8 boy)

'I hate romantic novels with phrases like "He grasped me firmly, his arms enclosed my waist (he'd have a hard time enclosing mine), his hard lips sought mine" — what utter garbage.' (Year 10 girl)

'I think the older generation think we, or other children like myself, have dirty minds and that we should read books like *Black Beauty* and *Lassie*. Their wrong, we're not dirty and those books are bull.' (Year 10 girl).

These comments give some idea of the range of tastes of students in any one class, even of the same sex, and indicate the difficulty of finding what a teacher called 'sure-fire texts'.

They certainly highlight the need for negotiation between teachers and pupils over choice of texts, for the organisation of small sets of texts in classrooms so that groups of pupils can each work on different texts at the same time, and for a wide-reading programme.

*Boredom and purposelessness of routine written exercises:* Many students strongly criticised the kinds of written exercises they were forced to do in response to literature. The strongest major resentment was of comprehension exercises on poetry and fiction, and chapter-by-chapter plot summaries of novels, which were seen as exercises in time-consuming, industrious futility:

'I like reading at school or anywhere else, but I don't like being asked stupid questions, to write answers to about it as I don't see any point in it.'

'The only problem with reading books is the work you have to do, either write a book report or answer a whole lot of questions.'

*Implications:* these kinds of comments clearly imply the need for:

- more small group discussion to replace much of the tediousness of summary writing and written comprehension;

- replacing externally imposed comprehension exercises on literary texts with the invitation to students to produce their own questions on texts for further discussion, with such questions being specified as having to be ones they don't know the answers to and want to know the answers to; and

- offering students a greater range of activities to engage in in response to literature, both of written and more performance-oriented kinds. There are many exciting ways of exploring literature imaginatively, ways which are more effective in helping students explore texts more deeply and enjoyably without resort to the arid, routine summaries and comprehension exercises they so bitterly resent.

NB: Some constructive suggestions for dealing with the problems raised here are made by students themselves (p.28) More detailed consideration is given in Chapter Five.

## Expressions of the status of literature in life

For a minority of the students, literature is seen as deepening their understanding of themselves, other people and the human condition:

'Reading literature helps you learn about life. The books take you far beyond what you have experienced yourself, so you understand something about the way people behave in the sorts of situations that haven't happened to you, but might happen sometime.' (Year 8 boy)

However, for many more students, reading literature is seen as an activity to be engaged in only when there is absolutely nothing else to do. It is a sort of last ditch anodyne for extreme boredom or a late night sleeping-pill substitute:

'Sometimes I like reading when there's nothing else to do, or nothing on television to watch, or nothing on radio to listen to, or nothing to do outside, or I'm not going anywhere. I read *TV Times* but not often. Publishers should make books more interesting. They should put more pictures in them.'

'I love reading when I'm sad or bored in my room.'

'I really enjoy reading if I have nothing to do or feel like it, but unless I'm ready to read a book I don't enjoy it, which is usually what happens.'

'I read only at school most of the time. When I haven't got anything at all to do I might read. Reading is OK. I wish I had more time to do it.'

'I would like to be able to read more books but living a very busy life I don't have much spare time for reading.'

## Pleas for assistance

'I have a lot of troble reading.'

'I don't like reading because I can never consentrate or sit down for a long time.'

'There should be more help in reading throughout the school.' (From a Year 8 boy who has difficulty in reading.)

'I can't read very well although I'd like to be able to. Why do you think I'm in 10E4 English?' (second to bottom class).

'I don't read much because I'm not that good of a reader and if I want to understand them I have to read real slow and it takes so long it gets borrowing and I lose interest.'

'I'm not a good reading they say I read like a Year 8 class. and I would like to inproof my reading so I can spell and reading as much as I like. but I try to read and when I can't say a word I get crankly with it and put down and do something else.' (Year 10 girl)

'I am not in the habit of reading but would like to start and get in the habit. I would like to improve my reading skills.'

'I would read a lot more if I could find some books I like – I start reading that I think interest me but never finish them.'

'If I don't like a book emmensely in the first few pages I don't seem to be able to read it.'

'Sometimes the beginning of the book stopped me from reading them or take me a long time to begin it.'

These comments reveal a great deal of self-knowledge on the part of the students as well as a desire to improve their reading so as to be competent and enjoy reading. Their insights have important implications for teaching.

*Improving concepts of self as learner:* The poor self-images these students have suggest that being placed in low ability classes and thus labelled as 'slow learners' or 'backward readers' is detrimental to their learning. To learn successfully, students need to see themselves as potentially competent. Many of these students don't see themselves as potentially successful learners because they have been streamed and labelled since they commenced Infants School.

*Removing guilt and finding satisfaction:* They need help in finding a book they could really enjoy. None of them is so bad a reader that he or she couldn't enjoy a book if it were appropriate for him or her. What they need is to be helped *not* to feel guilty and incompetent when they start to read a book they find boring or too difficult. In such cases they should, perhaps, be actively encouraged to put such a book back on the shelves and keep looking for and trying out books until they find one they can really enjoy.

*Assistance with reading strategies:* The last few comments suggest clearly that there are students who would welcome assistance with their reading strategies. They need, and can be helped to find, appropriate ways of actively questioning literary texts, of asking questions of texts in the act of reading and holding unanswered questions in the mind, trusting the author to provide clues, eventually, to the answers to those questions. That is, they need help to become active readers rather than passive ones.

*Recognising one's own productive strategies:* Another important kind of assistance needed by these students is to be helped to recognise their own productive reading strategies. Too often their school experiences have led them to see only the weaknesses in their reading, only the errors they make. Much of what they do is productive, and these productive strategies can be identified, made explicit to them and built on. For example, this is what one unsuccessful Year 8 student said about his reading, after making the point that he enjoys reading but is not good at it: 'I'm not to good at reading out loud in class 'cause when I read to myself I skip words I can't pronounce.' What this student identifies as a reading weakness is actually a most productive silent reading strategy. He needs to be encouraged to continue avoiding sub-vocalising in silent reading. Such knowledge would give him confidence and power as a reader and learner. (See Chapter Five for more detailed consideration of these issues.)

**Constructive suggestions**

Many students offered — explicitly or implicitly — many positive suggestions for the improvement of the teaching of literature, or they gave clues as to how they themselves could be helped in various ways.

*Awareness of reading satisfactions and strategies*
'I like books which have suspense, that even after the first paragraph intreagues you so much that you must read on and find out what happens in the book.'

This student, like many others who made similar comments, reveals an elementary awareness of one of the great satisfactions of reading, and of one of the important strategies for deriving satisfaction and understanding. Such students are ready to be made conscious of their own productive reading strategies. They are also ready to learn to use strategies they don't, as yet, possess.

## Sustained silent reading

'I would like more time to read at school. At Kirrawee High School when I went there, there was a time every day from 11 to 11.20 when everyone read, even the teachers. I really enjoyed it because you could choose your own books.'

'I would like a lot more time to read at school, because most of the time we write. The teachers shouldn't always pick the books we are to read.'

## Ways of organising more student choice and replacing routine exercises with more productive writing

'I feel that we shouldn't have to read one set book and answer set questions and write set essays. If you had a choice of ten to twenty books and you could write about what you felt about a book and whether you liked it, this would make reading much more enjoyable and essay writing more interesting and easier.'

'I think there should be a lesson each week where you can go up to the school library and pick out your own books, not the ones the teachers bring into class which have been in the book room for hundreds of years but ones we can choose that the teachers permit.'

## More dialogue with teachers, less lecturing

'I think we should read more and discuss our opinions about it instead of listening to teachers, because it's boring and you sometimes don't listen to the teacher.'

'I would like teachers to talk over with us what books we read and let us tell them if we think they are interesting.'

'The teachers think they should give kids what they think is interesting but our taste isn't quite with it. I think we should pick our own books and read them in the class and when we have finished we should tell everyone about it and hear what their books are like too.'

## Recognition of value of teacher as expert helper

While the students make clear that they don't want imposed, compulsory texts all the time, they also show they recognise the value of the teacher and her/his expert knowledge of books in helping them to find the books they might enjoy.

'I enjoy reading out of school most because I can pick what I want to read. Reading in school can be an advantage, though, because you don't know a good book until you have read it, and the teachers can help you find ones you might like.'

*Recognition that one's reading tastes go through stages, and of how reading can help in finding self-identity*
'The books I've written down on page 5 are just some of the books I've read in the past few months. I go through stages and I'm at the horror stage (as is obvious) at the moment. I also go through romance stages (*not* Mills and Boon or *Sweetdreams*, but Virginia Andrews), comedy stages, fantasy stages and stages of reading books I've read before. It just depends on how I feel.'

'It is difficult to say which type of books I like to read as I know I have not yet fully experienced the broad spectrum of written works. So at the moment I am reading as much variety as possible so as to compare and appreciate all types of written works.'

Teachers can help students to find the books they might enjoy and to find their own identities. For example, the student who wrote the following would be helped to explore more deeply issues that interest her if a teacher were to suggest to her that she might enjoy books like *The Summer of My German Soldier* (Bette Greene), *The Summer After the Funeral* (Jane Gardam), *Fireweed, Goldengrove* and *Unleaving* (Jill Paton Walsh), *The Pleasure Garden* (Leon Garfield) or *Jane Eyre* (Charlotte Brontë).
'I have 29 of a set of Sweet Dreams romance. I have a set of Secret Seven. I have a set of Moonglow romances. I have horse books (which I enjoy immensely). I read at least once a day.'

*Publicising literature*
'In school and out of school I think that more emphasis should be applied to reading. For example, there should be placards and posters everywhere showing different books that people might enjoy and letting people know how reading can help them.'

This recognition that many people (both inside and outside schools) just don't know either the pleasure of reading or the particular books that might help them discover them, is most important. For example, another student in answer to an earlier question of the survey, *'Which stories/articles/features do you like most in magazines you have read?'* wrote, 'Nothing, I just read them because they're there.' It would seem that good children's and adolescent literature would profit considerably from a 'higher profile' or the physical presence that television, magazines and newspapers have.

*Gratitude for imaginative teaching schemes*
Many students commented favourably on various activities teachers had organised for reading and/or responding to literature. There was particular commendation of an imaginative wide reading scheme being introduced into one of the high schools when the 1978 survey took place. In this scheme, many paper-back books were placed on shelves in the main corridors of the school and children were able to borrow on an honour system by merely writing the title and author of the book borrowed on sheets left by the bookshelves. This scheme appealed to students because it gave books a physical presence in informal surroundings allowing them to browse freely and choose at leisure. It also made borrowing less troublesome. (There seems to be great antagonism towards what they see as rigid routines, bureaucracy and the oppressive atmosphere they associate with the traditional formal library and its procedures.)

'Reading in school for subjects is very boring because they are rotten books. Most of the books in the library are rotten, some are okay, but it's a hassle borrowing them and you can easily get into trouble in there. The new Reading Programme at our school now is terrific.'

(Obviously the programme allows the students to find what they think is 'terrific' without imposing on them what they think is 'rotten'.)

'Some books are good, but lots in the library are hopeless. The thing Mr. Payne's got going now is real good, he's got good books out.'

'I like reading any book that looks interesting, such as encyclopedias, science books, science fiction, fiction. I am glad they put in the wide-reading scheme because they will get a lot of support from me.'

'In our school they have at last found lots of books that look like their worth reading.'

## PROBLEMS FOR THE TEACHER

In the English Schools Council study, Frank Whitehead and his colleagues found that teachers were imposing adult literary works on children before they were ready for them. This practice was most evident in the 14 to 15 year age group in which the Brontes, Dickens, Wells, Shute and Golding were far more frequently mentioned than Leon Garfield, Alan Garner, K.M. Peyton, Cynthia Harnett, Rosemary Sutcliff, Jill Paton Walsh and the many others who have contributed to making the past 30 years a golden age of children's and adolescent fiction. Whitehead says that the follow-up interviews with individal children confirmed the impression that making 'inappropriate recommendations of books that were too difficult or too mature for the child's particular stage of development'[6] was a general practice of the secondary schools.

The Bathurst survey shows that this is also a problem in Australia. The two major causes of it are the Higher School Certificate examination, which influences the selection of texts and the way English is taught right through the secondary school, and the inability of teachers to motivate students to read widely in contemporary children's and adolescent literature. While much of this literature is popular when read in class, not many students are reading it outside class. Apart from the English authors mentoned above, contemporary Australian writers such as Ruth Park, Victor Kelleher, Patricia Wrightson, Eleanor Spence, Lee Harding and Colin Thiele remain unknown to many students. The texts and authors set for study in the Higher School Certificate examinations indicate the chasm that exists between the demands of texts and the reading levels of most students. Many of the Year 12 students who are expected to respond intelligently to D.H. Lawrence and Patrick White have not, for years, chosen freely to read anything beyond the level of Mills and Boon and The Hardy Boys. Whitehead is similarly strong in his condemnation of the public examination syllabuses in England:

> Particularly regrettable is the influence of the O-level English literature syllabus, which is unduly constricting in its emphasis upon a small number of set texts which bear too distant a relationship to the natural tastes and interests in reading of adolescents at this stage in their development.[7]

It would appear that as students progress through secondary school, the gap between what they choose to read and what the school provides and recommends becomes increasingly wider. The fact that most students are not well acquainted with outstanding contemporary children's and adolescents' authors indicates that teachers are not generally succeeding in the task of matching pupils and books, and may justifiably be seen as widening this gap rather than bridging it. Many teachers are obviously not familiar with this literature themselves. This is a situation that urgently needs to be remedied, among other ways by the provision of more courses in children's and adolescent literature in University English departments and Colleges of Advanced Education where teachers are trained academically and professionally and by giving teachers time to attend full-time post-graduate, and part-time in-service, courses. As Whitehead says, as one of the conclusions to the Schools Council survey, 'It is impossible to overstress the influence of the teacher's own knowledgeability about books. The right book brought forward at the right time can make all the difference to a child's reading development.'[8]

The need for the teacher to be able to help individual students to find individual books that are likely to be most meaningful to them is important for all readers, whatever their reading experience or level of response. For example, both the Schools Council and Bathurst surveys brought to light some enthusiastic but undiscriminating readers: students who read lots of mediocre books. It would not be difficult for a teacher well-read in contemporary adolescent fiction to identify these students and their particular interests and to guide them to books that might give their appetites a deeper and more enduring satisfaction. These students enjoy some of the texts read in English classes, but need help and encouragement in finding other books by the authors they know and by other authors who are likely to appeal.

One of these students, a Year 8 boy who read impoverished literature enthusiastically, said that Henry Treece's *Legions of the Eagle*, read as a class text, was by far the best book he had ever read and he only wished he could find some more like it. He had no idea that there are other books written by Henry Treece or that there are other authors who have written about similar historical topics. All of the evidence of the Bathurst survey points to the need for a comprehensive, well-organised and attactive wide-reading scheme in each school and class. In his study, Ken Watson found that in those classes in which wide-reading programmes were in operation there was a considerably greater amount of reading done. For example, in Year 9, whereas the average number of books read in the past month over all the schools surveyed was 2.9, the average of classes in which wide-reading programmes operated was 3.8.[9]

Both the Bathurst and Schools Council surveys show that students who own many books, and whose parents are habitual readers, become committed readers themselves. In a study of the reading of Year 7 students (12 to 13 year-olds) in Victorian secondary schools in 1979, Elaine Pascoe offers striking evidence of the significant role of parents in developing an interest in reading. She found that:

1. the more books the students read, the more satisfaction they got from reading;

2. very few (19 per cent) of those who read least (0 to 5 books in the year) read books at home;

3. most of the parents of children who read a great deal offered their children books to read, while most of the parents of children who read least did not offer their children books to read;

4. almost all the parents of the heavy readers did a great deal of reading themselves, while most of the parents of those who read least did little or no reading; and

5. the heavy readers had family members who read to them often, while those who read least were rarely read to by others.[10]

For students whose parents show no interest in reading or in encouraging their children to read, the teacher's role is obviously crucial. Teachers can have a significant influence by encouraging book ownership (through reading clubs, for example), and more importantly, by demonstrating that they value reading themselves by being seen to enjoy reading. This can easily be done, for example, by often reading aloud to pupils and communicating an infectious enthusiasm through the quality of the reading, and by organising regular (daily?) periods of 'sustained silent reading' in which pupils and teacher do nothing but read.

There are, however, some students who are put off reading by the kinds of books made available to them in their homes. For example, as one girl in Year 10 put it, if your parents give you *Pilgrim's Progress* for your birthday, it's not surprising that you don't like reading until a friend passes on a copy of *Ten Boy Summer!* The implication for the school is that it might well be helpful in promoting children's reading habits if a letter to parents (particularly to Year 7 parents) were sent early in the year, explaining the school's policy on reading, suggesting a range of authors and titles for outside school reading and inviting parents' cooperation. At the very least, this would stop educationally concerned and cooperative parents from offering inappropriate literature to their children.

The major sources of all the books mentioned by students were personal ownership, borrowing from a friend and, in 1984, the English class. Only seven per cent of books read were borrowed from the school library and three per cent from the town library. This is a cause for concern. The library's comparative insignificance as a source of students' reading is confirmed by the responses to the question, 'Do you borrow books from the school library? Tick one of the boxes — often, occasionally, rarely.' (Table 2) Many students offered an unsolicited and emphatic 'never'.

Table 2: Frequency of borrowing books from school library

|  | Year 8 | | Year 10 | |
| --- | --- | --- | --- | --- |
|  | 1978 | 1984 | 1978 | 1984 |
|  | % | % | % | % |
| Often | 7.2 | 5.2 | 8.9 | 3.2 |
| Occasionally | 27.6 | 16.8 | 34.3 | 26.1 |
| Rarely | 65.2 | 78.0 | 56.8 | 70.7 |

It is clear from the responses of the committed readers that they very rarely borrow fiction from the school library. These students come from homes with plentiful supplies of good literature, both of contemporary writers and from the heritage. They also own many books of their own and purchase contemporary children's literature regularly. The problem is that those pupils who have few, or inappropriate, books in their home, don't borrow much from the school library either. This reflects a need for close collaboration between the library and the English Department to implement a wide-reading scheme and to make borrowing books from the library an attractive and rewarding experience.

## The National Reading Project: 'Children's Choice'
In a report of their findings about teachers' perceived difficulties in teaching literature and their methods of assessing students' response,

the members of the Australian National Reading Research project on students' reading attitudes and interests ('Children's Choice') show that teachers believe their main difficulties are the distraction of television, pupils' reading abilities and pupils' negative attitudes to reading.[11] Here is a summary of the report.

### 1. The main difficulties experienced in teaching fiction

- *The distraction of television* (36 per cent of comments). Many teachers feel that, without parental support, they are fighting single-handedly and powerlessly to encourage students to read more books and to watch less televison. (Whitehead's Schools Council findings also showed that while many capable readers watch a lot of television, poor readers are particularly heavy viewers.)

- *Pupils' reading abilities* (19 per cent of comments). This is a very serious problem with those children for whom English is a second language, and particularly with those who come from homes in which reading is not highly valued. 'The teachers considered the life-long habits of non-reading were substantially established before secondary school and were confirmed by the failure of the School to provide sufficiently interesting, accessible material.'[12]

- *Pupils' negative attitudes to reading* (31 per cent of comments). Many of the replies teachers gave to the question about the methods they use to motivate reluctant readers are illuminating. Working with a lack of suitable reading material and setting exercises such as reading aloud around the class and writing summaries and book reviews are activities more likely to exacerbate negative attitudes than to foster positive ones. The teachers who read exciting excerpts and entire texts aloud to pupils, who organise regular periods of sustained silent reading, who organise wide-reading schemes, who emphasise choice and a pupil's right to dislike a book without being penalised, who organise small-group discussion for sharing of opinions, and who arrange for more performance-oriented activities using a diversity of media (e.g., audio tapes and video cameras), are more likely to interest students in reading. For many secondary teachers 'the assumed learning environment [is] the whole class reading of a set text'. As Rhonda Bunbury and her co-researchers so pertinently say about some of the negative teaching practices:

'The research team wants to ask teachers what it is in unsupervised library visits and hearing pupils read aloud which they feel encourages reluctant readers to read, given that the negative attitudes to reading probably arose from such activities in the first place. [13]

## 2. Methods of assessing children's responses to fiction

Apart from obvious informal ways of assessing pupils' ability to respond to fiction, such as observing their behaviour in class, their reading interests and their borrowing records, and paying attention to their spontaneous comments and questions, teachers' most frequently used methods include oral and written book reports, oral and written comprehension questions, written essays and tests or examinations. Significantly low in teachers' priorities are methods of exploring literature imaginatively: for example, writing from personal and imagined experience, dramatisation, recreation in other media and the use of music, tapes, slides, video, etc., for presentational reports to the class. The infrequent use of methods that have been widely publicised in English teachers' professional journals for the past 15 years might well be explained by the finding that only 27 per cent of Australian teachers are members of the English teaching professional associations. [14]

It is crucial that we find out what satisfactions teenage readers seek in their reading, and what they bring to and take from it. It is in this important area that the English Schools Council research is weak. Whitehead admits that his accounts of the appeals of literature to young readers are 'speculative and impressionistic'[15] rather than empirically tested results of investigation. His team examined what they considered to be the appeal of popular books. When it came to finding out what actually happens in the minds of young readers while reading, the Schools Council report is evasive. On the basis of interviews with individual children, Whitehead and Capey conclude that 'the young reader seldom finds it possible to be articulate in any very specific way about what he has liked and valued in his reading'.[16] As Jean Blunt points out, in an important article in *English in Education:*

> Still we go on teaching literature not knowing what the young readers are really making of it . . . Is it fair to continue basing hours of our teaching time on mere speculations and impressions? Can we not somehow probe a little more into questions of what teenage readers bring to and take from their reading?[17]

It is in the exploration of response to literature and its profound implications for the classroom that the Bathurst research fills in the major gaps left by the Schools Council project. This is the theme of Chapter Four, 'Exploring Response'. It is these findings that might help teachers best in matching individual pupils with individual books and so give a more reasoned substantiation than hunches from teaching experience of Whitehead's quite reasonable assertion that 'there are very few children, if indeed any, who cannot be "hooked" on books if the right ones are put in their way'.[18] We need to know how to 'hook' all children on books, and while anecdotal evidence from experienced teachers is most useful, general principles and generally productive strategies need to be identified and formulated if it is at all possible to do so.

## THE IMPACT OF TELEVISION

*only a flicker*
*Over the strained time-ridden faces*
*Distracted from distraction by distraction*
*Filled with fancies and empty of meaning*
*Tumid apathy with no concentration.*

T.S. Eliot, 'Burnt Norton'

*How strangely the mind of the criminal is stocked*
*with images from that other anarchy, the legitimate*
*one.*

Albert Corde, protagonist of Saul Bellow's
novel, *The Dean's December*

There is no doubt that television is one of the most powerful influences shaping the lives and attitudes of children. The average Australian child spends more hours watching television than attending school.[19] While children are watching television they are not reading, being read to, or talking to others — activities important to language development and learning. Nor are they involved in other kinds of activities important to their physical, social, emotional and intellectual growth: exercising, playing and interacting with other people, exploring their environment, experimenting, wondering, reflecting and thinking. Watching television is particularly detrimental to children's growth when it occupies large chunks of time and is an essentially passive activity. For most children it is like this pretty well all the time.

## TELEVISION, READING AND THE IMAGINATION

The consistent, passive, unreflective and undiscussed viewing of television is undoubtedly destructive of the work of teachers who are trying to develop the reading habit in their students. Television was mentioned by the teachers surveyed in 'Children's Choice', the National Research Project, as the greatest single difficulty they experience in teaching fiction. As Dr George Gerbner, a leading American researcher of the effect of television on children, says, 'T.V. has profoundly changed the way our children become human beings.'[20] The impoverished language, simplistic plots and the brutalised and sentimentalised attitudes of the most popular American soap and action/adventure programmes watched by the Bathurst students condition their expectations of the possibilities of language and the satisfactions of fiction.

Habitual heavy television viewing also has an adverse effect on the development of children's imagination. Elin McCoy reports the research of the Singers at Yale University, which indicates that:

> a steady diet of the powerful images found on TV tends to displace a child's own capacity for private image-making so essential to reading, problem solving, and the ability to empathise with the feelings of others.[21]

Even the viewing of well-produced television films and serials of outstanding contemporary childrens books (e.g., of *The Eagle of the Ninth* and *The Machine Gunners*), a practice often recommended by teachers as a way of enticing children to read the books, is of dubious value. If the film is seen before or during the reading of the book, the imagination of the film-maker, so powerfully realised and communicated in explicit visual images, dominates the imagination of readers, preventing them from forming their own mental images of characters, places and events, including their feelings about these things which are even more significant than the imagined pictorial visualisations which generate them. If the film or serial is seen after the reading of the book, children are often disappointed because what they see on the screen is different from the ways they had imagined and interpreted the story. No matter how sensitive the interpretation or skilled the production, a film version is a product of someone else's imagination, not the viewer's own.

Of course the differences between children's imaginative interpretations and visualisations of books they have read, and television and film versions can be used constructively by teachers as the basis for explorations of the ways meanings are constructed and communicated in different media. This practice of encouraging constant reflection on what has been seen and read is a much-needed antidote to the reflection-inhibiting character of television as a medium. But unless work like this is done in schools, many students become disappointed with themselves as readers and disenchanted with reading, because they measure the success of their readings against the interpretations they see on the screen and attribute the obvious and inevitable differences to their own inadequacies. Only the most assured and competent readers interviewed in the Bathurst research were able to resist the power of the eye of the Cyclops, making comments like the following, from a Year 8 boy:

'I was very disappointed with the television production of *The Eagle of the Ninth* because it made everything too neat and simple. The book was much better. It was more complex and believable because in the book Marcus didn't have to choose between straight good and straight evil, but between two kinds of loyalty each with points for and against it. I didn't see the characters the way they looked on the television either. On the television they looked just dressed up without giving you the feelings the book did. People like Marcus and Guern with real problems, moral dilemmas, looked *too* confident or *too* worried, if you know what I mean. They were sort of overacted. I saw them as being more thoughtful, more troubled and more thinking than they were shown. You didn't see inside them enough, but in the book you did.'

Most students, however, focused on what they wrongly saw as their own inadequacies as readers in describing the differences between the reading of a book and their later viewing of a television version.

The general reaction to stories they were motivated to read after seeing on television was that the reading was not as good as the film, because, as one student put it,

'When you've seen it on television you know what's going to happen, how it's all going to end up. The television is much clearer and easier to understand because you can see what the characters really look like and how things happen.'

In other words, someone else's imagination is so powerfully imposed that your own never gets a chance to begin operating. Many students in this situation failed to complete the reading of books they had begun under the stimulus of the television production. Not only are words crowded out by pictures in television programmes, but also are fiction readers' mental images crowded out by film-makers' mental images. Forming mental images is one of the productive strategies of reading to be examined in action with young readers in Chapter Four.

## TELEVISION AND HUMAN VALUES

From the responses in both the written questionnaires and personal interviews, it is my conclusion that the content of students' television viewing does have a significant effect on their attitudes and values. The more extensive research of others confirms my findings.

The impact of television-portrayed violence on children's behaviour and attitudes has been extensively researched, particularly in the United States. In summarising and evaluating this research, a team of Australian researchers from the Audio Visual Centre at Sydney Teachers' College, Kevin Tindall, David Reid and Neville Goodwin, conclude that:

Major research evidence indicates that the viewing of television violence increases aggressiveness in children, leads to an acceptance of violence as a way of life, and consequently changes the nature of the social structure.[22]

In 1972, the most comprehensive study of all concerning the effects of television violence, that of the United States Surgeon General's Scientific Advisory Committee on Television and Social Behaviour, after reviewing all the major published research on the subject and undertaking some of their own (representing 60 studies and a sample of over 10,000 children), concluded that watching violence on television does contribute to children's anti-social behaviour.[23] The

Surgeon General, Dr Steinfeld, in presenting the final report of the Advisory Committee to the Senate Sub-Committee, said:

> Certainly my interpretation is that there is a causative relationship between televised violence and subsequent anti-social behaviour, and that the evidence is strong enough that it requires some action on the part of responsible authorities, the TV industry, the Government, the citizens.[24]

Dr Pool, Professor of Political Sciences at the Massachusetts Institute of Technology, one of the members of the Surgeon General's Advisory Committee, said:

> Twelve scientists of widely different views unanimously agree that scientific evidence indicates that the viewing of television violence by young people causes them to behave more aggressively.[25]

I am not suggesting that there is a simple equation between watching violence on television and behaving violently in life, but I am saying that violence in television certainly influences the interpretation children make of the world and of human behaviour. They learn to accept violence, exploitation and insensitivity in relationships as the norm in their world. The moral lesson of 'Starsky and Hutch' and many other crime programmes is that good triumphs over evil through violence, the manly as well as the only course of action. Violence is not only legitimised but approved of when it is used by the people with whom we are invited to sympathise, whether they be the police or forces of enlightenment or merely the victimised hoodlum who really wants and tries to be lovable but who is continually and unwittingly manipulated, blackmailed and exploited to serve the nefarious purposes of those portrayed as grotesquely evil miscreants. In this dramatisation of an ends-justifies-the-means philosophy, there is an indestructible bond between violent authoritarianism and saccharine sentimentality, with the audience invited to approve the final triumph of hypocrisy and materialist self-interest which is crudely engineered but carefully timed to reduce their resistance to its lowest ebb for the arrival of the sponsor's message.

Research carried out by Dr Bradley Greenberg of Michigan State University focuses on the importance of family discussion in helping children reflect on and evaluate the television programmes they watched: 'We found that in homes where parents talked with children about the violence on the program they almost wiped out the effects of viewing anti-social behaviour.'[26] For those children whose parents don't even monitor, let alone discuss programmes with them (the majority in Bathurst), it is essential that teachers do, by making the classroom a place where viewing habits and individual programmes are regularly and openly discussed and their methods and values explored.

Many of the girls in the Bathurst interviews said that they watched soap operas like 'The Restless Years', 'Dynasty' and 'Dallas' because they were important programmes illuminating both the real world and their own emotional experiences. One Year 8 girl from the top stream said,

'I don't like "The Restless Years" but you can't afford not to watch it. People like me, we won't all be able to get jobs in Bathurst when we leave school, with all the unemployment, so we'll have to go to Sydney, and you need to know what it's like out there and how to look after yourself. It's all going to happen to us. We're going to have the same problems they have. They left school in Year 10 and they have problems finding a job, normal teenage problems with their parents and boyfriends and girlfriends.'

A representative comment from another Year 8 girl was,

'Shows like "A Country Practice", "Dynasty" and "Dallas" are real. They show you the sorts of things that really happen. They put in the real problems that real people have to cope with, and this helps you cope with them too because they'll happen to us in a few years.'

This kind of apparently naive reaction to television is widespread, as research in Western Australian schools carried out by Pingree and Hawkins makes evident. Pingree and Hawkins found that children aged two, five, and eight construct their pictures of the reality of Australian life from what they see on American television programmes:

From viewing crime and adventure programmes, cartoons and game shows, these children may be constructing a distorted picture of reality that is far more mean, violent and sexist than Australia really is . . . And the children seem to apply this television picture of reality, a picture that is largely derived from American programmes, to what they believe Australia is like.[27]

In a study of Australian teenagers' responses to the extremely popular American television programme 'Happy Days', Noble and Noble found that many confused reality and fantasy:

> While adolescents knew the programme originated in America and was set in the 1950s, nevertheless half the sample said the show was true to life rather than acted as in a school play. One can understand why wreaths and wedding presents flood in when a fictional death or marriage occurs in a serial programme.[28]

This distorted view of the world that many television programmes provide leads many teenagers to adopt negative feelings towards their own capacities to control and direct their lives. Many made it clear in the interviews that they see the world as a place of violence, injustice and irrationality, in which the only course of action for individuals is to accept the harsh realities and adapt to them. Television creates and reinforces their own feelings of powerlessness, leading them to accept and tolerate with a shrug of resignation what they might otherwise humanly resist. Dr George Gerbner, dean of the School of Communications at the University of Pennsylvania, endorses the validity of this pessimistic view from his own research:

> In the world of TV, crime and violence are ten times more frequent than in the real world. Since children who are the heavy viewers are more prone to believe the real world is the same as the TV world, they develop a very distorted view of how much violence there is in the actual world. We've found that by junior high, children who are heavy viewers have already developed the "mean world" syndrome — they are more likely to be anxious and insecure, and more likely to think of people as mean and selfish and the world as a mean, cruel place in which they must protect themselves.[29]

As well as giving children a view of the world as 'mean', many television programmes portray different social groups in stereotyped ways. Appropriate activities in school to give children an understanding of the processes by which their attitudes towards other people are shaped by television would include investigations of the characteristics of different social, racial and religious groups as depicted on television; for example, portrayals of children, adults, parents, the police, old people, girls as opposed to boys, black people as opposed to white people, blue-collar workers as opposed to white-collar workers, etc. The images of the groups could then be compared with their portrayal in other media, including literature, and with the realities of children's experience of them in the world to examine the ways meanings are constructed by different media, and to evaluate the degrees of fidelity of the representations and the purposes of programme makers and authors.

## TELEVISION AND COMMERCIAL VALUES

The television industry in Australia is predominantly controlled by and for commercial interests. While this statement is not directly applicable to the ABC, such a small percentage of the population watches it that it has become alarmingly preoccupied with presenting mentally undemanding ephemera in order to compete with the commmmercial channels for ratings. By definition, television advertising aims to create a demand for goods, to persuade people to buy what they often don't need. It is not surprising, then, that children and teenagers develop a materialistic consumer mentality when exposed to the plethora of commercials that fragment programme narratives.

This disruption to narrative coherence also has a negative effect on viewers as learners: it helps to impair their capacities for sustained concentration. Teachers talk more and more frequently of the unsettled nature and poor attention spans of children who are heavy television viewers. The reading of an entire novel becomes for such students an insuperable task, as it requires the holding in the memory of many events and making connections between them through continual processes of mentally hypothesising and testing possibilities. Watching programmes on commercial televison, then, can well be described as learning how not to read.

There are many extremely popular television programmes that impair reading ability, promote a selfish materialism, and communicate stereotyped and socially undesirable attitudes and values. When these facts are made known, the vested interests of those who control the industry ensure that nothing is done. There is insufficient public accountability because the main concerns of the industry are making profits, not educating taste, improving public morals, or making people better informed. Television advertising creates and strengthens consumer demand, and television programmes create and strengthen attitudes and values. As a congressman said in the United States House of Representatives in 1972,

> Television's ability to influence the behaviour of its viewers can hardly be disputed. Advertising firms spend $2½ billion a year on that assumption. The high-paid corporate officers of the networks enthusiastically agree with them, yet they act with feigned surprise when anyone suggests that their programmes of violence influence children.[30]

The commercial principle of profits first and disinterested values second prevails. If large numbers of consumer-viewers will watch programmes such as 'Starsky and Hutch', 'The A-Team', 'Dallas' and 'The Restless Years', the producers see no point in offering more literate alternatives. As Arthur Capey, a member of the English Schools Councils research team, says so perceptivly about the powerful role of the media in a society such as ours, '[a] society that unquestioningly accepts what the (producer) offers can be made to appear actively to demand it.'[31] and 'Demand in an industrial society is a desire created by the advertiser to match the economic capacity of the producer.'[32]

Behind the advertisements and the more ephemeral and sensational television programmes and the spurious values they communicate, there is an implicit contempt for viewers. As part of their active exploration of media messages and their methods of construction, students in their English classes should be examining the images of viewers that different programmes imply, and drawing conclusions about programme motives and values. The image of the implied viewer is just as much a construct of the medium as a character in a soap opera, and many of the implied viewers constructed by the specific programmes bear only as close a relationship to real viewers as fictional characters do to the actors playing their parts. Unfortunately, many real viewers begin to see themselves as being identical to the constructed implied viewers and to behave accordingly. They are being socialised by the medium into becoming compliant servants of the commercial machine, both as citizens and consumers. Richard Hoggart, in *The Uses of Literacy*, expresses exactly what it is that an excessive diet of television does to people, in his comment about all ephemeral entertainment:

> The strongest objection to the most of trivial popular entertainments is not that they prevent their (consumers) from becoming highbrow but that they make it harder for people without an intellectual bent to become wise in their own ways.[33]

With seemingly all the power and technology in the hands of the controllers of the media, it might well be asked what teachers can do to help their students withstand the debilitating effects I have mentioned. Certainly, as Basil Bernstein pointed out in 1970, 'education cannot compensate for society'.[34] Education in Australia has been more successful in transmitting and reflecting the beliefs, attitudes and behaviours of society than it has in transforming them. Simply put, this means that if adults read very little, and of that even less great literature, neither do their children; if adults spend most of their leisure hours watching commercial television, so do their children. What, then, can teachers do?

## WHAT CAN SCHOOLS DO?

Although this is the subject of Chapter Five, which focuses primarily on teaching literature (although not excluding television narrative as literature), some general comments about television specifically are appropriate here.

Teachers and students have at their disposal the most powerful technology of all, one that although used by television can be used far more effectively by people to exert their control over television and pretty well everything else. This is language. Language is the most powerful instrument of learning and thinking we have, for, as Douglas Barnes said in *From Communication to Curriculum*, 'language not only transmits thought but shapes it':

> The importance of language is that it makes knowledge and thought processes available to introspection and revision. If we know what we know, then we can change it. Language is not the same as thought, but it allows us to reflect upon our thoughts.[35]

Where television uses language only to transmit thought, through a one-way speaking tube as it were, the teacher can organise interactions in the classroom for the discussion of television or anything else; situations in which language can be used for clarifying ideas, sharing ideas and making meanings (shaping thought) as well as for transmission-tube communication. Teachers who create open situations for discussion can promote that active exploration of television that might transform passive viewers into critical ones.

Primarily, media studies in school should be aimed at understanding how the media 'works you over'. Television meanings are constructed by programme makers. As a television programme is a construct, a structured artefact, then activities in class should be designed to explore the constituent elements of that construct as well as how they were put together, for what kinds of audiences and for what purposes. In other words, teaching television should involve students in processes of deconstruction or of unravelling the manufactured article.

Evidence has already been provided of students believing that fictional television programmes such as 'The Restless Years' and 'Happy Days' are transcripts of life. Documentary programmes are also constructs with their messages being predetermined and their presentations carefully packaged. One of the great dangers of television news and documentary programmes is that because we think we are watching immediate experience we believe we are seeing 'facts' or 'the truth'. The objectivity of 'factual' reports on television is a mirage. The events portrayed are carefully selected and arranged, as are the words used to comment on them. The soundtrack of words, music and special effects, like everything else, is a construct, creating feelings to accord with the producer's message. In the presentation of a news story, the shots of events which purport to be representative are, in fact, carefully selected. All documentary is constructed like fiction and we should study it that way. The reason that news and documentary programmes don't often aim to explore what may be the truth of an event but instead impose created meanings is that real objectivity is boring, and the aim of sponsors is to present programmes that are entertaining rather informative.

The kinds of investigations and activities teachers and students can undertake as part of the deconstruction processes of demythologising television include the following:

1. Keep individual viewing diaries and make surveys of viewing habits of the class so that all can consider the implications of the kinds of programmes they watch and evaluate the satisfactions they think they get from them.

2. Track the incidences of violence in each episode of particular programmes (including cartoons) and discuss the effects and possible purposes of each of the violent scenes.
3. Study programmes for their portrayal of stereotypes; for example, the characteristics of 'goodies' and 'baddies', women, school teachers, the police, etc.
4. Examine the language characteristics of different kinds of programmes; for example, the favourite words used by quiz comperes, the way character is revealed by accent, vocabulary, etc.
5. Deconstruct different programme genres: the news, documentaries, children's programmes, soap operas, crime shows, etc., to consider how they work, how specific meanings are manufactured, how certain illusions are sustained and what values and ideologies they are communicating, either explicitly or implicitly.
6. Involve students in the processes of construction of programmes if video cameras are available. If they are not, students can still construct their own advertisements, quiz programmes, etc., and then discuss their processes of construction.

Above all, such work should always be followed by reflective evaluation so that students develop the habit of examining the significance and implications of what they have been doing. As in every other aspect of teaching, teachers should make the purposes of any activity they organise in the classroom explicit to their students, and encourage them to ask questions about what they are being asked to do. The problem is one of student power: either they learn to control television or it controls them.

In adopting questioning attitudes and in being engaged in deconstruction activities, students are not only learning about television and how it works; in exploring their own responses and those of others, they are learning about themselves and their world. Students can learn to control not only their reactions to the media but their reactions to all experience, by learning to understand them. In learning the processes of cultural shaping and media manipulation, students are empowered to control and direct their own responsive behaviour.

As part of this student empowering programme, teachers might well draft a letter to all parents, setting out the main details about television's effects and inviting their cooperation in the education of their children by limiting television viewing in the home, monitoring the programmes watched and discussing them regularly with their children. Those parents who are concerned will appreciate getting some expert advice on how they can help their children. An excellent 'Letter to Parents' published by the Primary English Teaching Association as a guide or model contains the following paragraph introductory to a detailed outline of the kinds of suggestion I have mentioned above:

> Every minute of TV teaches your child something — about unreal situations, violence, glamorised products, or sport, wild life, some fine drama, much shoddy drama, and so on, depending on choice of programmes. The content is worry enough, but even worse is the passivity of the learning — instead of seeking answers, the child just waits for them to appear on screen. So what can parents do?[36]

The clear suggestions that follow are offered in a most civilised and unpatronising way.


## READING BEHAVIOUR

### SATISFIED AND DISSATISFIED READERS

The most sensitive, responsive and voracious Bathurst readers read a great deal of both of what Whitehead calls 'quality' and 'non quality' fiction. These committed readers are also wide-ranging in their other reading interests. In their reading of newspapers and magazines, they go beyond the sports pages, the comics and the beauty hints to politics, current affairs and sociology. Their television viewing, while incorporating both soap and highbrow programmes, is accompanied by more reflective evaluation than the viewing of the more passive consumers. The difference is between reflective readers and viewers on the one hand and unreflective readers and viewers on the other; between those who know from experience the difference between being active and passive in reading and viewing and those who don't; between those who can choose the way they will read or view (depending upon the demands of the material and the reader or viewer's purposes) and those who have no choice at all (being unable to vary their strategies according to the material); between those who have some control over their reading and viewing, and those who are controlled by them.

Between the group of committed readers and the group of those who choose not to read at all is a large group of students who choose to read only 'non quality' books outside school. What is most significant about these students is that they enjoy more and respond more sensitively to the set texts of the English class than do those students who read nothing beyond set texts. Those girls, for example, who read only teenage romance outside school, respond more positively and perceptively to mainstream fiction such as *A Wizard of Earthsea, To Kill a Mockingbird* and *The Eagle of the Ninth* than those students who choose not to read. The reasons for this seem to be pretty clear — they have experienced the satisfactions of reading, at whatever level of response they are operating, and they have learned to use at least some of the more rudimentary strategies that all good readers use. They are potentially good readers and they can be helped by teachers to find books that will offer deeper satisfactions and to use more productive strategies that will enable them to experience those satisfactions.

The least successful, most dissatisfied readers watch more television and home videos than than the other groups, watch more cartoons and read more comics. They are also mainly in bottom stream classes, but this does not mean that they cannot be helped to become more satisfied and successful readers. Almost all of them have been in bottom stream classes since they began school. Having been labelled early as 'slow learners' or 'linguistically disadvantaged', they have since performed in accordance with teachers' expectations. Labelling is a self-fulfilling prophecy in education, with children's poor performances arising from their negative self-concepts developed out of the low expectations of teachers.[37] As many of the least successful Bathurst readers pointed out in their different ways, if you're in a bottom stream English class you're hardly on target to become an English professor. Obviously, being consigned to a 'remedial' class, which is for most a school-life sentence, doesn't do much for your sense of your own competence. The most significant effect of being placed in a 'remedial' class is to make students realise that they can't accomplish what they may have otherwise thought they may have been able to do.

In the comments of these non book-readers the word 'boring' appears again and again. Boredom in reading is something they have learned to experience in schools. It starts in those Infants Schools in which mechanistic approaches to the teaching of reading prevail, the reading schemes of phonics-based readers which ensure that when a child has reached the stage of being allowed to read a real book with a real story she no longer wants to. The boredom factor begins with such quick-fried junk food reading and language programmes as SRA, Distar, Peabody and Ladybird with their repetitive behaviouristic methods of drilling decontextualised skills, and it flourished in those primary and secondary schools in which teaching practices such as the following prevail:

1. imposing on students received critical judgements of texts, thus stifling genuine discovery and exploration of honest personal responses;
2. denigrating emotional responses as being academically inappropriate;
3. causing students to feel incompetent and guilty by criticising the immaturity of their initial responses;
4. using literature texts for unimaginative and uninspiring routine written exercises, such as plot summaries and comprehension tests; and
5. failing to associate reading with enjoyment.

As one Year 8 girl said, 'I'm not a very good reader. I do badly at comprehension. I like reading the books and I understand them okay, but I'd like to get more right answers in Comprehension.' Perhaps she would get more right answers if she were asked the right questions, or allowed to participate in the formulating of questions herself, or if her first, honest responses were given some respectful consideration.

Many of the non book-readers see reading as being very good for you in some vaguely unspecified way, something like a dose of old-fashioned castor oil if only you can bring yourself to stomach it. Most of them can't because it's distasteful: it reinforces their sense of their own impotence. They haven't been helped by the prevailing kind of school syllabus in literature that emphasises the cultural heritage model of literature teaching and the necessity of finding the exploits of Gaspar Ruiz, or even of Ratty and Mole, more inspiring than those of James Bond, however much we secure readers might deplore the values and impoverished language of the latter. The self-confidence and sense of personal worth and dignity of these students can be developed if they are introduced to books that will speak to them about their real concerns, because it is from such purposeful engagement that they can develop powerful reading strategies to give them some mastery of their own meaning-making.

All the Bathurst students are quite explicit about what is important to them in their lives. They feel a need to be accepted, to be valued by their peers, to have their accomplishments recognised and what they see as their significant identities respected. They are concerned and fascinated with people's life roles, the problems of relations with parents and members of the opposite sex, and with sexual activity itself. Sometimes the pressures of these problems and roles become overbearing; for example, the need to be seen as physically attractive when acne breaks out or your body starts to go lumpy, or the need to live up to the machismo image of the Australian male if you see that as the most important thing you've got going for you. It is not surprising, then, that teenagers are enticed by television programmes that, exploitative as they may seem to teachers, appear to offer insights into the issues that concern them (like sex and violence) or present models of behaviour they would like to emulate in their own less ambitious ways. As one Year 8 boy said about Fonzie in 'Happy Days':

'I like the Fonz. I like the way he acts — real cool and tough without having to make a lot of noise, and funny too. He's always in control, he doesn't worry about anything much, but he can look after himself and no one ever makes a fool of him. Nothing gets him down. He's always on top. I like to be cool like that and I kinda talk like him and muck around like him.'

Much of what teenagers really like to watch on television (as opposed to what they watch desultorily because it happens to be on) gives some insight into what their real needs and interests are. All of these interests can be served by fiction, if their teachers know of the appropriate authors and books available. As D.W. Harding says,

Fiction can contribute to the search for identity or role definition that is a crucial task at the stage of adolescence. It allows you to try on various personalities, each of which selectively emphasises some fear or potentiality of your developng self.[38]

Adolescent fiction is a rich and growing field. From the life interests these teenagers specify, from the television programmes they like most, and from the magazines and fiction they choose to read, the implication for the school is very clear. Teachers must begin where the pupils are and must try to introduce into their pupils' discussions of their interests and problems other voices, those from adolescent fiction that are appropriate to their particular concerns and levels of response. Chapters Three and Four have a great deal more to say about recognising levels of response and the strategies of reading employed at each level.

## LITERATURE AND LIFE: THE APPEAL OF FLOWERS IN THE ATTIC BY VIRGINIA ANDREWS.

It is time to examine the appeal of a particular book, to see how it 'works over' teenage readers. An obvious choice is the Virginia Andrews' trilogy (Flowers in the Attic, Petals in the Wind and If There Be Thorns) as it was by far the most frequently mentioned title on the Bathurst lists, although mentioned only by girls and all but one of those in Year 10. The popularity of this work shows that it is seen by 15 and 16-year-old girls as illuminating their emotional experience more fully than any other book known to them. In analysing the appeal of the trilogy I will concentrate on the first novel, Flowers in the Attic, which is all I could bring myself to read. The book is very long (398 pages) and so would provide difficulties for slower readers.

**The relationship between author and teenage reader**

The first person narrator and main character is Cathy, aged twelve at the beginning and 15 at the end of Flowers in the Attic, the first novel of the trilogy. By creating a character moving from childhood to adolescence as the novel's 'centre of consciousness' and 'reflector of values' (Henry James' terms) the author takes the first step in forming a relationship of strong empathy between reader and narrator. As Aidan Chambers explains it, in an important article on the 'implied reader' in children's fiction:

> Tone of voice, style as a whole, very quickly establishes a relatonship between author and reader; very quickly creates the image of the implied reader. In books where the implied reader is a child, authors tend to reinforce the relationship by . . . putting at the centre of a story a child through whose being everything is seen and felt.[39]

Several top stream Year 10 girls put it this way, in interview:

> 'Having a character my age telling the story helps you to relate

to how she's feeling. The characters, Cathy in particular, has dreams that all girls have — to be beautiful like her mother and to become a ballerina. It's all about Cathy growing up, which is what we're going through.'

'They're (the three novels of the trilogy) easy to relate to. They explore problems that concern me. Your emotions are strongly involved, you can identify with the characters, mainly Cathy because she's a girl my age and has problems like mine, only worse.'

The potentially close relationship between narrator and reader is strengthened by the author's introductory claim that the novel is based on real events and by the narrator's comments in the Prologue that titillate the curiosity and fascination of teenage readers with hints that explorations of taboo topics are in the offing. Cathy writes, she says, to exorcise shame and guilt. Readers are thus offered the double attraction of having their own shameful and guilty longings, fears and curiosities both fed and assuaged. Cathy also writes, she tells us, to gain revenge on her hated mother who has betrayed her four children for money. Cathy hopes that 'some understanding publisher will put my words in a book, and help grind the knife that I hope to wield.' (Prologue).

As well as offering both to stimulate and resolve deep-seated latent feelings of hatred, selfishness, greed and desire for revenge, the book goes on to deal explicitly with taboo subjects. However, as it turns out, it deals with them not in such a way as to explain them honestly to readers or to help them to understand their own ambivalent feelings towards parents, other adults and the opposite sex, but rather in ways calculated to foster morbidity and to arouse rather than resolve anxieties. The first person narrator is portrayed as being a well-intentioned, naïve and totally innocent victim of circumstances. The adolescent reader is manipulated by an author who deliberately and wilfully cuts down the distance between inexperienced adolescent as reader and victimised adolescent as narrator. The author's narrative method and sensational treatment of taboo subjects are engineered to make it extremely difficult for adolescent readers to be sufficiently detached to respond in any evaluative way that might deepen their understanding of themselves or their problems. Rather than being invited to explore these problems honestly and from a safe distance, they have their noses rubbed in them. The catharsis readers might think they are experiencing will resolve nothing for them.

The taboo subjects include:

1. Sexual exploitation in various forms: incest, between sister and brother, and between niece and uncle; rape: Cathy is raped by her brother, Chris; adultery, between the children's mother, Corinne, and her husband's brother; seduction: 15-year old Cathy, dressed in a flimsy, diaphonous nightie, 'unwittingly' seduces her mother's young husband by kissing him 'innocently' and 'experimentally' while he is asleep, causing him to 'dream'. (Presumably, if he thinks he is dreaming, or is only half-awake, he is not as blameworthy as he would be if he were more deliberately engaged, so the moral shock of the teenage reader is supposedly cushioned. This is the kind of hypocrisy the book revels in.)

2. Sado-masochism: Corinne, the mother, is lashed by her mother, and the children are shown the blood-encrusted stripes on her back. Cathy and Chris are both whipped by their grandmother.

3. Sexual rivalry between mother and daughter: The relationship between Cathy and her mother changes from affection, through envy and jealousy, to hatred as Cathy reaches puberty. Each sees the other as a sexual rival for the affections of Chris (Cathy's brother and Corinne's son) and of Corinne's second and considerably younger husband.

4. Murder: Cathy's younger brother, Cory, is murdered by their mother, who attempts to poison all the children by adding arsenic to the sugar dusting on the doughnuts she regularly provides as a 'treat'. (Her motive is one of greed: she will not inherit her father's wealth if he gets to know that she has had children by her first, strongly-disapproved-of husband, who has conveniently been removed by a car accident at the novel's opening.)

5. Religious fanaticism: The grandparents inflict violent physical punishment on all those who stray from the narrow puritanical path into sexual awareness and/or behaviour.

6. Mutilation: Chris slashes a wrist to feed his blood to his brother and sisters when the grandmother is attempting to starve them as a punishment for Chris's having seen Cathy naked.

A touch of subtlety for advanced literary readers is the symbolism of the family's adopted name, Dollanganger (Doppelganger) or double. The doubles include Cathy's younger twin brother and sister, Chris and his dead father, Chris and his mother's new husband, and

Cathy and her mother.

The plot is ludicrously impossible. The four children live imprisoned for years in an attic in their grandparents' house without the grandfather or the maids ever finding out. When Corinne, the mother, marries a much younger man, he moves into the grandparents' house and lives with her without ever finding out that she has four children from her first marriage or that they are living in the same house. The first novel ends with Cathy, Chris and the surviving younger twin sister escaping from the house to make their way in the world: the 'flowers in the attic' are now 'petals in the wind', torn adrift from their roots. Indeterminacies in the action are multiplied at the end, as in each episode of a television or popular magazine serial, so as to increase the desires of readers to follow the fortunes of the hero and heroine, whose total lack of experience of the outside world (they have never been to school) promises the likelihood of continued wicked exploitation. As one of the Year 10 girls said about the trilogy:

> 'You couldn't put them down, they were all so fascinating and full of mystery. That's what makes you want to read it all as fast as you can, wanting to know what happens next and how they solve the sorts of problems they've got. Their problems are the kinds we could all have, only their problems are much worse because they have been sheltered [sic] from the world outside the attic.'

Give me the wicked world any day! The same girl told me that in *Petals in the Wind* 'they grow up' and in *If There Be Thorns* 'brother and sister marry and have two children, and she has to learn to love someone else rather than her brother'.

In *My Sweet Audrina*, the other Virginia Andrews novel at the top of the Year 10 girls' popularity list, 'a girl who is raped at the beginning of the novel has fallen in love with the guy who did it, at the end'. This is the kind of neat structure Virginia Andrews provides: violence is transformed into 'love' so that the 'happy ever after' ending conveys a spurious impression of moral triumph. ('My books exploit teenagers, your Honour? The very idea!')

### The fairy tale disguise

*Flowers in the Attic* has the form of a perverted fairy tale. In Chapter 1, entitled rather insensitively 'Goodbye Daddy', the perfect father (the King) is killed in a car accident on his 36th birthday. The mother is a Queen of dazzling beauty, and Chris and Cathy, emerging from childhood into puberty, are the young prince and princess, both extraordinarily beautiful. Every incident in the novel draws on the repertoire of the fairy tale: the scene in which Cathy seduces her mother's new husband by kissing him while he is asleep, is a reversal of 'The Sleeping Princess'; and the relationship between Cathy and her mother is a version of the Snow White/wicked stepmother-queen relationship, both involving the sexual jealousy of an older woman for a younger woman and an attempt to poison the younger rival. The second novel of the trilogy, *Petals in the Wind*, obviously begins with Chris and Cathy as Hansel and Gretel.

A consideration of the functions of the traditional fairy story and its appeal and value to younger children might help to indicate the measure of the exploitation of adolescent readers by the Virginia Andrews novel which mimics the form of the traditional fairy story at the same time as it perverts its traditional effects. Fairy stories have the attraction and value of offering children an understanding of problems and threatening situations in their own lives because their events take place outside the familiar frameworks of daily life. The fantasy element provides the safety factor, the distance, enabling readers to explore and find answers to problems that if set in their own familiar surroundings would cause only a confusing embarrassment or guilt. This is explained very well by Arthur Applebee in a passage from his book, *The Child's Concept of Story*[40] where he quotes Bettelheim[41]:

> Many of the (fairy) stories depicting "unacceptable" actions are used by children to discover for themselves some of the consequences of such actions as killing their parents – actions which, we must suppose, they never have attempted and never will attempt "in real" instead of "in story". These explorations do not have to be interpreted as expressions of unconscious conflicts or wish fulfilment (though in a few cases they may be): it is more to our present point to recognise that these actions derive directly from the conventional set of social expectations. To set a norm is to create the possiblity of violating that norm; to understand the norm means learning what counts as violating as well as what counts as observing it. By removing the characters and setting from their own immediate sphere of experience, children are given a simple way to explore these norms without threatening other important constructs. They can see what happens to "bad people"

without doing anything that would conflict with their expectations about what they, as "good people", do. Or as Bettelheim (1976) describes it in discussing a more particular example, "The fantasy of the wicked stepmother not only preserves the good mother intact, it also prevents having to feel guilty about one's angry thoughts and wishes about her – a guilt which wold seriously interfere with the good relation to Mother". Bettelheim goes on to suggest that a child's fantasies are also an important means of understanding, or figuring out "what the specific consequences of some action might be . . . It is his way of playing with ideas."[42]

In reading *Flowers in the Attic*, teenage readers are deriving perverted understandings of the norms of the society in which they live. The fairy-tale elements are only too thin a disguise for a novel which offers its young readers too direct an emotional involvement in the events it depicts. The characters and settings are not removed sufficiently from teenagers' 'immediate sphere of experience', with the result that the norms are not explored honestly and so cannot be rationally and sympathetically understood. 'Other important constructs' are certainly threatened. The portrayal of realistic adults as entirely vicious, exploitive and selfish, and of realistic children as entirely innocent victims of violent physical, sexual, emotional and spiritual manipulation and deprivation, is not likely to help adolescents to understand human relationships or to develop any meaningful relationships with adults or with each other. Instead of the fantasy of the wicked stepmother preserving the good mother intact and preventing the reader from having to feel guilty about having angry thoughts and wishes about her – as happens with the reading of *Snow White* – in *Flowers in the Attic*, the fantasy takes place in a much more real setting with characters who are much more real. The wicked stepmother is replaced by an all too realistically portrayed mother, and her empathic closeness to the first person narrator almost guarantees that the reader will feel guilty about having angry thoughts and wishes about a real mother whose goodness is shattered rather than preserved intact. The novel portrays a world of perverted relationships and represents a serious threat to teenage readers' perceptions of themselves, of parents and other adults, and of members of the opposite sex.

I have already quoted D.W. Harding's explanation of the way fiction can contribute to 'the search for identity or role definition', so important to teenagers: 'It allows you to try on various personalities, each of which selectively emphasises some fear or potentiality of your developing self.'[43] The personality *Flowers in the Attic* invites its young readers to 'try on' is one that can result only in their fears being strengthened and their feelings about the 'potentialities of their developing selves' becoming more and more guilt-ridden and morbid.

Binding the novel together is the most cloying sentimentality. The same indestructible bond between violent authoritarianism and saccharine sentimentality that was mentioned as characterising some of the more irresponsible crime programmes on television is to be found here. There is no attempt on the author's part to establish any emotional or psychic distance between narrator and reader to involve the reader's social and moral judgements more deeply. Young readers are very vulnerable to the emotional blandishments of this novel. They are blatantly deceived into hating the adults, weeping with and for the children, and experiencing a guilt-inducing prurient fascination in the perverted events portrayed in such a nastily suggestive manner. *Flowers in the Attic* has nothing to do with art or life. The way to help students to withstand the shoddy allurements of books like this is to bring them out from under the desk for open discussion and deconstruction work. Reading this novel strengthens my conviction that Neil Postman and Charles Weingartner made a profound contribution to educational theory when they said that we need to equip each of our students with 'a shock-proof crap detector'.[44]

## INVITING THE COOPERATION OF PARENTS

At the end of my discussion of 'The Impact of Television' (p.49) I mentioned the value of drafting and sending a letter to all parents inviting their assistance in a programme of empowering their children to withstand the exploitive effects of television. Such a letter could and should cover every aspect of English teaching, including reading. The Primary English Teaching Association publication, 'A Letter to Parents', which I recommended as a guide before, does just this. Its concluding paragraphs to the section on Literature, appropriately called 'Help Your Child to Use Reading' (with 'use' being a key word) is:

> Reading must be enjoyed. Be sure that anything you ask your child to read is something s/he *can* read and *wants* to read. Neither

nagging a child to read nor heavily criticising taste in reading will help.

Having problems with behaviour? Many adults admit difficulty in "knowing what the kids are on about". One source of help is paperbacks which explore the problems of young people in today's fastmoving world. If your child is reading such books they will help. [Not *Flowers in the Attic!*] Better still if you read them too and then offer them for comment.[45]

## REFERENCES

1. Frank Whitehead, A. C. Capey, Wendy Maddren, Alan Wellings, *Children and Their Books*, Schools Council, Macmillan Education, London, 1977.

2. Ken Watson, 'The Reading Habits of Secondary School Pupils in NSW', in *English in Australia*, no. 46, November 1978, pp. 68-77.

3. Kevin Tindall, David Reid, Neville Goodwin, *Television: 20th Century Cyclops*, Sydney Teachers' College Audio Visual Research Centre, 1977, p. 9.

4. Watson, 'The Reading Habits of Secondary School Pupils in NSW', p. 76.

5. Whitehead *et al.*, *Children and Their Books*, p. 55.

6. Ibid., p. 289.

7. Ibid., p. 195.

8. Ibid., p. 291.

9. Watson, 'The Reading Habits of Secondary School Pupils in NSW', p. 69.

10. Elaine Pascoe and Margaret Gilchrist, 'A Study of Reluctant Readers, Children Who Least Enjoy Literature', in Stuart Lee (ed.), *Issues 1984*, Primary English Teaching Association, Sydney, 1984, pp. 91-92.

11. Rhonda Bunbury, Ern Finnis, Geoff Williams, 'Teachers Talk About Their Teaching of Fiction, A Preliminary Report of the National Reading Project, Children's Choice', in *English in Australia*, no. 64, June 1983, pp. 3-15.

12. Ibid., p. 9.

13. Ibid., p. 12.

14. Ibid., p. 15

15. Whitehead *et al.*, *Children and Their Books*, p. 206.

16. Loc. cit.

17. Jean Blunt, 'Response to Reading: How some young readers describe the process', *English in Education*, vol. 11, No. 3, Autumn 1977, p. 34.

18. Schools Council Working Paper 52, 'Children's Reading Interests', Evans/Methuen Educational, London, 1975, p. 47.

19. Kevin Tindall and David Reid, *Television's Children*, Sydney Teachers' College Audio Visual Research Centre, 1975.

20. George Gerbner, 'Violence in Television Drama: Trends and Symbolic Functions', in G. A. Comstock and E. A. Rubinstein (eds), *Television and Social Behaviour, Vol. 1, Media Content and Control*, U.S. Government Printing Office, Washington DC, 1972, quoted in Elin McCoy, 'What TV Is Doing to Children', reprinted from *Parents* magazine, in *Education*, August 17 1981, p. 12.

21. Elin McCoy, 'What TV Is Doing to Children', *Parents* Magazine, Gruner and Jahr, New York, reprinted in *Education*, August 17 1981, p. 13.

22. Tindall, *et al.*, *Television: 20th Century Cyclops*, p. 108.

23. Report of the Surgeon General's Scientific Advisory Committee on Television and Social Behaviour, *Television and Growing Up: The Impact of Televised Violence*, US Government Printing Office, Washington DC, 1972, quoted in Kevin Tindall, David Reid, Neville Goodwin, *Television: 20th Century Cyclops*, p. 110.

24. Sub-committee on Communications of the Sub-committee on Commerce, US Senate, The 92nd Congress, March 21st to 24th, 1972, quoted in Kevin Tindall, David Reid, Neville Goodwin, *Television: 20th Century Cyclops*, p. 114.

25. Loc. cit.

26. McCoy, 'What TV is Doing to Children', p. 12.

27. Research paper by Dr Suzanne Pingree and Dr Robert Hawkins, reported in David O'Reilly 'TV "hypnotises" children', *The Australian*, October 26, 1978.

28. G. Noble and E. Noble, 'A Study of Teenagers' Uses and Gratifications of the *Happy Days* Show', mimeograph, University of New England, Armidale, 1978.

29. Quoted in McCoy, 'What TV Is Doing to Children', p. 12.

30. Quoted in Tindall, *et al.*, *Television: 20th Century Cyclops*, p. 110.

31. Whitehead *et al.*, *Children and Their Books*, pp. 260-1.

32. Ibid., p. 257.

33. Richard Hoggart, *The Uses of Literacy*, Penguin, 1962, p. 338.

34. Basil Bernstein, 'Education Cannot Compensate for Society', in Asher Cashdan (ed.), *Language in Education: A Source Book*, Routledge and Kegan Paul and The Open University Press, London, 1972, pp. 213-218.

35. Douglas Barnes, *From Comminication to Curriculum*, Penguin, 1976, pp. 19-20.

36. 'A Letter to Parents', P.E.N. 7, (Primary English Notes), Primary English Teaching Association.

37. See, for example, R. Rosenthal and L. Jacobson, *Pygmalion in the Classroom*, Holt, Rinehart & Winston, New York, 1968, and Jack Thomson, 'Social Class Labelling in the Application of Berstein's Theory of the Codes to the Identification of Linguistic Advantage and Disadvantage in Five-Year Old Children', in *Educational Review*, vol. 29, no. 4, November 1977, pp. 273-283.

38. D. W. Harding, 'Considered Experience: The Invitation of the Novel', *English in Education*, vol. 2, no. 1, Summer, 1967, p. 9.

39. Aidan Chambers, 'The Reader in the Book', *Signal*, 1977, p. 71.

40. Arthur Applebee, *The Child's Concept of Story*, The University of Chicago Press, Chicago, 1978.

41. Bruno Bettelheim, *The Uses of Enchantment: The Meaning and Importance of Fairy Tales*, Alfred Knopf, New York 1976, pp. 69, 119.

42. Arthur Applebee, *The Child's Concept of Story*, p. 83.

43. D. W. Harding, 'Considered Experience: The Invitation of the Novel', p. 9.

44. Neil Postman and Charles Weingartner, *Teaching As a Subversive Activity*, Penguin, 1971.

45. 'A Letter to Parents', P.E.N. 7, Primary English Teaching Association.

# 3 CONTEMPORARY THEORY: SOME CLUES FOR FINDING ANSWERS

This chapter looks at the kind of clues offered by contemporary theory to finding answers to the why, what and how questions asked of the activity of reading literature. Why read? What kind of an activity is it? and How is it best done? The answers that theory suggests are exemplified and tested in the experience of readers as they retrospectively outline their reading processes, reactions and satisfactions in response to specific texts. The aim is to try to identify both specific strategies of productive reading and the kinds of satisfaction readers experience at different levels of response.

## WHY READ AND TEACH LITERATURE

Art is a fabrication of reality which reveals a clearer truth.

Alan Garner, in Greg Shepherd, 'Alan
Garner's Visit', in *English in
Australia*, no. 64, June 1983

Art, especially literature, is a great hall of reflection where everything under the sun can be considered and reflected.

Iris Murdoch, *The Fire and the Sun*

The unique significance of literature and drama is that by their means we are enabled to 'live through' an experience which is not our own but which . . . we make our own. It is this 'living through' of imaginitive experience which affects us at the deepest level and is capable of altering the very grain of our being . . . Literature is a supremely potent mode of significant experience.

Frank Whitehead, 'Why Teach English?'
in Denys Thompson (ed.), *Directions in
English Teaching*

Literature is a GAME played for FUN, in which the reader *pretends*
that he is playing at life. But it is *not* life. It is a pretence. When
you read a story you are pretending a lie.

Charge number 4 against literature, by
Morgan, sixth form student in Aidan
Chambers' novel, *Breaktime*

Opinions about the value of reading and teaching literature range
from the exalted claims of the post-Romantics (from Matthew Arnold
to I.A Richards and F.R. Leavis) that it is a profoundly ennobling
quasi-religious experience, a remedy for the disorders of industrial
and post-industrial society, to the blunt dismissiveness of countless
school students, like Aidan Chambers' Morgan, that 'literature is a
sham, no longer useful, effluent, CRAP'. Certainly, the way we test
students' literary responsiveness in public examinations, and the way
we are led to teach them as a consequence, seem to undermine the
notion that reading literature might be of significance for the way
we view our lives and those of others. The Australian Association
for the Teaching of English claims that 'Literature is centrally
concerned with exploring and defining the value and meaning of
human experience', and that literature's 'uniqueness lies in the way
it does this; through the imaginative re-creation and shaping of
experience in language'.[1] However, very few secondary school
students see it that way. The evidence from the surveys examined
in Chapter Two suggests that whatever value we believe literature
has, many of our students are missing out on it.

To test the claims that literature can perform the 'miracle of
overcoming man's characteristic weakness of learning from his own
experience' (Solzhenitsyn) and develop our personal sensitivity and
social and moral awareness, as well as being pleasurable in itself,
and to examine these generalisations and abstractions in action, I
offer the following reflective evaluation of my own reading of the
literature text I have most recently completed and enjoyed, *The Raj
Quartet* by Paul Scott.

## *A PERSONAL EXPERIENCE: REFLECTIONS ON A READING OF THE RAJ QUARTET*[2]

The four novels of *The Raj Quartet* are set in India between 1942
and 1947, covering the last years of British rule leading to

independence and partition. The novels explore the responses to major political and historican events, and to daily social events, of a vast range of English and Indian people, their interrelationships, aspirations, social and racial atitudes, foibles, successes and tragedies. The two main events and focal points of these attitudes and reactions are: the assumed rape of a well-connected English girl by an Indian boy whose English upper-class upbringing and education at a prestigious English 'public' school make him an English gentleman in all respects except colour of skin and country of birth; and the mass desertion of Indian soldiers from British regiments to the Indian National Army fighting with the Japanese to 'free India'.

Both events appear to involve treachery, and the apparent betrayers of trust in each case — Hari Kumar, the assumed rapist, and the members of the Indian National Army, the assumed deserters — are hunted and persecuted by an agent of the British civil and military law, a policeman become intelligence officer, Ronald Merrick, a man of working-class origins and deep-seated insecurities, whose excessive zeal for his work arises from class and racial hatreds.

Like many of the girls who spoke about their enthralled reading of the Virginia Andrews trilogy, I found *The Raj Quartet* difficult to put down. There was the pleasure of playing the author's games: wanting to know what would happen next and what would be the final outcome of the events. I had read enough history of modern India to know that the partition of India and Pakistan occurred in 1947 accompanied by mass slaughter of Hindus by Muslims and of Muslims by Hindus, and it seemed likely that the Quartet would end about the time of partition or just after. At each reading moment there were short-term and long-term expectations being continually generated and modified. Would Hari Kumar be justly exonerated? Would Ronald Merrick's corruption, hypocrisy and manipulation of others in the name of justice be exposed? Would Sarah Layton be recognised by anyone, apart form the reader and the admirable elderly spinster Barbie Batchelor, as the person of charm and integrity she is in the empty society of English army officers, public servants and clergy and their wives, most of whom are parasites, snobs and sycophants with naive and narrow loyalties to what they still see as the white man's burden to civilise India.

There was also the pleasure of trying to solve the puzzles created by the author, by recognising and piecing together the occasional clues that are dropped in a studiedly casual way. Was Daphne Manners raped? If so, by whom? What was the exact nature of Hari's involvement? And there were the more complex pleasures of working out enigmas and formulating for oneself what the author never formulates. Who is the unnamed narrator of the first novel, *The Jewel in the Crown*, and will we get enough information in the remaining novels to fill in this gap in our knowledge? Is this visitor to post-partitioned India, this person with a detailed understanding of contemporary Indian history and an intimate knowledge of all the main characters and local events, actually the civilised intelligence officer, Guy Perron, introduced into the text by name for the first time in Volume 4, *A Division of the Spoils*, and mentioned in a subsequent Paul Scott novel, *Staying On*, as a Professor of History and husband of Sarah Layton? There is no question of the pleasures of reading to find what happens next in this novel, and to work out what happened in the past and why. However, while these kinds of pleasure might be necessary satisfactions of reading literature, they are not sufficient to justify its significance in education and life. What else do we want our students to get beyond enjoyment?

What knowledge and understanding of the world have I got from a reading of *The Raj Quartet* that I didn't have before I read it? Certainly, my knowledge and understanding of colonialism and historical events in India in the 1940s has been deepened. I know more about the kinds of lives led by English civil and military personnel in India, and by Indians from a variety of social levels. I have a deeper understanding of the ethos of the British Raj and what it meant to the public and private lives of a social range of British and Indian people of different loyalties and aspirations. I have a deeper understanding of the disparate behaviour of people in crises and how some react according to the social and vocational roles they are given and accept, while others transcend such cultural shaping.

I have measured myself against characters in the book I admired, and recognised something of my own strengths and limitations as well as those of other people I know. For example, not being as socially assured or as intellectually sharp as Guy Perron, I admire his superior accomplishments because he uses them to pursue selflessly humane ends. The fact that I did find some of his accomplishments irritating — a trace of glibness in his intellectual sharpness and of smugness in his assurance — makes me recognise something about myself in my reaction against him for the upper-class upbringing which has made his way in life easier. So, in terms of knowledge, I think I have extended and deepened my own understanding of the historical period and, more importantly, of the human condition, of other people and of myself. The novels have made some of the great abstractions of life — love, loyalty, patriotism, integrity — accessible in ways the reading of philosophy and history has not.

Was my reading of this work morally educative? Has it influenced my values, my set of beliefs about what is right and wrong? Scott's dramatisation of the ironies and inequalities of life is most convincing, but I think my values have been confirmed, strengthened and more deeply understood rather than transformed. I am appalled but not shocked by the fate of Hari Kumar. That a person can have his life wrecked by incurring the jealousy of someone in a more powerful position is no surprise. Nor is it a surprise when the victim is an Indian and the perpetrator a white Englishman. However, the theme of racial tension is given greater depth by the additional complications of social class and sexual relationships. The Indian male, Hari Kumar, is an English public-school-educated gentleman and his persecutor is an English policeman with a working-class background. Hari Kumar, if not a rapist, has had sexual relationships with a woman Merrick would like to marry to improve his social image. While destroying Kumar for his sexual activity with a white woman, Merrick himself can have sexual relationships with Indian males and continue to be admired as a champion of order and moral right. All this indicates the skill with which Scott dramatises complex issues, avoiding the stereotyped plots of sentimentalised fiction. What continually impresses in these novels is the apparent even-handedness in the presentation of numerous opposing viewpoints so that none is a caricature and each creates genuinely sympathetic understanding of the character whose perspective it is. In matching my moral universe with that portrayal in *The Raj Quartet*, while I acknowledge that my values have been more confirmed than modified, I believe I have emerged from the experience with a greater understanding of what is meant by nobility, loyalty, self-knowledge and moral consciousness, and with a greater awareness of the range of manifestations of these values and their opposites in daily life.

Throughout the reading of these novels my emotions were powerfully engaged. I felt strong sympathy for those characters, both English and Indian, whose understanding of other people and of the moral issues of their historical moment transcends that of characters whose responses to events are more immediately egocentric and materialistic. I felt both outraged and sad at the horror and injustice of the cold-blooded murder of a character whose moral growth is charted through the four volumes. There is no question of the success with which Paul Scott controls 'the flow and recoil of sympathy' which, as D.H. Lawrence says, 'determines the quality of our lives as human beings'[3]. Literature certainly seems to extend our range of emotional experience through empathy. In our daily preoccupations with immediate concerns, we often find it difficult to imagine the political or moral significance of events around us, or the feelings of those more deeply involved in them. In reading literature, we become more emotionally responsive and morally aware because the writer makes us see and understand the significance of events in terms of their consequences to the lives of human beings. It is this emotional response to the imaged world of literature that distinguishes literature from history and philosophy, and makes literature so powerful a way of enabling readers to understand issues about which other forms of discourse might often leave them relatively unconcerned and apathetic.

This resumé of the values and satisfactions of reading *The Raj Quartet* has so far ignored a whole range of higher level or more complex pleasures that I will call aesthetic understanding. However, experiencing the kinds of pleasures I have in mind involves more than recognising the author's methods and acknowledging his skills as an artist, for that recognition and acknowledgment lead to a deeper understanding of the meanings and a sharper experiencing of the effects already mentioned. The profundity of Paul Scott's moral vision cannot be experienced without a recognition of the structures of the text, the way language is used to control tone, or the methods used to arouse the reader's curiosity and to delay its satisfaction. Merrick is portrayed as a thoroughly efficient police officer. However, less through what is shown of him and said about him than by what is not shown and said, we feel something sinister about him. We fill the gaps left in his characterisation with the suspicion that there is something about Merrick that is not under conscious control, some weakness that might have significant consequences and, perhaps, ultimately betray him.

If we detect the recurring motifs in the structure of the work, the parallelling and counterpointing of episodes and characters, we will discover that for each theme in the novel there is a clearly portrayed range of human responses that we are intended to compare in order to derive a scale of moral worth. On the theme of sexuality, we recognise that Daphne Manners' rape, Mildren Layton's animality and adultery, Sarah's experimentation, Susan's timidity and Ronald

Merrick's homosexuality invite us to compare their moral responses. On the theme of leadership and authority, we compare and discriminate the moral worth of the values and behaviour of Mohammed Ali Kasim, Count Bronowski, Captain Rowan, Colonel Layton, Brigadier Reid, Teddie Bingham and Ronald Merrick. On the themes of feminine love and devotion, we are invited to compare the kinds of love shown by the Christian teachers, Edwina Crane, Barbie Batchelor and Sister Ludmilla; by the different ladies of the Layton family, Susan, Sarah, Mildred and Mabel; and by the Indian ladies, Mrs Kasim, Mrs Gupta Sen and Lady Chatterjee. On the theme of patriotism, the four members of the Kasim family, amongst others, are counterpointed, each with a different priority as to his or her highest loyalty. At least six quite disparate characters all attended the same English 'public' school, and that connection invites us to compare their sets of values in the light of colonialist notions that the British Empire was won on the playing fields of Eton.

Our attention is drawn by the frequent changing of narrative perspectives to the range of viewpoints on display. Ironic juxtapositions, the structural ordering of events by principles outside chronology and other rhetorical elements lead us to see the major characters as members of different groups that we are invited to compare with one another. We are also invited to compare the members within each group with one another and with their counterparts in other groups. For example, there are sensitive characters like Sarah and Mabel Layton, Guy Perron and Mohammed Kasim with almost instinctive understanding of human relationships and the significance of the events they are involved in; there are those who learn to understand these things, who grow during the course of the novels; there are those whose good intentions and sense of responsibility are restricted by the limits of a moral vision determined by their social and historical roles; and there are those whose evil acts are the outcomes of more complex psychological and political motivations which the novel explores. Each major character belongs to a number of the different structural networks of the novels. For example, Guy Perron is, like Ronald Merrick, a British official involved in detective work. He shares with Mohammed Kasim and others an ability to understand history and the consequences of actions which transcends the historical situation of his race, class and occupation. He is also a member of a group of old boys of Chillingborough School, so we are invited to compare his behaviour and attitudes with those of his old school chums who belong to the group of those who grow in self-knowledge during the course of the novels, as well as with those who remain eternally ignorant and those who manipulate others for selfish purposes.

My reading of *The Raj Quartet* was an enjoyable and enlightening experience. Much of the enjoyment and enlightenment arose from a whole complex of mental activities performed during the process of reading. These will be examined in the following section on contemporary literary theories (pp. 86-146) However, what is important to mention at this stage is that the initial satisfaction of reading is an emotional one. Empathising with characters was a powerful source of my enjoyment. D.W. Harding is right to emphasise the importance of emotional verification from personal experience as a source of literary satisfaction:

> The "that's me" may well reveal a very partial and too selective selection from the work, but the teacher will get nowhere in the attempt to make the work meaningful as experience if he does not begin with "me".[4]

> A developing interest in fiction is tied up in some way with an interest in other people. Like gossip, it depends on a wish to follow their doings to try to understand their motives, and to join with someone else in making an emotional response to their behaviour and supposed experience.[5]

## THE VALUES AND SATISFACTIONS OF READING

As we have seen, emotional response precedes intellectual understanding and seems to be a prerequisite for such understanding to have a significant impact. Louise Rosenblatt explains:

> Because the literary experience tends to involve both the intellect and the emotions in a manner that parallels life itself, the insights attained through literature may be assimilated into the matrix of attitudes and ideas which constitute character and govern behaviour. Hence the opportunity for students to develop the habit of reflective thinking within the context of an emotionally coloured situation.[6]

At this stage it has to be asked whether this habit of reflective thinking developing within the context of an emotionally coloured situation can't be just as powerfully stimulated by film. My reflections on my own processes of interpreting *some* films suggest that this is possible. For example, in the film *Missing*, starring Jack Lemmon as a politically conservative middle-aged American searching for his missing son in post-Allende Chile, a central image is that of the shooting of a magnificent white horse of striking beauty as it gallops through the streets of Santiago during an evening curfew. The first reaction is one of shocked revulsion. One is sickened by the barbarity of those who so gratuitously destroy such a beautiful free creature. The reflective interpretation of the event follows the emotional reaction. One recognises that the scene is a metaphor, a symbol of the destruction of freedom, purity, beauty, imagination and vitality by the fascist military regime after the coup in Santiago. This kind of visual metaphor exemplifies Susanne Langer's point that significant form in art is an articulate expression of feeling: 'art is the creation of forms symbolic of human feeling'[7]. Such techniques as this when used in film are often called 'literary', because we are more familiar with their use in literature. The scene is dislocative of the reader's absorption in the narrative action. Attention is directed, momentarily, away from 'What happens next?' to 'What am I to make of this horrible scene?' The film-maker leaves a gap in the text for the reader to fill in. The scene is not part of the realistic narrative sequence but a non-realistic symbol illuminating the significance of the action the narrative portrays. The significance is formulated by the viewer whose initial reaction is an emotional one. The best films, such as *Missing*, can activate the viewer's imagination in this way and so overcome, to this degree at least, the essentially passive role assigned to the viewer by the nature of the medium. The American film actor, James Stewart, on a recent visit to Australia, made the point in a radio interview that the films he liked best were those that don't need so much dialogue; that is, films which don't tell viewers everything but leave some space to activate viewers' imaginations to formulate meanings for themselves.

If film, at its best, can accomplish for viewers what literature can for readers in terms of developing understanding of self, other people and the human condition, some of the excessive claims made for literature's uniqueness and humanising capacity might well have to be questioned. I have not noticed that the professional readers of literature—English lecturers in academic institutions—are more sensitive in human relationships and more highly developed morally than people in other walks of life. In fact, when I ask what is unique to the study of literature, what the discipline has provided that other disciplines and activities have not, all I can think of is the kind of arid literary criticism that is taught in those universities dominated by the influence of Leavis and the New Critics, and imposed on the schools through the Higher School Certificate English syllabuses. This is the kind of activity that has turned most people off reading.

Reading literature can be of tremendous value. It accomplishes for us many things that a range of other activities can also accomplish, albeit in many cases less well. Perhaps it would be more sensible to see literature as one of many important activities promoting human understanding rather than as the unique civilising pursuit. Film and television are more passive media than literature, but films such as *Missing* are more valuable than novels like *Flowers in the Attic*. Literature can make the abstractions of life powerfully felt and understood, but so can the best films. The best literature does activate the reader's imagination and invite reflection on its significance, which is more than can be said for most of the television programmes that children watch. In comparison with film, literature does generally leave more space for readers to match their values and experiences with those of authors and to come to better understand their own beliefs and how texts have influenced them. The role of the reader of literature is something we pursue in the section on literary theory (pp. 111-128) when we consider Wolfgang Iser's contribution to our understanding of reading processes.

The question 'Why read literature?' is one that has to be asked and answered by each reader. The values and satisfactions can (must?) be intensely personal. What is important is that we as teachers invite our students to ask the question continually and that we help them to find meaningful personal answers that are both satisfying to them and justifiable to others. Here are two such personal answers from outstanding English teachers, Helen Drewe of Lithgow High School and David Moss of Ingleburn High School.

My attitudes to people have been developed through reading, as many of the characters in novels are reflective of people I would not normally meet. I find myself 'empathetic' to the point of tears on many occasions, such as when I read *The Summer of My German Soldier* this year. The naive way in which the main character in that book believed she could help an escaped prisoner of war was heart-breaking.

Helen Drewe

Reading literature of any sort emphasises the reader's own awareness of his or her humanity, his or her membership of the human race. There is a world of difference between an activity which can make a person more human and one which can make a person more humane. The quality of being human can well exist without or before the quality of humaneness . . . Reading literature is a means to an end. Humanising is the process; humaneness one of its goals. But humaneness is only one of the goals, and an idealistic one, of the process of humanising. Being human can involve the opposite of humaneness: cruelty, barbarism, sadism. This also is part of being human. The writing and reading of literature makes a person more human, that is more aware of (and susceptible to?) the frightening range of possibilities encompassed by the human experience — from humaneness to barbarism . . .

The range of the 20 or so books I read over the Christmas holidays reveals something about the different satisfactions involved in reading — from Desmond Bagley to Peter Carey, from Colleen McCullough to Jack Fingleton, from Mark Twain to Christopher Koch, from Michael Crichton to Len Deighton. Some of these were pure escape, some I found more intellectually stimulating. Some satisfactions ended where and when the books ended, whilst other caused me to contemplate aspects of my own existence. Some allowed me to do the travelling I've never done, some confirmed old ideas and prejudices, some made me feel vengeful and violent, some left me at peace with the world. Each one struck at least some vibrant chords, whilst some played symphonies. Each confirmed the humanity of myself, the writer and (most of) the characters.

David Moss


## THE POSITION OF LITERATURE IN THE ENGLISH PROGRAMME

From the conflicting attitudes towards the value of reading and teaching liteature prevalent in contemporary literary theory and in university and school English departments in Australia and overseas, there has emerged a number of different positions in the teaching of English. Each of these schools of thought gives literature a different definition and a different status in the English curriculum. These postions can be briefly summarised, recognising that in any one secondary school or university English department the teaching approach might well represent a compromise between several of them. Often, there are straight out conflicts between teachers in the same department, which must be confusing to students, particularly when the teachers do not make explicit to them the approach they are adopting and the theory or ideology underpinning it. The positions, or approaches are:

## Literature at the centre

Imaginative literature is the raison d'être of teaching English. Literature is usually defined as the great works from the heritage, and popular literature, film, television and students' own imaginative writing are likely to be excluded from consideration because they are seen to be inferior uses of language. Almost all the writing done by students taught by this approach is formal, literary critical essays. Informal writing, personal writing and imaginative writing are usually not encouraged.

The critical theory held by the proponents of this approach is almost certain to be American New Criticism or some amalgum of it and one or more of the theories of Matthew Arnold, I.A. Richards, F.R. Leavis and T.S. Eliot. This position is very strong in Australian universities and in Years 11 and 12 of the secondary school. It is not popular with most students because it emphasises detailed analysis of specific classic texts, imposes received critical judgment on them, denigrates their emotional responses as being inappropriate in a educational setting, causes them to feel incompetent because their own genuine responses are often deemed immature, and uses literature texts for uninspiring, routine written exercises such as comprehension work and plot summaries.

## Language at the centre

The main purpose of teaching English is to improve the abilities of students to use the language appropriately in the range of situations required for participating in our culture. This practical approach is underpinned by the work in contemporary sociolinguistics of people like Michael Halliday, Geoffrey Thornton, Peter Doughty and Basil Bernstein. Work in the classroom emphasises the use of oral language in small groups, and explorations of the varieties of language used by different people in a range of social situations of varying degrees of formality and informality. Although there are people holding this position who would omit imaginative literature entirely from English, most adherents would recognise how easily this approach can be combined with the 'personal growth' model.

## Exploring and using the personal experience of pupils

This approach has at its centre the personal development of the individual in terms of linguistic growth, aesthetic growth, social growth and moral growth. It is concerned with developing students' competence in using language for a range of practical and imaginative purposes, so that 'a growing mastery of language relates to a deepening awareness of self, of others, and of the human condition'[8]. In this position literature includes, as well as works from the heritage, contemporary children's and adolescent fiction, students' own imaginative writing from personal and imagined experience, film and television fiction, and writing in class covers a whole range of functions and audiences. This approach has been developed by the work of people such as James Britton, Douglas Barnes, Andrew Wilkinson, John Dixon and Leslie Stratta, and is supported by contemporary research and theory in psychology, psycholinguistics, sociolinguistics and literary criticism. As Stratta, Dixon and Wilkinson explain it in their important book, *Patterns of Language*, 'pupils and teachers are involved in specific explorations: into personal experiences and those of others, into the visions of life offered through literature; and into language itself and its relationship to living experience.'[9]

## The skills approach

The approach is influenced by the work of B.F. Skinner in behaviourist psychology and held by people with a colossal ignorance of the nature of language itself, of how it is learned, and of its central value as a tool of learning. The aim of the skills-oriented people in making public calls for a 'back-to-basics' movement in education is to isolate the discrete skills of reading, talking, listening and writing and to drill these so that all are successfully learned by all students who will never thereafter make any errors in using the language.

Unfortunately there is no such thing as a form of correct English that is appropriate in all contexts, and people don't learn to use the language as a set of discrete skills. There is a range of correct Englishes, each one appropriate in a particular social situation. For example, the boy who says in the school playground, 'May I play chasings with you boys?' could well be said to be using a wrong form of the language in this informal situation. Language is learned in the context of social situations, not in situations isolated from meaning. The main criticism I would make of the skills approach is that it is unsuccessful in teaching the skills. Language skills are only taught effectively when they are embedded in meaningful contexts and it is the responsibility of the teacher to create these.

## THE IMPORTANCE OF NARRATIVE: 'STORYING' AND 'THE ROLE OF THE ONLOOKER'

### Storying

> The anecdotes and stories honed to perfection through countless retellings in the front bar, testify to man's seemingly innate need for "storying".

> Garth Boomer, 'Eternal Triangles
> — Language as Literature in
> Senior English', in *The Teaching
> of English*, no. 27, September 1974.

> In every language, in every part of the world, story is the fundamental grammar of all thought and communication. By telling ourselves what happened, to whom, and why we not only discover ourselves and the world, but we change and create ourselves and the world too.

> Aidan Chambers, 'The Child's
> Changing Story' (in *Signal* 40)

We construct narratives out of the events of our lives in order to make sense of them. 'Narrative is a primary act of mind' Barbara Hardy tells us, and she goes on to suggest that the novel is only a more refined form of an activity we all engage in: 'The novel merely heightens, isolates and analyses the narrative motions of human consciousness.'[10] Turning our lives into narratives is our way of helping ourselves to understand them. As James Britton says, 'We do not learn from the higgledy-piggledy of events as they strike the senses, but from the representation we make of them.'[11] When we look back over the events of a day or a year or a longer period of our lives, we select those that we can connect with one another in such a way as to create order and meaning out of chaotic, undifferentiated experience. In this process of abstracting from the flow we impose a narrative shape or pattern so as to interpret our lives to ourselves. The pattern of meaning is constructed by us in language. As Britton, again, puts it:

> We construct a representation of the world as we experience it, and from this representation, this cumulative record of our own past, we generate expectations concerning the future; expectations which, as moment by moment the future becomes the present, enable us to interpret the present.[12]

As we shall see in the section on literary theories (pp. 111-128), the German phenomenologist Wolfgang Iser shows how we read literature in much the same way, continually constructing representations or interpretations and, at each reading moment, generating expectations about the kinds of things that might happen ahead in the text, and modifying our interpretations of what we have read in the light of what we are reading now.

Storying is important in the growth of the mind. The process of selection involved in the construction of narrative is a necessary part of the capacity to generalise. In her book *Children's Mind's,* Margaret Donaldson shows how important a sense of story is to the development of language and thinking[13], and Michael Halliday, in *Learning How to Mean,* a study of the developing language functions of a pre-school child, shows how narrative first develops as a strategy for learning[14]. In an important study of factors accounting for success in early schooling, Gordon Wells found that listening to stories was clearly the most significant[15]. Wells argues that the main reason why listening to stories is so much more beneficial to young children than other literacy-related pre-school activities is that hearing stories develops the sense of narrative so important in reasoning and making sense of the world as well as in learning to read and write. About the two or three or four year-old child listening to stories read aloud before he can read himself, Wells says,

> Most importantly, he is beginning to come to grips with the symbolic potential of language — its power to represent experience

in symbols which are independent of the objects, events and relationships which are symbolised, and which can be interpreted in contexts other than those in which the experience originally occurred.[16]

Wells suggests that reading stories aloud and discussing them with chidren in a way which encourages them to relate their own experience of the world to the imagined world of the story, and to reflect on both, is a productive way of helping them to direct and control their own thinking and languaging processes. This relationship between storying and the growth of literacy and reasoning is apparent at all stages of human development. It is just as important for English teachers to spend time reading stories to secondary students as it is for parents to read stories to pre-school children. Our sense of story continues to develop as our language and our reasoning powers develop. These processes of growth are interactive and mutually supportive. The better we read literature the better we think and the better we use language, *ad infinitum*.

### 'The Role of the Onlooker'

Through contemplation after the event, we may, by
becoming a spectator or onlooker to what has happened,
rearrange our view of the world. Now . . . the literary work is
an itensified form of spectatorship. It serves the purpose of
allowing the writer both prospect and retrospect on his world.
It allows the reader to share in the new perspectives and from
a new vantage point, to get fresh perspectives on his own life.

Garth Boomer, 'Eternal Triangles
— Language as Literature
in Senior English'

In his article, 'The Role of the Onlooker'[17], D.W. Harding shows how the activities of reading literature, daydreaming and engaging in gossip with a friend are essentially similar. In all these activities we are offered or offering symbolic representations of life events which enable us to contemplate the possibilities and consequences of our own and others' experience, including that of characters in fiction. In reflecting on our own experience or that of others we sort out, make sense of and come to terms with ourselves and the world.

The anecdotes we construct and share with others are indicative of our representations of the world. They reflect our sense of our own identities and beliefs and we share them to convey that sense of identity to others, so that in being amused, shocked, outraged, sympathetic or whatever these others confirm for us that our representation, if not exactly the same as theirs, is appropriate or worthy of respect. In reading literature, just as in listening to anecdotes of others, we can extend our understanding of ourselves, of other people and of the human condition. As Harding puts it, 'In literature . . . the author invites his audience to share in an exploration, and extension and refinement of his and their common interests; and as a corollary to refine and modify their value judgments.'[18]

Because we have a consuming interest in the possibilities of human experience, pleasant and unpleasant, we find the role of onlooking deeply satisfying. It is also crucial in our development as human beings, socially, intellectually, emotionally and morally. As James Britton has made clear, we take up the role of participant to operate in the real world by way of our representation of it, but we take up the role of onlooker or spectator in order to operate on the representation itself, to savour or to come to terms with past experiences, and to enter into other people's experiences. By doing so, we make our representation of the world as complete as possible, improving our predictive equipment.

> As spectators, we use language to contemplate what has happened to us or to other people, or what might conceivably happen; in other words, we improvise upon our world representation — and we may do so either to enrich it, to embroider it, to fill in its gaps and extend its frontiers, or to iron out its inconsistencies.[19]

To be in the role of spectator or onlooker is, in one sense, to generate hypotheses about the way things are without the present intention of putting them to the test. When we participate in the world's affairs feeling is worked off in action. When we are spectators or onlookers we are able to savour feeling as feeling and perceive the form it takes, attending to its pattern as well as the patterns of events and the form of language itself. In the spectator role, freed of the need to act, we can re-evaluate our own experiences and evaluate other people's in the full light of the beliefs we have derived from living. In this role as readers of literature, we can match our world representation with the representations of authors, with the possibility of improving or refining our own. As Harding says, whatever else a novelist or playwright is doing, he is conveying his own evaluation of what his characters do and feel, presenting their actions and reactions as funny, heroic, contemptible, sensitive, pathetic and so on, and implicitly inviting readers to share his attitude: 'Our task as readers is not complete unless we tacitly evaluate his evaluation, endorsing it fully, rejecting it, but more probably feeling some less clear cut attitude based on discriminations achieved or groped after.'[20]

These extracts from the transcript of an interview with a Year 8 Bathurst boy about his response to literature illustrate the paradoxical combination of emotional involvement and cool detachment that characterises the reflective and evaluative processes of a reader in the role of the spectator.

"In *I Am the Cheese* (Robert Cormier) you feel really sympathetic with Adam and you like him, but you only realise at the end that the journey was a dream world, his imagination. I found the ending terrifying, not because it was hard to understand but because it became so clear. It was so straightforward it was terrifying. Adam was a total victim. He is treated as a threatening thing, not as a boy or a person. He had no chance. If he knew anything they'd kill him. If he didn't they have to keep him permanently drugged in case he remembered something. It is not until the last section that you completely understand his problem and it's a bit of a shock . . .

"Sitting back reading, you don't have the same feelings as the character himself has because you are not in his position but judging. A character might misjudge his predicament but you as reader don't because you're not in the situation creating fear, panic or happiness or whatever it is. It's like looking at a soccer match from the Stand where you can see the mistakes and the tactics that go wrong, but the person playing is doing his best under pressure and he can't see the patterns that you can. I have no wish to be a backseat driver. Some kids like to be backseat drivers in reading but they might think the novel is life when it's only a picture of life. It's not actually happening. It shows you what the writer thinks life is like, what sort of things are likely to happen, and you're trying to learn what his view of life is like . . .

You assess, judge where the character might misjudge because of his emotions. You know more than they do. You are ahead of them. Even in *I Am the Cheese* where you don't know more than Adam until the last bit you are not him, but you know the author will let you know even if Adam doesn't find out. So you will understand something about life and something about him that he mightn't understand himself."

This student shows that in his reading he adopts all the main elements of Harding's spectator role, essential for reading at the highest levels. He sees the world as the character he empathises with sees it, but he understands it as the author does. His sympathies and his critical faculties are equally engaged.

It is a matter of the utmost importance that students be able to examine themselves and their world with some detachment, to step outside themselves and look at their experiences and feelings, as well as those of others, from another perspective beyond the immediately subjective one. This is a way of coming to know themselves and their world, a process of discovering who they are and what community they inhabit. Very few of the Bathurst students respond to literature at the high level reached by the 14-year-old quoted in the last paragraph. However, many showed the potential to read at this level. Many seemed to recognise that some of the books and poems they read and enjoyed offered some deeper satisfactions that were just out of reach. Unfortunately, they blamed their sense of dissatisfaction on their own intellectual limitations as readers rather than on the limitation of the range of reading strategies they were using. In Chapter Five we consider some of the kinds of practical classroom activities that teachers can organise to help students to read with higher levels of insight and satisfaction. It is pretty clear that three guiding approaches for teachers should be:

1. to encourage students to make links continually between the world of the text and the world of their own personal experiences outside it, between literature and their own lives;
2. to ensure that students do a great deal of spectator role writing, sometimes from personal experience, sometimes from imagined experience, and sometimes in response to literature read; and
3. to assist students to find the books that speak to them of their immediate concerns, and try to help them to progress from the kinds of books that merely confirm prejudice and strengthen self-ignorance and self-indulgent emotionalism, to those which promote reflection, understanding and human growth.

In 'The Role of the Onlooker', Harding says that, 'if we could obliterate the effects on a man of all the occasions when he was merely a "spectator" it would be profoundly to alter his character and outlook.'[21] A 'pure' participant in life, a completely non-reflective person, would, of course, be a victim of the vagaries of his environment. Such a person would experience the world as pure sensation, as a random collection of unconnected events. No one is entirely a spectator or entirely a participant, for to be human means to be to some extent reflective, even in the midst of action. There are obviously degrees of spectating and participating. The most contemplative recluse is 'onlooking' with some kind of participation in mind, however slight. The literary experiences which will be most valuable to our students (as they are to us) will be those in which they are, in the sense, both spectators and participants. They will be spectators of authors' representations of the possibilities of life, and they will be participants in the act of reading. Literature will be of value to them in so far as it is useful in improving the quality of their participation in life. They also need to be spectators of their own participation, observers of themselves as readers in action and of authors as creators, but more of this in later chapters.

The distinction Britton makes between spectator and participant roles offers a clue as to how we might construct an integrated English syllabus. The dichotomy between language-centred English and literature-centred English is based on narrow and essentially false notions about the nature and value of language and literature. The trouble with the literature-centred approach is that it makes literature remote from our students' lives. It defines literature as great artefacts from the heritage, each one to be admired and studied in isolation and treated as an object in itself but not *used* by ordinary people. The language of literature is seen as a superior form of expression, different in both quality and kind from the language in which we conduct our daily lives. If we define literature as language in the role of the spectator — and therefore incorporate gossip, oral tales, students' own spoken and written stories from personal and imagined experience, as well as printed children's, adolescent and heritage literature — we bridge the gap between literature and life, between literary language and personal language, between language read and language used. We demystify literature and make its processes accessible to students.

We use language in the spectator role for organising the subjective aspects of experience. As Britton says, we 'use talk and writing and reading to explore and shape our inner lives' and 'it is by such means that an individual preserves his picture of the world as a world worth living in.'[22] But we also use language in the participant role as an instrument of learning about the objective aspects of experience. We talk and write as participants to inform or persuade others – by reporting, explaining, analysing and theorising in rational discourse. In explaining things to others, we are also sorting them out and understanding them better for ourselves. For example, in talking and writing about literature in the participant role, we come to understand how literature works, how its language creates its representations of the world. In reading and interpreting literature, in being emotionally involved in the world of a novel or poem, we are in the spectator role, improvising on our representations of the world. In thinking and talking and writing about the way literature works, in analysing it and our own reading processes, we are in the participant role.

All the aspects of the English Syllabus that are often fragmented can and should be integrated through language. Mastery of language comes from using it purposefully. In writing stories and poems (participant role), students become better readers of stories and poems (spectator role) and thus better able to analyse the way stories and poems operate on them (participant role). In writing an advertisement for the latest teenage novel purchased for the library (participant role) students are better able to understand how advertisements they read in magazines and see on television achieve their effects. Reading and writing in both spectator and participant roles are mutually interactive and supportive activities.

To derive value from reading literature students need to have their own representation of the world extended or modified. To derive value from their work in language, students need to have their range of language functions extended and their performance in each function developed. We have seen that reading appropriate literature, and talking and writing about it openly and honestly in both spectator and participant roles can extend students' representations, value systems and emotional and intellectual understanding. Just as students bring to their reading and discussion of literature their present representations of the world, so also do they bring to these activities their habitual range of language functions and competences. Just as reading and talking about literature can extend their representations of the world, so can it extend their control of a range of language functions and their competences in performing each function. For example, to invite students to discuss and/or write about an incident in a novel from the point of view of a character whose viewpoint is not presented in the text itself is, at the same time, a productive strategy of reading, in requiring readers to explore the text more deeply for implications as to how such a character might consistently see the events narrated, and a productive means of developing competence in the speculative and imaginative functions of language. The speculative function of language, considering what might happen or what might have happened under certain given circumstances, is most important in the development of conceptual thinking as is shown by the research of Vygotsky, on the relationship between language and thinking, and of Britton, Halliday and Bernstein on the development of language abilities.[23]

## HOW EXPERT READERS READ AND THE SATISFACTIONS THEY GET: CLUES FROM LITERARY THEORY

No story is ever told by the author of the book: the telling
is done by the reader who takes the text for his scenario
an produces it on the stage of his own imagination with
resources furnished by his own experiences of life.

Ronald Morris, *Success and
Failure in Learning to Read*

"But that's absurd Madge. What we said doesn't mean that . . . "
"Whoever are you to say what it means? The words mean what they
mean to Patrick as much as they mean what they mean to you."

From *Unleaving*, a novel for teenagers
by Jill Paton Walsh

What happens when we read? What kinds of interaction occur between author, text, reader and reality? As with any other learning process involving the use of language, reading is an active process of making meaning. Development in reading and response to literature is a process of getting better and better at making a text have meaning, of becoming more intellectually and emotionally active while reading.

Recognition of the essentially active nature of learning is shifting the emphasis in education from what teachers transmit to what learners do, and from the products of learning to learning processes. In the teaching of writing, we have learned from researchers such as James Britton[24] and Donald Graves[25] to begin where the students are, to work with and develop the experiences and skills they possess rather than to impose structures and contents on them and then evaluate the worth of their written products by measuring them against finished products of mature writers. We no longer see them as passive recipients of information, and no longer expect them to arrive without having travelled, to have learned without actively experiencing the processes of learning. It is from the research of people such as Britton, Graves, Nancy Martin[26], James Moffett[27], and John Dixon and Leslie Stratta[28] that we know so much about developmental processes in writing, and that is far more than we know about developmental processes in reading and responding to literature.

In this section we consider the work of some of the contemporary literary critics who have shifted attention from the text itself as the sole repository of meaning and value to the process of reading, to what happens in the minds of readers as they actively engage with texts. In Chapter Four, we examine students' processes of reading and responding to literature. In matching what students actually do with what theory tells us are the productive strategies of ideal or expert readers, we might be better able to develop appropriate programmes to help students to read and respond with greater autonomy, power and control. Until now we have had insufficient knowledge of these processes and have been forced to rely too much on intuition in our teaching. Also the public examinations we have set have led us to assess the quality of a student's response in relation to specific texts and in terms of its approximation to the interpretations of eminent critics. The emphasis in students' literary education has therefore been on learning *about* specific texts rather than in developing their powers of responsiveness. We and our students have been concerned too much with literary information and not enough with response processes.

All literary theories are ideological because, as Terry Eagleton says, each one is informed by a 'largely concealed structure of values . . . modes of feeling, valuing, perceiving and believing which have some kind of relation to the maintenance and reproduction of social power.'[29] If you believe that literature is the respository of eternal values; that it deals with universals of human behaviour; that it is primarily concerned with improving the faculties that mediate experience, with refining taste and sensitivity, but not with inciting any particular feeling or form of behaviour; that each text is an autonomous and sancrosanct, organically unified object which is to be judged by the harmony of its internal relationships rather than by any criteria outside itself; then whether you know it or not your literary education has been shaped by the theories of I.A. Richards, F.R. Leavis and American New Criticism, which have dominated the reading and teaching of literature in the 20th century.

In an important historical essay on the shifting interests of criticism from the Classical period to the 20th century, Jane Tompkins explains that it is only in the 20th century that the text itself has become the major critical concern.

> Instead of moving the audience and bringing pressure to bear on the world, the work is thought to present another separate and more perfect world, which the flawed reader must labor to appreciate. The work is not a gesture in a social situation, or an ideal model for human behaviour, but an interplay of formal and thematic properties to be penetrated by the critic's mind. The imputation that a poem might break out of its self-containment and perform a service would disqualify it immediately from consideration as a work of art. The first requirement of a work of art in the twentieth century is that it should do nothing.[30]

There is nothing wrong in holding any one theory of literature as long as its adherents recognise that, like all human constructs, it is ideological and not the only, or the most 'natural', theory possible. Different theories have held sway in different periods of history. For example, as Tompkins points out, to readers in classical antiquity 'language was a form of power and the purpose of studying texts was to acquire the skills that enabled one to wield that power'.[31] In the Renaissance, literature was 'defined as a shaper of public morals'[32], and in the Augustan Age in England of the late 17th and early 18th century, poetry dealth explicitly with political issues and was seen as a 'weapon to be hurled against an opponent'[33] rather than as an organic system of relationships.

Where the New Critics focus on 'the poem itself' as precious artefact, on what a poem is rather than what it does,[34] contemporary reader-response critics focus on the reader and his or her creative and imaginative activity in constructing meaning under the guidance of the text. The reader is not the passive consumer of a completely formed product but involved actively in bringing the text to life in his or her mind. Whereas Leavis and the New Critics took it as axiomatic that literary meaning is contained in the words on the page, reader-response critics emphasise that meaning has no existence outside the mind of a reader who interprets the text in the light of his/her own experiences and values, assimilating its represent-ations of the world into his or her own, and/or accommodating his or her own representations to those of the text.

In their preoccupation with objectivity, order, harmony and structure in the analysis of literary works, the New Critics avoid political, social, historical and material issues like the plague. Terry Eagleton attacks the convenient hypocrisy of this stance of claiming to be non-ideological while being most ideological:

> Reading poetry in the New Critical way meant committing yourself to nothing: all that poetry taught you was "disinterestedness", a serene, speculative, impeccably even-handed rejection of anything in particular . . . It was in other words, a recipe for political inertia, and thus for submission to the political *status quo*.[35]

To New Critics, social and political questions are 'non-literary' or 'extra-literary' concerns, and thus conveniently ignored. For example, when William Styron's novel, *The Confessions of Nat Turner* was published in the 1950s in America and many black critics attacked it because they said Styron's fictional portrayal of the historical Turner was false to the negro mentality, the reaction of white New Critics was to ignore the criticism as being 'extra-literary'. The impression of 'female' created by the roles and behaviour assigned to girls in a children's novel would similarly be considered as lying outside the scope of critical interest. In making literature such a formal esoteric study and ignoring important human aspects of it, the New Critics have been most effective in turning students off reading.

All writers, readers, critics and producers bring to their literary activity their own values and beliefs, some more consciously than others. For example, in the past ten years I have seen three productions of *Twelfth Night*, each presenting its own distinctively different world view. The first one was a lyrical BBC television production which created feelings of optimism, harmony and reconciliation: the impression that all problems were soluble was appropriate to the mood of political optimism in England early in the Labour Government of Harold Wilson. The second was a production at the Nimrod Theatre in Sydney in the early confident years of the Whitlam government: it was an exuberantly comic triumph as befitted the mood of the Australian theatre under the first government that was serious about promoting the arts. The third production was at Stratford in England in 1983, and it expressed quite powerfully a sense of meanness and cruelty, appropriate, many would say, to what is happening in Britain under the government of Margaret Thatcher. The emphasis throughout was on social divisiveness, the dominance of privilege and wealth, and ineptitude in leadership. Orsino and Olivia were portrayed as insensitive and incompetent heads of households; Feste and Sir Toby Belch were nasty rather than funny; and Malvolio, the loyal well-intentioned victim of all the meanness, was given the status of an almost tragic hero.

## RICHARDS, LEAVIS AND NEW CRITICISM

### I.A. Richards

'All the pupils were given the same amount of class time to read *Let the Balloon Go*. A stencil/study guide was issued covering general questions, punctuation, vocabulary, creative writing, language – specific comprehension.'

'We always analyse poems under headings like theme, meaning, tone, imagery and diction.'

These approaches to the teaching of literature, outlined by two English teachers, inevitably lead students to see the skills and concepts as ends in themselves rather than as helpful strategies for exploring and articulating meanings. This fragmented approach to literature is an unfortunate and unintended outcome of the attempts in the 1920s of I.A. Richards, the Cambridge critic, to transform literary education by creating new reading methods 'for those who wish to discover for themselves what they think and feel about poetry'.[36] In his book of 1929, *Practical Criticism*, Richards used the terms sense, tone, feeling and intention as guides to readers of poetry. Margaret Meek, in a study of adolescents learning to read, identifies the weakness of teaching reading as discrete skills:

We confirmed our conviction that reading has to be taught as the thing that it is, holistically. To break it down into piecemeal activities for pseudo-systematic instruction is to block the individual, idiosyncratic moves that pupils of this age make to interact with a text and to teach themselves how to make it mean.[37]

Here, Meek is speaking specifically about the teaching of reading to adolescents who can't read, but her comments are equally applicable to improving the performances of readers at any level of accomplishment.

## F.R. Leavis

There hardly exists an English teacher who has not been influenced, either consciously or unconsciously, by the literary criticism of F.R. Leavis, Fellow of Downing College, Cambridge, and active critic from the 1930s to the 1970s. English syllabuses and teaching methods in Australia have enshrined his favourite authors, his attitudes and his critical vocabulary. It is difficult to avoid using Leavis's own language in talking about literature: expressions such as 'moral concern', 'discrimination', 'concrete realisation', 'achieved actuality', 'specificity', 'textual exploration', 'vitality', 'felt experience', 'life promoting', 'the great tradition', and the equation of 'moral consciousness' and 'literary sensitivity', are all his. Also widely accepted are Leavis's beliefs that there is a close relationship between our capacity to respond to literature and our fitness for life, that a refined sense of literary 'discrimination' makes us better people, ethically, morally and socially. As he puts it himself, the concern of the critic is not with any particular moral viewpoint or doctrine but with 'the quality of life that is concretely present in the work in front of him'[38]. As Terry Eagleton says, under the influence of Leavis and his followers literature became 'less an academic subject than a spiritual exploration coterminous with the fate of civilization itself'[39].

Leavis believed so passionately in the moral efficacy of literary discrimination that he ordered English poets and novelists in a hierarchy of excellence. Among the authors he found most 'significant in terms of that human awareness they promote of the possibilities of life'[40] are Chaucer, Shakespeare, the 'metaphysical' poets Donne and Marvell, Pope, Jane Austen, George Eliot, Wordsworth, Hopkins, James, Conrad, T.S. Eliot and Lawrence. A glance at the list of set texts for the Higher School Certificate examination in any Australian state over the past 30 years will indicate just how influential Leavis's 'great tradition' is in Australian education. Apart from the 'essential Englishness' (his term) of these authors and their concerns, and the problem of Australian syllabuses being dominated by great works from the English cultural heritage, there is the far more important one of any 'great tradition' being imposed on students; so that instead of discovering, exploring, testing and developing their own values through reading literature, they are taking over the values of another classifier; instead of discovering, exploring and articulating their own personal responses, they are taking over the critical judgments of master critics about master works. Discrimination and taste are not developed by taking over the discriminations and tastes of others.

To Leavis, literary education offered some kind of antidote to what he saw as the materialistic and meretricious values of modern industrial society which has destroyed the sense of community and harmony between man and environment characteristic of the 'organic' agrarian pre-industrial world. Leavis and his followers hoped to maintain the values of the past by educating a minority whose task would be to create an intelligent reading public. Despite the admirable intentions and the energy Leavis expended in gathering a group of committed followers, it would seem from research that the 'great tradition' of English literature, that collection of essential works perpetuating the values of English life, has not succeeded in delighting many readers in England or Australia. While Leavis might not be directly responsible for selecting the texts set for study in American and English schools today, his influence is dominant in these selections.

Leavis's concept of what Terry Eagleton calls 'an embattled cultivated minority' keeping 'the torch of culture burning in the contemporary waste land[41]' to pass on to posterity by way of their pupils is narrowly elitist and ambitiously idealistic. The notion that a group of people engaged in sensitive discussion of the literature of 'the great tradition' could transform the nature of post-industrial society is whimsical. 'Was it really true,' asks Terry Eagleton, 'that literature could roll back the deadening effects of industrial society and the philistinism of the media?'[42] The idea that readers of great literature are necessarily morally superior to those who haven't heard of John Donne is dismissive of the virtues of people whose moral and emotional sensitivities have been highly developed by other means than the reading of English at Cambridge. Reading literature is not the only 'civilising pursuit'.

The disinterested liberalism of the latter-day Leavisite intellectual with his moral seriousness and well-meaning ineffectuality is affectionately and amusingly portrayed in Malcolm Bradbury's characterisation of Stuart Treece, Professor of English Literature at a provincial English university, in his novel, *Eating People Is Wrong*:

> Each year he planned to send out into the world, at last, a little group of discontented men who would share his own disgusts, his own firm assurance in the necessity for good taste, honest feeling, integrity of motive, and each year the proposition came to seem odious as he foresaw the profound weariness and depression of spirit that would overcome such people.[43]

Stuart Treece is so sensitive, civilised and tolerant that he sympathises with everyone else's point of view. The result is that, despite his discrimination, he has lost the power to act: he can't do anything to help other people; he can only understand them. As Bradbury says, 'The liberalism that makes Treece virtuous also makes him inert.'[44] Perhaps this is also the failure of Leavis: his naïveté in believing that literature is above and beyond ideology, politics, economics and history. In emphasising the intellectual, emotional and civilising experience of reading, Leavis ignored the practical moral problems of people who had to live with the economic reality of the wasteland of contemporary post-industrial society. Treece explains the dilemma to a colleague:

> Why are we teaching in a university in the first place? Goodness knows it's not for the money. It isn't because we want to teach or because, simply, we love scholarship. Isn't it because we want to live in a world of circulating ideas and critical valuations? If our function isn't to talk about what is good when the rest of the world is talking about what is profitable, what can we do?[45]

The reply of a young Economics lecturer is significant:

> . . . it's necessary to accept the fact that university graduates must go into business and industry. Some can stay outside, a lucky few like ourselves; and we can *afford* to know better than anyone else. We don't have to face the moral problem of living with it.[46]

It is as though Leavis is saying that while a proper reading of the canon of 'the great tradition' increases our sensitivity, that sensitivity is not to result in any action in the real world; that after reading *Cry The Beloved Country*, for example, and empathising with the black father, we are not to *do* anything in the world about racial prejudice beyond understanding its evil and sympathising with its victims. Spectating is of little use if it doesn't make us all, ultimately, more human and more humane participants.

Terry Eagleton exposes the limitations of Leavis's liberal humanist theory of literature when he explains that, like religion, which it replaced as the moral ideology of the modern age, it may have been successful in developing a 'rich organic sensibility in selected individuals here and there', but there was never any serious consideration of actually trying to *change* such a society: 'It was less a matter of seeking to transform the mechanised society which gave birth to this withered culture than of seeking to withstand it.'[47]

What Leavis failed to recognise was that reading and teaching literature is, like all education, a political activity. Ideological neutrality is not an option. To read the books and authors Leavis recommends, to read them in the ways he has taught us to read, and to evaluate them as he has evaluated them, is to be ideologically shaped without knowing it. He and his followers transmit a culture to us as given. Attractive as this culture is, a teacher's priority should be to help students to explore, interpret and shape their own.

## New Criticism

> The Affective Fallacy is a confusion between the poem and its results (what it *is* and what it *does*) . . . It begins by trying to derive the standard of criticism from the psychological effects of the poem and ends in impressionism and relativism. The outcome . . . is that the poem itself, as an object of specifically critical judgment, tends to disappear.[48]

This declarative statement by W.K. Wimsatt and Monroe Beardsley in 1949 is one of the prime articles of faith of New Criticism which has dominated the teaching of literature in American and Australian universities since the 1960s. While the New Critics share with Leavis an emphasis on close reading and careful attention to the constituent parts of an organically unified literary work, the differences between them were sufficient to cause a split in the Sydney University English Department in the 1960s resulting in the departure of many of the

Leavisites to Melbourne, leaving the New Critics in unfettered control in Sydney.

As Wimsatt and Beardsley's statement suggests, the New Critics countered the risk of disorderly, emotional, idiosyncratic and untrained reponses of actual readers messing up their notions of the purity and objectivity of the literary text, and of the appropriate methods for analysing it, by completely rejecting their relevance. The New Critical pedagogical focus is on the literary product, the 'words on the page', and on rigorous and objective ways of interpreting them. The notion of the poem as a solid object to be consumed by a self-effacing reader who clears her mind of everything except the words before her is evident in the titles of critical works written by the New Critics — *The Verbal Icon* by Wimsatt and *The Well-Wrought Urn* by Cleanth Brooks[49]. In their influential anthology for students, *Understanding Poetry*, Brooks and Robert Penn Warren condemned the use of poetry for any purpose beyond itself, whether historical or moralistic.[50] In their insistence on the autonomy of the text, the New Critics banished the author and historical contexts from consideration, as well as the extra-textual experience of the reader. In their article 'The Intentional Fallacy'[51], Wimsatt and Beardsley assert that consideration of the author's intention in a work distracts attention from the work itself in the same way as a consideration of the 'affects' of the reader or of the context does.

To the New Critics the main function and value of literature is to harmonise or make coherent conflicting meanings, attitudes or possibilities of experience; to reconcile for example, the temporal and eternal, mind and body, spiritual and physical, thought and feeling, love and hate. These dualities, so the theory goes, can only be made whole in art, by the unifying power of the imagination of the artist expressed through metaphor and symbol. This notion is pretty well straight from Coleridge's *Biographia Literaria* of 1817 which explained how the 'primary imagination' balances or reconciles opposite or discordant qualities such as the general and the particular, the idea and the image, the individual and the representative, and so on. Because the possibilities balanced and harmonised are conflicting or contradictory, the coherence of literature is always associated with complexity. As John Docker explains, because these conflicts are only 'momentarily' reconciled, because 'such contradictory moral and metaphysical ideas and possibilities' can only be 'held in balance' in the work of art and not permanently reconciled, the work must always be ambiguous, ironic, paradoxical'.[52]

In *The Verbal Icon*, Wimsatt cites the last line of a stanza of John Donne's poem, 'A Valediction: Forbidding Mourning', as an example of the way this balance and reconciliation of opposites is achieved through metaphor:

> Our two soules therefore, which are one,
> Though I must goe, endure not yet
> A breach, but an expansion,
> Like gold to ayery thinnesse beate.

In the poem Donne's imagination fashions a series of startling images to communicate the paradox of physical separateness and spiritual oneness. The comparison of the lovers' relationship with gold metal is an apparently discordant juxtaposition. The separation of the lovers changes the physical state of their relationship but not its spiritual quality, just as the hammering of the gold into leaf changes its shape but not its value. The equivalences established between gold and the lovers' relationship suggest further connections: the relationship of the separated lovers, like the thin gold leaf, is delicate, tender, permanently valuable and adaptable to changed circumstances. Certainly such an analysis demonstrates the subtle skill of the poet, but I suggest that this kind of image, so admired by the New Critics, communicates a profound intellectual 'meaning' and a sense of the author's imaginative dexterity, but not the emotion appropriate to this precious union of spirits. The author displays too self-conscious a virtuosity in the creation of this image, which I see more as a product of what Coleridge called the 'fancy' than of what he meant by the more powerful 'imagination'.

The kind of close reading that led to the recognition for myself of the inappropriateness of tone in Donne's 'conceit' is a central part of New Critical methodology. Whether other readers agree with my evaluation or not is irrelevant to the point that the emphasis on close reading by the New Critics represents an important and positive contribution to pedagogy. Through careful scrutiny of details and possible connections in texts, we discover our own feelings and make our own interpretations. However, these creative acts of the reader are the very kinds of outcomes the New Critics wanted to prevent because of their potential for idiosyncracy and self-indulgence in response. You will realise that the analysis of Donne's image is primarily mine and only partly Wimsatt's, that where Wimsatt applauds loudest I most strongly demur.

The critical emphasis on coherence and harmony through the integration of the parts is designed to leave the reader in a state of contemplative admiration – and contemplative acceptance. John Docker points out this limitation in New Criticism: 'dualities like thought and feeling, mind and body, and so on, can only be made whole, reconciled in art'.[53] In reconciling all discordance, in abolishing all friction in the harmonious interrelation of its opposite qualities, such art risks becoming cut off from reality altogether and descends into aestheticism and even mysticism in the way it activates and disappoints wistful yearnings for a perfection and a wholeness that are unattainable. This is fine for readers who don't want literature to reconcile anything in terms of their understanding of the real world and whose interest is primarily in aesthetics and in the skilful uses of language. The trouble with 'the text itself' is that its world is just such a self-contained alternative to the real world whose social and political issues and implications can be conveniently ignored as irrelevant.

Northrop Frye, in *The Anatomy of Criticism*, points out that an unfortunate result of the New Critical rejection of the importance of the 'conceptual framework' the reader brings to the text is that readers see their task as merely to identify the literary devices of the text, 'to take a poem into which a poet has diligently stuffed a specific number of beauties or effects, and complacently to extract them, one by one, like his prototype Little Jack Horner'.[54]

A rigid New Critical approach in the secondary schools often creates this very impression in students. Many miss experiencing the 'harmony' of the whole because they are too busy looking for the separable parts: 'techniques' they think an author has deliberately 'chosen' or 'used' to 'get across a theme', as they often put it. When the more advanced students describe this as a search for symbol, metaphor, tension, paradox and ambiguity we know they have learned the New Critical jargon even if they haven't experienced the aesthetic delight produced by the coherence or synthesis or resolution that the concepts the words stand for are meant to achieve.

The vocabulary of the New Critics indicates this exclusive interest in the contemplation of moral, metaphysical and psychological dilemmas and tensions and the ways these are resolved in the language of symbol. As Terry Eagleton says, in his condemnation of the New Critics' rejection of social and political concerns as being unworthy of their attention, reading literature in the New Critical way is: 'a recipe for political inertia, and thus for submission to the political status quo . . . Oppositions were to be tolerated as long as they could finally be fused into harmony.'[55] Where Leavis believed that literature had a social purpose in restoring to society the highest values of the past, the New Critics remain aloof from such commitment.

The New Critical belief that writers are important in so far as they express the moral and metaphysical rather than the social and political has been the orthodoxy of the Higher School Certificate examination for many years, as a glance at the lists of set texts will confirm. In his important study of the 'struggles for control of Australian literature', *In A Critical Condition*, John Docker shows how the New Critical establishment in Australian universities has excluded from students' attention, 'all Australian literature except for the Australian metaphysicals, or writers with a presumed major metaphysical aspect.'[56] Docker provides conclusive evidence that the social realists of the 1930s, writers such as Vance Palmer, Eleanor Dark, Leonard Mann, Kylie Tennant, Dymphna Cusack, Xavier Herbert, K.S. Prichard and Miles Franklin, and those of the 1950s such as Alan Marshall, Judah Waten, Frank Hardy, Gavin Casey and Dorothy Hewett, have been institutionally ignored or 'actively repressed and silenced'.[57] As Docker so rightly says, 'The worth of these writers remains to be investigated — but the students should have been and should be given the opportunity to find out for themselves.'[58]

If a non-metaphysical, social-realist text is listed on university courses by the Australian New Critics, as occasionally happens with Xavier Herbert's *Capricornia* and Katharine Prichard's *Coonardoo*, it is because 'the inessential social and ideological surface can be bared to reveal a text's true metaphysical presence, authority and value.'[59] The leading Australian New Critics, constituting a kind of national literary selection panel, are G.A. Wilkes and Dame Leonie Kramer (Sydney), Vincent Buckley (Melbourne) and H.P. Heseltine (Brisbane). Their first XIII to represent Australia in international competition would appear to be Christopher Brennan, John Shaw Neilson, R.D. FitzGerald, Kenneth Slessor, Judith Wright, A.D. Hope, James McAuley, Douglas Stewart, Francis Webb, Henry Handel Richardson, Christina Stead, Martin Boyd and Patrick White. These are the writers most frequently mentioned in the selector's reports, and they are the ones who fit best into the selectors' ideological frameworks. The preponderance of poets, the shortage of novelists, and the presence of only two playwrights whose main strengths are in poetry and 'densely textured' poetic novels, is all in accord with New Critical orthodoxy. This team has considerable depth in metaphor and offers readers the promise of many hours of metaphysical contemplation. John Docker's analysis of *The Oxford History of Australian Literature*, published in 1981 and edited by Dame Leonie Kramer[60], shows that New Critical criteria for condemning the critical arguments of other schools of thought are based on irrationally subjective notions of what constitutes 'literary' as opposed to 'non-literary' judgments. In the Introduction, Dame Leonie criticises the literary nationalists for bringing 'extra-literary' considerations into criticism by examining the social attitudes expressed in literature. Vivian Smith's chapter 'asserts Kramer's and the orthodoxy's distinction between the "historical, cultural and sociological" interests of writers and "real aesthetic concerns".'[61] Everything that runs counter to the a-historical aesthetic ideology of New Criticism is dismissed as being an 'extra-literary consideration'.

The eminent English critic Raymond Williams takes the New Critics to task for treating writing as an object and readers as consumers of objects. He says this attitude misrepresents the active nature of both writing and reading, and ignores the interrelationship between writer, reader and work, and between writers' and readers' social experiences.[62] Despite what the New Critics demand of literature and of readers, there is no such thing as an ideologically innocent text or reader. The fact that the Higher School Certificate syllabus and examination in New South Wales are controlled by New Critical academics means that students are being culturally shaped by an ideology of middle class non-committal liberal humanism. The syllabus, the examination and the teaching methods that go with them, represent a form of social control, preserving the *status quo* by initiating students into habits of high-minded contemplation of eternal truths and beauties. The students who react favourably to the course and its methods are thus rendered socially and politically tractable. Most of the other students, the least 'successful' ones, suffer a loss of confidence in their own meaning-making interpretative abilities because their own honest responses have to be subjugated to the so-called purely 'literary' concerns of New Critical interest.

Any method which curtails the reader's response or imposes on it artificially predetermined patterns needs to be rejected. New

Criticism as a method for teaching and assessing literary response seems to succeed best in inhibiting it. I remember my own attempts at school and university to convey an impression of critical respectability by using a borrowed vocabulary to describe counterfeit responses. 'Evocative sensuousness' is an expression I regularly used about the Romantics, and 'the density of the texture' or 'the lack of density of the texture' was always worth an approving marginal tick from one lecturer. (You will have noted by now that some habits die hard.) Let us not kid ourselves that students swotting up critical information about texts for an examination are really deepening or strengthening their enjoyment of literature or improving their responsiveness. What most of them are really deepening and strengthening is their resolve never to renew their acquaintance with any of the set authors or their friends.

New Criticism's positive contributions to the methodology of reading and teaching literature are few. Certainly, in its insistence on close reading and careful attention to the textual details, it provides a rigorous basis for a training in interpretation. However, its weaknesses and negative effects on readers are all too evident. Emphasis on the objectivity of the text and the objectivity of the methods for interpreting it, ignores the reciprocity between text and reader and the relevance of a reader's individuality and extra-textual experience. It is easy for young readers to draw the conclusion that technical skill is more important than felt literary experience, and to rely solely on expert critical commentary for 'understanding', or to engage in dreary routines of device hunting. The preoccupation with the words on the page but not with the contexts that produced them, and the absurd affectation of ideological innocence are responsible for the drawing of the all too ideological distinction between 'literary' and 'non-literary' concerns and thus for the indoctrination of readers, as John Docker points out.

If you argue that literature is essentially moral and metaphysical, then in fact you are trying to pass off ideological considerations (of class, sex, race) embedded in moral and metaphysical themes as if they belong not to society but to the universal order of things.[63]

## READER–RESPONSE CRITICISM

### Structuralism

Structuralist criticism grew out of the application of linguistics to the study of literature, and the attempt to make literary theory more systematic and objective in the increasingly technological society of the 1960s, with its pressures on the arts and humanities to eliminate the sloppiness of subjective value judgments and to adopt more rigorous scientific methods consistent with their status as academic disciplines. Literature is no longer a pseudo religion or the perfect artefact. Nor is it of interest because of any psychological or sociological insights it offers. The structuralists see literature as a particular organisation of language and focus on the way its meanings are produced rather than on the meanings themselves. Structuralism is part of semiology, a general science of signs, which analyses all cultural artefacts as 'signifying systems'. A literary text is just another system of signs like a newspaper article, a comic, a photograph, a boxing match, a committee meeting, a film, a menu and so on, all to be analysed in the same way to discover how they construct meaning. As the purposes of structuralism are analytical and not evaluative, its methods implicitly threaten literature's prestige as the highest form of linguistic creation: the work of art may no longer be seen as society's most valued 'sign system'.

Just as structural linguistics attempts to describe the grammar (or system) of language — what it is that a native speaker implicitly knows in order to make sense of a sentence — so structuralist literary criticism attempts to find and make explicit the 'grammar' of a literary text, the understanding ideal readers have of how to read literature according to socially determined notions of appropriateness. Jonathan Culler calls this understanding that good readers have and which enables them to make literature texts have meaning, 'literary competence'. He says that readers gain literary competence by assimilating or internalising a set of conventions or 'grammar' of literature (how to read a detective novel, a sonnet, a tragedy, etc.) which 'permit them to convert linguistic sequences into literary structures and meanings'.[64] Analogously to the way linguistics examines the rules governing the relationships of words in a sentence, a structuralist poetics is interested in finding, for example, the rules governing the relationships of events, details and characters in a novel. Particularly useful for teaching is the way structuralism demystifies literature by showing that it is an analysable construct and not a holy artefact written by the divinely inspired for the edification of a sensitive elite. As Terry Eagleton says, in describing the structuralist emphasis on the constructedness of literary meaning as a liberating notion for learners, 'Meaning was neither a private experience nor a divinely ordained occurrence: it was the product of certain shared systems of signification.'[65] If the mechanisms of literature can be made explicit, then everyone can have access to them and they can be taught.

However, other linguistic-derived structuralist ideas are far from liberating for either readers or teachers of readers. The fact that there is no natural connection between word and thing, between a sign and what it signifies, that language is thus arbitrary and conventional has led some structuralists to the extreme view that all knowledge is a product of language rather than of experience. If we do see and interpret the world through the classifications of it imposed on us by our language, then our reality is produced rather than reflected by language. If language is all there is, the literary text is nothing more than a closed system and is about nothing else but itself, a collection of signs that don't signify anything beyond other signs. As Terry Eagleton points out, 'the structuralist view of the literary text as a closed system is not really much different from the New Critical treatment of it as an isolated object.'[66]

In order to examine the structure of signs more scientifically, structuralists ignore the reality the signs are intended by users to signify. Structuralists would argue that to talk about human intentions in language is to perpetuate a humanist myth that we create meaning. They believe that meaning is structured by the language itself and the rules that govern it. This denial of a reality and human intentions outside language is an extremely deterministic view which I cannot subscribe to. The realities of daily work, class, race and political power might, as Terry Eagleton says, 'be inextricably caught up in discourse, but they [are] certainly not reducible to it.'[67] Eagleton goes on to summarise this weakness of structuralist criticism:

> The work neither refers to an object, nor is the expression of an individual subject; both of these are blocked out, and what is left hanging in the air between them is a system of rules. This system has its own independent life, and will not stoop to the beck and call of individual intentions . . . Though language may not be

best understood as individual expression, it certainly in some way involves human subjects and their intentions, and it is this which the structuralist picture leaves out of account.[68]

Structural analysis concentrates on the forms of language in literature, the way signs are combined into meaning rather than on what they themselves say. I will try to illustrate, briefly, this structuralist concentration on the internal relationships of signs in literary analysis. In John Wain's comic picaresque novel of 1954, *Hurry On Down*, about the progress of a young man's career from the time he graduates from university until he attains a job that is temperamentally satisfying (as a comedy scriptwriter for radio), the focus is on the English social class system and the class orientation of all occupations. The aim of the protagonist, Charles Lumley, is to avoid class identification in his job and his lifestyle. A structuralist critic would schematise the events (signs) in terms of Lumley's horizontal and vertical progress through the social-economic world of 1950s' England. Each job he takes has a social class affiliation despite his attempts to avoid becoming socially stereotyped through occupation and to achieve an independent personal identity. Structuralist criticism would classify each career choice as 'high' or 'low' or 'equal' in terms of its relationship with previous career choices, so that the structure of the novel could be shown in the form of a diagram tracing Lumley's rises and falls and movements forward along vertical and horizontal axes. Such a formal analysis might well help a reader to recognise the irony of Lumley's naïve attempts to avoid inevitable social class identification, to understand that his attempted 'neutrality' is impossible to attain, and to draw some conclusions about Wain's representation of English society, but these would not be the prime concerns of structuralist critics. In other words, while a structuralist analysis can be helpful to interpretation, its main concern is with the laws and structures that govern texts. *Hurry on Down* is more than its structure; its details, events and characters have significance as well as an internal pattern of formal relationships.

Incidentally, if the jargon of structuralism, or of any of the other reader-response theories, strikes you as being pretentious, and if you feel much more comfortable with words and expressions such as symbol, image, tone, sensitivity, the synthesising power of the imagination, irony, theme, characterisation and plot — the jargon of the Romantics, Richards, Leavis and New Criticism — you will recognise how easy it is to see the most familiar theory as the most natural and best. We don't challenge the language of the theory we have 'naturalised'. Nor do we often think of trying to discover the ideology conveyed by the language of the theory we uphold and which is embedded in that theory. If we did, we might find just how much the language we have internalised constructs the reality we experience and believe. Here is another example. Just as the New Critics' concern with tensions between opposites causes them to favour those works in which this can be observed, and causes readers trained in New Critical methodology to look for symbols that reconcile opposites; so the structuralists' practice of seeing every event, every descriptive detail and every character in a novel as part of a formal pattern of parallels, contrasts and correspondences ('binary oppositions') can easily make us see the text and the world as more neatly structured (or more 'binary') than it is. Structuralism's exclusion of the author, extra-textual reality and human motivation from interpretative consideration, its concentration on the ways meaning is produced rather than on the meaning itself, is an ideological product of its particular history.

Structuralism's similarities and dissimilarities with New Criticism are interesting. Both critical positions scrupulously ignore the author and realities outside the text. Both place great importance on internal relationships in textual analysis. These similarities make it not coincidental that both are a-historical, and thus ideologically conservative despite claims of being non-ideological. In their concern to be more scientific, structuralists, unlike the New Critics, show no interest at all in literary evaluation; they are interested only in the characteristics of a poem, for example, rather than in the qualities that make it a good or a bad poem. Structuralism does annihilate the New Critical myth of the innocent reader approaching a completely self-contained text with no preconceptions. The structuralists have taught us to think of the literary work not as a self-contained organism as the New Critics think of it, but as something that has meaning because of publicly agreed upon conventions which readers have internalised. While the various value systems, experiences of the world and individualities that readers bring with them to the text hold no more interest for the structuralists than they do for the New Critics, the structuralists do shift the location of meaning from 'the text itself' alone, to the reader's activity in applying the conventions.

In his book, *Structuralist Poetics*, Jonathan Culler outlines the task of a 'structuralist poetics' as making explicit 'the underlying system which makes literary effects possible'. [69] This underlying system is the set of conventions that enable us to read, for example, a poem as a poem and a novel as a novel, and both as works of literature rather than as textbooks of metaphysics or psychology. Culler identifies and illustrates some of these conventions in an analysis of William Blake's poem 'Ah! Sun-flower'. The conventions include:

the rule of significance: read the poem as expressing a significant attitude to some problem concerning man and/or his relation to the universe.

[the sunflower is given the value of an emblem of human aspiration];

the convention of metaphorical coherence, meaning that the literal and metaphorical levels of an image make sense separately and have a consistent relationship (sunset is identified with the death of the flower which expresses human death);

the convention of thematic unity, which enables the reader to make connections between objects and events in the same poem to make an overall meaning (Youth and virgin and sunflower must be connected in an overall meaning. These relationships are 'binary oppositions').[70]

Readers operate these conventions, derived from their experience of reading literature, to produce meaning. For example, take this Haiku of Basho:

You light the fire
  I'll show you something nice —
    A great ball of snow.

The connection between the details is left for the reader to work out from his or her internalised understanding of the conventions of poetry, and of haiku poetry in particular. The reader knows that there is a connection from his understanding of the rule of significance. An obvious point of contact is the contrast ('binary opposition') between fire and snow, and whatever interpretation we make will derive from seeing this as being thematically significant.

Another rule we may have internalised is that haiku uses the simplest type of natural speech to communicate an often profound perception by holding still the observation of a moment of apparent aimlessness. Placed in opposition here with the fire/snow image are parallel emanations of warmth/cold and light/darkness. To produce light and warmth the fire has to be lit, but the snow is already there. It may be that Basho is trying to make us see the irony of this situation and to communicate to us as felt experience the speaker's mood of optimism at a time of intense cold and darkness. It suggests something about the experience of enduring winter, perhaps, and, by metaphorical extension, about enduring the wintry seasons of our emotional lives. Whatever interpretation we arrive at will have something to do with recognising and connecting the binary oppositions, and with seeing the world, for a brief moment at least, in a strikingly fresh way.

You will recognise that in this kind of commentary I am applying structuralism to interpretation. Structuralists are interested in the binary oppositions and the fact that they have extra-textual significances, but they are not interested in what those significances are, or in the emotions of response they elicit. I make this point to emphasise both the valuable uses of structuralist criticism and its limitations. A structural analysis of a text can help us to get beyond the narrative surface of a text to its deep structure, but it is not enough in itself. Authors and readers bring more to a text than a knowledge of language, as Culler has pointed out, but where Culler sees the additional experience brought by both authors and readers as being 'expectations about the forms of literary organisation' and 'implicit models of literary structures', he emphasises literary experience and neglects equally important life experience.[71] As well as their knowledge of other literature and cultural sign systems, authors and readers bring to new texts their knowledge of life, their emotional representations and their values. Their expectations about the motives and consequences of the behaviour of fictional characters derive at least as much from this 'extra textual' experience as they do from their experience of other literary texts.

Roland Barthes, the French literary theorist, contributes to our understanding of the conventions we have internalised through his idea of 'codes' which constitute texts and reality alike and which help us to interpret both. In his book, $S/Z$[72], Barthes analyses Balzac's short story 'Sarrasine' as an interplay of five codes or conventions that readers have learned from their experience of both living in a society and reading literature. These codes, shared by both author and reader, create a kind of network through which a text passes to become a literary work; or, to put it another way, readers construct a work of literature out of text by filtering the text through the network of codes they have internalised. The codes are the source of the text's meanings and involve the reader in producing those meanings. The value of Barthes' codes to the teacher of literature is that they recognise the importance of readers' life experiences to literary understanding, and thus expose the limitation of the exclusive focus of the New Critics on 'the words on the page'. There are numerous codes at work in any text*, but the five that Barthes identifies as most important in his analysis of the Balzac story are:

1. The code of action (proairetic code): our understanding of the sorts of events that go together, which enable us to place details in a plot sequence. We bring from experience and from reading and hearing narrative ideas of the kinds of events involved in falling in love, a kidnapping, a perilous mission and so on, so we can connect the details we encounter as we read into sequences, plots and sub-plots.
2. The code of puzzles, enigma and mystery (hermeneutic code): this helps us to recognise what counts as a puzzle so that we can arrange details of the text in our mind as possible contributions to its solution. The satisfaction is that of interpreting the significance of events and solving problems.
3. The code of character discernment (semic code): the knowledge we have of human behaviour, motives and consequences, that enables us to generalise about the personalities of people we know and of characters in novels.
4. The code of symbols (symbolic code): the knowledge we have that one thing can represent another. For example, there is no causal connection between riding a white horse and moral rightness but the symbolic code permits such associations, at least in cowboy movies. This is very important in helping us to

---

* Examples of other codes beyond those listed would be a code of tone (the reader's ability to relate items that characterise an author's attitudes) and a code of narrative perspective (the reader's ability to group items which characterise a narrator, and which distinguish narrator and implied author; e.g., Huck's naivety and Twain's irony in *Huckleberry Finn*).

interpret themes, or to move from surface narrative structures to deep structures.

5. The code of societies and cultures (cultural or referential code): the cultural information we have which we need to understand the cultural backgrounds and references of texts. For examples, a knowledge of Byzantine civilisation is helpful to the understanding of Yeats' poem 'Sailing to Byzantium', and an Australian bush yarn might be interpreted very differently by Australian and European readers.

To illustrate, here is a passage from the story, 'Sarrasine', and a summary of part of Barthes' analysis of it in *S/Z*: 'The Italian woman was armed with a dagger. "If you come any closer", she said, "I will be forced to plunge a dagger into your heart".' The Italian 'woman' is, in fact, a male castrated in boyhood so as to retain the soprano voice. Sarrasine, who is carrying 'her' off to his bedroom is thus a victim of deception. On the action or proairetic level the event is one in a series we will recognise as constituting 'rape' or the 'woman's' defence of her virtue. But on the hermeneutic level 'she' is really 'he'; 'she' is practising a deception. On the symbolic level the dagger signifies castration, which is the thematic core of the whole story as Barthes interprets it.

These codes, particularly the proairetic and hermeneutic, are crucial in understanding the satisfactions and dissatisfactions of reading that students experience, as we shall see in Chapter Four. Generating expectations and formulating and solving puzzles while reading are important features of active reading, and those students who don't do these things inevitably find reading very boring. 'What will happen next?' (proairetic code) and 'what significance has it got?' (hermeneutic code) are the kinds of questions that good readers keep asking of texts while they are reading, and a great deal of their reading pleasure comes from asking, speculating about and solving them. Making connections, drawing inferences, and forming and constantly modifying expectations as the text unfolds are hermeneutic activities that good readers have learned to perform almost automatically. They are also teachable.

Although the investigation of structures to see how literature works might be justifiable as an end in itself for literary theorists and linguists, it is only of value for students if its findings can be used to help them to become better readers. Barthes' codes and the conventions Culler makes explicit can help to identify the kinds of knowledge readers bring to their reading and how they might be used more productively by students in their reading. All students have internalised some of the conventions and codes, and, therefore, they have a potential 'literary competence'; but what they possess they often don't use, because they don't know they have it or how to use it. As Margaret (Spencer) Meek has often pointed out, we have a responsibility to pass on that 'list of secret things that all accomplished readers know, yet never talk about'.[73] In *Achieving Literacy*, her important study of adolescents learning to read, Meek and her teaching colleagues studied 'the scores of unexplained textual conventions that the reader has to learn' and show that adolescents can learn them as they learn to read comics, which are equally governed by rules, without much trouble.[74] In an address to the Third International Conference on English teaching in Sydney in 1980, Meek outlined some of the literary conventions mastered by good juvenile readers at various age levels. Among the 'literary competences' of experienced twelve-year-olds are these:

> They can relate one incident in a novel to another. If the hero fails in a trial of strength or understanding near the beginning of the story the reader knows that he must face the same danger or test later, often in a more acute form . . .

> They know that princesses in fairy tales are not misrepresentations of female status but symbols of moral worth . . .

> They can distinguish the voice on the page in terms of humour, irony, anger and cajoling. They can recognise a narrator who is not so honest as he might be. They share the author's jokes at the expense of some characters . . .

> They know that reading links the outer world of events with the equally real inner world of feeling so that events and responses are held in equilibrium, thought about, reflected upon and responded to.[75]

If narrative is 'a primary act of mind', as Barbara Hardy tells us, it is not surprising that children master many of its conventions easily. However, much of this naturally acquired and precious knowledge has not been recognised or valued by schools. We need to help students to value their own experience and the conventions they have internalised, and to be able to specify what these conventions are and to understand why they are valuable.

Maureen Worsdale has found a close relationship between students' tacit knowledge and use of the codes identified by Barthes and their ability to generalise. This is perfectly in accord with the work of Hardy, Gordon Wells, Margaret Donaldson and Michael Halliday concerning the relationship between children's sense of story and the growth of the mind.

It is only through an act of generalisation, involving searching out information, instances of behaviour and action and abstracting from these that we come to a knowledge of character, plot and theme. It is also an act of abstraction to recognise and understand elements of our own and others' culture in stories. In the same way it is only through our knowledge of character, plot, theme and culture that our discernment of the key points in a story comes, and therefore our ability to perceive structure and reach higher levels of generalisation. Progress in reaching the higher levels of generalisation, achieving fluidity between these levels, and development of the codes of reading is parallel.[76]

The 'interdependence between knowledge of the codes and generalising ability' can be used by teachers to develop students' understanding of the skills they possess and how to strengthen them. Worsdale suggests that helping pupils to be aware of their present abilities to generalise and of their present 'literary competence' can be liberating to them.

Through making explicit an activity which appears to be natural the pupil gains in self-awareness. Also becoming aware of what readers do to a text and what they bring to it makes it easier for the pupil to see how and why some texts are difficult, and why increased reading experience can help.[77]

Also potentially liberating to learners is the realisation that literature is a construct; that things don't just happen of their own accord in stories but by the design of a controlling author. Once this is understood by students, the questioning of the text can be made a reading habit. Teachers should make explicit to their pupils what David Jackson calls the 'shaping and patterning decisions involved in story-making'[78] so that they can be controllers of the literature they read rather than consumers of it. This control can come from exploring the ways language and texts do structure reality.

Even the extreme position of the Russian Formalists in basing their study of narrative on a distinction between the events of a story on the one hand and the construction on the other can be useful with some texts. For the study of novels such as *Catch 22* (Joseph Heller), *Nostromo* (Joseph Conrad), and *Free Fall* and *The Pyramid* (William Golding), in which the chronological order of events is dislocated, a comparison between the chronological sequence and the order of the presentation in the text can effectively reveal the purposes and effects of the author's logic beyond the conventional chronology. Involving students in writing their own literature is another activity that makes them better readers of other people's. Writing and reading in the spectator role are mutually supportive activities. Constructing their own stories and poems serves to make students very conscious that other people's stories and poems are constructs, products of choices and linguistic mechanisms that can be manipulated to achieve one's own purposes.

### Reception Theory: Wolfgang Iser's account of the reading process: "The Act of Reading"[79]

Thus author and reader are to share the game of the imagination, and, indeed, the game will not work if the text sets out to be anything more than a set of governing rules. The reader's enjoyment begins when he himself becomes productive, i.e., when the text allows him to bring his own faculties into play.

Wolfgang Iser, *The Act of Reading*

What [do] people see when they read a book, and why [does] one person see one pattern and nothing at all of another pattern? . . . How odd it is to have, as an author, such a clear picture of a book that is seen so very differently by its readers . . .

The book is alive and potent and fructifying and able to promote thought and discussion only when its plan and shape and intention are not understood, because that moment of seeing the shape and plan and intention is also the moment when there isn't anything more to be got out of it.

Doris Lessing, Preface to *The Golden Notebook*

. . . reading for learning will be most effective when the reader becomes an active interrogator of the text rather than a passive receiver of words.

The Bullock Report

I'm like a power, as if everything is happening because I'm there.

Claire, 3rd year secondary
school student, describing
her experience of novels.[80]

The most coherent account of the reader's actions in responding to literature is given by Wolfgang Iser in his book, *The Act of Reading*. Iser's literary theory is the most important of all in terms of implications for teaching, offering a way of breaking out of the stifling pedagogical box fashioned by New Criticism and incorporating the more useful and relevant contributions of structuralism without its arid, formalistic view of literature as a self-enclosed linguistic system unrelated to reality. To Iser, literature is not an object but an experience, and readers are not 'consumers' but active performers who bring texts to life in their minds. However, the reader's activity is not independent of either textual or cultural constraints. Reading is guided by the text and influenced by the personal experience and cultural history of the reader, his or her present representation of the world and the reading conventions s/he has internalised. Iser argues that literary meaning is not some hidden object or substance that can be extracted from a text like juice from an orange, leaving what remains to be discarded as worthless like the orange skin. The text activates the reader to produce meaning so that literature is an event, something that happens when we read.

As an aid to understanding Iser's theory of reading, here is Seymour Chatman's diagrammatic representation of the way narrative works in communication. It is based on Iser's concept of the 'implied reader' and Wayne Booth's concept of the 'implied author'.[81]

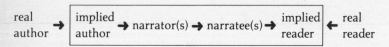

The box represents the boundaries of the text. The categories within the box are aspects of the functions of the text. The real author and the real reader are outside the text.[82]

The narrator is the narrative voice or speaker of the text (for example, Huckleberry Finn in Twain's novel, and the unnamed 'frame' narrator in *Heart of Darkness*, or the author writing in the first person, as a version of Henry Fielding does in *Tom Jones*); and the narratee is the narrator's directly addressed audience (for example, the men to whom Marlow tells his story on the deck of the ship in *Heart of Darkness*, or the versions of the reader directly addressed in *Tom Jones*). Narrators and narratees are not always present in texts. The implied author and the implied reader are constructs assembled by the reader from the textual details and they are always present in the text. The implied author, Booth says, is the 'real author's second self', the kind of person the text implies the author is, and possessing the kinds of values the text implies the author has. For example, from reading *Heart of Darkness* we get a strong impression of the moral rectitude, integrity, strength of character and even radical pessimism of the person who wrote it. The implied author usually represents the ideal aspirations rather than the fallible reality of the author himself. The concept of the implied author is important for young readers because, as Aidan Chambers tells us, 'they need to find within the book an implied author whom (they) can befriend . . . and thus (be) wooed into the book.'[83]

The implied reader is the kind of reader that the real reader is invited by the implied author to become so as to participate in the production of the text's meaning. For many students there is often a problem of imaginative entry into the world of the text when the setting is remote in time and place, the society on display different from their own, the textual language a strange dialect, or the author's world view an alien one. To become the implied reader that the text demands might mean having to take up, temporarily, attitudes the real reader might want to resist. It requires a willing suspension of scepticism or resentment if the reader is to give a text a chance to work on him or her. For example, many students refuse to become Jane Austen's implied readers because it seems to them to require a sympathy with wealthy people who never work and have unlimited time to gossip.

Aidan Chambers explains how authors establish relationships of trust with implied young readers through a tone that is warm and sufficiently responsibly adult to give them a sense of security but without feeling patronised. He points out that in much children's and adolescent fiction authors often, 'reinforce the relationship by giving the book a very sharply focused point of view . . . by putting at the centre of the story a child through whose being everything is seen and felt.'[84] Chambers makes the important point that many of those children's books which adults like but children don't have an implied author who is too detached, 'a watcher rather than an ally', and he cites William Mayne's books as examples.

I find that Richard Hughes' *A High Wind in Jamaica* is unpopular with all but the most accomplished student readers for the same reasons: the author's dispassionate examination of childhood requires a similar detachment on the part of the reader, and this is too demanding for those young people whose major satisfaction in fiction comes from empathising with characters and being absorbed by the narrative action, rather than from reflecting on its significance. On the other hand, Enid Blyton's 'allegiance becomes collusion in a game of "us kids against them adults".'[85] She fails her readers through her implied author role of 'king of the kids'.

When the author has established a trusting relationship with the young reader, 'he can manipulate that alliance as a device to guide the reader towards the meanings he wishes to negotiate' so that 'the implied reader [becomes] an implicated reader . . . the last thing he wants to do is to stop reading . . . He finally becomes a participant in the making of the book.' [86]

The evidence of the Bathurst research (to be reported in Chapter Four) suggests that teenage readers do become implicated readers as they become implied readers. They seem to become 'implicated' or absorbed in the text first, through the trusting relationship created by the tone of the implied author and/or the excitement of the narrative itself, and are then more likely to be prepared to make the effort to engage in the complex interpretative operations that are involved in becoming the text's implied readers.

The concept of the implied reader is particularly useful in helping teachers to choose appropriate texts for class work and to guide choice of individual reading. It is also useful in helping teachers to understand why some books are very popular and why others, that they themselves like, are not. It is crucial that inexperienced readers find in the text an implied author with a sharply focused point of view that makes them feel secure. It is a necessary stage of development of response before they are able to gain satisfaction from more complex and indeterminate books with more detached implied authors, unreliable narrators and apparently unconnected episodes.

Iser characterises the relationship between the text and reader as being quite different from that between an object and its observer: 'Instead of a subject-object relationship there is a moving viewpoint which travels along *inside* that which it has to apprehend. This mode of grasping an object is unique to literature.'[87]

The text can never be perceived as a whole at any one time as, for example, a painting can. At each reading moment the reader is operating within one of the textual perspectives, whether it be that of a narrator or one of the characters or of the plot-line or of the narratee. In being led through these shifting viewpoints the reader is manoeuvred into taking up a position from which all these different perspectives can eventually be fitted together in such a way as to make sense. The reader is engaged in a continual process of constructing meaning, organising the text's elements into coherence, generating expectations about what might come next and, in the light of what does happen next, forming new expectations and retrospectively modifying previous understanding. Thus, our response to a text is a dynamic process of self-correction: we formulate interpretations we have continually to modify because textual information comes gradually and we have to start inferring, connecting and synthesising details from the beginning: 'Throughout the reading process there is a continual interplay between modified expectations and transformed memory'[88]. If, for example, the 'theme' of the present reading moment is the conduct of the hero, what he is actually doing (a plot perspective), our attitude towards him will be influenced by the 'horizon' of expectations we have formed about him from previous plot events and from the perspectives of the narrator(s), other characters and himself. The action of the hero in that part of the text we are reading at the moment might confirm our expectations about his behaviour, or modify them, or cause us to reject them altogether.

The very nature of the reader's relationship to the text, the unavoidability of 'travelling along inside' that which our perceptual powers have to 'apprehend', involves us in processes of synthesising an assembly of constantly shifting viewpoints, of continually forming and modifying both expectations of what is to come and interpretations of what has previously been read. Here are examples.

• In *Catch 22*, the perspectives of many other characters and of the plot (events) show the hero, Yossarian, to be insane and a coward. However, the deficiency of each of these perspectives is shown when viewed from the standpoint of others. The reader has to sort out the contradictions. When the reader relates these opposing viewpoints to one another, she or he produces a kind of reciprocal negation with themes and horizons in continual conflict. What Yossarian says and does looks sane from one point of view but insane from the points of view of characters who are revealed more and more clearly to be insane themselves as the novel progesses (Havermeyer, Cathcart, Aarfy, etc.). The reader's full recognition of Yossarian's real sanity (if unconventionally displayed) coincides with a clear recognition of the sanity of the eccentric and superficially apparently irrational characters who like and support him (Orr, Dunbar, etc.).

• There are other variations of the theme and horizon structure where perspective segments are more mutually supportive to produce gradually increasing emotional effects of eventually great power. In such cases each 'theme' adds incrementally to the effects of the already established 'horizon'. For example, in E.M. Forster's *A Passage to India*, there is the recurring motif of different sounds — the echoes in the Marabar Caves and the noises of wheels of more and more powerful trains. As the novel progresses the echoes in the caves reverberate more and more as do the noises made by the trains. Each time one of these sounds is mentioned, it has more significance for the reader than it had the previous time it was mentioned.

• Perspective segments can 'reciprocally spotlight' one another. For instance, in Saul Bellow's novel, *Herzog*, the characters Moses Herzog and Valentine Gersbach are paralleled for vanity but contrasted for sense of humour. We are not told this; it is enacted in the combination of the details. Structures of binary opposition, parallels and oppositions, counterpointing techniques are identified or created by the reader, or at least by those readers who have mastered the structural conventions of literature.

Iser's account of the reader's activities under textual guidance (generating and modifying expectations and connecting events to form patterns of meaning) bears an obvious similarity to Barthes' account of the proairetic and hermeneutic codes. In generating expectations readers are asking the questions, 'What might happen next that fits with what has gone before?' (proairetic) and 'Will what happens next provide an additional clue to the solution of the puzzle?' (hermeneutic). In subsequently modifying expectations and past interpretations, readers are developing hitherto unforseen plot connections to identify different plot strands and to discriminate major from minor events (proairetic); they are also considering what these potential connections signify in terms of interpretation or problem-solving (hermeneutic).

Generating expectations, modifying, correcting and extending impressions, and solving puzzles are active, moment-by-moment activities which can be developed by teaching. They are also the origins of a great deal of the pleasure we get from reading, as my analysis of my reading of *The Raj Quartet* shows. Often we underestimate students' interpretative potential. If 'narrative is a primary act of mind' as Barbara Hardy tells us, then narrative anticipation is a skill children develop early as a means of sorting out and interpreting their own experience. We can encourage pupils to predict while reading and to argue in support of their deductions, as well as to reflect on their own productive processes so as to make them explicit to themselves and thus better understood as tools for use. We can also encourage pupils to identify clues within the story that might help them to guess possible outcomes more intelligently. We can also help them tremendously by letting them know that it is not a sign of poor reading to be wrong in making predictions. If our expectations are completely fulfilled by a book, we are bored. We say it was 'too predictable'. If our expectations are totally inappropriate we are baffled, as we would be to read Blake's 'The Sick Rose' as a guide to gardening.

Of course the text itself does not formulate expectations or their modification. It is the reader who formulates connections, following a moving viewpoint. The complexity of the networks of possible connections partly explains why there are many interpretations of texts. For example, take my evaluation of the character Scobie in *The Heart of the Matter* by Graham Greene. To me, the episode where Scobie tells a sick child his improvised story of 'Bishop Among the Bantus' establishes his humanity, his imagination and his sense of humour. It reciprocally spotlights and modifies all the other textual perspectives of him. It is part of my interpretion of Scobie's character but not of any critic's interpretation I have read. To most readers Scobie seems to be a one-dimensional, self-apppointed protector of life's less successful citizens whom he pities in the time he can spare from agonising over the problems of sin and guilt. Imagination, inventiveness, and a capacity for pretence-puncturing jokes are not generally attributed to him.

Each reader builds up a coherent interpretation of a text for himself or herself, and each reader will do it differently because the decisions that have to be made depend to some extent on individual disposition and experience both of the world and of literature. Not only will different readers read the same book differently because their 'repertoires' of personal and literary experience predispose them to focus on some aspects more than others, but the same reader can never read the same text again the same way. When you know what is going to happen next, guessing is closed off as an avenue of pleasure and you direct more of your attention to other areas. What readers bring to a novel shapes the way they go about making it mean. The 'repertoire' I brought to the reading of The Raj Quartet included a first-hand rudimentary knowledge of Indian society from having travelled through India and Pakistan for some months in 1960, a knowledge of 20th century Indian history from teaching it on the Higher School Certificate Modern History course, a measure of competence in some of the literary conventions from reading lots of novels (including A Passage to India which I was reminded of time and time again while I was reading The Raj Quartet), some understanding of human behaviour from having survived for nearly 50 years in the world so far, and certain values and beliefs about human rights and the offensiveness of 'benevolent' paternalistic government. They all helped me read the book 'well', but they also ensured that I read the book my way.

However, my reading of The Raj Quartet did not merely reinforce the beliefs, knowledge, attitudes and ways of seeing I had before reading it. If I read the book my way, it modified me its way too. Iser explains how literature enables us to understand things about the social and historical 'norms' of our civilisation that we may not have grasped any other way. Here are some examples of the way literature helps us to see the familiar in new ways. The examples are mine but I think they illustrate the processes Iser describes.

• Distancing situations in space and time is a way of getting readers to see their own social norms and values with some objectivity or freshness of vision. In The Crucible, Arthur Miller portrays the values of 1950s McCarthyist America set in 1692 Salem, so a contemporary audience could see their own society's values 'depragmatised', out of the context in which they had got so used to them as to see them as natural and accept them. Distance in historical setting allows for critical distance in response. The success of historical fiction (e.g., Rosemary Sutcliff) lies in the way it reworks and resets the patterns and values of its own world in terms of ours.

- In fairy stories, as we have seen earlier, norms are distanced in space and time but their themes are 'foregrounded'.

- In Ernest Hemingway's short story, 'Hills Like White Elephants', we are forced to see our customary attitudes ('prevalent thought systems') to the grand tour of Europe and young love as being romantically idealised.

As Iser puts it, 'the repertoire reproduces the familiar, but strips it of its current validity'[89], enabling readers to take a fresh look at forces and beliefs which influence their lives, and whose rationality and validity they may have hitherto accepted without question. The literary work can teach us new ways of understanding, so we can recognise the limitations of our habits of perception.

Authors also use literary conventions, familiar literary patterns, and recurrent literary themes to help us reach deeper levels of awareness of social and historical norms and literary processes if we have sufficient knowledge to make the implied connections. James Joyce's *Ulysses* is built on a framework of Homer's *The Odyssey*, as *Lord of the Flies* is a reconstruction of *Coral Island*, and Cervantes' *Don Quixote* fosters expectations of the conventional tale of the brave knight which it then parodies. In 'The Waste Land', T.S. Eliot alludes to Spenser's 'The Faerie Queene'. He juxtaposes the romantic past and the spiritless, decaying present to place both in an ironic light; the past was not romantic, being decadent too; and the present's decadence is highlighted ('foregrounded') by comparison with the apparently romantic past. Eliot de-romanticises the past as well as emphasising the sordidness of the present. The film *Apocalypse Now* parallels Conrad's *Heart of Darkness* and achieves profound effects by having Wagner's music intermingle with the noise of bullets in a scene in which helicopters are strafing innocent people. Iser explains how the plot of *Tom Jones* combines elements of the picaresque and the conventional romance: the fact that the hero is an outcast on the road offers the reader a critical perspective on the norms of society, and the conventional romance elements assure the reader that the hero will not remain an outlaw but will triumph in the end; this triumph endorses the implied criticism of society offered in the hero's perspective.

The implications of Iser's analysis of the 'repertoire', the social-historical knowledge and literary conventions that both author and implied reader share, are clear. It is important to encourage students to correlate their own personal experiences of life with those imaged in literature. (Iago is more understandable if you've been fooled by a friend.) Personal experience is not an intrusive irrelevance to textual understanding, as Richards and the New Critics would have it, but essential to it. Forming connections between personal life and textual events through anecdote is a constructive reading activity and can be developed as a habit of mind in class discussion.

An important part of the process of making books 'mean', says Iser, is the action of transforming words into 'mental images'. As meaning is not entirely in the text or in the reader but is the product of the text-reader interaction, it has to be 'ideated' by the mind of the reader:

> A reality that has no existence of its own can only come into being by way of ideation, and so the structure of the text sets off the sequence of mental images which lead to the text translating itself into the reader's consciousness.[90]

Iser goes on to say how the 'content' of these mental images will be 'coloured' by the personal experience of the reader, that the only way the reader can assimilate new and unfamiliar experience is to link it to what is known or seen already. This is certainly true of the mental images I formed while reading The Raj Quartet. The fictional hill station town of Pankot I saw in terms of my memories of Simla in the Himalayan foothills, and so on. But what is perhaps more significant about mental images is that they are not just sense impressions of sight, sound, taste, smell and touch, but feelings about places, people, events. To say that 'I see' Marlow's steamer on the Congo River in Africa (where I have never been) involves not just a pictorial image of an old steamboat with him at the wheel and the white traders and Africans on the decks, or the sounds, smells and tastes of the river, the vegetation, the rotten hippopotamus meat and so on. Sharper and more powerful than such sense images, important as they are, are the associated emotions and significances of these details. I can visualise Kurtz's spectral appearance ('that apparition'), but the dominant impression I have is of its sinister overtones. I can see and hear (and smell) Kurtz crying out his dying words in a whisper, '"The horror! The horror!"' but the dominant impression is of moral rather than physical corruption.

In forming our mental images we incorporate sense impressions, emotional effects and significances in a progressive movement of increasing depth and sophistication of response. Iser puts it this way:

> 'our mental images do not serve to make the character physically visible; their optical poverty is an indication of the fact that they illuminate the character, not as an object, but as a bearer of meaning.'[91]

Leavis, in writing about the poetry of Blake, said much the same thing in *The Living Principle:* 'The essential objects. . . . are not susceptible of visualisation; they belong to inner experience, emotional and instinctual life, the inner life of the psyche.'[92]

Ted Hughes writes of his experience of getting the clue as to what the Elizabethan philosopher Sir Francis Bacon was like by reading that he had 'peculiar eyes — eyes like a viper'. This made Bacon come alive for Hughes. He did not form a purely pictorial image, but the selected details suggested a mood that made Bacon 'near and real'.[93] When our imagination is unfettered, our mental images are certainly more powerfully affective and interpretative than optical. This applies to students' mental images too. Here is Jane, age 13, writing about the way *Lord of the Rings* affected her. She claims clear visualisation but communicates the greater power of emotion and interpretation — feelings about, rather than explicit visualisations of the text.

> I would visualise very clearly the scenes, characters and movements, feel sadness, happiness, joy, pain, love, tenderness, fun, experience everything. I was wrapped in the pictures in my mind and the plot. I was sort of tranced in my thoughts and the characters. The hobbits were especially clearly pictured. I could sense the aura of peace, tiredness and wisdom in Gandalf, the elf king, the wisdom, shyness, jolliness, weariness surrounding the characters'.[94]

We often resent the visual determinacy of film and television versions of novels we have read because the mental images we have formed are not pictorially sharp, so no matter what the photographic portrayals are like they inevitably exclude our own images. Iser says that we resent the photograph because it, 'reproduces an existing object and it also excludes me from a world I can see but which I have not helped to create'.[95]

We have already seen in Chapter Two how the explicit visual images of film and television versions of a novel overwhelm the mental images of those children who have read it. In overpowering children's visualisations, which Iser says is inevitable because of the 'visual poverty' of our mental images, they also overwhelm the emotional effects and significances personally imagined by readers. These are important idiosyncratic elements of common response processes like forming mental images and they should be treasured and nurtured rather than obliterated. For example, to me, Saul Bellow's Herzog is not so much a balding middle-aged man with horn-rimmed glasses and crows-feet under his eyes (the stereotypic visualisation) but a brilliantly intellectual and comic person with a range of clearly distinguished characteristics that I feel more powerfully than I see. He is partly a mixture of different key physical and behavioural characteristics of people I know and others I have seen in films, the street and other books, but he is quite unlike any of them in physical appearance or total personality. The fact that I see characteristics of many of my friends in Herzog and of Herzog in many of my friends indicates how much I admire and value both him and them. My mental image of Herzog is all my own work, created at the point of interaction between the text and my 'repertoire' of social and literary experience. This is the way students create mental images too. Here is part of the response of 14-year-old Sandra to a novel called *Beautiful Girl:*

'One of my favorite books would have to be *Beautiful Girl.* I enjoyed it because I could relate to my own surroundings as in friends, school etc. even though nothing like that has ever happened . . .

'In the book when the author described things I imagined them, but sometimes I changed them to suit what I thought they should be. Example, say the author described a kitchen of a home, I would sometimes imagine my own kitchen at home, but if they described say, a galley in a ship (I haven't seen a galley) I would sometimes change it around to what I imagine.'[96]

Readers of literature use their experience of the world and their knowledge of the conventions of literature to fill in what the words of the text do not tell them. In the analysis of the haiku of Basho in the last section (p.105) we have seen how the reader has to formulate unstated connections in texts to make meanings. To fill in these indeterminacies in the text we employ our 'repertoire' of 'social and historical norms' and conventional rules such as the rule of significance, the rule of metaphorical coherence and the rule of thematic unity. We could also say we read the text by filtering it through the grid of codes we have internalised. The hermeneutic activity of reading, for instance, involves finding a gap or a puzzle to fill in or solve. What Iser calls the 'gaps' or 'blanks' in the text are spaces between sentences, chapters, events, details, characters, narrative viewpoints, textual perspectives and so on which are left for the reader to fill out. Thus, Iser sees the gaps as the stimuli to the reader's creative participation, invitations to the reader to become collaborator or co-author in the creation of meaning. We do exactly the same in real life too, in building, for example, a total and coherent impression of another person from the few instances of contact we have with him or her, and no matter how many contacts we have or how deep the relationship, we always have gaps to fill in to make an interpretation.

> Whenever the reader bridges the gaps, communication begins . . . the blanks leave open the connections between perspectives in the text, and so spur the reader into coordinating these perspectives — in other words, they induce the reader to perform basic operations *within* the text[97]

Here are some examples of gaps which spur the reader into mental activity in the texts concerned:

- Ernest Hemingway's carefully selected (and omitted) physical details to describe and evoke apparently inconsequential moments in war time, have profound emotional significance. The reader formulates the horror, injustice, lack of dignity from the details and omissions. For instance, in *A Farewell to Arms*, the first person narrator, recovering from unconsciousness after an explosion, mentions that one of his boots was 'warm and wet', and the reader realises immediately what the shell-shocked narrator is temporarily too numb to deduce — that the boot is filled with blood, and its wearer is in a bad way, physically and mentally.

- In *Heart of Darkness,* we are continually forced to fill in the gaps, find the missing links, formulate the connections between apparently disparate observations of Marlow's, like the upturned railway truck and the scrupulously neat accountant (the details are juxtaposed) at the first station in Africa. The implications about the incompetence and decadence of colonial administration are formulated by the reader under the guidance of the text.

- To demonstrate how a blank can be used to arouse not only the reader's activity but also his or her commitment, Iser gives the example of the famous scene in *Oliver Twist* in which Oliver asks for more food. In this scene, Iser tells us, Oliver's emotions are deliberately omitted to emphasise the indignation of the authorities at the presumptuousness of this request. The apparent lack of sympathy on the part of the narrator ensures a flood of it in readers.

- Reinbert Tabbert offers interesting examples of gaps in books for young children. Reporting a conversation with Maurice Sendak, author and illustrator of *Where the Wild Things Are,* he says that Sendak explained his deliberate omission of the young hero's mother from the end of the story (which people had complained about), saying, 'I leave the mother to the imagination . . . You feel her there. By her absence she is more available.' Max's mother is present in the text by way of the supper he finds in his room when he returns from his journey to the Wild Things.[98] Aidan Chambers mentions a crucial gap in the same book that children seem to have no trouble filling in but which some adults certainly do, going by the number of those who complain that the book is frightening for young children. The gap is the one 'which demands that the child reader supply the understanding that Max has dreamt his journey to the Wild Things, that in fact the Wild Things are Max's own creation.'[99] The clue to filling in this gap is given by the first picture in the book, one of a room which includes on its wall a framed portrait of a Wild Thing signed by Max.

- With writers such as Harold Pinter and Eugene Ionesco, the blanks become thematic: they draw attention to themselves; meaning is conveyed by a subtext; words are used as weapons of assault;

intentions and motives are not explicated. The focal point is not what is said but what is unsaid. Blanks are foregrounded, with our expectations and understanding of 'normal' conversation in the background. The process exposes the limitations of our usual interactions with one another.

In much contemporary literature, including literature for children and adolescents, the authoritative orientation supplied by the author in the novels of the 18th and 19th centuries is gone. There is no definitive frame of reference by which to judge the events of the narrative. There is an increasing complexity of narrative structures with a range of perspectives, some or even all of which may be misleading or unreliable; there is an increase in the number of blanks; the logical, linear plot is a thing of the past, and so on.

The more gaps authors leave, the more demanding are their books to readers. Didactic and propaganda fiction, such as *The Pilgrim's Progress*, leaves few gaps for the reader's active participation. Andrew Stibbs compares Jill Paton Walsh's novel *Fireweed* with C.S. Lewis's Narnia series and draws the conclusion that where Lewis's books brainwash their young readers (leaving few gaps), *Fireweed* invites them to make life-like decisions and judgments (having many gaps).[100] Geoff Fox describes the gaps as space readers need for reflection, a kind of middle ground where text and reader meet. He considers the amount of space left by various children's authors and suggests that W.E. Johns and Enid Blyton don't leave much while in Alan Garner's later novels such as *Red Shift* and *The Stone Book* series there are chasms.[101] Research conducted by Robert Protherough shows that children prefer stories with more gaps to fill rather than those which leave little space for the reader.[102] As a result, Protherough says that teachers 'should give more thought to selecting texts that will extend children's sense of what fiction is and does, rather than simply looking for novels that will fit a given theme or provide interesting follow-up activities.'[103]

The productive reading strategies can be taught. Students can be helped to actively question and argue with the text by being encouraged to formulate their own questions arising from their own puzzlement, rather than being directed to answer questions set by the teacher. When students are reading to answer other people's questions, they inevitably see the text as an object and the reader's role as one of extracting meaning. They become passive ciphers rather than active and reflective meaning-makers. They also learn boredom.

Further, when answers to other people's questions are assessed as being right or wrong, the textual puzzles and problems become sources of anxiety rather than of pleasure, and reinforce students' feelings of their own inadequacy as readers. The construction of textual meaning requires the correlation of details to form patterns, the holding of unresolved questions in the head, the constant generation and modification of expectations — tough, vigorous mental activities which are certainly not encouraged by the kinds of exercises demanding instant and 'correct' answers. Speculation and hypothesising, so essential to literary interpretation, as well as to the development of language and thinking, are stifled by methods which penalise 'error'. You don't make guesses when you are likely to be penalised for being wrong.

In order to become more active readers, students need help during the process of reading. It is possible to develop in students the habit of asking questions such as the following while they are reading, and to help them to realise that any answers they formulate at one reading moment are provisional, and will almost certainly require subsequent modification. In fact, as the Bathurst research shows, students can find it liberating to discover that in guessing ahead you are likely to be wrong, and if you are, the text is far more interesting than if you're right. These are the kinds of questions that students can learn to ask of texts and can find considerable enjoyment from so doing. Formulating and solving puzzles is a source of pleasure when the rewards are so great, so long as penalties are not imposed for perfectly productive 'wrong' answers.

1. What is the significance of this particular detail, event, form of words?
2. How does it connect with other details, episodes?
3. What is this preparing us for? What kinds of things might happen?
4. How does this event affect my interpretation of what has gone before?
5. What am I learning about this person and his/her relationships with others? Why was he/she included in the story at all?
6. Whose point of view is being presented here? Why is the author offering this character's point of view here?
7. What is the implied author's view of this character, that behaviour, the human condition? How is s/he making me feel about this character, that behaviour, the human condition? How is s/he doing it?

Once it is recognised that reading is a creative activity, it becomes clear that the practice of imposing interpretations (whether of the teacher or the literary critic) on students is unhelpful in developing their literary perception.

Students respond positively to the discovery that meaning is something you make for yourself rather than an object you borrow or steal from others. As Bryant Fillion has pointed out, people only solve problems that they represent to themselves, [104] and poor readers aren't helped by being given other people's questions to answer. Further encouragement to students to become active interpreters of literature can take the form of requiring them to formulate their own questions about texts. For example, Penny Blackie reports on very successsful classroom work in poetry in which it was stipulated that the only questions to be discussed would be those formulated by the students, and the questions students asked had to be questions they didn't already know the answers to and wanted to know the answers to.[105]

Activities in the classroom to assist students to speculate and infer about events and characters could include filling in the gaps in some of those sections in narrative texts where long periods of time are summarised. For example, in Rosemary Sutcliff's *The Eagle of the Ninth*, one sentence at the beginning of Chapter 12 covers a whole summer: 'All that summer Marcus and Esca wandered through the abandoned Province of Valentia crossing and recrossing from coast to coast, and making steadily northward.'[106] Students could be asked to discuss, dramatise and/or write about an experience of Marcus and Esca during these early months in the north as they went about becoming known to the tribes and familiar with their lore. For example, some students might write a story about Esca meeting a group of people from his own tribe to bring out his divided feelings about going back to his own tribal lands as the slave/sword-bearer/companion and friend of a Roman officer.

Such work would be condemned by New Critics as lying outside the boundaries of the text, but just because the characters are constructs does not mean that their significance *in* the text and to the reader is limited to the 'words on the page'. What is on the page is connotative of what isn't on the page. Readers do have to infer about characters' lives beyond the text. Such a passage as that from *The Eagle of the Ninth* invites the kind of speculative interpetation or gap-filling that my suggested classroom activity involves readers in making. To engage in that activity, students are drawn deeper into the text to understand more fully and evaluate the motives of the characters, the seriousness of the risks they are undertaking, their awareness of possible consequences, and the way they go about fulfilling their purposes. Such imaginative recreation work, in writing particularly, also serves to make students realise that novels, stories, poems and plays are constructs, products of choice and literary mechanisms that they can become conscious of and learn to use for themselves.

In involving students in activities which require them to explore texts creatively, we must also make them enquire into their own reading processes. Not only can reading literature help us to better understand our emotional selves and our identities, but it can help us to become aware of our own intellectual processes if we focus attention on them reflexively. Leslie Stratta, John Dixon and Andrew Wilkinson have made it clear to us that in the imaginative exploration of texts, students' 'active engagement' should be followed by 'reflective evaluation'[107] of what they have learned. However, this reflective evaluation of textual understanding should itself involve reflexive evaluation of their own reading and learning strategies and processess. Further, helping students to be conscious of their own contribution to textual meaning is an effective way of undermining both the old Romantic notion of the text as divinely inspired unitary artefact to be admired but not investigated or analysed, and the old formalist notion of the text as an orange to be squeezed dry for its literary significance. Iser makes it clear that for most readers the processes of interpretation are unconscious:

> the syntheses (made by connecting signs and representing their equivalences) take place below the threshold of consciousness, unless they are raised above this threshold for the sake of analysis, though even they must first be formulated before they can become an object of scrutiny.[108]

Iser calls such syntheses 'passive syntheses' because they are unconscious, and goes on to suggest that if we can make our reading processes explicit and understood, we gain a greater control over them as well as a greater understanding of how authors influence and interest us. Such kinds of knowledge are forms of personal power which we can use to direct our own lives rather than have them under the direction of others.

# Psychoanalytical criticism

Modern psychoanalytical critics such as Norman Holland and David Bleich argue that the way we interpret and respond to literature has more to do with our individual consciousnesses and personalities than with any intrinsic qualities in the texts. Where the New Critics see the mind of the reader as a *tabula rasa* on which the objective text inscribes itself, extreme psychoanalytical critics such as Bleich see the text as a *tabula rasa* on which the subjectivity of the reader inscribes itself. Holland, while recognising the role of the text in initiating performances of meaning, locates meaning primarily in the reader, who 'shapes the materials the literary work offers him'[109] so as to re-create his or her own unique identity and transform his or her unconscious wishes and fears into socially acceptable meanings.

> All of us, as we read, use the literary work to symbolize and finally to replicate ourselves. We work out through the text our own characteristic patterns of desire and adaptation . . . We interpret [the text] in such a way as to cast it in terms of our characteristic ways of coping with the world. That is, each of us will find in a literary work the kind of thing we characteristically wish or fear the most.[110]

So, according to Holland, we re-create the text according to our characteristic patterns of adapting to real life, and we project on to it our characteristic fantasies. Our enjoyment comes from the transformation of our anxieties and desires into aesthetic, moral, intellectual and social coherence and significance.

An example Holland gives to illustrate his theory is the range of responses to *Hamlet* of different readers who all see authority figures as the 'central desire and danger in their worlds' but who deal with this wish/fear in different ways. As one of these responses is very close to my own response, I believe there might be something useful in what Holland says. One of the ways Holland specifies of coping with such authority figures is by 'establishing limits and qualifications on their authority', and the people who cope this way tend to relate to *Hamlet* 'by discovering and stressing irony and occasional farce' and emphasising the failures and contradictions of corrupt and easily manipulable characters such as Osric, Polonius and Rosencrantz.[111] As this is certainly one important way I relate to *Hamlet*, I have to acknowledge that Holland's analysis has enabled me to see more

clearly some things about myself that I was less aware of before —
namely that I am very concerned with authority figures and the
agencies of social control, both in the immediate work place and
in the larger organisations of society, nationally and internationally;
and that the way I cope with them is to 'establish limits and
qualifications on their authority' in various ways. Suffice to say that
my immediate and startled recognition of the application to myself
of the significance of one of Holland's specified responses to *Hamlet*
has enabled me to see how my interpretation of literary works might
well reflect my characteristic life strategies for dealing with my
deepest fears and wishes. One of the main uses of psychoanalytical
criticism, then, is that it can help readers to gain self knowledge if
we reflect on our own interpretations of texts, asking ourselves the
question, 'What am I learning about myself from my unique response
to the text? ' or 'What does my interpretation, in relation to other
people's interpretations, tell me about myself?'

As well as helping us to discover aspects of ourselves that we were
only vaguely aware of before, psychoanalytical criticism can tell us
a great deal about 'sub-texts' of works, those aspects or meanings
which the works themselves unconsciously imply. Terry Eagleton,
in an analysis of *Sons and Lovers*, shows that Lawrence's overt
downgrading of Walter Morel is countered by unconscious sympathy
for him in scenes which enact his warmth and vitality, while Mrs
Morel's admirable encouragement of Paul to develop his aesthetic
life is balanced by covertly communicated life-denying
characteristics. Eagleton explains how the novel which *tells* us that
Morel has denied the god in him also *shows* us the opposite:

> in such telling incidents as the final reunion of Baxter Dawes (in
> some ways a parallel figure to Morel) with his estranged wife
> Clara, the novel "unconsciously" makes reparation for its
> upgrading of Paul (whom this incident shows in a much more
> negative light) at the expense of his father. Lawrence's final
> reparation for Morel will be Mellors, the "feminine" yet powerful
> male protagonist of *Lady Chatterley's Lover*.[112]

Without wanting to exaggerate its uses or to take its methods to
extremes, psychoanalytical criticism can be of great value in helping
readers to decipher the unconscious motivations and ideologies of
authors as these are embedded in texts. In his book on Marxist
literary criticism, Terry Eagleton examines a scene in Joseph Conrad's
novel *Nostromo* to illustrate the complex, indirect relationship

between literary works and the ideological worlds they inhabit, a relationship of which authors are often quite unaware.[113] Eagleton argues that the scene in which two characters (Nostromo and Decoud) are adrift on a barge in the Placido Gulf, isolated from contact with civilisation, and with nothing to sustain them but their own values, dramatises Conrad's 'individual psychology', which is itself a product of attitudes and values deriving from the imperialist/capitalist structure of his society. Conrad portrays Nostromo and Decoud as men whose reputations disguise a moral emptiness that only becomes evident when they are isolated from the props of their society and the adulation of its citizens. Eagleton focuses on the way Nostromo communicates a sense of humanity's failure to learn anything from history, a feeling of human disharmony and isolation, and of the relativism and irrationality of human values, and says that this ideological pessimism was rife in conservative middle-class intellectual circles at the beginning of the 20th century when the novel was written. Eagleton concludes that Conrad's individual psychology is embedded in the novel in ways he himself couldn't recognise. The psychoanalytical critics claim that every literary work has a 'sub-text' or 'unconscious', that this unspoken element may be as significant as what is articulated, and that it is available to readers who care to reflect pyschoanalytically on literature.

The psychoanalytical critics also emphasise the pleasures of reading which are often ignored or forgotten in the schools and universities with their concentration on the high moral seriousness and solemnity of reading literature, and their preoccupation with developing students' responsiveness through a knowledge of literary devices and techniques. This approach to teaching is conditioned by the demands of public examinations. Freud saw human behaviour as being motivated essentially by the desires to gain pleasure and avoid pain. Initial enjoyment of literature is a necessary prerequisite to deeper understanding which, in turn, might well increase the enjoyment. However, there is no point in trying to involve inexperienced student readers in the closer and deeper analysis of texts which they initially find essentially boring. Further, if all readers interpret any one text slightly differently from one another in terms of their individual identities, it becomes essential to make sure students are not made to feel guilty (experience pain) when they don't enjoy reading what their teachers enjoy reading, or when they don't see in texts exactly what their teachers see in them. This suggests that not only should teachers allow lots of choice in reading by developing wide-reading schemes, but that they should encourage and help all students to find those books which they will enjoy immediately.

For example, an appropriate strategy at the beginning of the school year would be to give each student the task of finding (with some guidance and/or assistance) one novel which is so powerfully exciting an experience to read that she or he is impelled to tell others about it. Such a strategy needs clearly stated rules to make it both liberating to students and workable in practice. One of these rules would be that after choosing a book to try, if the student is bored after reading one chapter she or he puts it back on the shelf and chooses another to try. It is counter-productive to make reading unpleasant or too difficult for students in the early stages of literary development. A primary aim of teaching literature should be to involve as many students as possible in enjoying it. All the people who read literature outside an educational institution do so because they find it pleasurable. It would seem that many English Departments in schools and universities are often so concerned to establish the status of the discipline of criticism, that they emphasise the intellectual rigour of reading and responding to literature, and academic standards, at the expense of the pleasures, and consequently turn many students off reading altogether.

The psychoanalytical critics' insight that people deal with literary texts in the same way as they deal with life experience suggests that students should be encouraged to make continual connections between events in literary texts and their own lives; and, further, to make predictions about plot developments and character behaviour in the light of understanding drawn from life, all during the process of reading. This view is supported by the English psychologist, D.W. Harding:

> We need to encourage, very warmly, verifications from personal experience, not frown on the "That's me" identification with a character . . . People who need to use the concept of "discipline" in talking about response will be uneasy about the freedom of "That's me", but it can perhaps be accommodated even to a literary respect for the work of art. "That's me" has two components, and our aim is to move dynamically from the "me" of personal identification to the "that" of the poem or the object in the poem. The discipline lies in the attentiveness to the "that", and it should be made plain that there is no real dichotomy here, but a natural movement from subject to object and back again.[114]

Wolfgang Iser would claim that the distinction between the reading subject and the text as object disappears in the reading process as the reader thinks the thoughts of another and creates the world of the text in his or her reading. However, the essential points that both Harding and Iser make support psychoanalytical criticism's emphasis on the importance of readers making connections between literature and life. An example of how this can be done in teaching practice is given by Ernie Tucker, Head of English at Maroubra Junction High School. In introducing Reginald Maddock's *The Dragon in the Garden* to a junior class, he used prediction questions to get the class making life-literature connections before they began reading:

> For instance, what would happen when a twelve year old boy who talked posh, came to school for the first time in his life? As they began to read I asked them to tell each other when they came to a part they had predicted. The small group talk emerged with questions such as, "Do they offer him cigarettes? Does he smoke? Do they try to scab money off him? Will they bash him up after school?"[115]

Psychoanalytical criticism supports Wolfgang Iser's reception theory in showing us why no two readings of a text will be exactly the same. With this knowledge, teachers will be aware of the danger of imposing interpretations on a class, and will see their role as one of helping students to explore texts to make their own meanings. The personal response of the reader is all important in the development of literary judgment. The process of deepening and refining response involves a valuing of students' initial responses as a starting point and giving them the opportunity, through small group talk and a range of imaginative activities, to test that initial response against the responses of others and against the text itself. As meaning is created by the reader, and as literature is the outcome of the interaction between text and reader, the teacher's job should not be conceived of as raising ignorant inexperienced readers to the level of sacrosanct text, but rather as helping readers to value their own experience and to see literature as offering an extension of it, with students' present understanding and value systems being recognised as their points of imaginative entry to the world of texts. To bring the experience of the student and the world of literary texts into a cooperative relationship, teachers must be well acquainted with both students and the literature written for them.

Psychoanalytical criticism has obvious weaknesses that would make it dangerous to use as a sole guide to the teaching of literature in schools. It does not allow for a critical faculty that can escape its own subjectivity enought to see literary significance at different levels. In its extreme form of seeing the literary work as being nothing outside the mental processes of the reader, and thus identical with the reader's mental state during the act of reading, it could be used to support any kind of self-indulgence or mental laziness in reading and response, and this would not be helpful in teaching. Teaching literature means trying to help students to read better. We all acknowledge that there are levels of response, and that some responses can be readily identified as being more penetrating than others. A theory which implies that one response is as good as another is certainly not going to help teachers to develop their students' reading.

However, as we have seen, there are many useful and liberating implications of psychoanalytical criticism for teaching. Norman Holland's theory that we interpret literature in accordance with our own identity destroys the belief in an autonomous text and the objectivity of literary criticism. It suggests the need for a new kind of critical writing which acknowledges its own subjectivity. Hugh Crago has argued for and exemplified a form of criticism which 'avoids projecting on to the book the critic's own feelings and responses', and honestly recognises them as being personal and subjective.[116] He presents the process notes he made while reading Jill Paton Walsh's novel *A Chance Child*, together with his analytical commentary on his responses, considering how much the book and how much his own repertoire of life and literary experience contributed to these responses.[117] His analysis is not only far more honest an interpretation for being acknowledged as subjective, but seems to me to be far more valuable to readers.

Further, Crago's commentary offers a guide to a kind of writing we should be encouraging our students to use in place of the formal literary critical essay demanded by public examiners and, therefore, by schools, presumably because of its spurious appearance of objectivity. To justify the prohibition of the first person pronoun and to insist on the use of the impersonal 'it' and the passive voice in the name of objectivity is absurd and hypocritical. If response is a personal matter then it is more honest, as well as more useful to students and their readers, to encourage them to write in more personal and informal ways. As Holland says, 'Many, perhaps most, critics write not as though they themselves were actively discovering forms and synthesising ideas in what they read, but as if they were just passively reporting what is "objectively" there.'[118] This practice is misleading and quite unhelpful to young readers for whom the critical writing of others is only of use if it teaches ways of reading texts more deeply and satisfyingly.

Crago also writes wisely about another implication for teaching that he derives from his reading of the psychoanalytical critics. His experience as a teacher convinced him that the activities of reading literature and discussing it with others are not sufficient of themselves to ensure that students will extend and refine their understanding of themselves and of other people and the human condition, the main contemporary justifications for teaching literature. My experience as a teacher strongly supports what Crago says:

> access to the attitudes of others may broaden a person's mind provided that no deep-seated values are involved for that person. If they are, then simply hearing other people's ideas will make very little difference. It seems to me that in discussion or in the act of making a written evaluation, most of us put our energy into defensive behaviour—shoring up our own values by rationalisation rather than genuinely opening ourselves to the ideas and values of others. Similarly, within the literary work itself, we respond favourably to characters who embody our own modes of coping with life and find boring or even actively repulsive those who are too different from ourselves.[119]

This is, of course, partly what Holland means when he says we interpret literature in accordance with our own identities and our characteristic ways of coping with the world. If literature is to be therapeutic in any way, we must help readers to go beyond recreating texts in terms of their own identities. If students' feelings and values are to be educated by literature, work in the classroom must obviously go beyond reading and discussion. Here the practical activities of imaginative exploration, already mentioned in earlier sections, can be most productive. Crago particularly urges the value of involving students in the role playing of fictional characters as a way of developing deeper human understanding through literature:

> Once a person begins to improvise action and words around a fictional scene or character, she begins to give that character life from within herself, to the considerable increase of her own

understanding and involvement. Paradoxically, it is by entering further into *ourselves*, by drawing on our own affective resources, that we come to empathise with others. By role-playing characters we dislike, we may (sometimes) be able to acknowledge that what we dislike in them is something we dislike and deny in ourselves . . . Once we speak our feelings directly, instead of merely talking about them or writing about them, things do start to happen — feelings are stirred up and insights can occur.[120]

Just as students' anecdotes from personal experience are not an intrusive irrelevance to understanding literature, neither are their emotional responses. If we ignore students' personal experiences and feelings in their responses to literature, if we suppress them in the name of objectivity and scholarship, we effectively teach them to ignore literature as a source of pleasure in their lives.

## Political criticism

Political criticism considers the relationship between a literary text and the ideology embedded in it. All political theories of literature have in common the premise that literature is produced by a particular historical consciousness and can only be properly understood within its social and historical context. The conviction of F.R. Leavis that there is a point of view above history, that there can be intellectual, aesthetic and moral activity that is untainted by social and economic circumstances, is seen by political critics as naive. Novels, plays and poems are manufactured like television news and can be analysed the same way. The New Critical reification of the literary artefact has created the myth that what is really culturally constructed is 'natural' or a product of divine inspiration. English teachers, influenced almost exclusively by Leavis and the New Critics, have traditionally seen their task as transmitting to their students the cultural heritage of the world's great books as the repositories of eternal values uncontaminated by history. This practice is characterised by Gary MacLennan and Robert Lingard as 'lighting a candle and hoping the barbarians will go away'. As we have seen already, this image certainly applies to Leavis, whose aim in teaching literature was to help a cultivated minority withstand rather than combat the barbaric elements of post-industrial society. MacLennan and Lingard go on to say that the role of English teachers should be to find 'curricula and pedagogical alternatives which [might] produce individuals who can control their lives and their world.'[121]

In holding that all literature is political or ideological, political critics argue that any theory is misleading which treats a literary text as a purely aesthetic object, or as an objective structure, or as a product of a writer's uniquely individual mental processes, or in any way that isolates it from society and history. Only political criticism will explain how texts enshrine ideology and how they produce ideological effects on readers. Further, the notion of the ideologically innocent reader is as preposterous as the notion of the ideologically innocent text. Just as we saw in the last section on the psychoanalytical critics that Joseph Conrad's individual psychology was at least partly socially determined, so are the individual psychologies of readers. There is no such thing as an a-theoretical or non-ideological text. Walter Benn Michaels and Stanley Fish say that readers' interpretations of literature are the results of interpretative strategies possessed by being members of 'a community of interpreters',[122] that 'the self that interprets is also an interpretation . . . that what the self wants has already been constituted by the canons of interpretation.'[123]

Post-structuralist criticism, deriving its insights from the findings of modern linguistics, claims that meaning is not simply expressed or reflected in language but is actually produced by it. If, then, the text and its author's psychology are products of history; and if the reader's self is a product of socially determined interpretative strategies; and if language, itself socially created, is the source rather than the vehicle of meaning; then reality is a product of language. As Jane Tompkins says, this situation 'repoliticizes literature and literary criticism' because literature and literary criticism create reality for us:

> The insistence that language is constitutive of reality rather than merely reflective of it suggests that contemporary critical theory has come to occupy a position very similar to, if not the same as, that of the Greek rhetoricians for whom mastery of language meant mastery of the state. The questions that propose themselves within this critical framework therefore concern, broadly, the relations of discourse and power. What makes one set of perceptual strategies or literary conventions win out over another? If the world is the product of interpretation, then who or what determines which interpretive system will prevail?[124]

The main recent shift of emphasis in literary criticism is from the text itself to the reader. Those critics who wish to shift the emphasis on the reader to the reader's socially determined interpretative strategies raise the notion of language (in this case, literary rhetoric) as a form of power which can be used, and this has important implications for teaching literature. If our interpretative strategies are socially/historically influenced (conditioned? determined?), and if all texts and all critical theories are ideological, then knowing this can itself be a source of power, enabling us to recognise the processes of our own cultural shaping. If you don't agree with this statement, consider your criteria for distinguishing between literary and extra-literary judgments of texts. If you consider that there are issues about literature that are 'non-literary' or 'extra-literary', then ask yourself who says so and why. We have already seen, in the section on New Criticism, how Australian New Critics privilege those writers who express the moral and metaphysical over those who express the social and political. John Docker provides detailed evidence of this being the major trend in Australian literary criticism since the 1950s.[125] As one example, he analyses an essay, 'The Eighteen Nineties', by the Sydney University New Critic, G.A. Wilkes, which describes the social and political aspects of literature as superficial, minor, local, temporary, temporal and 'non-literary' considerations and the metaphysical issues as profound, major, universal, permanent, eternal and 'literary':

> If we were to evaluate the nineties by strictly literary standards, then, we should find that the mass of writers are men of minor talent . . . Furphy's work is important not for its democratic temper or offensively Australian bias, but for its exploration of issues that are not local, but universal in their references . . . The nationalistic, patriotic, radical tendencies in the writing of the period assure it a place in Australian social history, but its place in Australian literary history must remain in doubt . . . [126]

About *Such is Life*, Wilkes goes on to say,

> The value set upon the novel by the social historian is largely irrelevant to its value as literature: *Such is Life* is memorable not as showing a stage in the evolution of the Australian democratic ideal, but as an exploration of the abiding problems of destiny and free will, moral responsibility, and the operation of chance in the universal scheme — problems which have engaged writers

not of Furphy's period only but of all periods, and which are still in no imminent danger of solution.[127]

The political critics represented in *Re-Reading English*, edited by Peter Widdowson, all assert that literature is a construct of criticism, and literary value is determined by the ideology of the literary theory currently in vogue. Some of the critics represented in the collection show how Leavis and the New Critics canonise those works of literature which are consonant with their own values of liberal humanist individualism and, at the same time, reject much popular poetry and working-class oral literature as being of little merit. Widdowson's contributors also show how such criticism is most ideological when protesting its abhorrence of ideology most vehemently: 'Literary value, therefore, as perceived by criticism in the "great tradition" of master works or "classic" texts, correlates closely with the values of liberal individualism in general, and substantially helps to underpin them.'[128]

In the 18th century, street ballads and the drama did not qualify as literature, but philosophy, history, and essays did. Those writings that had high prestige according to the values of the age were given the status of literature, but those without it were not. In the 18th century, the novel was a doubtful case, just as today film and television drama is in the eyes of conservative critics.

Such judgments are value saturated, just like those that distinguish between literary and non-literary readings of texts. I remember, when teaching Higher School Certificate History in a Sydney secondary school years ago, being attacked by a number of teachers (indoctrinated by New Critical theory) for setting Bernard Shaw's play *The Apple Cart*, as reading for my students on the topic of the British and American systems of government. That the students enjoyed reading the play, and gained a great deal of understanding of the British system of government from seeing and talking about such things as the responses of cabinet ministers to King Magnus's exercising of his right of royal veto of legislation were irrelevant to those who condemned what I did.

When I produced evidence that the students had gained more political insight and historical knowledge from Shaw's play than from the set readings of historical texts, this made the situation even more regrettable; here was a barbarian perverting literature for 'non-literary' purposes. It appears that the worst of all literary crimes is to gain valuable, usable, practical knowledge from literature. It was from that moment on that I began to recognise that literary critics are not disinterested literary commentators but usually academics or teachers employed by the State to prepare students ideologically for their roles in society. Unfortunately, I didn't have the foggiest notion of this when I was a university student being prepared for my role.

Where the New Critics' major purpose and satisfaction in literary analysis seems to be aesthetic contemplation of the way parts of a work cohere in an harmonious metaphysical whole, contemporary post-structuralist or deconstructionist critics emphasise the indeterminancy of meaning and structural disharmony of literature. Roland Barthes, for example, prefers texts that emphasise the incoherence and arbitrariness of meaning and challenge the notion of literary unity because he believes they portray more honestly the true state of the world's incoherence and disorder. Works which self-consciously draw attention to their own artifice and to their own plurality of meaning subvert the bourgeois faith in metaphysical order, certainty, causation and the transparent understandability of the world. The post-structuralist critics see the logical resolutions and determinate meanings of realistic fiction as the false constructions of bourgeois ideology. Anything which draws attention to the arbitrariness of meaning undermines the naturalisation of concealed ideology. For example, Bertolt Brecht's dramatic methods and structures are highly approved of by Barthes because they emphasise the methods of communicating meaning rather than concealing them, and thus bring audiences to see such meanings as constructs. If each event in a play is seen as *not* being the logical and necessary outcome of preceding events, then the world is seen not as fixed but as alterable.

Modernist writers such as Samuel Beckett, John Fowles, Vladimir Nabokov and Flann O'Brien, in experimenting with form and flouting the conventions of the novel, show that what they communicate is artifice, not reality, and thus indicate that the patterns imposed upon experience by traditional fiction are illusory. In Beckett's novels there is a pervading mood of despair, emanating from the futile attempts of his rootless narrators to make sense of experience. However, the futility of the effort doesn't obviate the need to make it, as in *Molloy*, for example, where the hero tries desperately to organise the circulation of his 16 sucking stones so that he will suck them in the same order in each cycle. Where no metaphysical order exists, human beings find it necessary to impose one, no matter how irrational and absurd it is. In *S/Z*, Barthes describes the literary text as being like an onion, consisting only of enveloping layers with no kernel or heart of finite meaning:

> The text is not a line of words releasing a single "theological" meaning (the message of an Author-God) but a multi-dimensional space in which a variety of writings, none of them original, blend and clash. The text is a tissue of quotations drawn from innumerable centres of culture.[129]

The contribution of post-structuralism to political criticism is its identification of the processes of ideological concealment implicit in the constructedness of literature, and its emphasis on the necessity of disentangling the 'codes' or threads of structure and meaning, the fabricating devices that constitute texts. This work of deconstruction enables readers to see exactly how texts are the constructed products of ideology. Deconstruction was mentioned in Chapter Two as a necessary part of media studies in schools to enable students to see how television, magazines and newspapers 'work them over'. Deconstructive activities should also be central in the school exploration of literature.

In her book, *Children's Minds*, Margaret Donaldson emphasises the importance to children's intellectual growth of their being taught in ways that develop their reflective awareness of both the way language works and the processes of their own minds. English teachers need to ensure that the activities they organise in the teaching of literature include those that will require students to reflect on the way texts work to influence their attitudes and on their own response processes. As Donaldson puts it, 'If a child is going to control and direct his own thinking . . . he must become conscious of it.'[130]

This kind of knowledge, derived from reflective and reflexive thinking about the ways texts work on us and about the ways we work on texts, is a form of political power, as Paulo Freire has pointed out:

> Attempting to liberate the oppressed without their reflective participation in the act of liberation is to treat them as objects which must be saved from a burning building; it is to lead them into the populist pitfall and transform them into masses which can be manipulated.[131]

Barbara Hardy, as we have already seen, describes narrative as 'a primary act of mind transferred from art to life'. Young readers can be helped enormously by recognising that 'the novel merely heightens, isolates and analyses the narrative motions of human consciousness'[132], that the stories of published writers are constructed in much the same ways as we construct narratives about our own lives in order to understand them. Those writers who play with narrative and draw attention to its nature are valuable in helping readers to stand back and evaluate texts as authors' creations embodying world views and ideologies. It is the task of the teacher to encourage and nurture personal responses to literature and the pleasure associated with making them, but it is also the task of the teacher to help students to understand the way texts and their own minds interact to produce such enjoyment, and this understanding can lead to a more rewarding pleasure as well as to greater control of texts and of themselves.

Political understanding of the processes of the literary transmission of values and ideology, and the reflexive understanding of one's own reading processes are not separate issues. A novelist who is acutely aware of this, and who writes for children and adolescents, is Aidan Chambers. His novels, *The Present Takers* (for younger adolescents) and *Breaktime* and *Dance on My Grave* (for older adolescents) teach young readers the fact and methods of literary artifice and ideology in the process of their reading of them. The conventions and techniques of fiction required for understanding these novels are communicated in the act of reading, and readers are challenged to consider the ways ideology is embedded in the fiction. Chambers says that 'It is one of the responsibilities of children's writers, and a privileged one, so to write that children are led how to read: how to accept the challenge.[133]

In my first year of teaching, an amiable and well-meaning senior English teacher offered me what he saw as a simple but spectacularly successful practical teaching model:

1. Tell them what you're going to tell them (introduction)
2. Tell them (transmission of information)
3. Tell them what you've told them (summary/conclusion)

In these enlightened days of universal pedagogic understanding of the central importance of the need for learners to use language actively for learning to take place, no English teacher would take this model seriously. However, while rejecting the middle transmission step, I would make a strong claim for the efficacy of the first step. I believe that at every stage of education from kindergarten to university, learners should have certain things made explicit to them at the outset. These include the purposes of the learning; the uses, in the world outside the educational institution, of the particular concept or knowledge to be taught; what the learners are expected to gain from learning it; the forms the learning will take (the organisation of the learning situations); what the students are required to do; and the criteria of assessment. Applied to the teaching of literature, this means making clear to students the reasons why literature is included in the curriculum, what they are expected to get out of reading, what committed readers get out of it and what good readers do to get these benefits.

Making explicit the values of literature and the ideology associated with the answers provided by different literary theories should be part of the literature curriculum. Questions of value and purpose, and of reflective and reflexive understanding, are policical and this fact should be recognised. Answers to these questions vary according to the answerer's critical theory. Therefore, the kinds of answers offered by critics, teachers and pupils should be all respected, examined and regarded as provisional, so that the curriculum becomes a negotiated one in which the role of the teacher changes from fount of all knowledge and expert transmitter of orthodoxy as truth, to experienced partner in the joint exploration of common concerns. In developing literary competence, students should also be learning about literary ideology and how it works, and about themselves. They learn about themselves by becoming interpreters of their own life behaviour and languaging processes, and of the way the language of others works to influence them. This kind of reflective and reflexive understanding can give them power to control their own responses to reading and their own lives. As Humpty-Dumpty put it to Alice, it is a question of 'which is to be master' — the words we read and use or we who read and use them.[134]

Marxist critics believe that the development of individual literary sensibility is not of itself an adequate educational aim in a world of inequality. They believe that students need the power conferred by control over language to operate in society effectively. Terry Eagleton[135] and the contributors to Peter Widdowson's *Re-Reading English*[136] call for the incorporation of literature into a larger discipline of Rhetoric or Cultural Studies, which would include other forms of writing and cultural production, and would analyse all these forms of communication, setting them in their social and historical contexts. Eagleton suggests that in studying the kinds of effects discourses produce and how they produce them, students can learn to practise the rhetoric for their own purposes. This would, as Jane Tompkins suggests in a passage quoted earlier in this section, give literature the status it had in classical Greece as Rhetoric. Eagleton argues that we should, like the Greeks, 'grasp' discursive practices as 'forms of power and performance' to be used.[137] Certainly, students need to learn to narrate, describe, criticise, plan, argue and justify in meaningful contexts to real audiences, and the study of discourse methods can help in this. The internalised effects of reading literature have always been powerfully available to committed readers. Eagleton merely suggests that the study of discourse methods should become more conscious and more systematic. To implement such a programme in schools would mean drawing on the whole range of contemporary literary theory, as Eagleton says.

> Rhetoric, or discourse theory, shares with structuralism and semiotics an interest in the formal devices of language, but like reception theory (Iser) is also concerned with how those devices are actually effective at the point of "consumption"; its preoccupation with discourse as a form of power and desire can learn much from deconstruction and psychoanalytical theory, and its belief that discourse can be a humanly transformative affair shares a good deal with liberal humanism.[138]

I think that studying literature in the context of Cultural Studies or Rhetoric has much to recommend it. Literature, biography, technical publications, textbooks, television, radio and the press all shape our ways of knowing and they should all be subject to deconstructive analysis in the classroom so the processes of this shaping are understood by students. In fact through this work, students can gain a deeper understanding of the communication networks of their whole society as well as of its values and its ways of maintaining them. One can't help but recognise the truth of Terry Eagleton's criticisms of Leavisite elitism and New Critical snobbery in education.

> While literary critics have been cultivating sensibility in a minority, large segments of the media have been trying to

devastate it in the majority: yet it is still presumed that studying, say, Gray and Collins is inherently more important than examining television or the popular press.[139]

A sensitivity for Romantic poetry is certainly worth cultivating, but so is a hard-nosed understanding of the spuriousness of romantic advertisements for scented shaving cream and hair shampoo. It is just as important for students to understand how Mills and Boon novels stimulate the interest of young readers as to have one's own interests stimulated by *Wuthering Heights*. However, while I believe that literature should be considered as a form of discourse and deconstructed as such in schools, I would also argue that literature should, as well, be sustained as a separate discipline. What is unique about literature as a 'cultural sign system', what justifies its independence, is its humanising and humane-ising potentiality in a world becoming increasingly mechanised and mechanistic. By all means let us study the rhetoric and signifying processes of *The Raj Quartet* to understand how it achieves its effects on us and to gain control of its discourse methods for our own use; but reading it as a novel, as imaginative literature, offers something more than rhetoric and more than a better historical understanding of modern India. If offers the possibility of a broadening and deepening of our human understanding and imaginative sympathy, an extension of our representation of the world in terms of values and feelings as well as of cognition.

Finally, if students are to be empowered politically by the study of literature as a structure of cultural transmission, and if they are to achieve deeper understanding of self, others and the human condition through the study of literature as imaginative creation, they need to be engaged in production as well as in reception. This means that as well as actively reading and discussing the texts of others, they should be actively producing their own literature in all its forms of writing and dramatic inprovisation, and presenting reports on their explorations and discoveries of texts to others. This emphasis on production is also appropriate, of course, for other forms of discourse. With the emphasis on student productivity and creativity in literature teaching, rhetoric can indeed become a form of power. Gary MacLennan and Robert Lingard outline the way teachers can empower students, by linking the language and experience they already have with the language and experience they get from literature, and building the latter on the base of the former:

We should restore the rhetorical dimensions to our English teaching. In other words . . . children should be given the language skills necessary to impose themselves on the world. Appropriate English teaching would begin with the life experiences of the children, but then the whole field of discourse, including the "High Culture" literature, should be used to help them go from their own experiences to an understanding of the wider society.[140]

## Implications for the teaching of reading

There is much that English teachers can learn from the reader-response critics. The teaching of reading at all levels from Infants School to University would improve significantly if English teachers started to follow Margaret Meek's advice from her work in teaching illiterate adolescents how to read, and that is 'to look at reading not as reading experts but as expert readers':

> When we began to be concerned about those who could not read the class texts and to take an interest in the teaching of reading, we found the territory occupied by those whose studies were derived from psychology: experts in learning difficulties, diagnostic assessment, remedial methodology and child guidance.[141]

In the methods of teaching reading derived from psychology, the emphasis is on what pupils can't do rather than on what they can do. As Margaret Meek shows in *Achieving Literacy*, when 'attention is paid to what inexperienced readers actually can read[142], the productive strategies can be identified and built on. The trouble with much of the teaching of reading at the Infants School level is its focus of discrete reading skills identified by studies in educational psychology and transmitted in isolation from meaningful contexts. In these circumstances many children never discover that 'reading is worth the trouble it takes to learn'.[143] Teachers who direct children's primary focus of attention to sight-sound correspondences so that reading becomes a process of phonic decoding, are teaching them to see the skills as ends in themselves rather than as means to ends. This model of reading development derives from that branch of psychology known as behaviourism, which aims to perfect techniques of operant conditioning and skill reinforcement. Its mechanistic methods have been produced from laboratory tests with rats which are tortured in the interests of learning about human behaviour.

Behaviourism's equation of children and rats is indicative of its contempt for any theory of learning which sees human behaviour as being directed by anything higher than instinct. Significantly, the success of Margaret Meek and her colleagues in teaching illiterate adolescents to read resulted from their rejection of the decontextualised skills approach of behaviourism, and their use of strategies deriving largely from reader-response theories of literature and reading. When the reluctant adolescents concentrated on 'what happens next' rather than in words and sounds, there was the beginning of progress. In recognising that reading involves more than taking meaning from the page, that the meaning of the text is the outcome of a dialogue between the reader and the text, Meek and her team encouraged their adolescent pupils to link textual events with personal experience, and to identify and respect the value of their present skills and knowledge.

> We strove to help them to predict and guess their way through narrative texts outside the remedial reading schemes, we discovered how "readability", the measurement of text, vocabulary and sentence length is not what makes a text difficult. Instead, we studied the significance of what the author doesn't say, about the world inside the story and the world outside it, with the scores of unexplained textual conventions that the reader has to learn.[144]

Reader-response criticism suggests the need for a change in the teacher's role and methods. If teachers begin to see their task primarily as one of improving students' reading processes in all the ways outlined in this chapter, rather than passing on to them the received wisdom of self-appointed arbiters of taste as to what constitutes literary excellence, then new ways of selecting and exploring texts in schools are called for. These are outlined in Chapter Five. Initially, it is important for teachers to consider the new critical positions, to examine all their present assumptions about literature, and to deconstruct their own teaching practice so as to make explicit to themselves, about every detail of it, why they are doing exactly what they are doing and what it is accomplishing. I believe that each teacher should take from each of the contemporary critical theories exactly what s/he finds useful in helping students to become better readers and more integrated and independent human beings. In the context of teaching, it is no more profitable to construct a hierarchy of critical theories than it is to construct a hierarchy of the world's greater and lesser writers. We need to be eclectic, practical and responsible. While not endorsing any one theory or the ideology underpinning it, we must recognise that all are ideological, and we must take from each what serves our purposes as teachers.

## POSTULATING A DEVELOPMENTAL MODEL OF RESPONSE

### THE VALUE OF A DEVELOPMENTAL MODEL

The literary theories and research findings outlined in this chapter provide many clues as to how a developmental model of response might be constructed. They also provide some tools for this construction work in their identification of specific productive activities involved in the reading of literature.

The need for a developmental model has been recognised by English teachers for a long time. A reading programme needs to have some logic of sequence, or at least coherence, in terms of helping students to progress from the stage they are at to the next attainable stage, if such staging points or levels can be established. Teachers need to be able to match the content of their literature programmes with the developmental levels of the students they are teaching, recognising that the students in any one class (streamed or non-streamed) will vary considerably in the developmental stages they have reached; there is unlikely to be much homogeneity in any class in terms of levels of reading performance. By the content of their programmes, I mean: the literary texts chosen for shared class reading; the literary texts suggested or recommended to individuals for wide reading; and the literary satisfactions, concepts and reading strategies that are appropriate to teach to each student on the basis of his or her perceived need and identified developmental stage.

It has been an orthodoxy in teaching for some time to begin where the students are, to build on their present states of understanding, to link new knowledge and skills to what they know and can do already. The simple, practical logic of the situation is that each student *does* begin from his or her present store of experience and knowledge, because there is nowhere else she or he can possibly begin. The problem in the teaching of literature is to know where the students are. When teachers begin above or below each student's level, problems arise. When the reading programme is too far above a student's level, she or he finds the literature incomprehensible and the work on concepts and strategies irrelevant, as they are out of reach. When the programme is too far below a student's level, she or he finds the literature unsatisfying, and the work on concepts and strategies unhelpful, as they have already been mastered. This is not to suggest that by hypothesising a developmental model of response I am trying to make literary response into a measurable and marketable quantity, or that I see a simple, linear developmental model as a possibility. I am well aware that in literary and language development there are no simple straight lines, that progress probably occurs in 'nebulous spirals', as John Stephens put it in an article in *English in Australia* in 1967.[145] However, if some kind of progression can be identified — and the evidence of contemporary theory and research suggests the possibility — then it might provide a helpful framework on which to structure a more coherent literary programme, even if not a perfectly linear, non-recursive sequential one.

We have already seen in the report of the written questionnaire responses of the Bathurst students in Chapter Two that in imposing on students received critical judgments and introducing the categories of literary criticism too early, we are asking them to arrive without having travelled. As Barbara Hardy puts it, 'it is very foolish to teach our children imagery and symbols before we teach them about themselves.'[146] A developmental model that helped teachers to work out fairly easily each student's level of response would be very useful in indicating what it is that each student already does competently. At present, teachers are more aware of what young readers don't understand than of what they do understand. Students are far more likely to progress in situations in which teachers build on the constructive strategies they do possess — and which they are shown they possess — rather than in 'remedial' situations which emphasise their inadequacies and draw their attention to them. In the Bathurst interviews many reluctant readers were amazed, and exceedingly gratified, to discover that many of their mental processes in response to literature were the same as those of expert readers. They also found how easy it was to enjoy reading and to learn new reading strategies when they started to believe in their own abilities and to concentrate on meaning and their own interests in a story rather than on what they had come to see as teacherly concerns.

## CLUES FOR IDENTIFYING DEVELOPMENTAL STAGES

In the Preface to *Lyrical Ballads* in 1800, Wordsworth indicates that the first and most immediate pleasure of literature is emotional. However, he also hints that more complex and deeper satisfactions are afforded to those who read reflectively. He says that poetry's 'object is truth . . . carried alive into the heart by passion'; that 'the end of poetry is to produce excitement in co-existence with an overbalance of pleasure'; and that poetry, 'the spontaneous overflow of powerful feelings', offers experience 'recollected in tranquillity'.[147] Wordsworth seems to imply that the mature reader's process of response is the counterpart of the poet's process of creation: both processes combine emotional involvement and cool detachment. It is this paradoxical combination that D.W. Harding and James Britton characterise as 'onlooker' or 'spectator' role activity.

Margaret Early describes the movement from 'immature' response to 'mature' and 'developed' response as a progression from a stage of 'unconscious enjoyment', in which 'the reader knows what he likes but doesn't know why'; through a stage of 'self-conscious appreciation', in which 'the reader gradually moves away from a simple interest in what happened' to an interest in psychological conflict and the motives of characters; to a stage of 'conscious delight', in which the reader's deepest pleasure is aesthetic.[148]

The most valuable contributions to identifying the stages that might be involved in responding to literature are those of D.W. Harding and Jean Blunt. In his article, 'Considered Experience: The Invitation of the Novel'[149], Harding analyses the psychological processes involved in the reading of fiction, and in her article, 'Response to Reading—How Some Young Readers Describe the Process'[150], Blunt organises Harding's categories into levels of response. Harding says that once readers have passed the elementary stage of becoming interested in a book and understanding it on at least a rudimentary level, they take up the role of the onlooker and can be described as 'serious' readers:

When we think of reading fiction seriously (including, of course, reading comedy seriously) we assume that three main processes will be occurring: first, empathising with characters; secondly, evaluating what they do and suffer; thirdly, in some measure accepting or rejecting the values the author implies by his interests and attitudes.[151]

Harding defines these 'three main activities' as follows:

1. *Empathising:* 'imaginative insight into, or empathy with, the experience of other people.'[152]

2. *Evaluating characters:* '[the reader] reacts *to* [the characters'] behaviour and feelings as much as *with* them. He evaluates them, sympathising in part, condemning, pitying, respecting, questioning.'[153]

3. *Accepting or rejecting the values of the author:* 'an awareness [by the reader] that fiction is a social convention, an institutional technique of discussion, by means of which an author invites us to join him in discussing a possibility of experience that he regards as interesting and to share with him attitudes towards it, evaluations of it, that he claims to be appropriate . . . An awareness that an author is offering his own values and preconceptions for acceptance or rejection . . . '[154]

In another article, 'The Bond With the Author', Harding describes the satisfaction experienced by those who reach this third level of response as

the sense that some other human being found it satisfying to contemplate such and such possibilities of experience and evaluate them in such a way, that when we share his satisfaction some mutual sanctioning of values is occurring.[155]

Blunt takes from Harding's work six elemental activities which she sees as constituting a full response to fiction when engaged in by readers who 'accept the role of the onlooker'. These elements, organised into two stages of increasing complexity, are as follows:

Stage One:
1. attending willingly
2. elementary perception and comprehension
3. empathising (Harding's 'empathising')

Stage Two:
4. analogising and searching for self-identity
5. distanced evaluation of the participants (Harding's 'evaluating what characters do and suffer')

> 6. reviewing the whole work as the author's creation[156] (Harding's 'accepting or rejecting the values of the author')

Harding omits from his summary of the 'three main processes' of 'serious' readers the first two elements of Blunt's system — 'attending willingly' and 'elementary perception and comprehension'— as he sees these two components as prior to the main processes and satisfactions experienced by the serious reader. The other element in Blunt's system not listed by Harding as one of the 'three main processes', is 'analogising and searching for self-identity'. Harding sees this process as being closely related to and emanating from that of 'empathising', and as involving more feeling and less detachment than involved in the next process-stage, that of 'evaluating characters' or Blunt's 'distanced evaluation of the participants'. He explains and exemplifies as follows:

> Closely related to this [empathising] but involving a rather different mechanism is the effect fiction can have of giving enhanced significance to the reader's own life by analogy with the events of the novel or play. The boy engaged in the routine of school chemistry can see it in a different light if he has been absorbed in a film of the life of Pasteur.[157]

About the three main processes that he assumes will be occurring as part of the experience of the serious reader, Harding goes on to say, 'These three processes are not successive stages of practised response to fiction. They can all occur in simple and rudimentary or in developed and subtle form.'[158]

If I interpret Harding correctly, what he means is that while all three processes might be taking place in the mind of a reader, the highest level process could not be occurring in a 'developed and subtle form' while the two lower level processes were occurring in 'simple and rudimentary form'. A prerequisite for the developed form of a higher level response is the developed form of the lower level responses. Experience in the interviews with the Bathurst students certainly supports this interpretation. For example, several students were able to 'evaluate what the characters do and suffer' only in a rudimentary way because their empathy with the characters concerned was also at a rudimentary level: that is, their feeling for the characters (or against them) lacked any strength, and in some cases was one of virtual indifference. To be of any practical use, then, a refined developmental model of response would need to distinguish between 'simple and rudimentary' and 'developed and subtle' forms of response which might well be closely connected with the degree of intensity of the reader's involvement in what she or he is reading.

Wordsworth, Early, Harding and Blunt seem to agree that the development of a mature response to literature involves a progressive movement from close emotional involvement to more distanced reflective detachment, and from an interest in self to an interest in other people and the human condition. After analysing the responses of her 15-year-old students, Jean Blunt draws attention to the 'formidable chasm' between empathising and more detached responses.

A conscious awareness of the role of the author as creator of the fiction is less manifest in this sample of teenage readers than their willingness and evident desire to discover characters in the novel with whom they can empathise in some depth. In adolescence it seems that emotional responses may come more easily than cognitive ones.[159]

Similarly, development in response means de-centring, learning to 'transcend our own egocentricity' as John Dixon put it in a talk in Sydney in 1974, or 'breaking through our egocentricity to new points of view not determined solely by our physical vantage point in time and space or by our emotional preferences', as James Moffett puts it.[160] Margaret Early expresses it this way:

A sign of maturity as a human being and as a reader is that a deep feeling for mankind replaces narrow concern for oneself. The mature reader no longer seeks only self-knowledge in literature but, with the artist, digs at the well-springs of life.[161]

With this dynamic movement of the reader's growing interest and satisfaction in literature from 'me' to 'outside me', and from emotional closeness to reflective distance, there is a parallel development of the reader's pleasure from simple emotional enjoyment to the more contemplative satisfactions of understanding the social, psychological, aesthetic, structural and ideological aspects of texts, as well as his or her own interpretative strategies. At each stage of reading development, pleasure in one form or another is paramount. Without pleasure, no-one would learn from reading literature because without it no one would read. Harding, too, reminds us that 'feeling is first': 'empathising' precedes 'distanced evaluation'; an interest in individual people and their motives and emotions precedes matching one's world view against that offered by an author.

> It would certainly seem that a developing interest in fiction is tied up in some way with an interest in other people. Like gossip, it depends on a wish to follow their doings to try to understand their motives, and to join with someone else in making an emotional response to their behaviour and supposed experience.[162]

## EXAMPLES OF IDENTIFIED PROCESS STAGES IN ACTION

The following comments made by Bathurst students in interview are offered at this stage as illustrations of the processes identified by Harding and Blunt as components of a developed response to fiction.

### Adopting the role of the onlooker or spectator

In answer to the question, 'While you are reading a book you are enjoying, where do you feel you are in relation to the characters in the story?' a Year 10 boy said,

> 'You don't feel you're actually in the story as a part of what's happening, but you do feel you've got an eye on the characters and what they're doing, following them around. You are like a ghost — you can see them but they can't see you.'

A Year 8 girl said,

> 'I don't feel that I'm in the action with the characters but I don't feel I'm right outside either. I'm more on the outside looking in, but my feelings are in there with them.'

and a Year 8 boy said,

> 'I'm not in the book but I'm not uninvolved either. You want to understand how it feels to be in the situations the characters you

like are in without necessarily being in there yourself. What's happening is not happening to you, but you experience what it might be like in your imagination.'

These comments are very similar to Harding's own explanation of the reader's onlooker role vantage point.

It could be said that the reader of a novel is in the position of a ghost, watching unseen the behaviour of a group of people in whom he is deeply interested; he can imagine what they are feeling, he takes sides in their conflicts, regrets this bit of behaviour, applauds that, and he has hopes and fears about the outcome but can say nothing and do nothing to affect it.[163]

## Empathising

'I was very concerned for Luke Skywalker, how he gets involved in so much action and how he gets out of it. I worry about how he's going to get out of his predicaments. When he's fighting against his enemies, I feel for him because I know he's feeling frightened, and I admire him because he comes out on top of his fear.'

Year 10 boy

## Analogising and searching for self-identity

In answer to the question, 'Do you think your reading has helped you to understand anything about other people or your own life in any way?' a Year 8 boy said,

'In your own life you often display the irrational thinking of people in the book you have read. In real life you make similar mistakes to characters in books because you are involved and you can't think logically.'

My question and the boy's generalisation in reply emerged from his comments about his reading of Rosemary's Sutcliff's *The Lantern Bearers* and his recognition of the way his understanding of the main character, Aquila, helped him to understand himself.

'Aquila felt a sense of bitter revenge for the bird man – you know the fellow who went around the countryside selling birds and passing messages from one farm to another — who betrayed his father under torture. Aquila condemned him bitterly without knowing the full facts — that he was tortured to give the information. This brings you to like the hero, Aquila, because he is lost, you feel sorry for him because you know more than he does and you sympathise with him because he is human. We all condemn other people for doing things to us when sometimes if we knew the problems of the person we condemn we would be more sympathetic.'

## Distanced evaluation of the characters

In answer to the question, 'What were your feelings and attitudes towards David Copperfield?' asked about the novel he had just finished reading, a Year 8 boy said,

'When David was sad I *wasn't* necessarily sad because you're trying to think what caused it, if he brought it on himself and that. You don't feel exactly as he does because you can't help him. You know more than he does. You can think about what you'd do. You might feel more sympathy for him but not have the same feelings. When he's happy you mightn't be happy if you can see he won't be happy for long. For example, when he marries Dora you wonder if he's doing the right thing, and when you get the information to answer that, you're on the way to understanding and judging him.'

## Reviewing the whole work as the author's creation

Following her account of what had most interested her in Ursula le Guin's *A Wizard of Earthsea*, a Year 8 girl made the following generalisation, showing her awareness that the text is a construct.

'While I read I'm thinking about what the author is doing as well as the characters. Sometimes I think, "Now why did she write that in there?" or "Why did that event happen?" And a few chapters later you find out why. What didn't make sense comes to make sense.'

A Year 10 girl, in expressing some disappointment in certain aspects

of the plot of John Wyndham's *The Day of the Triffids*, made it clear
that she saw literature as a 'social convention' by means of which
an author presents 'his own values for acceptance or rejection':

> 'In *The Day of the Triffids* all the characters you are concerned
> about just manage to avoid death and live happily on. It would
> be more dramatic if someone close to the main characters died.
> It would make you think more at the end. Some of them should
> have been killed by the triffids so you could see more clearly that
> the triffids represent man's punishment for being lazy and greedy
> and destructive. There were things about the triffids they said
> they'd have to research, but they were too greedy for the oil they
> produced to bother studying the harmful effects of them.'

## PROCESS STRATEGIES

The reader-response critics, and particularly Wolfgang Iser, have
contributed enormously to our understanding of the strategies
adopted by good readers. However, about these strategies, there are
several questions I have to ask, which, if answered, might make Iser's
work even more useful for teachers.

1. Are the reading strategies Iser specifies developmental? Can they
   be ordered as logically connected, progressively more complex
   interpretative operations?
2. Does each strategy have its own developmental sequence?

My speculation, based on observation of educational attempts to
reduce multivarious human behaviour (including learning behaviour)
to a simple linear cause-effect logic (for example, Bloom's Taxonomy
of Educational Objectives), is that the answer to each of these
questions will not prove to be a simple 'yes' or 'no' but, more likely,
'a bit of both'. I anticipate that:

1. each strategy does have its own developmental sequence, from
   simple to complex; and
2. while the highest levels of some strategies are probably more
   complex and more powerful than the highest levels of others, the
   strategies themselves will resist any neat hierarchical or vertical
   ordering.

I assume that in any one reader's reading of any one text at any one time, there will be a whole range of strategies in operation, each at a different level of performance. However, below, I list the process-strategies derived from Iser and other reader-response critics, in roughly hypothesised stages of complexity, recognising that each strategy almost certainly has its own developmental sequence, but also that there is probably a complex network of connections between all of them.

## Stage One reading operations

1. *Generating expectations:* from an elementary interest in what happens next to rigorously questioning the whole text.
2. *Forming mental images:* from pictorial stereotypes to complex emotional associations.
3. *Using the resources of the repertoire:* which obviously becomes more extensive with more life and literary experience if that experience is reflected on.
4. *Filling in the gaps:* formulating connections of increasing subtlety and complexity; i.e., at the highest level, apparently random clues can be linked to create significant patterns of meaning.
5. *Synthesising an assembly of constantly shifting viewpoints:* following the 'wandering viewpoint' to reconcile all the textual perspectives, from synthesising a few of the most easily reconcilable perspectives to synthesising the perspectives that seem most resistant to reconciliation.

## Stage Two reading operations

6. Recognition of the 'implied author', and of the need to take up the role of the 'implied reader', involving an explicit understanding that the relationship between the implied author and the implied reader is a literary convention.
7. Reflexive monitoring of one's own reading processes, and developing understanding of the productive strategies and of how they can be developed. (A reader at this level would be able to solve the puzzles of form posed by an experimental text that defied the 'established' conventions, and make it mean.)

With these tentative formulations as hypotheses, the next step is to test them in action with young readers. In doing this, I have to ask another question. Can the reading strategies of Iser's processes model be related to the psychological processes of the Harding/Blunt developmental model to produce one powerful model of reading development? If we could easily identify, for each of our students, both the reading level and the strategies being used at each level, we would be able to take some of the guess work out of teaching literature and develop more appropriate reading programmes for individuals, groups and classes. It is certainly worth trying to find the answer to this question, because between our present state of ignorance and our intuitions we have not been very successful in developing the reading habit in our students.

## REFERENCES

1. The Australian Association for the Teaching of English 1984 Conference brochure, 'Literature: Connected Learning'.
2. Paul Scott, *The Raj Quartet: The Jewel in the Crown* (1973), *The Day of the Scorpion* (1973), *The Towers of Silence* (1973), *A Division of the Spoils* (1977), Granada, St Albans.
3. D.H. Lawrence, *Lady Chatterley's Lover*, Penguin, 1960, p. 104.
4. D.W. Harding, 'Response to Literature', in Margaret Meek, Aidan Warlow and Griselda Barton (eds), *The Cool Web: The Pattern of Children's Reading*, The Bodley Head, London, 1977, p. 390.
5. D.W. Harding, 'Considered Experience: The Invitation of the Novel', in *English in Education*, vol. 2, no. 1, Summer 1967.
6. Louise Rosenblatt, *Literature As Exploration*, revised edition, Noble and Noble, New York, 1968, p. 274.
7. Susanne K. Langer, *Feeling and Form: A Theory of Art*, Routledge and Kegan Paul, London, 1953, fifth impression 1973, p. 40.
8. Leslie Stratta, John Dixon and Andrew Wilkinson, *Patterns of Language*, Heinemann, London, 1973, p. xi.
9. Ibid., p. xii.
10. Barbara Hardy, 'Narrative As a Primary Act of Mind', in Meek *et al.*, *The Cool Web: The Pattern of Children's Reading*, p. 12.
11. James Britton, *Language and Learning*, Allen Lane, Penguin, 1970, p. 72.
12. Loc. cit.

13. Margaret Donaldson, *Children's Minds*, Fontana, London, 1978.
14. M.A.K. Halliday, *Learning How To Mean*, Edward Arnold, London, 1975.
15. Gordon Wells, *Language, Learning and Education*, Centre for the Study of Language and Communication, Bristol, 1982.
16. Ibid., p. 184.
17. D.W. Harding, 'The Role of the Onlooker', in Asher Cashdan (ed.), *Language in Education: A Source Book*, Routledge and Kegan Paul and The Open University Press, London, 1972, pp. 240-244.
18. Ibid., p. 244.
19. J. Britton, *Language and Learning*, p. 8.
20. D.W. Harding, 'The Bond With the Author', in *The Use of English*, vol. 22, no. 4, Summer 1971, p. 307.
21. Harding, 'The Role of the Onlooker', p. 242.
22. James Britton, 'English Teaching: Retrospect and Prospect', in R.D. Eagleson (ed.), *English in the Eighties*, Australian Association for the Teaching of English, Adelaide, 1982, p. 5
23. L.S. Vygotsky, *Thought and Language*, MIT Press, Cambridge, Massachusetts, 1962; James Britton, Tony Burgess, Nancy Martin, Alex MacLeod and Harold Rosen, *The Development of Writing Abilities (11-18)*, Macmillan, The Schools Council, 1975; M.A.K. Halliday, *Learning How to Mean;* Basil Bernstein (ed.), *Class, Codes and Control*, vol. 2, Routledge and Kegan Paul, 1973.
24. James Britton, *et al.*, *The Development of Writing Abilities (11-18)*.
25. Donald Graves, *Writing: Teachers and Children at Work*, Heinemann, Exeter, New Hampshire, 1983; see also Jack Thomson, *The Writing Process*, Australian Studies in Language in Education, Curriculum Development Centre, Canberra, 1980.
26. N. Martin, P. D'Arcy, B. Newton and R. Parker, *Writing and Learning Across the Curriculum, 11-16*, Ward Lock, London, 1976.
27. James Moffett, *Active Voice—A Writing Program Across the Curriculum*, Boynton/Cook, Upper Montclair, New Jersey, 1981.
28. John Dixon and Leslie Stratta, *Achievements in Writing at 16 +* , a series of booklets, The Schools Council, 1980-1984.

29. Terry Eagleton, *Literary Theory: An Introduction*, Basil Blackwell, Oxford, 1983, pp. 14-15.
30. Jane Tompkins, 'The Reader in History', in Jane Tompkins (ed.), *Reader-Response Criticism*, The John Hopkins University Press, Baltimore, 1980, p. 210.
31. Ibid., p. 203.
32. Ibid., p. 207.
33. Ibid., p. 211.
34. W.K. Wimsatt Jr and Monroe Beardsley, 'The Affective Fallacy', in W.K. Wimsatt, *The Verbal Icon: Studies in the Meaning of Poetry*, The University of Kentucky Press, Lexington, 1954.
35. Eagleton, *Literary Theory*, p. 50.
36. I.A. Richards, *Practical Criticism*, reprinted by Routledge and Kegan Paul, London, 1970 (first published 1929).
37. Margaret Meek *et al.*, *Achieving Literacy*, Routledge and Kegan Paul, London, 1983, p. 214.
38. F.R. Leavis, *The Common Pursuit*, Penguin, 1978 (first published 1952).
39. Eagleton, *Literary Theory*, *p. 32.*
40. F.R. Leavis, *The Great Tradition*, Penguin, 1962 (first published 1948).
41. Eagleton, *Literary Theory*, p. 34.
42. Loc. cit.
43. Malcolm Bradbury, *Eating People is Wrong*, Arrow Books, London, 1982 (first published 1959), p. 14.
44. Ibid., p. 296.
45. Ibid., pp. 113-114.
46. Ibid., p. 115.
47. Eagleton, *Literary Theory*, p. 33.
48. W.K. Wimsatt and Monroe Beardsley, 'The Affective Fallacy', from W.K. Wimsatt, *The Verbal Icon: Studies in the Meaning of Poetry*, Lexington, Kentucky, 1954, reprinted in David Lodge (ed.), *20th Century Literary Criticism*, Longman, Harlow, 1972, p. 345.
49. Cleanth Brooks, *The Well-Wrought Urn: Studies in the Structure of Poetry*, Dennis Dobson, London, 1949, reprinted 1960.
50. Cleanth Brooks and Robert Penn Warren, *Understanding Poetry*, Holt, Rinehart and Winston, New York, 3rd edition, 1960, pp. xiii-xiv.

51. W.K. Wimsatt and Monroe Beardsley, 'The Intentional Fallacy', reprinted in Lodge (ed.), *20th Century Literary Criticism*, pp. 333-344.

52. John Docker, *In A Critical Condition*, Penguin Australia, Ringwood, p. 47.

53. Ibid., p. 48.

54. Northrop Frye, *The Anatomy of Criticism*, Princeton University Press, Princeton, New Jersey, 1957, pp. 17-18.

55. Eagleton, *Literary Theory*, p. 50.

56. Docker, *In A Critical Condition*, p. 93.

57. Ibid., p. 131.

58. Ibid., p. 95.

59. Ibid., p. 93.

60. Leonie Kramer (ed.), *The Oxford History of Australian Literature*, OUP, Melbourne, 1981.

61. Docker, *In A Critical Condition*, p. 174.

62. Raymond Williams, 'Literature in Society', in Hilda Schift (ed.), *Contemporary Approaches to English Studies*, Heinemann, 1977.

63. Docker, *In A Critical Condition*, pp. 181-2.

64. Jonathan Culler, *Structuralist Poetics*, Routledge and Kegan Paul, London, 1975, p. 114.

65. Eagleton, *Literary Theory*, p. 107.

66. Ibid., p. 111.

67. Ibid., p. 107.

68. Ibid., pp. 112-113.

69. Culler, *Structuralist Poetics*, p. 118.

70. Loc. cit.

71. Ibid., in chapter entitled 'Greimas and Structural Semantics'.

72. Roland Barthes, *S/Z*, translated by Richard Miller, Hill and Wang, New York, 1974.

73. Margaret Spencer, 'Children's Literature: Mainstream Text or Optional Extra?' in R.D. Eagleson (ed.), *English in the Eighties*, p. 126.

74. Meek, *Achieving Literacy*.

75. Spencer, 'Children's Literature: Mainstream Text or Optional Extra?' pp. 121-123.

76. Maureen Worsdale, 'Literature in the Fourth and Fifth Year of the Secondary School', in *English in Education*, vol. 16, no. 1, Spring 1982, p. 36.

77. Loc. cit.

78. David Jackson, *Encounters With Books*, Methuen, London, 1983, p. 125.

79. Wolfgang Iser, *The Act of Reading*, Routledge and Kegan Paul, London, 1978.

80. Geoff Fox, 'Dark Watchers: Young Readers and their Fiction', *English in Education*, vol. 13, no. 1., Spring 1979.

81. Wayne Booth, *The Rhetoric of Fiction*, The University of Chicago Press, Chicago, 1961.

82. Seymour Chatman, *Story and Discourse*, Cornell University Press, Ithaca, New York, 1978, p. 151.

83. Aidan Chambers, 'The Reader in the Book', *Signal*, no. 23, 1977, p. 72.

84. Ibid., p. 71.

85. Ibid., p. 74.

86. Ibid., pp. 75-6

87. Iser, *The Act of Reading*, p. 109.

88. Ibid., p. 111.

89. Ibid., p. 74.

90. Ibid., p. 38.

91. Ibid., p. 138.

92. F.R. Leavis, *The Living Principle*, Chatto and Windus, London, 1975, pp. 89-90.

93. Ted Hughes, *Poetry in the Making*, Faber, London. 1967, pp. 42-3.

94. I am indebted to Barry Cooper, Head of English at Woolooware High School, for this piece of writing.

95. Iser, *The Act of Reading*, p. 139.

96. I am indebted to Helen Drewe, English Department, Canowindra High School (now Lithgow High School), for this piece of writing.

97. Iser, *The Act of Reading*, p. 169.

98. Reinbert Tabbert, 'The impact of children's books: cases and concepts (Part I)', *Children's Literature in Education*, vol. 10, no. 2, 33, 1979, pp. 92-102.

99. Chambers, 'The Reader in the Book', p. 77.

100. Andrew Stibbs, 'Honour Be Blowed', *English in Education*, vol. 14, no. 3, Autumn 1980.

101. Fox, 'Dark Watchers: Young Readers and Their Fiction'.

102. Robert Protherough, 'Children's Sense of Story Line', *English in Education*, vol. 13, no. 1, Spring 1979.

103. Robert Protherough, 'Evaluating Children's Responses to

Literature', in *Children's Literature in Education*, vol. 14, no. 1, Spring 1983.

104. Bryant Fillion, 'Reading as Inquiry: An Approach to Literature Learning', *English Journal*, vol. 70, no. 1, January 1981, NCTE, Urbana, Illinois, pp. 39-45.

105. Penny Blackie, 'Asking Questions', *English in Education*, vol. 5, no. 3, Winter 1971.

106. Rosemary Sutcliff, *The Eagle of the Ninth*, Puffin, 1977, p. 149.

107. Stratta *et al.*, *Patterns of Language*, p. 44.

108. Iser, *The Act of Reading*, p. 135.

109. Norman N. Holland, 'Unity Identity Text Self', in Tompkins (ed.), *Reader-Response Criticism*, p. 125.

110. Ibid., p. 124.

111. Ibid., pp. 124-5.

112. Eagleton, *Literary Theory*, p. 178.

113. Terry Eagleton, *Marxism and Literary Criticism*, Methuen, London, 1976.

114. D.W. Harding, 'Response to Literature', in Meek *et al.*, *The Cool Web: The Pattern of Children's Reading*, p. 390.

115. Ernie Tucker, 'Help Them to Get Started', in R.D. Walshe, Dot Jensen and Tony Moore (eds), *Teaching Literature*, Primary English Teaching Association and English Teachers' Association of NSW, Sydney, 1983, p. 103.

116. Hugh Crago, 'Cultural Categories and the Criticism of Children's Literature', *Signal*, No. 30, September 1979.

117. Hugh Crago, 'The Readers in the Reader: An Experiment in Personal Response and Literary Criticism', *Signal*, No. 39, September 1982.

118. Norman Holland, *Poems in Persons*, Horton, New York, 1973, p. 3.

119. Hugh Crago, 'Talking to Real People', *English in Australa*, no. 47, March 1979, pp. 38-39.

120. Ibid., p. 40.

121. Gary MacLennan and Robert Lingard, 'Class, Culture and the English Teacher: Beyond Reproduction', *English in Australia*, no. 63, March 1983, p. 121.

122. Stanley Fish, 'Interpreting the Variorum', in Tompkins (ed.), *Reader-Response Criticism*, pp. 164-184.

123. Walter Benn Michaels. 'The Interpreter's Self: Peirce on the Cartesian "Subject"', in Tompkins (ed.), *Reader-Response Criticism*, pp. 199-200.

124. Jane Tompkins, 'The Reader in History', in Tompkins (ed.), *Reader-Response Criticism*, p. 226.
125. J. Docker, *In A Critical Condition*, pp. 90-92.
126. G.A Wilkes, 'The Eighteen Nineties', in Grahame Johnston (ed.), *Australian Literary Criticism*, OUP, Melbourne, 1962.'
127. Ibid, pp. 36–39.
128. Peter Widdowson, 'Introduction: The Crisis in English Studies', in Peter Widdowson (ed.), *Re-Reading English*, Methuen, London, 1982, p. 3.
129. Barthes, *S/Z*.
130. Donaldson, *Children's Minds*.
131. Paulo Freire, *Pedagogy of the Oppressed*, Penguin, 1972, p. 41.
132. Barbara Hardy, "Narrative As a Primary Act of Mind", in Meek et al., *The Cool Web: The Pattern of Children's Reading*, p. 12.
133. Chambers, 'The Reader in the Book', p. 77.
134. Lewis Carroll, *Alice's Adventures in Wonderland* and *Through the Looking Glass*, Puffin, 1968, p. 274.
135. Eagleton, *Literary Theory*.
136. Widdowson, *Re-Reading English*.
137. Eagleton, *Literary Theory*, p. 205.
138. Ibid., p. 206.
139. Ibid., p. 216.
140. MacLennan and Robert Lingard, 'Class, Culture and the English Teacher: Beyond Reproduction', p. 46.
141. Meek, *Achieving Literacy*, pp. 8-9.
142. Ibid., p. 51.
143. Ibid., p. 224.
144. Margaret Meek, 'How Do They Know It's Worth It? The Untaught Reading Lessons', in Roslyn Arnold (ed.), *Timely Voices: English Teaching in the 1980s*, OUP, Melbourne, p. 151.
145. John Stephens, 'The Unanswered Questions', *English in Australia*, No. 7, June 1967, p.7.
146. Barbara Hardy, 'The Teaching of English: Life, Literature and Literary Criticism', *English in Education*, vol. 2, no. 2, Summer, 1968, p. 13.
147. William Wordsworth, "Poetry and Poetic Diction", Preface to the Second Edition of *Lyrical Ballads*, 1800, in Edmund D. Jones (ed.), *Nineteenth Century English Critical Essays*, OUP, London, 1916, reprint of 1959, pp. 13, 20 and 22.
148. Margaret Early, 'Stages in the Growth of Literary Appreciation',

166

*The English Journal*, vol. XLIX, March, 1960, pp. 161-167.

149. D.W. Harding, 'Considered Experience: The Invitation of the Novel', pp. 7-15.

150. Jean Blunt, 'Response to Reading: How Some Young Readers Describe the Process', *English in Education*, vol. 11, no. 3, Autumn 1977, pp. 34-47.

151. Harding, 'Considered Experience: The Invitation of the Novel', p. 14.

152. Ibid., p. 7.

153. Ibid., p. 11.

154. Ibid., pp. 13-14.

155. Harding, 'The Bond With the Author', p. 311.

156. Blunt, 'Response to Reading: How Some Young Readers Describe the Process', pp. 34-44.

157. Harding, 'Considered Experience: The Invitation of the Novel, p. 9.

158. Ibid., p. 14.

159. Blunt, 'Response to Reading: How Some Young Readers Describe the Process', p. 44.

160. James Moffett, *Teaching the Universe of Discourse*, Houghton-Mifflin, Boston, 1968.

161. Early, 'Stages in the Growth of Literary Appreciation', p. 167.

162. Harding, 'Considered Experience: The Invitation of the Novel', p. 15.

163. Ibid., p. 12.

To learn literature is to learn the processes of reading, responding
and reflecting on literature and to use these processes
autonomously. Consequently as teachers a major thrust should
be to develop procedural strategies in our students to help them
control these processes. To do this, however, we need to
investigate the processes themselves: the ways in which children
read literature; the ways in which they respond to it; and the ways
in which they reflect on it.

Robert D. Eagleson, 'Responding and
Reflecting'[1]

The pedagogic massivity of "correct" readings is being shifted,
slowly, towards the problematic of how students *do* internalise
and organise texts (and that is a useful starting point for a
definition of *reading*). For us, the crucial question is, what
processes underlie the meanings and values which students place
upon texts? (not, blandly, "what is student response to literature?")

Peter Moss, 'Literature: The Neglected
Situation'[2]

## THE STUDENT INTERVIEWS

The written questionnaires analysed in Chapter Two were followed
up by individual interviews of one hour each with five per cent of
the Year 8 and Year 10 student respondents. Fifty-one students,
covering a whole range of reading abilities and attitudes, were
interviewed out of the 1007 who completed the questionnaires. From
the 1978 interviews a tentative developmental model (process-stages)
was formulated, and this was tested and refined in the 1984
interviews, which were also used to determine the reading strategies
associated with each developmental level. In other words, following
the 1984 interviews, a developmental model (stages) and a process
model (strategies) have combined into a single model of reading
development.

For the 1978 interviews a question profile was constructed that draws heavily on D.W. Harding's analysis of the processes involved in the reading of fiction[3] and on Jean Blunt's organisation of Harding's categories into levels of response.[4] Its purpose was to establish developmental stages or levels of response. In the 1984 interviews, this profile (in a slightly modified form) was again used, but it was supplemented by another set of questions designed to identify the strategies used by the readers. This second profile of questions on process strategies draws heavily on the work of contemporary reader-response critics, particularly Wolfgang Iser. In the interviews neither question profile was used rigidly or unvaryingly with any student, but rather, each set of questions was used as a guide to the interviewer, who improvised on the basis of individual student responses in order to probe and explore specific attitudes, and to offer pupils the opportunity to particularise and exemplify.

## INTERVIEW PROFILE 1: IDENTIFYING DEVELOPMENTAL STAGES IN TERMS OF PSYCHOLOGICAL PROCESSES AND SATISFACTIONS

Each student (in 1978 and 1984) was asked to discuss some or all of the following questions with reference to specific favourite texts that she or he had identified in his or her written questionnaire.

The Role of the Onlooker: the student's definition of his or her stance to the story.

1. While you are reading, do you imagine yourself being with a character or characters?
2. Where do you feel you are in relation to the characters?
3. Do you think what it would be like to be one or more of the characters?
4. Do you take sides in their conflicts, wish they hadn't done certain things, feel happy when you agree with what they do as being right?
5. Do you imagine yourself as being with the writer, feel you're helping him write the book, deciding what characters might do next, how they should end up, how they should be feeling?
6. Do you like happy endings? Such as? Why?

## Attending Willingly

7. Do you get any pleasure out of reading?
   (a) Refer to favourite books on list from written questionnaire.
   (b) Which sections of which books did you enjoy most? Why?
   (Referring students back to their written questionnaires, try to get more explicit reasons for choices and sources of satisfaction.)

## Elementary Perception and Comprehension

8. Do you ever read books which you find difficult to understand in some ways?
9. Which books for example?
10. What did you find difficult to understand?
11. Did you finish the book(s)? Did you still manage to enjoy it (them) despite the difficulties of understanding?
12. Why, do you think, did you enjoy them despite the difficulties?

## Empathising

13. In reading a novel, do you ever feel you would like to be in the action, helping the character, for example. Why?
14. Do you ever think about what you would have done if you were in the situation the characters were in?
15. What feelings do you have when reading? Are your feelings the same as your favourite character's feelings, or do you ever feel quite differently from the way your favourite character feels?
16. Do you feel pleased or irritated with (i.e., judge) the characters' actions and feeling while you are reading?

## Analogising and Searching for Self-Identity

17. Have you learned anything important about the world you live in from your reading? What? How?
18. Do you think your understanding of other people has increased from your reading? In what ways? How? Give examples.
19. Do you think you have learned anything more about yourself from your reading of a book, something you didn't know or hadn't thought of before you read the book(s)? What? How?
20. Has any book ever influenced what you believe in, what you think is right, and true? What? How? Examples?

## Distanced Evaluation of the Characters

(The counterpart of Empathising: questions 13 to 16 cover this.)

## Reviewing the Whole Work as the Author's Creation

21. Is there anything apart from the story-line that interests you in a book? What? Examples?
22. Do you ever enjoy the way a book is written? Examples?
23. Do you ever reject a book because of the way it is written, even when you find the subject interesting? Examples?
24. Do you ever respond to a book by saying to yourself about the author such things as, 'Yes, he's right there. That's true', or 'No, that couldn't happen, it's unbelievable'? Give examples.
25. Do you think your reading as a whole has helped you to understand other people or the world any better?

### INTERVIEW PROFILE 2 : IDENTIFYING READING STRATEGIES

The questions below were used as the basis of discussion with each of the 1984 interviewees with reference to specific texts recently read and enjoyed, and the opening paragraphs of a short story or novel read to them by the interviewer. The text read to each student was one of the following:

'The Bad Deeds Gang' (short story) by Barry Breen (from L.M. Hannan and W.G. Tickell (eds), *The Bad Deeds Gang and Other Stories*, Australian Association for the Teaching of English, 1971).

'Too Early Spring' (short story) by Stephen Vincent Benét (from James Moffett and Kenneth McElheny (eds), *Points of View*, Mentor, 1966).

*The Present-Takers* by Aidan Chambers (Bodley Head).

*The Cartoonist* by Betsy Byars (Puffin).

*Trillions* by Nicholas Fisk (Puffin).

*Dragonslayer* by Rosemary Sutcliff (Puffin).

*Kes* by Barry Hines (Penguin).

*The Day of the Triffids* by John Wyndham (Penguin).

*The Catcher in the Rye* by J.D. Salinger (Penguin).

*The Wind-Eye* by Robert Westall (Macmillan).

The selection of which particular text to read to each student was governed by the likely appeal of the text to that student as far as this could be anticipated from the student's written questionnaire and the early stages of the interview dealing with process stages

(Interview Profile 1). No text which had been read previously by a student, or which seemed likely to be too complex for him or her, was used as the text read in that student's interview. The consideration of textual difficulty meant, in effect, that the least successful readers as identified by the school, and those most antagonistic to reading as indicated by the written questionnaires, were read the beginnings of 'The Bad Deeds Gang' or *The Present-Takers* or *The Cartoonist*, texts whose opening paragraphs seemed more likely to arouse the instant interest of unsophisticated readers than did the opening paragraphs of other texts.

I recognise that the texts used in the interviews make different demands upon readers and that each can be read at different levels. The problem was to choose a text for each reader that would arouse real interest and provide a sufficient challenge to call into operation all of the reader's strategies or skills. As I believe that enjoyment is a prerequisite for any meaningful response to eventuate, the first question students were asked of the opening section of a text read to them was, 'Would you want to read on?' and if the answer was 'No', that text was discarded and another tried, and so on, until a text was found that aroused interest. As it turned out, most students found the first or second text chosen to be of interest and in no case was it necessary to go beyond a third choice. I took it as an indication that a text had sufficiently interested and challenged a student when she or he asked at the end of the discussion how she or he might go about getting hold of a copy of it so as to be able to continue or complete the reading of it. Most did express the desire to do just this. Further, the interested involvement of all students in the interviews was apparent in the seriousness and quality of their talk. I believe the interviews were very successful in identifying the ways the students represent and interpret texts to themselves (i.e., their response processes).

**The questions**

Predicting/Forming Expectations

1. In response to the opening paragraphs of the short story or novel read: What is happening in your head while you are listening? Are you asking yourself or the text any questions?
2. Relating to a novel recently read and enjoyed: As you read, do you imagine or guess what might happen next, or consider how the story might develop?

The Repertoire

While you are reading/listening do you think of:

3. things that have happened in your life similar to some of the things that are happening to characters in the story?
4. other books you have read that the story you are reading reminds you of?

Mental Images

5. What impressions do you form in your mind of the people and places in the story? Are you (ever) able to see in your mind the characters and the places where the events take place?

Filling in the Gaps

Do you ever ask yourself questions like:

6. What is the connection between events that are seemingly unrelated?
7. What is the point of a particular event?
8. Why was a certain character included in the story?

The Implied Author

9. Do you ever think about the author and the kind of person s/he is? Did you find him/her someone you could like, or not?

The Implied Reader

10. Do you think about the kind of reader the book was written for? What kind of person do you think the author was writing for?
11. Did you have any difficulty in sympathising with the author's view of the world, or did his/her attitudes and opinions make the book difficult or annoying?

Most of the students said at the end of their interview how satisfying they had found it. There were comments like, 'I really enjoyed that, I learned something about how I can read better', 'I didn't realise that so many things happen in my head when I read', and 'I realise that sometimes guessing wrong can help you enjoy a book better — as long as you do guess'. It was, undoubtedly, a significant learning experience for the students because their reflections on texts and on their own reading processes were facilitated and supported in a way that couldn't happen in a classroom of 25 to 30 pupils, at least for such an extended period of time. What all the readers found appealing was the respect accorded to their individual responses. They said they found it liberating that their comments were not rejected, denigrated, 'corrected' or evaluated in any way, but listened to carefully and accepted as being of interest and importance. Some of those who were reputed to have very short spans of attention managed to sustain complete concentration and involvement for an uninterrupted hour, and expressed disappointment when the interview came to an end. All of these to whom I read the opening page and a half of 'The Bad Deeds Gang' asked me if I could finish reading it during their recess or lunch time break. The interviews were, in fact, a valuable teaching strategy for they provided what Geoff Fox calls the 'space' which readers need for reflection so that response can grow, or the 'middle ground' where book and reader meet:

> It seems useful to note that the "middle ground" exists whether or not an interviewer enters it . . . It deserves more attention in the teaching of fiction than we allow if our concern is limited to the text. It is the area where the possibilities suggested by the text are "discussed" by the reader.[5]

## A DEVELOPMENTAL MODEL *

I cannot provide conclusive proof of the validity of the model because of the relatively small number of students interviewed (51) and the restriction of the selection to students in Years 8 (13 to 14 year-olds) and 10 (15 to 16 year-olds). However, I can say that the model, in its present form, emerged from the reading behaviour of the 51 students, as elicited in interview, and that each student's reading process is accommodated neatly by the model. Therefore I offer it as a likely approximation to the reality of the processes of literary development that all readers experience. I cannot provide all of the detailed evidence from 51 interviews to substantiate this claim, as that would require several volumes of transcripts. Rather, I will use examples from the interviews to illustrate the way the model works — the developmental stages reached by students and the strategies used at each stage.

---

* This model is represented diagrammatically on page 360.

## DEGREES OF INTENSITY AND SOPHISTICATION OF RESPONSE
## (COLUMNS 2 AND 3)

By referring to the model (p.360 you will see that the process-strategies (column 4) are now linked to the process-stages (column 1) and that both are ordered in a sequence that emerged from the interviews. What also emerged clearly from the interviews is the existence of different degrees of interest and sophistication of response at each developmental level, just as D.W. Harding suggested would be the case.

We have already considered Harding's view that the processes of response 'can all occur in simple and rudimentary or in developed and subtle form', and the need for a developmental model to take this into account (p.152). It is in the same article that Harding mentions the 'variation in intensity' of readers' interests in literature:

> 'Our interest in the characters of novels or plays varies in intensity' from a 'faint flicker of interest we may feel' in other people and their actions to 'a high degree of empathy with [their] supposed experience and an intensely interested contemplation of the events [they] take part in.'[6]

Students who showed a strong and active interest in the characters and events of novels they had read varied considerably in their degrees of sophistication of response. For example, consider within the group of those who had reached Stage 2, empathising, the sub-group of those whose interest was strong and active. While all of those in this sub-group were highly sympathetic towards their favourite characters, and while all felt emotionally drawn to these characters, there was a range of sophistication in their responses from those who could not see beyond their emotional allegiances to those who, while no less emotionally drawn to characters, showed deeper psychological understanding of them.

In illustrating the different levels at which children evaluate books, Robert Protherough cites the following critical judgments of 13 to 14 year-olds as examples of 'more mature' level evaluations because they offer 'apparently objective justifications for their verdicts', even though they are 'clearly dependent on the teacher's example':

> '"There was a lot of descriptive words and I liked the characters",

"I think it was well written . . . it had a good start and ending", "The characters were too extreme, all good or all evil", . . . "I liked the story because I think the characters of the people came out effectively", [and] "It had a moral behind it, but it disguised it well".[7]

Despite his recognition that these responses are 'pretty thin', Protherough offers them as 'more mature' level responses because they are 'attempted critical judgments'. If such responses are to be categorised as high level responses because they represent 'the dawnings of an attempt to find apparently objective reasons for their evaluation', there certainly needs to be a discrimination between 'simple and rudimentary' and 'developed and subtle' responses within the categorisation. While I would tend to classify some of the responses quoted as 'dummy-runs' (James Britton's term), I would certainly classify two of them ('The characters were too extreme, all good or all evil', and 'It had a moral behind it, but it disguised it well') as being more 'developed and subtle' than all of the others.

Any classification system of levels of response would seem to need to make provision for the ranges of interest and sophistication shown by readers at each developmental stage. For another example, consider the responses of professional literary critics and university teachers of literature. Obviously these experts have reached the highest stages of response (5 and 6), which subsume and incorporate the preceding stages (1 to 4). However, even at this level, identifying the degrees of intensity of interest and sophistication of response at each reading stage might be useful in helping to determine the strengths and/or limitations of these experts as readers and as teachers. For example, some of the New Critics whose theory and literary criteria and judgments are examined and illustrated in action in Chapter Three, would certainly be recognised as reading with strong and active interest and in developed and subtly sophisticated ways at stage 5, reviewing the whole work as the author's creation. While they also consciously consider their relationship with the author (stage 6), the other aspects of stage 6 response — recognition of textual ideology and understanding of one's own identity and one's own reading processes — may not be as fully developed in them because these are not regarded as being of the highest importance by them. The New Critics, as we have seen, appear to recognise as ideological only those works with whose ideologies they don't sympathise, and there is not a great deal of evidence from their work that they consider the reflexive understanding of their own identity themes and reading processes as important reading satisfactions or useful forms of knowledge. To them, the critic's highest role is to review the whole work as the author's creation.

Further, while no doubt reading with a 'developed and subtle' degree of sophistication at all levels, the New Critics make it clear in their writing that their highest pleasures and strongest interests in literature are aesthetic, so their degree of intensity of interest at the levels of empathising and analogising would be far from reaching the strong and active end of the range. The same would be true of the structuralists whose deepest pleasures and interests in literature are linguistic or semiological rather than emotional. Considering the degrees of intensity of interest and sophistication of response can, therefore, be useful in helping to identify the reading priorities of high level readers of different theoretical orientations. The New Critics' relative disdain of close emotional involvement with the lives of characters (empathising) and of making direct connections between events in literature and readers' life experiences (analogising), helps to explain why their critical approach lacks appeal for young and unsophisticated readers, who find scholarly preoccupations with literary form and technique to be arid and irrelevant to their more immediate life concerns.

To illustrate the value of considering level of intensity of interest and sophistication with student readers I will consider the contrasting cases of Michael and Jenny, two Year 8 students, both aged 14. Both have a stong and active interest in action which they both respond to at a developed and subtle level of sophistication. However, where Jenny is strong and active in her interest in characters at the level of empathy, Michael is weak and passive because he has little interest in any characters apart from those he sees as versions of his potential self. At this level of empathising, both Jenny and Michael are at the simple and rudimentary end of the scale of sophistication, Michael because he has little sympathy for others, and Jenny because the strength of her feelings usurps her capacity to understand characters psychologically. Because of his quite conscious egocentricity, Michael does analogise from his reading in order to try to enhance the significance of his own life. However, Michael's egocentricity prevents his analogising activity from leading to deeper understanding of his own values and beliefs. He analogises strongly but not in a developed or subtle way. He learns from admired characters ways of behaving that he would like to practise, but reading is not for him an experience of self-exploration. He puts it this way:

'I'd like to be a pilot on one of the space ships in *Star Wars*. They were all good because they all did their job expertly and they never panicked when the going was tough. I liked them all. I didn't just admire one. I learn a lot from studying how head guys and guys with top jobs behave.'

However, on the level of action, there is no question of the sophistication of Michael's response. He shows interest in the patterning of action.

'It's not so much happy endings I like, but endings which are logical, like when the detective in a story solves his case and achieves some satisfaction about finishing his job or when Ged finds the monster chasing him and gets free of it [*A Wizard of Earthsea*].'

In contrast to Michael's cool detachment, Jenny's response is strongly emotive but not in any way analytical:

'I get completely involved with the characters. When they're crying so am I. When they're happy so am I. When I was a little girl I used to think I was Snow White, and now when I read I'm playing the part of a character too. When I watched *Seven Little Australians* on television I thought I was right in there with Judy and had some arguments with my father too. I still haven't got over her dying . . . I loved *The Silver Sword*, particularly the last three chapters when the four children and the father met up and there was lots of excitement in their meetings. It made you forget the troubles they'd had.'

## THE CONNECTION BETWEEN PROCESS-STAGES AND PROCESSING STRATEGIES (COLUMNS 1 AND 4)

In the developmental model, the kinds of satisfaction readers experience are ordered in successive stages of increasing complexity of response. These satisfactions are also cumulative: a good reader who reads at the highest levels also experiences enjoyments at earlier levels. The pleasure that comes from reviewing the whole work as the author's creation, for example, does not supersede but rather supplements the pleasures of empathising and analogising. Similarly, the strategies of reading are also progressive and cumulative. As a reader progresses from one level to the next, she or he does not, snake-like, shed old strategies like a worn-out skin, but develops those strategies for increasingly complex purposes, as well as adopting new strategies. For example, the reader's predictive and interpretative activity can range from merely anticipating what might happen next to a continual questioning of the text at each reading moment, reinterpreting the significance of short and long-term past events and modifying expectations of possible alternative short and long-term outcomes.

As can be seen from the chart (p.360), specific reading strategies were clearly identifiable at each developmental stage. Each kind of reading satisfaction or source of interest was found to be associated with particular strategies used by all students reading at that stage.

For example, consider the satisfactions and strategies of students operating at stage one, unreflective interest in exciting action. Students reading at this level enjoy books with cut-and-dried plots, and characters tailored to fit them. An interest in characters goes no further than concern for the success or failure of the actions they are engaged in. Characters are enjoyed as stereotypes, sympathised with if they are goodies or not sympathised with if they are baddies. Hermeneutic puzzles and subtleties of motivation perplex and bore such readers rather than arouse their curiosities. Their attention is fragile and requires the constant excitement of dramatic action for its maintenance. The characteristic strategies of this level are forming simple mental images and anticipating what might happen next in the short term. The mental images are mainly visualisations of place and character, together with stereotypic feelings about the characters and events, with both the pictorial and affective elements influenced substantially by film and television. In generating expectations, action level readers are actively interested in the outcomes of events beyond the present moment but not in the long term implications or significances of them. That a character succeeds or fails is the object of concern, not why she or he succeeds or fails, nor what view of the world his or her success or failure implies.

At the second stage, of empathising, readers are more deeply interested in characters and more sensitive to their feelings, and thus beginning to consider their motivations. Consequently their mental images encompass more complex feelings about characters, and their expectations encompass not only what happens in action but its implications for characters involved in it. At the stage of analogising (Stage 3), readers' satisfactions include not only an interest in characters like themselves, but a consideration of the implications of characters' behaviour for their own lives, and so conscious connections are made between what happens in fiction and personal experience. By the stage of reflection (Stage 4), the process of decentring (from 'me' to 'outside me') is well underway, and the growing capacity for detachment, with no loss of involvement, leads to deeper understanding of other people, their motives and aspirations, and of the human condition. The strategies associated with evaluating characters and interpreting themes include reconciling increasingly complex textual perspectives, filling in larger textual gaps and entertaining a range of alternative possible long-term outcomes. It is at this stage that readers have entered fully into Harding's onlooker role of making detached evaluative responses. Obviously, the fifth stage of seeing the whole work as an author's construction and matching one's world view with that of the author, involves recognising both the real author's creative role as artificer (and orchestrator of the reader's response) and the implied author's values.

In the final stage, (Stage 6), readers are fully aware of the textual functions of the implied author and the implied reader, and the relationship between them. At this stage readers are not only interested in analysing the text as a construct, but also in considering the ideological implications of its constructedness and in reflexively exploring their own identities and their own reading processes. They understand the implications of psychoanalytical, structuralist and political criticism and apply that understanding to their analysis of texts and of themselves. This reflective and reflexive thinking about the way texts work as structures of cultural transmission, and about the way they work on texts to interpret them, confers considerable power on readers. They can direct and control their own thinking when they are conscious of it; and control over their own thinking and over the rhetoric of texts gives them more power to operate effectively in their society.

As we shall see in the next section, reflexiveness can be taught at each stage of reading development. This is one of the most productive and unanticipated findings of the interviews, but in retrospect it can be seen as a function of the one-to-one relationship between student and interviewer and of the form of the enquiry into reading strategies. The purposes of the interview were made explicit to each student at the outset, and the activities organised to identify students' reading strategies, and the questions asked about these strategies, promoted students' interest in, and awareness of, their own reading processes. At the end of the interview all the students expressed some satisfaction in their newly acquired knowledge of their own reading powers. It also became clear that once readers become reflexively interested in their own reading processes they can be helped to progress to higher levels of reading, if the order of development is preserved in the teaching. This was evident in what happened with the most unsuccessful readers interviewed in 1984, those who at the time of the interview read no fiction at all from choice. In responding to a simple short story ('The Bad Deeds Gang'), the beginning of which appealed to them because the characters were mischievous children, every one of these readers learned the strategy of questioning the text sufficiently well to develop considerable interest in what might happen *next* in the action, and in some cases, in what the final outcome for the characters might be. Much of the trouble with the teaching of literature in school seems quite clearly to be that the perceived sequence of literary response is ignored. The Higher School Certificate examination, for example, has traditionally required responses at Stages 4 and 5 from students who have not experienced the satisfactions offered at Stages 2 and 3.

## ILLUSTRATING THE MODEL : TEENAGE READERS IN ACTION

Here are the opening sections of the short stories and novels read to the students in interview and used as the basis for identifying their reading strategies. They are reproduced to enable you to interpret and evaluate more easily the comments of the students about them in the analyses of responses in this section.

Mick read that if you put lights in a chook-house they'd think night was day and you'd get eggs twice in twenty-four hours. So we put a couple of old kerosene lamps in the shed.

The chook-shed burned down.

That was the end of our Good Deeds Gang. Nothing seemed to

go right with any of our good deeds, and there certainly wasn't
any money in it.

Barry Breen, 'The Bad Deeds Gang'

LUCY BEWARE MELANIE PROSSER SHE IS OUT TO GET
YOU Angus xxx
How do you know? And stop sending me notes.
I HERD x x x Angus.
"Wait here," Melanie Prosser said at the school gate. "Then we
won't miss her."
"In her daddy's posh car," Sally-Ann Simpson said. "Showoff pig."
"I'll put an armlock on her," Vicky Farrant said. "I'm amazing at
armlocks."
"Not till we've got her behind the cycle shed," Melanie said. "Be
all smarmy smiles till then."

Aidan Chambers, *The Present-Takers*


"Alfie?"
"What?"
"You studying?"
"Yes," he lied.
"Well, why don't you come down and study in front of the
television? It'll take your mind off what you're doing," his mother
called.
He didn't answer. He bent over the sheet of paper on his table.
He was intent.
"Did you hear me, Alfie?"
"I heard," he called without glancing up.
"Well, come on down." She turned and spoke to Alma. "Who's
the announcer that says that on TV? It's some game show. He
says, 'Come on downnnn,' and people come running down the aisle
to guess the prices."
"I don't know, Mom. I don't watch that junk," Alma said.
"But you know who I'm talking about. Alfie Mason, come on
downnnn!"
Alfie didn't answer. He was drawing a comic strip called "Super
Bird".

Betsy Byars, *The Cartoonist*


No one can tell you exactly who it was now, but it was quite
certainly one of the youngest children that invented the name

"Trillions". You can imagine a group of children squatting on the ground, scraping together heaps of brightly coloured, mysterious grit that had fallen from the sky . . .

"I've got millions!"

"I've got billions!"

"I've got trillions!"

Trillions it was from then on. The name fitted perfectly. It had the right hard, bright sound to it — and Trillions were hard and bright. It suggests millions upon millions — and the Trillions were everywhere, sprinkling roads and gardens and roofs and even the firesides of people's homes with a glittery dusting of tiny jewels (but Trillions were not jewels).

And the name Trillions had a foreign sound to it — a suggestion of other worlds, star-studded skies, the cold emptiness of space. That was right, too. For wherever Trillions came from, it was not this world.

So everyone — the children, then the adults, then the local newspapers, then the national newspapers and TV stations and at last the world authorities — came to call the strange, jewel-like dust by the name the children invented: Trillions.

Nicholas Fisk, *Trillions*

I'm writing this down because I don't ever want to forget the way it was. It doesn't seem as if I could, now, but they all tell you things change. And I guess they're right. Older people must have forgotten or they couldn't be the way they are. And that goes for even the best ones, like Dad and Mr Grant. They try to understand but they don't seem to know how. And the others make you feel dirty or else they make you feel like a goof. Till, pretty soon, you begin to forget yourself — you begin to think, "Well, maybe they're right and it was that way." And that's the end of everything. So I've got to write this down. Because they smashed it forever — but it wasn't the way they said.

Stephen Vincent Benét, 'Too Early Spring'

In the great hall of Hygelac, King of the Geats, supper was over and the mead horns going round. It was the time of evening, with the dusk gathering beyond the firelight, when the warriors called for Angelm the King's bard to wake his harp for their amusement; but tonight they had something else to listen to than the half-sung, half-told stories of ancient heroes that they knew by heart. Tonight there were strangers in their midst, seafarers with the salt still in their hair, from the first trading ship to reach them since the ice melted and the wild geese came North again. And their Captain sat in the Guest Seat that faced the High Seat of the King, midway up the hall, and told the news of the coasts and islands and the northern seas.

Rosemary Sutcliff, *Dragonslayer*

There were no curtains up. The window was a hard edged block the colour of the night sky. Inside the bedroom the darkness was of a gritty texture. The wardrobe and bed were blurred shapes in the darkness. Silence.

Billy moved over, towards the outside of the bed. Jud moved with him, leaving one half of the bed empty. He snorted and rubbed his nose. Billy whimpered. They settled. Wind whipped the window and swept along the wall outside.

Billy turned over, Jud followed him and cough-coughed into his neck. Billy pulled the blankets up round his ears and wiped his neck with them. Most of the bed was now empty, and the unoccupied space quickly cooled. Silence. Then the alarm rang. The noise brought Billy upright, feeling for it in the darkness, eyes shut tight. Jud groaned and hutched back across the cold sheet. He reached down the side of the bed and knocked the clock over, grabbed for it, and knocked it farther away.

"Come here, you bloody thing."

He stretched down and grabbed it with both hands. The glass lay curved in one palm, while the fingers of his other hand fumbled amongst the knobs and levers at the back. He found the lever and the noise stopped. Then he coiled back into bed and left the clock lying on its back.

"The bloody thing."

He stayed in his own half of the bed, groaning and turning over every few minutes, Billy lay with his back to him, listening. Then he turned his cheek slightly from the pillow.

"Jud?"

"What?"

"Tha'd better get up."

Barry Hines, *Kes*

When a day that you happen to know is Wednesday starts off by sounding like Sunday, there is something seriously wrong somewhere.

I felt that from the moment I woke. And yet, when I started functioning a little more sharply, I misgave. After all, the odds were that it was I who was wrong, and not everyone else — though I did not see how that could be. I went on waiting, tinged with doubt. But presently I had my first bit of objective evidence — a distant clock struck what sounded to me just like eight. I listened hard and suspiciously. Soon another clock began, on a loud, decisive note. In a leisurely fashion it gave an indisputable eight. Then I knew things were awry.

The way I came to miss the end of the world — well, the end of the world I had known for close on thirty years — was sheer accident: like a lot of survival, when you come to think of it.

John Wyndham, *The Day of the Triffids*

If you really want to hear about it, the first thing you'll probably want to know is where I was born, and what my lousy childhood was like, and how my parents were occupied and all before they had me, and all that David Copperfield kind of crap, but I don't feel like going into it. In the first place, that stuff bores me, and in the second place, my parents would have about two haemorrhages apiece if I told anything pretty personal about them. They're quite touchy about anything like that, especially my father. They're nice and all — I'm not saying that — but they're also touchy as hell. Besides, I'm not going to tell you my whole goddam autobiography or anything. I'll just tell you about this madman stuff that happened to me around last Christmas before I got pretty run-down and had to come out here and take it easy.

J.D. Salinger, *The Catcher in the Rye*

When they were all ready, and in the dining-room, Professor Bertrand Studdard made his expected plea for sanity.

"Why don't you come with us in the Volvo?" he asked in a hopeless voice.

Madeleine pretended to pause and think; until hope dawned on her husband's face. Then she said: "The Volvo? That thing? It's more like a bus than a car, and you drive it like a bus-driver."

"You can drive, if you like . . . "

"I wouldn't be seen dead in it. Besides, the clutch makes my leg ache."
The three children watched silently. Could this family never do anything without a row? thought Beth. Could they never go on holiday in one car, like other families? Heavens, the Volvo was big enough!"

Robert Westall, *The Wind-Eye*

Obviously each of these texts offers different pleasures to readers and makes different demands on them. It was felt that the most reluctant and unsuccessful readers would be most likely to find 'The Bad Deeds Gang' or *The Present-Takers* or *The Cartoonist* appealing, at least in their openings, because their implied authors are all sympathetic to the world of childhood, and the taking up of the role of implied reader requires little *initial* adjustment to attitudes such students are likely to possess already. In 'The Bad Deeds Gang', for example, the sympathetic narrator is a child, a member of a group of characters the reader is invited to sympathise with; the setting is an Australian country town; the mode of the story is realistic; the narrator's language is familiarly colloquial; and the thematic concepts are simple. The story is structured as a simple reversal: when intended good deeds achieve bad ends, a deliberately bad deed achieves good ends. A grumpy adult's mean sense of humour in slicing the gang's cricket balls in half and displaying them on top of his fence is outmatched by the boys' ingenuity in painting his bottom red while he is sitting on his backyard dunny.

## STAGE ONE: UNREFLECTIVE INTEREST IN ACTION

Readers at this level gain their satisfaction from the excitement of continuous action, spectacle and suspense. They tend to see characters merely as objects in the action playing out stereotyped roles, and thus they show little interest in, or imaginative insight into, their feelings and motivations ('You take sides with the good guy and hope he wins'). Many of these young readers are engaged in a process of wish-formulation, in that the stories they enjoy help them to define their wishes and to imaginatively contemplate their fulfilment. Reading is a kind of day-dreaming about lives more glamorous than their own. The hero-figures of such readers are characters whose lives are adventurous and romantic. One intelligent 14 year-old who reads very little but enjoyed *Star Wars* and some of the James Bond novels, outlined for me the kind of book that would make him a more enthusiastic reader.

| | |
|---|---|
| *The Story* | 'The brain behind the tough guys has a missile aimed at New York, and the spies come out to stop him. He's really after revenge for what has been done to him in the past by somebody in the American government.' |
| *The Places* | 'The main hero has his base in New York which is headquarters. He has to go over to Europe and live in lots of top hotels. The criminal has a big underground laboratory on an island in the Mediterranean.' |
| *The Characters* | 'The hero is a bloke about 25 and he's good looking. There are some big, tough, heavy blokes on the other side, and the brain behind them is small and crippled, ugly and mean. There's a string of girls, all good looking, and they like the hero.' |

A 14 year-old girl described her enjoyment of the Trixie Belden and Hardy Boys mysteries as arising from the freedom and excitement of the characters' lives which she contrasted with the boredom of her own life:

'They have good times with their friends and their parents let them have so much freedom. They lead really exciting lives. The Hardy boys' dad is rich, and they can go on planes and to lots of other countries, and I'm stuck in Bathurst miles out of town.'

A 16 year-old girl shows a complete lack of understanding of *The Chocolate War*, read as a class text, in explaining how it disappointed her because it did not satisfy her requirement of a happy ending:

In *The Chocolate War* it was wrong that Jerry got bashed up. It should have ended in good feelings, not bad. Brother Leon and all the boys should visit Jerry in the hospital and be sorry for all they've done, and look after him and forgive and forget so life will be better after.'

Associated with the appeal to these students of fiction that formulates their fantasies or portrays the world as they would like it to be is their dismissive evaluation of most of their school texts as boring: 'Cry the Beloved Country was boring compared with Star Wars. There were long sections of description of people and places when nothing was happening.'

What boredom really means to these students is an inability or unwillingness to participate in the creation of textual meaning, a failure to comprehend texts by filling in their gaps. Comprehension really means that the text answers the questions readers ask in their heads as they read. For many of the readers at this level boredom arises because they don't ask any questions or generate any expectations; or because they find the gaps between textual details and events so wide that they don't know which questions to ask and are, therefore, confused; or because they don't realise that the questions they do ask are not intended to be immediately answerable, that the information required for formulating an answer is deliberately withheld for some time or disclosed only gradually.

'If the starts don't have enough action I don't read them. It's boring when writers go into great details on one event. When there's a lot of stuff about a character's feelings and the way he sees things it's boring. If it's got nothing to do with the proper story it bores me.'

'In The Bridge to Terabithia there were lots of boring bits that dragged on and on, and had nothing to do with the story, only descriptions of the house and people and what they thought.'

'I don't understand it when they switch from action to ordinary scenes where nothing is happening. This happens with the books we read at school; they shift from one scene to a completely different scene and from action to description. When this happens I flip the pages to get back to the action, but it's never the same again because you've lost the excitement. I can't see why they have those bits in the book, about characters and what they think and how they feel. It spoils the exciting parts.'

About the opening section of Kes read to him, a Year 10 student said, 'No, I wouldn't read any more because it's not interesting. It's only about the feelings of the characters. They're not doing anything. It's boring.' The mental images formed by readers at this level lack visual and emotional richness. This is evident in the comparisons they make between works of fiction they have read and also seen on television or film.

> I like the TV shows better. If you're reading you can't visualise it. You can sometimes, but in the TV show it's done for you. You don't see it as well when you read. The best way to read is to see the first few chapters of a book on TV, and if you like it, go read it.'

> 'The TV was better than the book because you could see what was really happening.'

> 'It's a lot better if you've seen the movie first because then you can see it clearer in your head. With *Star Wars* I read the book first and when you read it, it described him but you couldn't see him very clearly — his clothing and hair and that. With *The Empire Strikes Back* I saw the movie first and then read the book. That was great because when you read the book it was like seeing the movie a second time. I like to see the action, the blood, the sword strokes and all that.'

Because of their lack of experience and satisfaction in the reading of fiction, many students had little understanding of literary conventions. Without a literary repertoire to draw on, they were not able to recognise many of the possibilities of textual meanings because they had little sense of such things as a plot, structure, genre, irony and tone. For example, the expectations one Year 8 boy formed from the title and opening paragraphs of 'The Bad Deeds Gang' was that it might be obscene. He said, 'I think it will have dirty bits in it. They might meet a gang of girls who want to do bad things too.' He had no awareness of other possibilities of meaning of the term 'bad deeds'. Another interpreted the dislocation of the chronological order of events in *The Amityville Horror* as a completely purposeless trick on the part of the author:

> 'It was always shifting about from time to time and place to place. They muddled up the time when things happened, starting with a thing today and then shooting forward to tomorrow and then back to yesterday and all over the place.'

A Year 10 boy who was half way through reading *Treasure Island* in class, when asked how he thought it might end, said,

'Long John will get the treasure if there is any. He will share it with Jim, half each. Trelawney and his mob won't get it because they're not as determined as Long John who will do anything to stop them. Jim will end up happy and wealthy.'

This boy's lack of understanding of the conventions of the children's adventure story in the portrayal of moral right and wrong, is matched by his unawareness of the conventional forms of expressing humour in fiction. He also assumed from the title of 'The Bad Deeds Gang' that the story would 'end up in tragedy', completely missing the tone of the opening paragraphs.

'Someone will have a bad accident. They'll make another shed, but it's not going to work out. They'll end up hurting themselves real bad. The chook shed's burned down, so something bad will happen to the new one they build.'

Although he was interested in finding out what happened in *The Catcher in the Rye*, another Year 10 missed the tone of the opening section in predicting that Holden Caulfield might end up as a tragically insane inmate of a lunatic asylum.

'He's got something wrong with him. He's probably very retarded because he's going off all the time. When he went mad at Christmas time it might be because he can't handle the pressure. He'll end up in an institution or a farm. They'll keep his brain numb so he won't have any more of his fits.'

The important point to make about such expectations as these students generate is that they are indicative of bad reading, not because they are wrong, but because they are so inappropriate, and this is the result of their lack of understanding of the conventions of fiction. As I mentioned in Chapter Three, 'wrong' but logical or apposite predictions about what might happen can be most productive, enabling readers to enjoy the unexpected or unforeseen. Importantly, the fact that these students do form expectations, indicates their reading potential. What they need is a course of reading that, as well as being enjoyable, begins at their level and teaches them the conventions their lack of experience in reading has prevented them from grasping. These students require any problems they find in text to be resolved very quickly. They do not formulate questions explicitly to themselves, and any simple puzzles they are vaguely aware of are not held in the mind. 'If it's really boring at the beginning I lose interest and don't read any more. If nothing starts to happen pretty soon I give it up.'

In response to the opening paragraphs of *Trillions* read to him, a Year 8 boy said,

'I can't understand what they're talking about. I was trying to work out what the little dust things are, but I couldn't think what they might be or what they might do. I want to know straight away. There is not enough action or explanation in this book. You don't understand it when you read it.'

A Year 10 boy curtly dismissed *The Wind-Eye* after hearing the opening half-page because the meanings are enacted (in dialogue) rather than explained.

'It's a bit boring. Two adults are obviously having a quarrel but it doesn't say why. It starts too abruptly. I don't like too much dialogue at the start where you have to work things out that have gone on before.'

The problem is summarised quite explicitly by a very intelligent Year 8 boy (Michael of the preceding section) who understands that books have different structural patterns but who has not been helped to consider the purposes and effects of unconventional principles of ordering narrative. His generalisation followed a comment about Roald Dahl's *Charlie and the Chocolate Factory*, the structure of which he found satisfying because 'Charlie was poor at first and all the others were rich and greedy and you thought it would be right if Charlie ended up with the factory, which he did.'

'I like books that start at point A and go to point B and so on to the end, in proper order. I like to make connections, but lots of books don't have connections. Like some of the ones we have at school. They skip about all over the place and you forget things and lose track of what's happened.'

How easy it would be to help this boy to read with some satisfaction the kinds of books he criticises. In his interview it emerged quite clearly that despite his condemnation of the school texts, he really believed it was his own inadequacy as a reader which caused his confusion. When he was told that authors sometimes deliberately confuse readers, and that the confusions are eventually resolved by readers who can hold puzzles in their heads while they read, he was quite cheered. It was a completely novel idea to him.

Although the interviews were not set up primarily as a learning experience for the students, it was hoped that they would gain some value from them. The students at this level did learn the pleasures and productivity of generating expectations, and mentioned with surprise and satisfaction that perhaps some of their earlier attitudes to both stories and their own competences as readers might have to be modified. In response to questions 1 and 2 about their reading strategies (What is going on in your head while you are listening? What do you think might happen in this story?), most of the students expressed surprise at the notion that they should be actively doing anything. They thought that text operated on readers rather than that readers had to operate on text; that the minds of good readers automatically processed print into understanding; and the fact that their minds didn't seem to do this too well indicated that they were 'bad readers' because they were unintelligent. The act of asking students what questions they were asking of the text read to them, led them to ask these questions, and the enabling security of the interview situation led them to think aloud while doing so. At the beginning of the interview, when the purposes and procedures were outlined to them, I made it perfectly clear that they weren't being tested in any way and that no evaluation of them would be passed on to their teachers. I emphasised that I was trying to find out something that no one knew much about, so they couldn't be judged right or wrong, and I told them that they were the experts about the way their own minds worked, and that I was trying to find out information that only they could give. Their reaction to this was one of relief, and as their apprehensiveness wore off they spoke openly, confidently and interestedly.

In answer to the opening questions about strategies asked of 'The Bad Deeds Gang', a Year 8 remedial class boy said, 'It's funny. The way it says it is funny. That bit about the chook shed getting burned down, it's funny because it didn't work out the way they wanted it to.' And in answer to the question about his expectations, he said,

'They might do bad things. The good things they try to do turn out bad, so they get annoyed with doing good things. They might as well do bad. When they start doing bad things they might turn out good! I like it because it seems it might be funny.'

Because of this boy's obvious enjoyment and shrewd perception of the possibilities of 'The Bad Deeds Gang', I read him the first page and a half of Betsy Byars' *The Cartoonist* to see if and how he would enjoy and interpret a more complex opening. In the passage, the comic strip ( entitled 'Superbird') being drawn by Alfie, the central character, is described as follows:

In the first square a man was scattering birdseed from a bag labelled "Little Bird Seed". In the next square little birds were gobbling up the seeds.
In the third square the man was scattering birdseed from a bag labelled "Big Bird Seed". In the next square big birds were gobbling up the seeds.
In the fifth square the man was scattering huge lumps from a bag labelled "Giant Bird Seed". In the last square a giant bird was gobbling up the little man.

The listener's response to this was a surprised laugh and the following unprompted commentary.

'I expected the giant birds to eat up the giant food instead of the man, and I thought it would go on to have super-giant seeds for a super-bird to eat. But that's great. I really like that, the way you expect one thing and it gets turned round on you. It gives you a surprise and it's very funny. I really like jokes like that. Are there lots more like that in the book?'

Later on he speculated that as Alfie would rather draw cartoons in his room than watch television with his mother, he might be a boy who 'does things on his own and mightn't get on with other kids'. This student has taken the first step to become an active reader.

What I think is most interesting about almost all of the readers at this level is that at the end of the interview they said things like 'I didn't know so much happened in my mind when I read', and 'I've never been much good at reading, but I know some of the ways to make it more interesting now' and 'I really enjoyed that; stories can be interesting if you learn to use your brains to think about what is happening in them'. The importance of the supportive interview situation is, I think, that in it the students became conscious of the constructive strategies that the questions led them to use. It was not that the students were intellectually incapable of reading with enjoyment and understanding but, rather, that they had not been placed in situations before in which they could learn how to go about it successfully. They possessed the capacity for reading productively, but seem not to have experienced situations that called on them to use that capacity. In the interviews, they also gained an inkling that their consciousness of their own productive reading strategies is a powerful educational tool.

## STAGE TWO: EMPATHISING

In the responses of readers at this level there is a range of imaginative insight into the experiences of characters and what they are feeling. Empathy for fictional characters varies both

1. in intensity of interest or commitment: from virtual indifference to deep absorption in what they do and feel; and
2. in sophistication of response: from rudimentary to more developed psychological understanding of, and imaginative sympathy for, their feelings and situations. The more psychological understanding there is of characters, the more imaginative sympathy for them. That is, there is a range of sensitivity towards characters' experiences and emotions.

In his article, 'Psychological Processes in the Reading of Fiction', D.W. Harding describes the experience of less and more sophisticated 'onlookers' at this level, as follows:

The onlooker not only enters into the experience of the participants (characters) but also contemplates them as fellow-beings. It is an elementary form of onlooking merely to imagine what the situation must seem like and to react *with* the participant. The more complex observer imagines something of what the participant is experiencing and then reacts *to* him, for instance with pity or joy on his account. The spectators who watch Othello as he kills his wife are not feeling simply what they imagine him to be feeling, they are also feeling, as onlookers, pity *for* him.'[8]

I would suggest that the pity felt for Othello arises from the recognition that a fellow human being is in an unenviable predicament, and that this pity may be felt by spectators whose empathy, while strong, is fairly rudimentary. I would qualify Harding's explanation with the point that only those with an equally strong but more sophisticated empathy are able to 'imagine something of what the participant is experiencing'; that is, to imagine how Othello is feeling as well as to pity him. Harding is wrong, I believe, when he says that empathising involves feeling what a character is feeling. Neither naive nor sophisticated spectators would actually feel what they imagine Othello to be feeling when he kills his wife; nor would many of them be so deluded as to think they were experiencing the same feelings as Othello. They would all have some idea of what Othello is feeling, and they would all sympathise with him to varying degrees of sensitivity. Contrary to Harding, I believe that merely to react *to* the predicament of a character (for instance, with pity or joy *for* him or her) is the elementary form of empathising; that the more complex observer, as well as reacting to a character, is able to imagine and sympathetically understand how he is feeling without feeling the same way himself. The more sophisticated empathisers respond with more psychological insight into behaviour, and this makes them more sensitive to the 'otherness' of fictional characters.

At a higher level on the developmental model (Stage 4), is the stage of reflecting on the significance of characters' experiences, which involves an understanding of complex motivations and the making of moral, psychological and philosophical generalisations about human behaviour. At the stage of empathising, readers are beginning to decentre, but they have some way to go before they could be said to have reached the stage of making the detached, evaluative judgments of Harding's spectator role. Fundamentally, at the stage of empathising, readers are emotionally involved. Their feelings towards characters are of varying degrees of strength and sensitivity. Harding describes the attitude adopted by the empathic reader towards characters she or he likes as 'that of a well-wisher who is not merely anticipating the joy that they will feel but enjoys the fact that they will be feeling joy.'[9] I would add that the more sophisticated empathisers have a greater degree of imaginative understanding of the quality of that joy and of its meaning to the characters than do the less sensitive empathisers.

Readers whose empathy is developed have more understanding

of the emotions experienced by both themselves and the characters they sympathise with, than do those readers whose empathy is rudimentary. They understand more deeply why characters feel as they do and why they as readers react to these characters as they do. Interestingly, and perfectly understandably, the act of asking students questions about their feelings about characters, and about their position as readers in relation to such characters, promoted the reflection that made them more reflexively conscious of such matters. At the rudimentary end of the scale of empathising are the kinds of responses described by readers in the following ways.

'I feel like what I'm reading is really happening. If someone's sad I feel sad. I'm laughing and crying with them. I cry in lots of books. In *The Outsiders* I felt I wished I was there to help because I was crying a lot of the time.'

'In the Nancy Drew books, I always feel very close to Nancy herself. In all the adventures and troubles she got into I felt I was there with her and feeling with her. When she was frightened I felt frightened for her.'

'In the Trixie Belden books, when Trixie's gone and done something wrong, I felt "it won't turn our right for you, Trixie, you should have done something else". I always get worried for them.'

'In Nancy Drew she's finding out different things, and I want to be there with her, helping her, being on her side. I think she's pretty good. My feelings are like hers. When she is waiting for someone to get better I want to be helping them to get better too. When Nancy is frightened I'm frightened. I'm not just sorry for her, but so frightened I want to get away from it too.'

The next two accounts are of more sophisticated empathic responses.

'In *I Am David* I really felt sympathy for David. He was told lies about his mother and father, and he travelled so many miles to find his mother, and it took so long. It showed you how much he wanted to get back to her. By the time you came to the end, after all his travels and all his troubles you felt really sorry for him and warm towards him, and you were glad for him and his mother to get back together again.'

'In *Flowers in the Attic* I felt very sympathetic with Chris, the biggest brother. He had most responsibility. He had to play mother and father. He tried to be hard and cold, but he was really soft and caring. I felt very sympathetic with him.'

Finally, the following descriptions are illustrative of the most sophisticated responses of students at this level.

'In one of the Hardy Boys' books, *The Talking Skull*, I was frightened a bit but not as frightened as the Hardy boys. At night the natives used to go to sleep and on top of the mountain they had a skull with a light inside, with real red bloodshot eyes and the mouth all moving. When they saw it first they were frightened, but although you were frightened too, you were not as frightened as them. You understood their fear and knew how they were feeling, but you didn't feel quite so frightened yourself.'

This student shows she understands the difference between empathising with characters and 'identifying' with them.

'In *Born Free* I really felt sorry for the lion and the lady who owned it. I cried. I felt for her, that she loved Elsa so much, and when Elsa came back with the cubs she wanted to pat them and she wasn't allowed to, and I understood why. She couldn't become addicted to them because they had to live in their own world, not the humans' world. But you still feel sorry for her feeling of loss. She'd feel happy, too, because Elsa had got back to her natural world, but sad because she'd lost a good friend. I think I know how she felt, and felt a bit the same myself, but not exactly the same because you're not her or in her position.'

In *Sweet Valley High*, I really liked Elizabeth but I didn't think I was her, or even that I was feeling just what she felt all the time. You feel like a fly on the wall of the household. You're looking at these girls all the time, and you imagine yourself in their place, but you don't think 'I'm them'. I think how they might feel rather than feeling the way they do. You get inside the mind of someone else, but you stay out of it as well.'

It is very clear, I think, from these comments describing the most developed empathic responses, that it would be easy to lead the students who made them to higher levels of response. It would also be easy to extend their reading repertoires by introducing them to more demanding and stimulating books. And readers who empathise as sophisticatedly as these last two are well on the way towards breaking out of their egocentric world into the universe of other people. A Year 8 girl put it this way:

> 'It's outlined for you in books how other people are feeling and why, and you get to understand others and become more tolerant of them. You understand the reasons why people sometimes react in strange ways. For example, they might be lonely and feeling rejected.'

Whereas readers at the action stage (Stage 1) are interested in characters primarily in terms of whether they win or lose, succeed or fail, readers at this level generate expectations about characters' motives and feelings. They are interested not only in what happens next but also in the effect of what happens on characters and what causes them to feel as they do. A bottom-stream Year 10 girl responded to the opening paragraph of *The Present-Takers* as follows:

> 'It looks like some rough girls are picking on Lucy and they are setting up an unfair fight. What interests me is what the boy [Angus] has got to do with it. He seems to like Lucy because he warns her and puts kisses on his note, but there are no kisses on her reply. You want to know why he likes her and why she doesn't like him, and what will happen — will they they develop a relationship with each other and with the girls who are picking on her.'

This is what a middle stream Year 8 girl said about her expectations of the short story, 'Too Early Spring', after hearing the opening paragraph.

> 'It sounds like the person writing is confused and angry. I think it's a boy, and people have confused him and so he wants to understand how he was led to be confused, so he's writing it all down. You want to find out what caused him to feel this way, and whether he's right to feel as he does. The way he talks, it's just how you feel when adults don't understand you. I think the title is hinting that he was probably trying to grow up too quick. He might have fallen in love too young.'

That the emphasis on characters' feelings and motivations is a major source of interest at this level is made explicit in this generalisation by a top-stream Year 8 girl:

'I hate books where you can tell right from the beginning that the good guys are going to win. I like twists that surprise you and make you think why characters behave as they do, so you get inside them more.'

The same girl's response to the strategy question (Number 5) about mental images ('What impressions do you form in your mind about the people in the story?'), makes it clear how mental images at this level are primarily affective.

'If they describe a character you get a picture in your head about what he looks like. You get feelings about them from the way they're described. In some television programmes if someone has a plastic moustache and narrow eyes you know he's going to be a baddie. Enid Blyton's books are a bit like that too. As soon as a character is described you know if you're for or against them. In more serious books you know pretty early on whether you sympathise with them or not, but your attention is on their feelings and understanding them, even when they do things that are sometimes wrong.'

## STAGE THREE: ANALOGISING

Readers' own lives can gain what D.W. Harding calls 'enhanced significance' by analogy with the events of fiction when they are emotionally drawn to characters whose experiences they recognise as similar in some way to their own. As Harding points out, the possibilities of the reader's own life that are contemplated need not always be 'flattering and agreeable' ones, but they are entertained only by readers who become 'deeply absorbed in the experiences of characters whom they like.'[10]

It is important that we distinguish between students who draw on personal experience to inform their understanding of fiction, and students who, as well, go on to derive implications for their own lives from their reading. Many readers at the level of *empathising* relate their personal experiences to the behaviour of fictional characters in order to better understand these characters, but they do not engage in the reverse process of drawing analogies from fiction to gain a heightened awareness of themselves and their lives. For example, a Year 10 girl at the level of empathising said, 'If someone's having a fight with their parents I think about fights I've had with mine, I just naturally think of them', but as she went on to talk about her reading of her favourite books it became clear that she did not draw analogies from her reading to discover something about herself. Making connections between personal experience and the experience of fictional characters helped her to empathise with them but it did not lead to any deeper understanding of herself. Fiction can, however, as Harding puts it, 'contribute to the search for identity or role definition'[11], and this process stage of analogising is exemplified in the following comments of a Year 8 girl about her reading of Madeleine L'Engle's novel, *A Wrinkle in Time*.

'In *A Wrinkle in Time* Meg is impatient, and I feel she's like me — with a temper. Sometimes I get angry for not being allowed to do things or for being kept in ignorance about things I think I ought to know, just like Meg was kept ignorant by Mrs Whatsit when they were first about to enter the town her father was in . . . After I've read about Meg losing her temper, I realise that people are often saying things about me behind my back like they were saying about Meg in the story. It's a great comfort to know you're not the only one who gets angry . . . Actually I would have hated to be Meg. Everything was going wrong for her — she was in trouble at school, the teachers didn't understand her and her father was out in space, and she got sent to the headmaster for not listening in lessons, so she got angry and moody and nobody understood how she felt . . . You don't hate her because of her anger and her moods. You learn to understand why she's moody, and you are sympathetic to Meg because you know what it is like to feel as she does. She didn't know why her father left her brother behind when she was just about to get hypnotised by the man with red eyes. Meg was angry with her father for taking her away from Charles Wallace when she didn't realise she was being taken over by *it* and the father was trying to save her. Other people didn't understand Meg, but we do because we learn more information about her. We can see the reasons for her behaviour that other people didn't like . . . I obviously enjoyed the book because of the resemblances between Meg and me, but it also made me look at how Meg learns to cope. It's not that I imitate her in any way, because I know I am me and I have to live my own life and not someone else's, but you do learn about yourself from being interested in the way characters you like and who are like you in some way, how they behave and face problems. You find out about them, but you also learn about yourself.'

This girl explains very clearly how reading has developed her understanding of other people and of herself. However, she is not yet at the stage of reflecting on the significance of fictional events and behaviour (Stage 4). She is not sufficiently distanced from action and character to be able to generalise about the portrayal of human values in fiction, as her following comment shows: 'When I'm reading a book I only think about the characters and what they're doing, whether they are doing silly or good things, and sometimes I think about what you find about yourself.'

Another Year 8 girl says that her main response to her most recently read novels (*I am David* and *The Diary of Anne Frank)* was to compare herself with the characters, to learn about them from her own experience, and to learn about herself from their experiences.

'I wonder what they're thinking and feeling and how I would be feeling if I were in that position. I always think of myself, I compare how I would feel and act. Would I have done that? Why has she done that? You learn what sort of things you like and why, and what I'm like to other people. I am looking at what they're doing, and what people think of them, so I can look at myself and think what people I know are thinking about me.'

In response to the question, 'Where do you feel you are in relation to the characters?' a Year 8 boy explained how he learned about himself through his feeling of empathy with the young Prince Arren in Ursula le Guin's *The Farthest Shore.*

I felt closer to Arren than to Sparrowhawk because I felt I was like him. It made it easier to imagine what it would be like in his position. He's like me because he's a boy, and he's with a powerful wizard, which is sort of like being with a teacher you like and trust. You're young and inexperienced like him, and you can learn about yourself from his mistakes just like you can learn from your own mistakes in life if there's a kind and experienced person to help you.'

Readers at the level of analogising are often quite explicit about the affective quality of their mental images. They recognise that physical descriptions are important primarily for the attitudes they communicate about characters.

'While I'm reading I have a continuous movie in my head, only it's slower than a real movie. When I stop reading and start again later I read again the last page I've read to pick up my picture again. But my movie is not one of clear pictures like on film. When it comes to details on the face you don't see too much. It's more a feeling about a person. For example, in the last book I read – I forget the name – the man who took on the position of leader was described as being tall and well-built and he had a few grey hairs. There were more details than that which I can't remember but they didn't give you a full picture of him that you could see him all clearly. But what details there were made you imagine him as the fatherly type, compassionate, brave, understanding, very intelligent. The features described were in agreement with that impression.'

'I have an idea of their personality in my mind, but not what they look like exactly. I was disappointed with the film of *The Railway Children*. The way they looked and the way they spoke was not the way I imagined them from the book. Sometimes I try to pick out a vision but I can't, but I get a strong feeling of their personality.'

Readers at this level have also developed a greater understanding of literary conventions. For example, this Year 8 girl showed her sophisticated sense of fictitional endings when she described the sad ending of C.S. Lewis's *The Lion, the Witch and the Wardrobe* as being appropriate, in her answer to the question, 'Do you like happy endings?'

'It depends what sort of story it is. In the Narnian books Aslan said the children couldn't go back – that is the older two, Peter and Susan couldn't go back to Narnia because they were too old for it. This was the right ending even though it was sad, because it would have been boring if Susan and Peter kept on going back and having the same experiences over and over again. They were growing up, and out of childhood, and losing their childish imaginations. I like stories that aren't so much happy — happy's not the right word — but stories where you feel at the end there's some hope for them in the future, they've got a chance of making a good life even it it's not certain.'

I think this last point the girl makes is a very important one for teachers to keep in mind, at least with younger readers, including the 13 to 14 year-olds of Year 8. The child protagonist as a complete victim of events beyond his or her control is not a theme of fiction that these readers want or should have to confront at this stage of their lives. I am not suggesting that teachers should choose fiction that avoids the harsh realities of life, but rather that they should eschew both extreme sentimentality and inexplicable horror and despair. When we are trying to give students a sense of their own competence to solve problems in life and school I think we need to offer them fiction in which the difficulties of youthful protagonists are shown as soluble, albeit after a great struggle.

Like readers at the level of empathising, readers at the level of analogising generate expectations about characters' motives and feelings. However, they show a greater ability to generalise about characters' predicaments, and greater reflexive understanding of their own reading tastes and strategies. These skills are exemplified in the following comments made by two students after the reading of the opening section of a novel to them. First, here is a Year 10 girl's reaction to the first paragraph of 'Too Early Spring'. She neatly captures the essence of the situation and considers appropriate possibilities of the story's development: 'It sounds like a teenage crisis about parents not believing what we tell them. This boy feels betrayed. The rest of the story might tell us what happened to make him feel that way.'

Secondly, this response of a Year 8 girl to the beginning of *The Present-Takers* incorporates a reflexive commentary about her own reading processes as well as her likes and dislikes in fiction. Again, the mere posing of strategy questions in the interview, and a secure situation in which to think aloud unselfconsciously, led students to question the text more confidently and to reach deeper levels of reflexive understanding.

'They are going to get a girl and bash her up. There's been something going on for a while between them, something to start it all off. It might be that Lucy has been acting as though she thinks she's better than they are — all posh and that, but I think it's more likely that the girls who are out to get her are to blame. They are possibly jealous of her for some reason that we're yet to find out. I am past all the Trixie Beldens and teen romances because I can tell what's going to happen in all of them from the start. They're boring because they're all the same kinds of plots. It might be that Angus has been told to write these notes to Lucy to threaten her and to get her having nightmares so she'll be all softened up, but he might really be trying to help her too. When I guess ahead in romance books you get so used to the plots you can tell what's going to happen. Melanie Prosser is the leader of the girls who are out to get Lucy. You can tell the others are her followers because they're trying to impress her. I try to figure out what might happen and my mind goes like a flash while I'm reading. While you were reading my mind was asking lots of questions: What were they going to do with her? Why? What has Angus got to do with it? What has Lucy done to deserve it? Is she friends with Angus? Is she rich? Are they jealous of her for being rich? or being friends with Angus?'

For students who have reached this level of response the meaning of boredom has changed. To them it means that a too predictable text all too readily answers the questions they ask in their heads, while to the most reluctant readers at level one it means that the text is incomprehensible because they don't ask appropriate questions of it.

## STAGE FOUR: REFLECTING ON THE SIGNIFICANCE OF EVENTS AND BEHAVIOUR

Readers at this level are able to make generalisations about the themes of fiction they have read and these generalisations show an awareness of the significance and implications of action and behaviour. Such readers see literature as making complex statements about the human condition and they recognise that these statements can only be understood by considering literary works as wholes. This kind of understanding is exemplified in the following comments of students.

'*To Kill a Mockingbird* had a strong effect on me. It was a real life situation about what the truth was at the time it was set. It shows the prejudice white people felt about black, and the way truth and justice are distorted where there is hatred between people. I relate *To Kill a Mockingbird* and its truth about the treatment of negroes in the southern states of America with the treatment of aborigines in Queensland and the Northern Territory which are our version of the American deep south.'

(Year 10 boy)

'A novel I really enjoyed was *Duncton Wood* by W. Horwood. It's about a colony of moles, but it's really a portrayal of our society simplified. There are two who go against convention — Bracken and Rebecca. They are inevitably destroyed. They represent people who don't conform in society . . .

'I liked the ending because it was thought-provoking. It made you think of the significance of the lives of the main characters. I thought it was appropriate they could find what they spent their lives looking for and couldn't share with others. Nobody can give you their experience of the world, you've got to learn for yourself. Finding this knowledge was portrayed as a judgment. Despite their dying, their lives were justified. They had some value, but only to themselves. They had made a private pilgrimage.'

(Year 10 girl)

'The main character in *The Collector* [by John Fowles] is representative of a range of people in our society, people without much individuality or strength of character who are always wanting to be accepted, and who treat other people as objects because of their own inadequacies.'

(Year 10 girl)

While these readers still empathise with characters, they also stand back and evaluate their behaviour by taking into account a range of textual perspectives of them.

'My feelings about the characters vary while I'm reading. In *Lord of the Rings* I was always sympathetic with Frodo. But with Gollum, at times when he was being nice to Frodo I felt really sympathetic, but you see him as a traitor when he betrays Frodo, even though you feel sorry for him too. Your judgments change as you read. Your final judgment has to take all the events into account, what the character does at different times that is good and what he does that is bad, and why.'

(Year 8 boy)

'In *A Wizard of Earthsea* Ged learned about himself and his faults. When he killed the shadow he showed he knew there were things greater than him. He stopped boasting. When he challenged Jasper he shouldn't have done that because it was arrogant to set himself up as superior to the wizards who made the rules of Roke and who knew more than he did. He did wrong because he wanted to show off and he thought he knew more than he did.'

(Year 8 boy)

'In *The Day of the Triffids* I got annoyed with Bill because I thought some of the things he did were stupid — like staying on with those blind people when he couldn't do anything for them and they were nasty to him. It would have been an act of mercy to kill them, as well as sensible for his own survival. That's what I thought when I was reading, anyway, but when you get to the end and think about what it all means, it's not so easy to judge them as there are lots of moral viewpoints to consider. When you're reading you've worried for the main character's survival, but when you stop reading and think about what it all means it's not so easy to make clear judgments.'

(Year 10 girl)

Concerning the development of the strategies of readers at this stage, questioning of the text is more rigorous and expectations about longer term possibilities of textual development and meaning are generated in the process of reading. After expressing interest in the opening section of *The Cartoonist* and specifying the questions he would want the text to answer, a Year 8 boy speculated on the problems Alfie's passion for drawing cartoons could cause him:

'He could become a good cartoonist, he might grow out of it, he might get sick of it, because he spends all his time on it and has no friends. These are the risks he takes if he pursues his talent at the expense of his relationships with his friends. People who have special talents often have to make choices like that.'

After considering a range of possible alternatives as to the nature and powers of the strange grit mentioned at the beginning of *Trillions*, a Year 10 boy showed his understanding of the literary convention that the beginning of a work of fiction is significant for its ending, and that a mystery at the beginning will be solved by the end. 'Although they're a mystery they are obviously important, and the book will have a lot to do with the power and value they might have. They will have important consequences.'

Here, a Year 10 girl also considers a range of possibilities of the trillions' long term significance.

'They might be seeds from another planet chucked on to the earth to grow and reproduce, to wipe us out. People from another planet might be surveying the land on earth, testing what it might be like — a sort of litmus paper to test the earth's atmosphere for a population migration. They might be like lights on an airport runway showing people from outer space where to land. It gets you interested because you're not sure whether it's evil or good, whether it's going to end this world or improve it in ways people on earth haven't imagined.'

When encouraged to make explicit the particular appeal of the opening few pages of Rosemary Sutcliff's *Dragonslayer* read to her, a Year 10 girl revealed her understanding of the conventions of mythic literature in considering the possibilities of the novel's development. In representing this knowledge to herself, she came to possess it in a way she had not properly done so before it was made conscious, and it was the questioning that brought this operational understanding to consciousness.

'I would like to read that. It's written very interestingly. Its plot is likely to be interesting, but not so much in itself as a story but because of its importance in revealing something about human power and endurance. I think the events are probably not so important in themselves as in their significance. The language is unrealistic, it's very dignified, and it gives you that feeling. It's not like the language of a realistic novel, but suggests a mythology, something old and permanent. You're pretty sure the hero will win, but the importance of it is most probably his inspiration to all of the people. It might be a story written to uplift a whole race of people — the Vikings or the Saxons or people who lived harsh lives long ago.'

Two Year 8 boys also show a high level of understanding of the conventions of myth in considering possible developments and long term outcomes in *Dragonslayer*. The first expectations are those of a boy who told me he enjoyed Susan Cooper's *The Dark is Rising* fantasy sequence (five novels) as much as anything he had ever read, and the second are those of an avid J.R.R. Tolkien reader.

'One of the people in the hall might go to Denmark and slay the dragon. He might be made the king's personal killer of evil, and he might then have to go and kill other monsters. It would be a bit boring if he didn't have challenges like monsters to kill. Dragons and ugly creatures are symbols of evil, and killing them is a way of showing how evil is overcome. Usually, to kill a dragon, the hero has to overcome his fear and show courage. Stories like this are usually about overcoming your own weakness to defeat evil.'

'They will try to kill Grendel and they will succeed. If there are any other evil magicians and monsters as well as Grendel they'll have to get them too, and they'll be tougher because in a story like that, the tasks get harder.'

To these young readers puzzles and enigmas are intellectually appealing challenges, sources of enjoyment in fiction rather than causes of boredom. With their understanding of many fictional conventions, they see order and design in different genres where less experienced readers see only random, unconnected incidents. Here a Year 8 girl is able to generalise about the pattern of detective fiction from her reading and enjoyment of Franklin Dixon and Carolyn Keene mysteries: 'At the end of every chapter something interesting happens. There are puzzles at the end of each chapter to arouse interest in the next. You can't put them down.' She is describing what Iser calls 'a controlled proliferation of blanks'[12] or gaps in the text. These blanks are sources of pleasure to those who know how to deal with them, as do the two Year 10 girls who made the following generalisations about their reading strategies.

'If you don't understand something you ask yourself why it is there. Some incidents don't seem to fit at first, but they do when you think about them. You don't understand until you read some more. A doctor committed suicide in *The Day of the Triffids* and you find out why later. These problems confuse you at first, but you realise you will probably understand it eventually.'

'Problems usually sort themselves out before the end of the book. In *To Kill a Mockingbird* I couldn't see the point of Boo Radley, how he fitted into the book's meanings. Towards the end you realise what he was there for. At the beginning he was just a frightening thing for children and at the end they realise he's just a well-meaning person. The children have to learn to put themselves into other people's shoes before they can make judgments of them. The story is about growing up and learning to be tolerant. Boo Radley is another kind of person in our society discriminated against, just like we discriminate against people of different religions and different colours to us. In Australia it's migrants and in American it's negroes. Boo Radley is discriminated against because he's not the same as everyone else.'

Another Year 10 girl, when read the opening section of *The Catcher in the Rye*, saw the title as an attractive puzzle or gap to be filled in while reading. It was her experience of similarly enigmatic titles of texts (her literary 'repertoire') that caused her to see it this way.

'The title doesn't mean much to me, but it certainly captures my interest. It might refer to something that happens in the story, or it's like *To Kill a Mockingbird*, full of meaning that ties together the main incidents. I don't know what it means now but I will when I read the book.'

A Year 8 boy who is a committed reader explained how he not only considered possible long term outcomes and modified his expectations in the act of reading, but systematically considered changes that occurred in stories by comparing the ending with the beginning. This enabled him to identify thematically important elements of texts.

'At the beginning I like to think what's going to happen towards the end, what changes might take place, and what things are going to be the same. You want to know if the characters will solve their problems, if they will continue to make the same mistakes, or if they will learn from them, and what all this shows about them as people. At the end I like to compare events with the beginning and think about what's changed and why.'

Again, the reflexive understanding promoted by the interview questions showed how easy it would be to help readers at this level to move to the next level. Many of the students said at the end of the interview that they looked forward to reading their next novel as they thought they would read and enjoy it better because of their new consciousness of the their own reading processes. That next novel was going to be, they said, *Trillions, Dragonslayer, Kes, The Day of the Triffids* or *The Catcher in the Rye.* The opening of Robert Westall's *The Wind-Eye* was not so appealing to these readers. Most of those I read it to were disturbed by the open hostility of one parent towards the other and the apparently resigned attitude of the children. They had little in their literary repertoires to draw on to help them to make an imaginative entry in to this text. (Perhaps, for some, the situation was all too close to personal experience.) The implication is that teachers need to introduce novels with unappealing beginnings by starting somewhere else, perhaps with an incident that arouses real curiosity while not threatening readers' emotional security. For example, with *The Wind-Eye,* an appropriate introductory section to read to a group would be where quarrelsome Madeleine, the step-mother, insensitively tramples on St. Cuthbert's tomb at Durham Cathedral, an incident with clearly ominous overtones, and the beginning of an enthralling mystery about the influence of the past on the present.

## STAGE FIVE: REVIEWING THE WHOLE WORK AS A CONSTRUCT

It was very clear from the attitudes and responses of many students that they see fictional works either as transcripts of reality, records of events which would be reported in much the same way by any author, or as invented tales embodying the accepted moral values and agreed wisdom of the community that produced them. In this view, there is little understanding of the individual writer's role as artificer or pattern-maker, communicating a personal (and often subversive) interpretation of the human condition and, as Harding puts it, 'offering his own values and preconceptions for acceptance or rejection.'[13] Such students, therefore, see the roles their teachers invite them to adopt as readers as being to accept unquestioningly the values and attitudes of authors rather than to match authors' representations of the world with their own, continually questioning their own and authors' values.

Very few readers in the Bathurst research reached the level of considering literature as the creation of idiosyncratic and fallible human beings, although some showed they had glimmerings of this knowledge without real understanding of its implications. Most of this section is, therefore, taken up with a detailed report of a more sustained interview with one of the few students whose responses reached this level. However, before proceeding to that, I think it is important to record some of the glimmerings of others as they are indications that the students who had them were ready to progress to this stage and could easily have been helped to do so.

Several students spoke of their irritation with the clichés of some of the genres of fiction they had encountered, and in so doing showed they were aware of weaknesses in the making of books they had grown out of.

'The teenage romances I've read all end up the same way. The girl gets the boy or, from the boy's point of view, the boy gets the girl. If it begins with a girl saying to herself, "I've loved Joe for so long", you know she'll get him in the end, or someone better. If they were more true to life and had a more varied story line I'd like them better.'

'In Science Fiction I get sick of phrases you've seen dozens of times before, like, "He blended into the shadows, the dark one among them". These writers seem to write to a formula. *The Hitchhiker's Guide to the Galaxy* sends those clichés up.'

Other students made perceptive generalisations about the value of fiction, in the midst of more commonplace comments about specific books.

'Good books are different. They are unpredictable. They look at unusual topics or ordinary things in unusual ways. They help you to think about things you take for granted, by letting you see ordinary things in ways you haven't thought about before.'

The above comment was made by a Year 10 girl in talking about *The Day of the Triffids* which she said influenced her view of the world. In the comment below she shows she also understands Iser's point that literature enables us to better understand our social and historical 'norms'.

'Books are about ideas and beliefs and they can help you sort out your own. *To Kill a Mockingbird* helped me to understand why I felt unhappy about some of the things that happened when I lived in [Greenville]. I thought about [Greenville] as having the same small town mentality.'

(Year 10 girl)

'The author shows his feelings about the world from his experience. The author's views dictate what happens. The important thing is not just what characters do but what the author tries to show about people by what he has them do. You're thinking about what you read in the book. Your view might be the same as the author's, but it may be the opposite.'

(Year 8 boy)

This Year 8 boy is not far from understanding one of Harding's arguments for the value of literature: 'The reader must make his own value decisions, but he makes them in the light of a much richer consideration of human possibilities than one lifetime's experience in his contemporary group could have given him.'[14]

A Year 8 girl explains how the emotional distance between herself and a character is often a function of the narrative mode of the story, but she was unable to go further to consider authors' purposes in choosing their narrative modes. Her comments are in response to the question, 'Where do you feel you are in relation to the characters?'

'It depends on the book. If my favourite character is writing herself [first person narrative], it's like I'm involved and close to her. If she's the one writing the book you agree with her, but if it's in the third person you know how everyone feels. If she's written it herself you sympathise more with her, but you don't know so much about what others are thinking.'

In response to the strategy question about the implied author asked of his reading of *To Kill a Mockingbird*, a Year 10 boy showed greater understanding than most other students of the author as one who offers readers his representation and evaluation of the world. Again, it must be pointed out that the question itself prompted this reflection on an issue which the boy acknowledged he had never considered before.

'What would the author have been like? What does the book show about the author? I've never thought about it. But you still have an idea, don't you, even though you've never thought about it much? It's something you know. Harper Lee may have had that kind of father [like Atticus, the lawyer], and then he's written about his own way of life through the eyes of another person — a young and unprejudiced person — Scout [Atticus's daughter]. He feels that prejudice is an unjustified emotion. People who are prejudiced are evil. He has an egalitarian view that people are the same regardless of their colour. A work of fiction conveys the writer's views of life or some aspect of it. My feelings are pretty well the same as the author's feelings. He's making me feel what he feels is the truth.'

Those readers who had read a number of works by the one author, or who had a wider literary repertoire to draw on, were more able than others to entertain the idea of texts as constructs of authors who had individual attitudes, interests and styles. For example, a Year 8 girl to whom I read the beginning of *The Cartoonist* proceeded to make connections between it and a number of other Betsy Byars novels she had read, before drawing some conclusions about Betsy Byars' concerns as a novelist.

'The mother reminds me of the mum in *The TV Kid*, only it was the opposite here. Alfie [*The Cartoonist*] doesn't want to watch TV and the TV Kid wanted to watch it all the time. In *The Eighteenth Emergency* the mother there was the opposite again. She ignored her son all the time. Mouse's mum [*The Eighteenth Emergency*] ignores him while these mums are on the kids' backs all the time. Betsy Byars is giving you in her books pictures of the way different sorts of mothers annoy their kids by not understanding them and by not wanting to understand them.'

## One Interview In Detail

The interview with Colin[15], a perceptive and highly committed 14 year-old reader, took place in 1978 and was, therefore, entirely taken up with the questions of Profile 1, designed to identify developmental stages in terms of psychological processes and satisfactions. However, in his answers to these questions, Colin had important things to say about reading strategies, and so the analysis of the transcript which follows includes commentary about both strategies and stages. Even though no opening sections of unfamiliar texts were read to him to test his reading strategies in action, it is easy to identify the strategies he uses from his detailed responses to the questions asked about process stages.

The experience of the 1978 interviews made it clear to me that it was impossible to formulate questions that would produce answers confined to the processes and satisfactions of each level separately. For example, questions designed to explore Colin's analogising processes elicited responses that went far beyong analogising, and so on. Because of this, no attempt has been made to reorganise Colin's comments in an ascending order of abstraction or complexity of response; they are presented simply in the order they occurred in the interview in reply to the questions asked. Interpretative commentary is printed in italics, as are the questions.

Q. 1. *While you are reading, do you imagine yourself being with a character or characters?*

I try to put myself in everyone's place, to see the point of view from every character's side. It gives you a clearer picture of what they're doing various things for, why they're doing what they're doing. I try to look at the claims of other characters, apart from the one the writer is trying to make you sympathise with. I don't like books in which the authors try to show a character as flawless-like. It's fun to try to discredit the hero because you are trying to beat the author in a way. Not always [do I do this], like when you're lazy you read the whole story through and accept it as the writer puts it down without thinking much about what it means. *That is, he suggests that a lazy reader is one who accepts all he reads without reflecting on its significance, one who misses the implications and focuses on events only to find out what happens next without thinking about why it happens, what*

*that reveals of the characters' motivations and what
interpretation of the world the author is offering.*

If it is a good writer he does win you over to sympathy
for one character.

*He then goes on to analyse C.S. Lewis in terms of what he
sees as the too obvious didacticism of the Narnia books.
Between the ages of eight and eleven the Narnia books had
had a compelling attraction for him and he read all of them
three or four times. Now at age 14 he is able to make
generalisations about the lack of space (few gaps) left in these
books for more mature readers to participate in the creation
of their meaning.*

For example, in C.S. Lewis, his Narnia books are good for
young readers because of the happy endings, but he leaves
out rational analysis of the characters. Edmund does bad
things in *The Lion, the Witch and the Wardrobe* but he always
makes up for them by rescuing people out of the clutches of
evil and becomes completely good. Eustace in *The Voyage
of the Dawn Treader* is *all* bad and then he becomes *all* good.
It is not believable. He's too bad and then too good. C.S.
Lewis is saying to you, "This kid is bad but if he learns to
be good, that is good in the way I think — Christian values — he
will become all good and never do any more bad things."

*Colin's suggestion that C.S. Lewis is guilty of superficiality
in his exploration of characters' actions and motivations is
quite sophisticated, but it shows he does not fully understand
the conventions of allegorical and epic literature and their
differences from the conventions of realistic literature.
However, he certainly shows that he sees the whole work as
an author's creation, and there is an explicit recognition of
the implied author and of the relationship between the implied
author and the implied reader. At age 14 he also identifies
the ideology of the Narnia books, and thus refuses to become
their implied reader, whereas at age eleven he was happy to
accept that role.*

I like Tolkien because a lot of the people you expect to be
heroes die by a not very honourable death; the one you expect
to be the hero, after defeating evil, dies young and doesn't
come to fame. It is more believable because there are no simple
material rewards for the heroes, and others who don't deserve
the big rewards, who played small parts in the triumph of

good, they become the famous ones, they get the reputation undeservedly — not with the writer, but with the common village people in the novel — and this is the way life is.

*He doesn't mean that those who played small parts in the triumph of good earn their reputation undeservedly as much as that they gain a reputation out of all proportion to their contribution. He is pointing out that in real life a perfect system of poetic justice does not operate and that Tolkien communicates his awareness of this to the reader.*

C.S. Lewis is too obviously directing your sympathies about what you should admire.

In *The Eagle of the Ninth* you feel critical of Marcus when he breaks into the northern tribe's religious centre to steal his father's eagle back. He was invited as a guest to that tribe and then he deliberately completely betrays them by taking their god. We can see Marcus's point of view and we sympathise with it, but we can also see the point of view of the Barbarians. Marcus's point of view is not the only one, we can see both points of view. Rosemary Sutcliff is a good writer because she keeps the options open, she makes you see all view points and life is complex like this. If you end up sympathising more with Marcus than the Barbarians, it is not just because he's *all* right and they are *all* wrong. You learn more about human behaviour from Rosemary Sutcliff than from C.S. Lewis. She is a more powerful writer than C.S. Lewis.

*Again, he shows he is unaware that C.S. Lewis and Rosemary Sutcliff are working with different conventions, but he recognises the omnipotent author, just as he fills in gaps in the text to evaluate characters from a distance.*

*Q. 2. Where do you feel you are in relation to the characters? Are you in the story yourself, in there with the characters, or are you on the outside looking in, a sort of unseen spectator?*
It is different for different books and different writers. Yes, you are an unseen spectator. The writers tell you things that the person living out the events doesn't know. You feel you're in that place with the characters but you know more than they do so you are sympathetic too, looking on. In *The Hobbit*, you feel you're in there with Bilbo Baggins, because he's not the hero, or I mean being a hero isn't easy for him, and he's

really trying and you like him. In *The Hobbit*, you don't sympathise with Gollum because you see things through the eyes of Bilbo Baggins, but in *Lord of the Rings*, you can sympathise with Gollum because you learn more about him and the more you learn the more you understand his problem and sympathise with him. You learn he's a kind of victim of the ring — the ring possesses you, it causes your mind to deteriorate, it takes you over, and that part of the novel is written from Gollum's point of view — you are being told why he is like that, Tolkien's explaining it and you can understand him [Gollum].

*Here he explains the way a good reader, as onlooker or spectator, is, in the act of reading, both emotionally involved and coolly detached, empathising with characters and reflectively evaluating their behaviour at the same time. His description of the reader's position (Iser's 'wandering' or 'moving viewpoint') as a continual shifting between being inside the story (lost in the book) and standing back to evaluate characters and the author's values and methods, shows how both activities are important in a developing response.*

Q. 5. *Do you imagine yourself as being with the writer, feel you're helping him write the book, deciding what characters might do next, how they should end up, how they should be feeling?*
No. I don't feel I am helping the writer write the book, I leave it to the author. My explanation [*if he were the manipulator of the plot*] would be too simple. I try to understand the characters and the events as the author presents them. That question [question 5] implies that the reader would want to change the story and I'd rather sit it out, following the events and trying to understand what the author has presented and what he is getting at.

It [*reading books*] often gives me ideas for writing stories, though.
*Here he acknowledges the debt he owes to authors in influencing his own writing, making the important pedagogical point that access to the rhetoric of fiction can empower young readers linguistically. Becoming a better reader can mean becoming a better writer, and vice versa.*

You might . . . something happens in the story and you feel it might have happened differently. After you have finished reading you think, if some of the early events had been slightly different the whole outcome would have been different. After you have finished the whole book, you think of these things and you think of writing stories of your own. That doctor in *Dr Who* says, "There are many corridors in time which the actual event could take and every time you have to make a decision you could take a different path". It is sort of like being in a forest and there are many directions you can go and the characters have to choose one. The same event would not happen twice out of the same circumstances because the character might choose a different path on a different occasion. There are many avenues, and the avenue the character chooses, he chooses without a full understanding of the implications of his choice. The reader sees this but the character is usually not in a position to know it, and even if he did have the knowledge his feelings at the time might make him choose not rationally.

*This is very similar to Iser's account of the reading process as a 'moving viewpoint', involving 'a continual interplay between modified expectations and transformed memory'.*[16] *At each reading moment, the reader is modifying expectations about what might happen ahead in the long and short term, and reinterpreting what has gone before, all in the light of the textual information being processed in the present. Here, Colin sees the way the reader and the author share a game of the imagination that places both of them above the characters.*

Q. 6. *Do you like happy endings? Such as? Why?*

Most of the books I have read haven't had a perfect happy ending. The main impression might be happy, but minor details don't turn out right. The predominantly happy ending is achieved only at some cost, and this is like life. When something is gained something is always lost. Ursula Le Guin sums it up [in *The Wizard of Earthsea*] "when you make a spell you must sum up the repercussions because you affect the balance". For example, if you make rain to end a drought in your area you take it away from somewhere else. In that television programme on China [*The Long Search*, episode on Chinese religion] they call it Yin and Yang, the balance. In China, like in Ursula Le Guin, the equilibrium is all important. If you defeat evil in Tolkien, there must be some loss as well as big gains.

*Here he focuses upon the tragic impression of waste and*

destruction involved in the restoration of order. *He shows he would understand the pattern of a Shakespearean tragedy.*

Life is really a matter of achieving balance. In *A Wizard of Earthsea*, Ged made a shadow out of spite, he brought up a shadow from the dead to prove himself cleverer than Jasper. He did this out of pride without understanding what would happen. Until he realised the evil he was looking for was himself and named it with his name, he was lost. He dealt in matters he didn't understand, out of pride. He created evil or the possibility of evil on earth because of weakness in himself, and he then had to restore the balance in himself. The evil he did could not be fully overcome because the Archmage [Nemmerle] died in saving Ged. You really have to think about her novels. There are things you don't understand that you have to think about, but even while you're not understanding you have a feeling that what she is saying is true, and right, and not simple. In C.S. Lewis the meanings are all easy and he's too obviously telling you, guiding your thinking too much.

Q. 7. *Do you get any pleasure out of reading? (a) Refer to favourite books on list; (b) Which sections of which books did you enjoy most? Why?*

Yes, of course, but sometimes you have trouble in school assignments. In lots of book reviews you're told to find the climax of the story, but that is very difficult, because although there might be one place where it all fits together, you have to consider all the events to understand. The whole book is one unit, not separatable parts and sometimes you're expected to divide it up.

*Here he focuses on school assignments which, in providing a framework designed to help pupils' understanding, often lead to over-simplification and fragmentation in response and interpretation. He shows that he is aware of the problem inherent in piecemeal analysis of literature. He recognises that a work of literature invites a response to the work as a whole.*

Q. 8. *Do you ever read books which you find difficult to understand in some ways?*

Q. 9. *Which books for example?*

Q.10. *What did you find difficult to understand?*

The Owl Service you had to think a lot about and *I Am The*

*Cheese.* I like those books with a trick in them. In *The Owl Service,* you have to see for yourself how the Welsh legend works out in the lives of the people living now. The other boy [that is, Roger as opposed to Gwyn, the protagonist] changed the legend by coming in to help, to rescue her [Alison], when his [Roger's] counterpart in the legend and in the other stories of the legend didn't intervene to change how the legend worked out, didn't show love or compassion, let the evil work itself out. This other boy [Roger] really saw the owls as flowers whereas earlier characters saw them as claws or feathers — he saw the good side where his predecessors only saw the bad. *There is no question of Colin's ability to fill in large gaps in the text to make complex connections between textual events. He sees puzzles as sources of intellectual pleasure in reading.*

Q.11. *Did you finish the book(s)? Did you still manage to enjoy it (them) despite the difficulties of understanding?*

Q.12. *Why, do you think, did you enjoy them despite the difficulties?* Yes. I enjoyed them more, because once you worked out what was happening, everything hung together so much better. You see what the writer is getting at. The difficulties are only there because the meanings are deeper and these books are more interesting.

Q.13. *In reading a novel, do you ever feel you would like to be in the action, helping the character, for example, or living at the time of the book? Why?* Just for curiosity's sake it would be nice to be living at the time of the book. You would like to see what the time was like, what it was like to live in that era. But not to help the character — that would ruin the story. The author is not likely to destroy the character meaninglessly. It is not for me to interfere in what the writer is presenting. He's got his meanings about his view of life, and I want to know what his view and his meanings are. My wishes and hopes and interference might wreck the deepness of these meanings and I want to find out what they are. If I wanted a character to do something that would make things better for him I wouldn't find out why the author had him do something different. What the author has him do is part of the meaning you're trying to get at. You have to ask yourself why the author had him do this instead of that.

220

*Colin asks very productive questions of the text which he consciously treats as an author's construct.*

Q.16. *Do you feel pleased or irritated with (i.e., judge) the characters' actions and feelings while you are reading?*
Yes, I do. You understand his behaviour better than he does. I don't want him to be perfect. I accept his errors. He mightn't know his errors are errors, but you as reader are cooler and much better able to understand.
*Colin seems to understand the difference between the position of the protagonist as a 'participant' in life and the position of the reader as 'onlooker' in Harding's terms. However, he not only evaluates characters with some detachment, but recognises the author-reader relationship which gives the reader his or her 'onlooker' role.*

Q.19. *Do you think you have learned anything more about yourself from your reading of a book, something you didn't know or hadn't thought of before you read the book(s)? What? How?*
Yes, you learn about the possibilities of life. You realise you could do what characters have done, and reading the book doesn't mean you won't do silly things any more, for example, do something in a temper that you shouldn't do, but reading books helps you to understand your own behaviour, because although you might say that a character in a book is doing the wrong thing, endangering his life in doing something when he is angry, you know you do these things too and you realise you aren't unique. Everyone has these feelings too.
*He focuses on two issues here: 1. how reading helps us to 'transcend our own egocentricity' (John Dixon)—we share our humanity, our emotions and our weaknesses with other people—this is the comforting dimension; and 2. the recognition that knowledge and understanding don't necessarily lead to altruistic action, but that reading helps us to reflect more coolly on deeply felt past experiences in our own lives, and to understand our own actions in retrospect.*

Q.20. *Has any book ever influenced what you believe in, what you think is right, and true? What? How? Examples.*
No, I don't think so. Actually, what I think is right and true might influence the way I read the book.
*Here is a half formed recognition that we interpret literature and experience in terms of the representation of life we bring*

to them. *He recognises that we bring prejudices to our interpretation of literature that might in fact distort what the writer is trying to communicate.*

I suppose what I read helps me to understand things better. In Ursula Le Guin [*A Wizard of Earthsea*] what happened didn't contradict what I already believed to be right and true, but it raised things I hadn't thought of. For example, it prompted things you hadn't thought of, like the idea of disturbing the balance. That is a way of explaining that made sense to me. Books extend your understanding more than they alter it.

*Here he shows that reading a book and coming to understand its meanings might give him a deeper awareness of aspects of life that he had only before understood in a vague and relatively abstract way. He also seems aware that a fiction writer communicates ideas more powerfully because abstractions are embodied in concrete imagings of life.*

In *I Am The Cheese* [Robert Cormier] the idea that government agencies could be so corrupt — I had thought of it, but not to the great powerful extent the book shows it. It made me *feel* that idea.

*Here again is the idea that we know something abstractly but that it has no real impact on us until we feel the emotions associated with its working out in concrete fictions.*

Q.21. *Is there anything apart from the story-line that interests you in a book? What? Examples.*

Yes, the ideas behind the events, understanding the book's interpretation of life and how it alters your understanding. *This comment summarises the arguments of all his previous answers. He explains how reading fiction can extend one's representation of the world through what Piaget calls the processes of assimilation (primarily) and accommodation (less pronounced).*

Q.23 *Do you ever reject a book because of the way it is written, even when you find the subject interesting? Examples.*

C. No, I always finish them, then I judge. I hold judgment to the end because you might reject a book before you have given the writer a chance to make clear what seems confusing. *Again the idea that response to literature is a response to the total work and not a matter of piecemeal contextualisation.*

Q.24 *Do you ever respond to a book by saying to yourself about the author such things as, 'Yes, he's right there. That's true', or 'No, that couldn't happen, it's unbelievable'?*
*Give examples.*

C.     Yes, I do, particularly the unbelievable, C.S. Lewis.

*As a 14 year-old, he looks back on his favourite author of some years before and sees the Narnia books as too obviously contrived, too apparently manipulated. He has become conscious of the methods of authors in their organisation and structuring of fiction. His response to Ursula Le Guin indicates that he does say things like 'yes, the author's right there', as is clear in his account of the idea of balance in A Wizard of Earthsea.*

Q.25 *Do you think your reading as a whole has helped you to understand yourself/other people/the world any better? Could you explain this?*

C.     Yes, that people and life are not so simple. What a person does is caused by many complex things. The same event . . . people will react to differently, and the same person will react differently to similar things on different occasions. People are not like numbers in mathematics which produce the same answers . . . numbers don't change but people are unpredictable. They have moods and feelings.

*Here again is the recognition of human diversity and the need for sympathetic understanding preceding judgement.*

Colin's responses in the interview show that he has reached Stage 5. He recognises that fiction is an artefact, a social convention by means of which authors present evaluations of human experience. Colin's high level of response emanates from the 'developed and subtle' degree of sophistication of his responses at earlier levels, and from the intensity of his interest at Harding's basic stages of 'attending willingly' and 'elementary perception and comprehension'. Colin has cultivated the reading habit. Because in his experience reading is associated with enjoyment, he does read ('attends willingly') and the more he reads the more competent and confident a reader he becomes ('perception and comprehension') and the more he looks, in order to satisfy his curiosity, to increasingly profound and challenging books, making more complex statements about the human condition. He has developed a genuine critical sense because of the amount and quality of the reading he has done.

Most literature teaching in schools operates at the levels of 'distanced evaluation' and 'reviewing the whole work as the author's creation'. Introducing the categories of literary criticism too early, before students have committed themselves to reading at the elementary stages, is like asking them to arrive without having travelled. Only a few of the students interviewed in the Bathurst survey are at the stage of being able to match their representation of the world with that offered by an author. If literature is to extend a young reader's understanding of himself, of other people and of the human condition — and these are the values we claim for literature in our teaching — Harding's 'detached evaluative response' would seem to be essential. However, for a reader to reach, for example, the stage of 'analogising and searching for self-identity', of being able to connect his own first-order experience to the second-order experience offered for his contemplation so that the processes of assimilation and accommodation might begin to take place in relation to his value system, the more basic stages must be achieved at a high level of commitment or in 'developed form'.

The interview was a valuable learning experience for Colin, just as it was for all the other students. He, too, saw it, retrospectively, as an exploration and discovery of his own reading processes. He said that in making his own satisfactions and strategies explicit to the interviewer he made them clear to himself. He came to recognise this reflexive understanding as a form of personal power.

## STAGE SIX: CONSCIOUSLY CONSIDERED RELATIONSHIP WITH THE AUTHOR, RECOGNITION OF TEXTUAL IDEOLOGY, AND UNDERSTANDING OF SELF (IDENTITY THEME) AND OF ONE'S OWN READING PROCESSES

The reading activities and satisfactions of Stage 6 are logical developments from the attainment of Stage 5. If it is understood that the literary work is a construct, then it would seem logical for readers to consider both the implications of its constructedness and the significance for them personally of their own ways of interpreting it. Perhaps it would be more appropriate to describe what I have called Stage 6 activity as constituting an overdrive of top gear (Stage 5) rather than as an additional and higher gear (or Stage) in its own right.

As has been pointed out several times, many readers gained some reflexive understanding of their own reading processes from the interview questions and situation. This comment from a Year 10 girl shows an exceptional degree of understanding which obviously preceded the interview, but she said it had never been previously acknowledged by anyone she discussed her reading with as being of any significance: 'The characters in a novel are inside my head. Everything that takes place in the book takes place in my mind. I produce the meanings in my head like a director of a play.'

While this girl showed she was reading at Stage 5 in commenting sensitively about the works of authors such as D.H. Lawrence and John Fowles, both of whom she had read widely, she did not go on to consider what her own responses revealed to her about herself as a person (her 'identity theme'). Like many of the other readers, she learned something about herself through analogising — recognising aspects of her own behaviour and her strengths and weaknesses in the behaviour of characters in books she read — but she did not reflect on her own interpretations of texts in relation to other people's interpretations and thus become more conscious of her own characteristic ways of coping with the world.

Similarly, the closest any of the student readers came to considering the ideology of texts was Colin in his comments on C.S. Lewis's didacticism in the Narnia books, and Colin's remarks belong to the world of orthodox New Critical evaluative analysis of authors' artistic achievements. He does not identify the ideology of the Narnia books in order to explore some of the processes of value transmission through literature; he is making an aesthetic, not a political judgment, and he does so because aesthetic judgments are valued more highly than political judgments in the world of his literary education.

The reason no students consistently engaged in the activities of this level is that there is no systematic discussion of such activities in the schools. New Criticism is the literary theory enshrined in secondary education. Reader-response theories have, as yet, little institutional power, but, as we have seen, they have much to offer and deserve to have a place in the curriculum. I think the report of the interviews demonstrates that the Stage 6 satisfactions of reading can be taught to those who are ready for them, and that one of them, reflexive understanding of one's own reading processes, can and should be taught at every Stage because it is a powerful and liberating form of knowledge that each reader needs and deserves to possess. Inviting students to write down in their journals what happened in their heads while they were reading a novel or a poem recently enjoyed is one way of getting them to develop this reflexiveness. For example, here is a 14-year-old's retrospective reflection on his own activity while reading *The Catcher in the Rye*:

'The novel that I have enjoyed most in my life has been *The Catcher in the Rye*. Whilst I read the book I began to identify and associate with the central character, Holden Caulfield. I placed myself within the book and began to live out every moment of it, as if I was Holden.

'Right from the very first page I began to visualise the different scenes and situations in the book with myself as the person that they were affecting and relating to. In my mind, I actually became Holden Caulfield, and acquired his views, his outlooks on life and his problems.

'When Holden began his journey of discovery I felt that I travelled it with him experiencing all the events as vividly as he did. I shared his sense of humour and found the same events amusing just as he did. Because I was able to identify with Holden so personally I was able to understand his motives and his goal. I felt that I knew his family and shared his liking for his sister, Phoebe.

'Whilst I read the book my mind was able to analyse and identify with the book, and particularly Holden. I associated myself with Holden and shared his feelings and emotions. Because the book and particularly the character of Holden was so effective my mind was able to identify with all the aims and desires in the book, and I felt for actually a while, that I was Holden.'[17]

The next stage in developing this boy's understanding of his own identity could be to invite him to consider and make explicit why he thinks he was so sympathetic towards Holden Caulfield, and what this and his other written interpretations show him about himself. Also, he could be asked to jot down his ideas about the way his mind processes text, and then to discuss with his teacher the implications of what he has discovered in the act of writing about it.

Here is what a 14-year-old girl wrote in response to her teacher's invitation to do just this after she had read a novel called *Beautiful Girl*.

226

'When reading the book I find myself looking in at whats happening but not seen, not heard by any of the characters. I don't take part in any of the events but I see them happening.

'Sometimes in the book things did not happen as I thought they might and I would stop reacting for a while and imagine something else, though I didn't get carried away.

'When I came to a boring part in the book occasionally I would skip a few lines but not too many as to lose what's happening.

'Not very often I would drift away from the book thinking of something else but still reading the sentences, then I would have to read it again (this only happened when I was tired or excited about something).

'When I read I can hear a voice inside talking, but I try to refrain from this as it makes you read slower.

'Occasionally I would come to an exciting part and I find I could not read quick enough to find out what happens.

'Before reading *Beautiful Girl*, I had to read the review to find out what it was about but I think it spoiled it and I found myself reading through the book looking for the things explained in the review.

'Overall I enjoyed reading the book but the books that I don't like are books that don't relate to me.'[18]

In the subsequent discussion the teacher asked the girl to consider the implications of her statements here for herself as a reader. Issues that were considered included the meaning of boredom, generating expectations about what might happen in the long and short term, the identity of the 'voice inside' — whether it is from the text or an outside distraction — and what we mean when we say books do or don't relate to us personally.

## MORE SUCCESSFUL AND LESS SUCCESSFUL READERS

Poor readers can't make the book mean: no voices speak to them, no meanings match in with the meanings they already possess; and even good readers have this difficulty at times, with some books

Mike Torbe, 'What Reading
Does to Readers.'[19]

He still sees reading as something that will happen to him rather than a process he has to take to further his own intentions.

Margaret Meek, *Achieving Literacy*

The confusion or puzzlement that all good readers necessarily experience, at least temporarily, in interpreting literature they enjoy is assumed by poor readers to be an indication of their own incompetence rather than a challenge or spur to their own mental activity. Unsuccessful readers have not learned that authors play with readers' expectations, deliberately withholding information to stimulate speculation, reflection, deduction and gap-filling.

As we have seen, readers at the early developmental levels of response can tolerate very little textual indeterminacy. They expect meanings to come to them automatically rather than to emerge from active mental questioning. The action-oriented readers of Stage One, for example, do show considerable interest in what might happen next (in the short term), but not in possible long term outcomes or the significance of ongoing events, behaviour or outcomes. Roland Barthes would describe them as 'readerly' readers who focus entirely on the surface narrative of a text, thus passively 'consuming' it. On the other hand, 'writerly' readers are those who read from the writer's point of view, rigorously interrogating the text and thus actively 'producing' it. In Barthes' terms, readerly readers stay on the proairetic level, while writerly readers operate hermeneutically as well. What is important, however, as the interviews show, is that hermeneutic activities such as speculating, filling in textual gaps and generating and modifying expectations during the process of reading are teachable. It is not that poorer readers are intellectually incapable of performing productive strategies but that they have not learned many of the conventions of reading because of the limited reading they have done, a situation which is itself often a product of their lack of satisfaction in the texts given them to read in school. Also, they have rarely had the constructive strategies they do possess endorsed by their teachers.

In both written questionnaire and interview, many of the unsuccessful readers told of unpleasant memories of early failures in mastering reading, emanating from infants' and primary school teachers' attempts to teach reading skills in isolation from meaning and enjoyment. Literary competence, as Margaret Spencer has pointed out, is not acquired from reading phonics-based readers but from real stories.[20] This early schooling experience convinced these students that they were incapable of becoming competent in an activity they didn't like anyway, and subsequent school experience has merely strengthened their conviction. We have seen how even a very successful reader like Colin hammers the inanity of some of the routine school assignments on literature, and many other students do too:

> 'What turned me off was all the work we had to do on it. We had to summarise every chapter and do vocabulary work, which didn't help you understand the story better but made you lose track of it. We spent more time writing about it than reading it. It killed the suspense, because you had to summarise or answer questions on a chapter before you read the next one.'

There were many instances cited of school exercises turning students off books they might otherwise have enjoyed. On the other hand, there were some students for whom the class text provided their first experience of pleasure in reading, but unfortunately, in many of these cases, students were not told of other books by the same author or on similar subjects or themes they might also have enjoyed if they had discovered them. 'The Legions of the Eagle [Henry Treece] was the best book I have ever read. I would like to read more like that, but I haven't come across any.'

Another cause of many students' sense of alienation from both literature and school approaches to it was their conviction that a gulf existed between their personal thoughts and feelings about texts, and what they believed their teachers valued as response and expected from them. They believed that their teachers disvalued the personal and emotional in favour of a detached, aesthetic response. However true this general characterisation of teacherly preference is, the important point is that many students believed it to be true. In this context, the following findings and tentative conclusions drawn from the research are significant:

1. When the experience of reading is enjoyable, students read voraciously.
2. The more students read, the more confident and competent they become as readers, and the more they look for satisfaction to increasingly complex books making more profound statements about the human condition.
3. The more students enjoy reading, the more curious they get about

how books work and, conversely, the more they come to know about how books work, then the more enjoyment they get. As J.R. Squire found back in 1964, readers who become emotionally involved in a story are likely to become interested in analysing the elements within it that aroused their feelings.[21] A genuine critical sense easily develops out of the increasing amount and complexity of reading experienced, so that it is not difficult to teach those who read with commitment how to reach higher levels of satisfaction and response. The track from Margaret Early's 'unconscious enjoyment' to 'conscious delight' is not a difficult one to follow. The real problem is that too many students never find where the track starts.

4. When literature teaching operates *only* at the high level of distanced evaluation or the detachment of viewing the whole work as an author's creation, when the categories and abstractions of literary criticism are introduced too early, then we are expecting students to arrive without having travelled. The travelling — the process required for reaching distanced evaluation and conscious delight — necessitates students' experiencing simple enjoyment in understanding and empathising with characters.

One powerful enemy to the development of conscious delight in reading is the public examination system — the whole nauseating business of assessing students' competence and future career prospects on the basis of hurriedly written first draft finished products. The influence of the Higher School Certificate papers seems to filter down through all the years of secondary schooling pretty often. The methods we have so far evolved for assessing response to literature seem to succeed only in inhibiting it. Let us not kid ourselves that students swotting up critical information about texts for the examination are really deepening or strengthening their enjoyment of literature. What most of them are really strengthening is their resolve never to read any of the other works of the set authors.

## SOME IMPLICATIONS

Perhaps only poetry had the strength to rival the attractions of narcotics, the magnetism of TV, the excitement of sex, or the ecstasies of destruction.

Albert Corde, in Saul Bellow's
novel, *The Dean's December*

What happened in the student interviews suggests the need for a change in the role of the teacher. As reading is highly active and as response is idiosyncratic, personal, felt responses cannot be transmitted from teacher to pupil. Literary conventions are best learned by those who do a great deal of reading rather than by direct instruction, but teachers who understand developmental sequence and the strategies characteristic of each stage can create the most facilitating contexts in which genuine response can grow. They are the teachers who will know when to intervene to assist individual students and when to desist from intervention. They will not impose texts or interpretations on students, but neither will they leave the development of higher level strategies to chance. They will also recognise most clearly that the readers in any class are likely to be at different stages of development, and that each student will need individual consideration as well as frequent experience of working co-operatively with others on shared texts.[22] In other words, such teachers will know how to 'negotiate' the literature curriculum[23] with their students, both individually and as class wholes.

Teachers need to start where their students are, with their tastes in reading and attitudes towards it. As Jean Blunt points out, this might mean beginning with 'comics, magazines, supernatural tales and thrillers' as 'the seedbed for the germinating response'.[24] Those teachers who might want to resist such an approach need to consider the simple, practical logic of the fact that each pupil has to begin from his or her present store of experience, knowledge and interest because there is nowhere else she or he can possibly begin. We have seen how 14 year-old Colin's comments on C.S. Lewis's Narnia books and some novels of Rosemary Sutcliff, J.R.R. Tolkien and Ursula le Guin, suggest that he has progressed beyond the Narnia stage. However, without his earlier fascination with the Narnia world he may not have been able to enjoy so readily the more complex representations offered by Sutcliff, Tolkien and le Guin. His teacher's wide-reading recommendations to him at this stage of his development include K.M. Peyton's *Pennington* novels, *The Silmarillion* by Tolkien, *The Dispossessed* by Ursula le Guin, Golding's *Lord of the Flies*, Alan Garner's *Red Shift* and Homer's *The Iliad and the Odyssey*. Others in his class are finding considerable pleasure in reading works such as the Narnia books, Henry Treece's historical novels, Astrid Lindgren's *Pippi Longstockings* books, Mary Norton's *Borrowers* series and so on, all on the recommendation of a trusted teacher who is sensitively trying to match book and reader, with important consideration being given to each student's stage of development. While Colin enjoys the activities in class on shared texts, it would be counter-productive for the teacher to recommend to him books by authors such as Mary Norton and Henry Treece, at least for the major part of his wide reading, as he has quite clearly outgrown their challenge.

The interviews were productive in helping young readers to understand and value the constructive strategies they already possessed. Many students began to see themselves as potentially competent, active readers rather than as the failures their experience of schooling had convinced them they were. This suggests that the teacher can do a great deal to improve the skills of young readers by being supportive listeners to the interaction between reader and book. Geoff Fox describes this support to textual reflection offered by teachers who listen as 'making the space of the middle ground between reader and book more available to be filled in by the reader/talker'.[25] What the students enjoyed so much about being listened to in the interviews was being able to explore and explain their opinions, interpretations and self-understandings without having them judged for their critical merit. Fox explains:

> It seems that each reader must be assured of the importance of the unique response he or she makes to the text. For it is this response and a sense of its value which seem to be the growth points of a reading life.[26]

At the beginning of each interview the interviewer's intentions and motives were made explicit to each pupil. This approach gained the cooperation and interest of the students, most of whom responded immediately by asking probing questions about the value and use their ideas and reactions might have, and went on to express some surprise that they were to be seen in the role of experts informing an ignorant adult researcher. 'Coming clean' with students is a most educationally productive practice and a basic courtesy. Teachers should be concerned to make their purposes explicit to students in all areas of the curriculum. If students understand what it is that teachers expect them to get from reading a particular poem or novel or literature in general, and from writing, reflecting or performing in a particular way in response to it, they are in a position of some control over their own learning. They have enough information to investigate the teacher's values, to test them and, ultimately, to choose to accept, modify or reject them. They are in a position of being able to negotiate the curriculum and to take some responsibility for their own learning. In choosing to accept or reject teacherly propositions, they understand the basis of their choice and are thus not alienated by school as they necessarily are when they are confused and bewildered by never being involved in considering the purposes, uses and values of the curriculum.

Just as teachers are trained to evaluate their own lessons in retrospect, so students should be encouraged to evaluate their own learning. Active participation in reading and responding in various ways should be followed by reflective evaluation of what has been achieved from the reading and the associated classroom activities. Students should also be encouraged to reflect on what they have learned about themselves — their identities and reading processes. When the only evaluation of lessons is a teacher's reflections on her own teaching strategies; and when this evaluation is made on the basis of pupils' observed behaviour alone, and does not arise in any way from open discussion with them; and when the teaching methods, purposes and criteria for evaluation of student work are not made explicit; then students are in the position of being manipulated . It is crucial that students enjoy reading, but it is equally important that they reflect on the significance of what Louise Rosenblatt calls that 'lived-through experience'. As Bill Green puts it in a recent review article,

> What matters [as well as] the pleasure and experience of the literary work — the 'indwelling' of the reader in the experience of the text, . . . [is] reflection upon that lived-through experience as a necessary part of that whole process.[27]

Similarly important is that students come to understand the artificiality, or constructedness, of literature. Too often the emphasis in literature teaching is on texts as finished creative acts, and too rarely do we examine their origins and processes of creation. Many of the Bathurst students indicated in writing or in interview that they regarded much of the literature they experienced at school as awe-inspiringly remote from them. They saw texts as divinely inspired artefacts they were bidden to admire and 'appreciate', but far beyond their own powers of emulation. They had no notion that in telling their own anecdotes and writing their own stories from personal and imagined experience they were engaged in essentially the same creative 'spectator role' activity as published poets and novelists practise in their craft. Peter Abbs gives a very clear explanation of the debilitating effect the great artefacts approach to literature can have on students:

Of course, it is necesary to disseminate finished work and struggle for its elucidation and appreciation but we must be careful not to allow the formal architecture of the completed artefact to hide the chaos that may have attended its creation. I suspect that many children and students, half consciously measuring their own powers of thinking and articulating against 'the great work', the set piece, secretly conclude that their minds function at a completely different level; being messy, spasmodic, confused, idiosyncratic, they decide that their thinking/imagining/ remembering cannot be worth cultivating. It is as if the intellectual giants think in vast chapters, their interpreters in lucid paragraphs, the teachers in good sentences and the pupils in muddled fragments, dislocated phrases trailing into silence . . .

I think, as English teachers, we should draw attention to the nature of the creative process and to the fact that poems are not given like manna from the skies but are made in a concentrated response to what is given in experience or to what rises up from beneath experience. The cry 'only the best' is important but in this context it can give birth prematurely to a hyper-critical attitude and engender in the would-be-creator an impending sense of sterility. And this is unforgivable because it means that many never discover their own powers, never shape their most intimate reflections, never realize the particular rhythm of their own identity, but live solely submerged in the reflections and images of others.[28]

In *The Making of Literature*, Ian Reid attacks the model of teaching that views literature as a 'gallery' of artefacts to be observed and admired but not touched, argued with, tested against the reader's own experience, or imitated as forms of expression. Against the 'gallery' view of literature and literature teaching, Reid offers his preferred 'workshop' model:

In the Workshop . . . literature is directly linked with students' own creativity, because reading what someone else has written

234

and writing something oneself are both seen as activities of constructing significance. Reader and writer alike are meaning makers, and while not identical, the two roles are more closely akin than Gallery curators would have us believe: each is the other's dialectical partner.[29]

In Chapter Five, we look at some of the ways Reid's workshop model can be implemented in the classroom to empower students and to help them to grow psychologically, intellectually and socially.

## REFERENCES

1. in R.D. Walshe, Dot Jensen and Tony Moore (eds), *Teaching Literature*, Primary English Teaching Association and English Teachers Association of NSW, 1983.
2. in *English in Australia*, no. 60, June 1982.
3. D.W. Harding, 'The Role of the Onlooker', in Asher Cashdan (ed.), *Language in Education: A Source book*, Routledge and Kegan Paul and The Open University Press, London, 1972, pp. 240-244; Harding, 'Psychological Processes in the Reading of Fiction', *British Journal of Aesthetics*, 1962; and Harding, 'Considered Experience: The Invitation of the Novel', in *English in Education*, vol. 2, no. 1, Summer 1967.
4. Jean Blunt, 'Response to Reading — How Some Young Readers Describe the Process', *English in Education*, vol. 11, no. 3, Autumn 1977.
5. Geoff Fox, 'Dark Watchers: Young Readers and Their Fiction,' *English in Education*, vol. 13, no. 1, Spring 1979, p. 34.
6. Harding, 'Considered Experience: The Invitation of the Novel', p. 7.
7. Robert Protherough, *Developing Response to Fiction*, Open University Press, Milton Keynes, 1983, p. 41.
8. Harding, 'Psychological Processes in the Reading of Fiction'.
9. Ibid.
10. Harding, 'Considered Experience: The Invitation of the Novel,' p. 9.
11. Loc. cit.
12. Wolfgang Iser, *The Act of Reading*, Routledge and Kegan Paul, London, 1978, p. 191.

13. Harding, 'Considered Experience: The Invitation of the Novel', p. 14.
14. D.W. Harding, 'The Bond With the Author', in *The Use of English*, vol. 22, no. 4, Summer 1971, p. 319.
15. This transcript and part of the analysis of it appeared in *English in Education*, vol. 13, no. 3, Autumn 1979, as 'Response to Reading: The Process as Described by One Fourteen-Year-Old'.
16. Iser, *The Act of Reading*, p. 111.
17. I am indebted to Martin Gooding, Head of English at Knox Grammar School, for this piece of writing.
18. I am indebted to Helen Drewe, English Department, Canowindra High School (now at Lithgow High School), for this piece of writing.
19. in *English in Education*, vol. 10, no. 3, Autumn 1976.
20. Margaret Spencer, 'Children's Literature: Mainstream Text or Optional Extra?' in R.D. Eagleson (ed.), *English in the Eighties*, Australian Association for the Teaching of English, Adelaide, 1982.
21. J.R. Squire, *The Responses of Adolescents While Reading Four Short Stories*, NCET, Urbana, Illinois, 1964.
22. See Ian Reid, *The Making of Literature*, Australian Association for the Teaching of English, 1984; in Chapter 2, 'Learning Through Exchanges', Reid emphasises the value of 'intensive collaboration between students, guided but not cramped by teachers'.
23. See Garth Boomer, *Negotiating the Curriculum*, Ashton Scholastic 1982; and Boomer, 'Negotiation Re-visited', *Interpretations*, vol. 16, no. 2, November 1982.
24. Blunt, 'Response to Reading—How Some Young Readers Describe the Process', p. 46.
25. Geoff Fox in an address to an 'Invitational English Conference' conducted at Sydney University in July, 1981.
26. Fox, 'Dark Watchers: Young Readers and Their Fiction', p. 34.
27. Bill Green, 'Yes, but . . . A Single Impulse', review of *A Single Impulse: Developing Response to Literature*, Education Department of South Australia, 1983, in *English in Australia*, 68, June 1984, p. 65.
28. Peter Abbs, 'English Teaching: An Expressive Discipline', in *English in Education*, vol. 11, no. 3, Autumn 1977, pp. 50-51.
29. Reid, *The Making of Literature*, p. 25.

# 5  PRACTICE: EXAMPLES OF TEACHERS AT WORK

Why don't you read what I have written and make up your own
mind about what you think, testing it against your
own life, your own experience.

Doris Lessing, Preface to
*The Golden Notebook*

I cannot think for others or without others, nor can others think
for me. Even if the people's thinking is superstitious or naive, it
is only as they rethink their assumptions in action that they can
change. Producing and acting upon their own ideas — not
absorbing those of others — must constitute that progress.

Paulo Freire, *Pedagogy of
the Oppressed*

If the culture of the community is to enter the culture of the school,
its stories must come too and, more profoundly perhaps, its oral
story-telling traditions must become an acknowledged form of
making meaning.

Harold Rosen, *Stories and Meanings*,
NATE Papers in Education

Traditional New Critical approaches to the teaching of literature have
largely ignored the active role of the reader and the subjectivity of
response. Trying to explain to students how a poem works before
they have experienced its effects is a sterile pursuit. This discursive
analysis of the literary critic, which is an attempt to explain the
qualities of the text which account for the experience of reading it,
does not transmit that experience to others. We can successfully
explain how the parts of a poem interact to produce certain effects
only to those who have experienced them. The experience of
literature involves more than a distanced appreciation of its linguistic
felicities.

The emphasis on objectivity, critical detachment and discursive analysis in the teaching of literature has led to the apotheosis of the essay as the highest form of literary response. Harold Rosen mockingly describes the essay as the 'state of achieved perfection' of expository prose, which is unfortunately seen by many as 'nothing less than the greatest intellectual achievement of Western civilisation':

> It is cleansed of ideology, purged of concreteness and the encumbrances of context. It soars into the high intellectual realm because, so it is said, it is "decontextualised" (as if that could be said of any kind of discourse). It is so autonomous that, if you interrogate it, it will speak for itself: speech without the imprint of the speaker![1]

The role of the teacher is to create contexts in which students will experience literature in a powerfully felt way, and respond honestly and deeply; contexts in which students of all reading levels will use productive strategies habitually and consciously, so that they might further develop these strategies and progress to the next level of satisfaction and achievement. I have found that teachers readily understand the limitations of traditional methods of teaching literature when they are asked to consider if there are any differences between the ways they talk about books with their friends and the ways they ask their students to talk about books in class.

In a very important article, Lola Brown explains how after reading and recording her most powerful impressions of a novel a friend had aroused her interest in, she reached the conclusion that there was a 'mis-match' between the way she read novels for herself and the way she 'taught' them.[2] She recognised that one of the ways she had made the world of *A Candle for Saint Anthony* (by Eleanor Spence) 'real' to herself was 'by filling it in with details from similar experiences of (her) own', and she quotes James Britton's comment that active response involves 'an unspoken monologue of responses — a fabric of comment, speculation, relevant autobiography'.[3] Brown concludes that in her teaching she had focused primarily on the 'literary devices, conventions and forms the author uses to create the fictional world', whereas in her own reading she habitually and consciously concentrated on constructing that world for herself while absorbing the forms 'subconsciously': 'My actual dialogue with the author has been at the level of remembering, speculating, associating.'[4] The implication of her article is that teachers should foster the 'unspoken monologue of responses' by involving students in activities which facilitate 'remembering, speculating, associating', before making the structural patterns of texts and the way readers process them matters for explicit study.

One of the main difficulties for teachers in the centralised states systems of education in Australia is that syllabus contents and objectives have been traditionally constructed by constituted authorities and handed down with little opportunity for all but token teacher participation in decision-making. While 'school-based curriculum development' is a fashionable slogan in the 1980s, there is little evidence of it in operation, at least in the teaching of literature in the senior years, and it is likely to be slow to make headway because teachers have been socialised into a system which has imposed on them definitions of the purposes and routines of their work.

In research conducted in the north of England, in circumstances more conducive to teacher reflection on their purposes than in Australia, Peter Medway found a considerable lack of curriculum theorising by teachers. Many of them could offer no justification for the curriculum they taught, nor any definition of English that their practice might imply. Medway reports:

> There was no reason to assume that teachers were doing whatever they did in English in order to achieve some aim beyond it. Quite conceivably they might be setting themselves simply to 'do teaching English' . . . Generally there is no indication that teachers are using the novels to achieve anything beyond whatever it is that reading books is assumed automatically to result in. No *particular* understanding of self or society, for example, seems to be sought. The books are simply run, and that is 'doing literature'.[5]

Just as students need to formulate knowledge for themselves if it is to be possessed, so teachers need to make explicit to themselves their own theories of learning and teaching. We can justify and evaluate the success of our methods only if we have some explicitly formulated and consistent purposes against which to measure them. Medway rightly describes the 'language for language's sake' notion 'inherent in the standard minimum version of English' as a 'disabling limitation', and points out that what literature teaching should be concerned with is not just an understanding of literature as an end in itself, but an understanding of life and an empowering of students, *through* reading and writing, 'not only to find their own voices but thereby to pursue for themselves the understandings they feel most in need of'.[6]

Teachers need to understand for themselves exactly how teaching literature involves helping students to improve their maps of the world and their understanding of the emotional and moral landscapes they encompass. Too often the teaching of literature, conditioned by the public examination syllabus of set texts, has meant in practice transmitting the approved interpretation of specific major texts. What we should be a teaching students is how to read, write, talk and listen better for a range of transactive purposes. Only as teachers continually reflect on their work and refine their theories of learning, can meaningful teaching and learning occur in classrooms, and the inertia into which they are socialised by centralised syllabuses be overcome.

Those teachers who have formulated coherent theories of teaching literature to which they are committed, and whc understand the political significance of their classroom acts in their effects on learners, are the ones most likely to make their purposes clear to their students and to encourage the development of their reflexive understanding. Garth Boomer has written wisely about what he calls 'the complicity of tact in schools, the phenomenon of keeping secrets for the so-called good of others', showing how keeping students ignorant of curriculum objectives and of the reasons for specific procedures devised to attain them, is 'a political act — an act of subjugation (securing) the power of those who have the secret'.[7] Boomer argues that keeping students in the dark about 'how school works, how the curriculum is constructed and how to negotiate for reward'[8], is a way of maintaining the dominance of teachers over pupils: 'By choosing not to tell . . . teachers are teaching a politics which condones information capital and privilege, cultural discrimination against the young and the division of mental labour.'[9]

However, Medway's research suggests that many teachers are not so much making a conscious choice about not telling but, rather, they are unaware of the relevance of telling. You can't pass on the secrets if you haven't thought about and made clear to yourself what they are. For example, you can't make explicit to students your criteria for evaluating any of the work you set them to do if you aren't exactly clear in your own mind what these criteria are because you have unconsciously absorbed them by accepting school routines and policies you've never questioned. Also, a teacher who has not reflected on the purposes of his or her teaching is unlikely to encourage students to reflect on their learning. The teacher who has not made it clear to students what she or he hopes they might learn from doing a unit of work in a particular way is unlikely to ask them to consider retrospectively what they have learned from doing it.

Teachers certainly need to 'come clean' with students, as Boomer says, if the latter are to develop some control over their learning. Students will not experiment and take risks if teachers are likely to penalise them for experiments and risks that don't result in highly markable finished products, even if the experience of producing them 'unsuccessfully' is successful in terms of learning outcomes. Students are unlikely to engage in exploratory, experimental approaches if teachers don't, or can't, make explicit to them the purpose and value of such approaches. Unless teachers make their intentions and methods clear, students' primary focus of attention will be on satisfying the demands of what they perceive as the teacher's real but covert curriculum (for example, by concentrating on avoiding mistakes in writing, rather than on exploring and making meaning, if the teacher's only response to writing is to mark out 'errors'). Students can be empowered to learn only by teachers who can help them to understand and take responsibility for their own learning processes.

For this to happen, teachers need to recognise that a centralised curriculum is only a set of guidelines within which they can construct and improvise and negotiate with their students more specific curriculums to meet the students' needs. You might have to select from a list of set texts for the Higher School Certificate examination, but even within the draconian constraints of the form of public assessment of literary response (the restriction to the essay), there is still room for approaches that liberate students rather than render them powerless. However, students can't be fully conscious of their own powers and purposes if their teachers aren't aware of theirs. In another article, Garth Boomer identifies the weakness in the 'negotiation of the curriculum' movement (which he himself has led) as 'trying to raise the consciousness (indirectly the power) of the relatively more *powerful*, the teachers, where the more radical drive would be to raise the consciousness of the relatively *powerless*, the students.'[10] I would say that the consciousness of students can be raised only by teachers of heightened consciousness. The most exciting classroom activities in the world will be of little lasting value to students who aren't involved in negotiating them and in reflecting on their purposes and uses.

In an address to the Australian Association for the Teaching of English in 1978, John Dixon clearly formulated the question about teaching literature that had been causing English teachers uneasiness for some time: how do we help our students to move from spontaneous, felt, non-analytical responses to texts to a more detached, critical reflection without destroying the initial response and without imposing the teacher's viewpoint? Dixon put it this way: 'How can I combine the invitation to remain involved, living in the world of the encounter, with the chance to contemplate the experience — to realise what nature offers if we look steadily in the mirror?'[11]

An outstanding drama teacher, John Carroll, made a significant contribution to answering this question two years later.[12] Although Carroll answers the question from the point of view of a drama teacher, his comments are relevant to the whole of English teaching. He argues that 'a major change in communication patterns occurs when drama is used in the classroom' because 'pupils respond by simultaneously becoming the entertainers and the audience':

As entertainers, they represent possibilities of experience. For example, in a dramatic exploration of the industrial revolution, pupils could take on the role of deprived children in a nineteenth century workhouse, or the role of rich capitalists living in a mansion. Simultaneously, in their role as the audience, they become capable of evaluating these experiences and drawing conclusions about them. So drama in the classroom develops into an area where "authors, players and audience are one".[13] (Britton).

Carroll uses a theatre analogy to explain the roles the teacher can adopt and those he can assign his pupils. When the teacher is in the role of 'actor' and the class is in the role of 'audience', we have a 'transmission-tube' model of teaching, as Douglas Barnes calls it, with passive pupils. When the teacher takes the role of 'director' and the class is in the role of 'cast' we have another version of the transmission model with the teacher manipulating pupils who are left ignorant of educational purposes and values and, therefore, powerless. As Carroll points out, the 'all-knowing teacher' has to 'discipline those "actors" who want to improvise on the classroom script'.[14] The third and preferred model Carroll offers is that of teacher as 'inventor' or 'releaser of ideas' or 'catalyst' for learning (rather than 'interpreter of ideas'), and class as 'ensemble'. In this situation, the pupils are 'participants in an activity and spectators of their own understanding of it',[15] so they both perform, or explore meaning more deeply, and reflect on the meanings they find and the significance of what they are doing. Carroll claims that students are able to manage their dual roles because 'they are protected by the "once-remove" that only the drama situation provides.'[16]

> They take on a lifestyle and the role provided by the drama while remaining themselves in the spectator framework . . . They become capable of taking a stand on an issue and then giving a view on their understanding of it . . . They are able, because of the "once remove" of drama, to reflect on their experiences, and *know* that they know a new range of thinking and action is open to them.[17]

What John Carroll shows the drama teacher can achieve when she or he sees his or her role as 'inventor' and that of the class as 'ensemble' can be achieved by any teacher of any subject who offers his or her pupils and him or herself the same creative roles. Such a teacher breaks down barriers in traditional social relationships between teacher and taught, becomes learning facilitator rather than punitive judge, emphasises learning rather than instruction, and creates a space, or penalty-free area, within which students can focus on making meaning rather than on impressing others, and can try things out for themselves, knowing that they can learn from mistakes rather than being penalised for them. For example, in teaching literature, a teacher as 'inventor' would see students not only as active readers and performers of texts but as creators of their own texts. As Harold Rosen says, we want to help students 'not only to engage with texts but to be the makers of them, to make reading and writing like speaking and listening genuinely complementary activities.'[18] Margaret Meek, too, argues for the privileging of narrative in the discourse of the classroom: 'You don't teach children to tell stories; you let them, and then help them to know that's how other authors — the ones who write books — do it too.'[19]

# WIDE READING

So I had a secret vice. So I hung around bookstores. I read what I could and when I could. I used to get kicked out. So I stole books. But what did these pieces of knowledge mean? What were these chunks of dreams, secreted away in my duffel-bag? I was safe in a book, looking inside. I was constructing a huge puzzle without head or tail, a puzzle that was continually expanding. I was trying to order my world.

> Seamus O'Young, protagonist of
> Brian Castro's novel, *Birds of
> Passage*

That a student should read more books with satisfaction may be set down as an objective; as a second, he should read books with more satisfaction. We need to foster, in other words, wide reading side by side with close reading.

> James Britton, in James R. Squire (ed.),
> *The Dartmouth Seminar Papers*, NCTE

Wide reading and close reading should go hand in hand in English. Without a wide-reading scheme in the school, the reading habit is unlikely to be developed in all those students who haven't picked it up in their homes. Without attention to close reading in schools, to assist in the deepening and articulation of response, students' reading is unlikely to make optimal progress to higher levels and to more demanding books.

As we have seen, those students who read a great deal with a great deal of pleasure inevitably, if unconsciously, pick up many of the conventions of literary discourse, making it easier for teachers to make conscious to them what they can already do and what they need to go on to do in order to progress. As Margaret Early puts it, voracious readers are left with 'a residue of insight into life and into the writer's craft, forming the basis for deeper perceptions.'[20]

It is not difficult to organise a successful wide-reading programme even in schools where assessment is a fetish. One can easily allocate a swag of marks for the end-of-year English assessment to the reading project, say 20 per cent to 40 per cent as part of a progressive assessment system. The problem in such a case is then to make sure the necessity of completing assignments on some of the books read doesn't destroy the pleasure of reading, so that the writing of responses doesn't become another hoop-jumping exercise. When literature is used only as a source for comprehension work, for example, the emphasis on the testing of information shifts the focus from the human concerns of literature to the uncontextualised skills of reading, or to the spotting of literary devices. It is difficult to develop in students a genuine love of literature when it is used as training-track work, skill-building drill divorced from meaningful communication. In this situation what were originally designed as means become ends. Reading becomes something done routinely in class rather then something voluntarily engaged in throughout life. Underlying this approach is the false assumption that the specific reading skills taught in 'comprehension' lessons will automatically transfer to all kinds of reading in different content areas, from literature to mathematics. Clark McKowen, an American teacher, adopting the persona of a high-school drop-out, describes those teachers of his school days who had the teaching of poetry well-organised for anything but a love of reading:

> They were geniuses when it came to poetry. We classified and sorted every poem we got our hands on. We put little marks above every syllable (some of them made awful pretty designs, especially if you used different coloured ink), counted the feet, which anybody can see is important when there's more than two of them, and found all sorts of figures of speech. I can tell you, I really developed a healthy respect for a poem. When there's that much work in something it has to be good. Besides, you have to protect your investment. We learned to step lightly around anything where the first lines all began with capitals but don't all end with periods. And I guess that's what they were after. You wouldn't want just anybody slopping around something as serious as all that.[21]

In organising a wide-reading programme, teachers need to value students' personal choices and protect their right to have them. This can be done by, for example, setting each pupil as a beginning assignment the task of finding one novel she or he would genuinely want to recommend to others. Pupils' reading interests are extremely varied, as one of the Bathurst teachers explains in her questionnaire response:

> 'I surveyed their in-class interests at the start of the year. It was

a mixed bag. For all those who said they liked mystery and adventure stories, there was an equal number who said they didn't. Similarly, some liked stories about people and romance and some said they couldn't stand them. I do not yet know much about their interests outside school, but expect that this will emerge as they write.'

Another teacher made an important point about the psychological effect on pupils of providing choice as opposed to having texts imposed on them.

'I have found that all the students are delighted with our Wide Reading Programme, for they can make their own choice of the books they read. Often the pupils are turned off a class novel simply because *everyone has* to read it.'

Many teachers emphasised the need to create an appealing reading environment in which students can discover for themselves their own favourite books, poems and authors and, through these, something about their own identities.

To help students choose books it is useful to provide them with lists of titles (available from the school or class library) under genre or thematic headings ('historical', 'teenage problems', etc.). The titles should be carefully selected to cover wide interests and varying levels of difficulty. Some teachers like to construct class libraries in which there are multiple copies (five to ten) of a number of titles to provide opportunities for group work and sharing ongoing reading experiences with others. Several of the Bathurst teachers suggested important ways of linking the wide-reading programme with the close reading work on the shared class text:

'With each novel studied, I'd like to provide an additional class library of novels by the same author, of the same period, similar topic, similar style or contrasting style. Often given an insight into one novel, students are eager to try another in the same vein. This would develop a greater awareness of style.'

'This term a wide reading scheme has followed from the class text, *The Otterbury Incident*. The follow up consists of:

     (i)    choice of one detective book (from list compiled by librarian)

(ii)   a book review of it
(iii)  a written report of an interesting detection in it
(iv)   a poster advertising the book.'

As many children get little opportunity or encouragement to read at home, it is important that class time be allocated to uninterrupted private reading or 'sustained silent reading', say for 15 minutes every day or half an hour once or twice a week. In these sessions teachers, too must read literature of their own choice and not mark students' work or prepare lessons or, in fact, do anything else but read or 'conference' with students about their reading.

Obviously, it is essential that teachers are well acquainted with children's and adolescent literature, as well as the reading tastes and developmental stages of their students, so they can help them to find books that will be read with pleasure and promote growth. This requires continual informal discussion with students about their favourite books and *why* they choose them. One of the Bathurst teachers who wrote of the value of such informal, judgement-free discussion, also mentioned the usefulness — for both students and teacher — of students keeping work-book logs to record their ratings of books read:

> 'Any book enjoyed and recommended is talked about in class. This is an informal couple of minutes about the book, and the first to ask gets to borrow the book next. The title and author of each book read is entered in the "Book Case" section of the Work Book and rated by the student on an A, B, C, D, E scale from "great" to "boring".'

Another teacher wrote of the value of attaching a sheet at the back of each book in the class library for students to write comments on when they have read it. I think this is a particularly effective way of extending the classroom discussion of literature as it enables students to find out what others have thought of a book, often leading to conversation, and it enables the teacher to keep a check on the popularity rating of the available books. Yet another teacher encourages students who have read and enjoyed the same book to work as a group to decide how best to persuade others to read it. This can result in the production of a tape recording of a scene, with music and sound effects, or a display with maps, posters, dioramas etc., or the prepared reading of an exciting section with the resolution omitted in order to arouse curiosity in the book. Iser would describe this last form of presentation as 'multiplying the blanks or gaps in the text'. The emphasis in all of these activities at this stage is on helping students to 'read more books with more satisfaction', not on evaluating finished product performance.

In a programme with activities such as these, the teacher is able to monitor individual progress and assist all students in the specific ways they need it. When time in class is devoted to selecting, reading and talking together about books, many students are far more likely to want to take their choices home for private discovery.

## THE CASINO HIGH SCHOOL WIDE READING PROGRAMME

An outstanding example of such a programme is in operation at Casino High School in northern New South Wales. Gary Whale, Head of English, and Ken Patino, Head of History, explain in their article which follows how their programme for Year 10 works and how it has been received by students. It would not be difficult for any teacher or school to replicate. If every English Department in Australia were to adopt such a programme, this alone would transform the quality of education and the lives of numerous students. I am sure that reading, listening to, writing and telling literature could become as popular with teenagers as watching television and listening to pop music: it merely needs more media exposure and more effective 'marketing'.

### Wide reading in the english classroom[22]

Preparing our Year 10 students for the School Certificate Reference Test in July 1984 imposed certain restraints on teacher and student alike. Students were compelled to confine their reading to uncontextualised extracts and their writing to single-draft products. We wanted to return them to the basic tenets of reading and writing espoused in the Junior English Syllabus.

Coincidentally, at a Parent-Teacher Night in July, a number of parents had requested that their children be encouraged to read more books, and had also expressed their concern that Year 10 students be helped to diversify their reading. Since the use of reading and writing contracts had been used on occasions as a successful teaching strategy at Casino High School, we saw this as an appropriate way to extend and diversify our students' reading.

**What did the contract contain?**

Each student was given a copy of the Wide Reading Contract, which included:

1. A statement of the aims of the unit (to read more widely, to read more critically, to read for greater enjoyment, to develop your written responses to literature).
2. Ten categories of literature, with an example of each, from which they were to choose their reading material. The categories were:
   - Australian fiction
   - Biography/autobiography
   - Children's 'classic'
   - Famous author
   - Fantasy fiction
   - Historical fiction
   - Poetry (ten poems minimum)
   - Science/speculative fiction
   - Teenage 'problem' fiction
   - Other fiction (crime, mystery, spy, etc.).
3. Details of the three levels (A, B or C) for which they could contract:

   *C Level*
   - read five books from at least four categories
   - keep a Reading Log for each book (five)
   - write an essay of about 750 words on a set topic.

   *Topic:* Imagine you are a member of the selection committee for Casino High School Memorial Library. Prepare a paper for the other members of the committee which ranks the five novels in the order you would recommend their purchase and which justifies your choice.

   *B Level*
   - read as for C *and* two additional books by one author already read
   - keep a Reading Log for each book (seven)
   - write an essay of about 1000 words on a set topic.

   *Topic:* Discuss the three novels of the author you have read for this unit, pointing out the similarities and differences among them. Decide which of them you would recommend as the first purchase for C.H.S. Memorial Library, and justify your choice.

   *A Level*
   - read as for B *and* two further books from another two categories

- keep a Reading Log for each book (nine)
- write an essay as for B *and* a further essay of
  about 500 words on a set topic.

*Topic:*      What have you learned about human problems and human nature from the nine novels you have read? (Do not try to cover the plots of the nine novels. Try, instead, to deduce common aspects among the novels, and to illustrate them by reference to the novels.)

4. Details of the level contracted for, the duration of the contract, the signature of the student and the counter-signature of the teacher.

Students were given an extensive Recommended Reading List to help them to make their selections. Most of the books listed were chosen specifically for their appeal to adolescents. They also received a suggested format for their Reading Logs which emphasised their personal response as readers.

---

*Suggested Format for Reading Log*
(Length: two to three quarto pages per book)

---

          *Title*         *(Date started)*

          *Author*       *(Date finished)*
      (Publisher; year of publication;
        place of publication; length)

*Characters:*  (List major character and particular characteristics.)

e.g.: Colin  - 14 y.o.; curious, but lacking confidence

Susan  - Colin's twin; the more dominant

Uncle Tom Cobbley  - gruff old Somerset farmer with heart of gold

Mabel  - his wife

Jack O'Lantern  - a mysterious cobbler

*Setting:*   Identify briefly both the time and the place in which the novel is set.

e.g.: The main action takes place in Florence, Italy, particularly in the vicinity of the Ponte Vecchio, in the early seventeenth century.

| | |
|---|---|
| *Plot Summary:* | Give a *bare* outline of the plot, no more; and try *not* to reveal the climax. Avoid such clichés as 'To find out what happens, you'll have to read this fantastic, engrossing, etc., etc., book'. |
| *Comment:* | Give your opinion of the novel, but do more than that. Discuss the major themes and issues the novel raises, and how they are presented. Give some thought to the characters and the setting. How 'real' are they? How convincing? Consider the language – is it natural? appropriate? Is the dialogue convincing? Think about the structure – is it linear (chronological)? Does it include flashbacks or foreshadowing? Is it more like a spiral or a circle? Does the novel remind you of any other novels? Which? Why? |

## How did it operate

In the first week, most of the English lessons were spent in the library, where students conferred with their teacher and/or the teacher-librarian about the categories and their selection of books. We found the assistance of a teacher-librarian well read in the field of adolescent literature to be invaluable. During the following five weeks, the students were encouraged to write each Log as they completed each book and to begin drafting their essays. While we intended to set an example by reading extensively in class ourselves, we found our time increasingly taken up in discussing with our students the books they were reading, the progress of their Logs and the development of their essay/s.

## How successful was it?

The first measure of success was the competent way in which the students completed all the requirements of the level for which they had contracted and the thoroughness with which they wrote both the Logs and the essay/s. Even students who contracted for the minimum level (C) attained a pleasing selection of books and a high level of perception in their writing.

Another indication of success was the enthusiasm of the students as shown in a follow-up questionnaire. Ninety seven per cent of the students said that they had enjoyed the unit, with comments such as 'Discovering books I didn't think I'd enjoy was great' and 'It made me read a variety of books that I wouldn't have dreamt of reading'. One girl went so far as to say:

> 'It enabled me to broaden my scope . . . I had to read books that I would under normal circumstances not have given a second glance to and having to write about the books afterwards really made me think about why I did like or dislike the book and analyse my feelings and thoughts.'

The number and quality of books read exceeded our expectations. Some 325 books were read by 46 students in the short space of six school weeks. In other words, they maintained an average of better than a book a week while at the same time completing both Reading Logs and essays. (They also had the ongoing responsibility of an entry in their Journal every week.) Both of us observed a progression to more demanding books such as *Capricornia, Moby Dick, Pride and Prejudice, Nineteen Eighty-four* and *The Left Hand of Darkness*. In contrast, several students who had read some demanding books and then returned to an easier one (for instance, a Children's 'classic') found it unsatisfying.

Students made a wide selection of books from all categories except Poetry. The most popular categories were Australian fiction (46), Fantasy fiction (46) and Teenage 'problem' fiction (45). We were pleasantly surprised by the number of books chosen from the Biography/autobiography (37) and Famous author (30) categories.

The students showed initiative in the choice of their books. The Recommended Reading List contained 176 titles, yet the students read in total 266 separate titles, of which only about 100 came from the list. This indicates that the students used the Reading List to find their first books. but then went on to other books by authors they had enjoyed or to books they discovered in browsing.

The Reading Logs were designed to serve two purposes. First of all, we needed to know that our students had, in fact, read the books! More importantly, however, we wanted to give our students the opportunity to respond personally and honestly in order to write their way to a deeper understanding of the books. This was even more successful than we had hoped, as shown by the evaluation of the students. Over 80 per cent indicated that they had found writing a Log for each book 'helpful and worthwhile', and gave as reasons: 'They helped you to be a more observant reader'; 'I could show my thoughts about a book'; 'It helped me gain a greater depth of enjoyment and understanding'.

The essays were designed to further their initial responses, to develop their comparative and critical faculties and, at the end of Year 10, to introduce them to the more 'literary' essays required in Senior English. While the majority of students (68 per cent) felt they were beneficial, some felt that the essays tended to duplicate the Reading Logs, while one student suggested that they were 'only set for the teacher to mark'. Some comments, however, supported our original intentions: 'Instead of just putting the book away after reading it and writing the Log, I was made to think about all the books and the issues they raised'; 'I could put all my thoughts on to paper and read them over later which somehow gave me an even clearer understanding of the books'.

We were pleased with the quality of the essays we received and with the insights they contained. Even though nearly one third of the students claimed they were no help, their enthusiasm for the books they had read was still patently obvious in their essays.

**What changes would we make?**

The only changes we would contemplate to the categories would be to delete the Poetry category and, perhaps, replace it with another. While there were a couple of excellent Poetry Logs in this category, it was significantly less popular than the other categories (only four students attempted it), and in two of the four instances it was clearly (and mistakenly) perceived as an 'easy option'.

It is worth recording, however, that another teacher at Casino High, Alan Moore, devised a contract along similar lines which dealt exclusively with Poetry, and found his Year 9 class responded most enthusiastically to it.

The clear desire of our students to discuss the books with us (and others) before they wrote suggests that time should be provided for this important aspect. We would not want to prescribe it — we could not possibly talk to all our students about each book they read — but we would want to provide time for them to talk with us or each other about their reading, thus allowing them to shape their ideas before putting pen to paper for either the Reading Logs or the essays.

# FACILITATING THE FORMATION AND DEVELOPMENT OF PERSONAL RESPONSE

Pupils only begin to make a reading experience their own by using talk and provisional jottings as ways of fitting new and unfamiliar experience into their already existing systems of understanding.

David Jackson, 'Dealing with a set book
in literature at 16 + '[23]

From the work and research of people such as James Britton and Douglas Barnes[24] in the 1960s and 1970s, and of many others since, we know that language is not only a means ofcommunication but an instrument of learning. Barnes has shown that using language in talking and writing not only transmits our ideas but shapes them, and Britton's writing research has demonstrated that 'we not only learn to write by writing, but we learn by writing'. If learning means making knowledge for ourselves and if in turn this means shaping, exploring, clarifying and developing our own thinking in our own language, then informal conversations with others about books and instant, exploratory jottings in response to first readings have an important place in the classroom. Unfortunately, there are still many people who see language, both spoken and written, only in terms of public performance and not at all in terms of learning; they want to assess it as finished product rather than foster it as learning process.

Informal, expressive, penalty-free talking and writing in response to literature provide the space for the growth of a conversational relationship between the reader and the text which the teacher's intrusive voice can often stifle. If the tensions of public display are to be avoided at the initial stage of sorting out ideas in response, so that students can concentrate, unselfconsciously, on making sense of texts for themselves, the teacher must encourage lots of exploratory discussion in informal small groups and much expressive writing in a reading journal. The first and most important audience for such journal writing is the student who writes it, but for it to operate as an instrument of learning for its writer, its other audience — the teacher — needs to be a trusted adult who reads and replies but does not evaluate. In these circumstances, students can sort out and clarify ideas in the act of jotting them down and/or discussing them.

## THE READING JOURNAL

Entries in the reading journal should include occasional jottings of immediate responses to completed texts – as a starting point for small group discussion, for example – as well as responses to texts *during* the process of reading them. In both situations, the writing not only helps the students to inspect and discover their own thinking, reading processes and problems, but it also helps the teacher to find out what their students' individual strengths and weaknesses as readers are so s/he can help them.

Teachers can begin to develop students' reflexive understandings of their personal identities and reading processes by discussing their journal entries with them, and helping them to identify those features of texts and themselves that make some texts (and textual features) appealing and others less appealing to them. Open discussion of the teacher's purposes and learning theory in encouraging the keeping of a journal can help students to start to explore their own reading and learning processes and develop their own explicit reading and learning theories. If teachers make quantity the only criterion for journal evaluation, they demonstrate in practice their belief that quality improves with quantity, and that writing is indeed an instrument of learning.

To facilitate this open dialogue between teacher and students it is appropriate that journals should be seen by students as written conversations with their teachers as well as with themselves. For example, students can be encouraged to address their teachers directly with questions ranging from requests for titles of other books similar to the one they have enjoyed to pleas for help with an identified problem of reading. If the teacher is a trusted adult, the journal becomes an arena in which problems can be articulated, shared and solved. As David Jackson puts it, 'playing around with hunches and intuitions [is] legitimised as a necessary learning stage'.[25]

As well as providing the opportunity for jotting down immediate first impressions and questioning the text in the act of reading, the journal is also useful for recording responses to situations that arise spontaneously in class discussions of literature. For example, here is a very informal piece of imaginative writing in response to Saul Bellow's novel, *Herzog*. Some 18 to 19 year-old first year students in a Communications degree course said that they found the obsessive letter-writing of the novel's main character, Herzog, to be puzzling. In a neurotic reaction to the tensions of his complicated life, Herzog composes letters to leading politicians, historical figures, religious leaders, intellectuals, friends and enemies, alive and dead, to contest a whole range of issues with them. Some of these letters are written on scraps of paper and some are merely formulated in his head, but none is ever sent. As many of the specific issues of these letters and most of their addressees were not part of the students' cultural repertoire, they found the letters boring in themselves and problematical in their significance. When the students made their difficulty explicit in class, the teacher realised he had to think of a way of getting them to relate Herzog's problems to their own lives and experiences. What he did was to ask the students to compose a letter to someone they would like to engage in debate, insult, censure or satirise but whom they would never write to in practice. To cover the range of Herzog's purposes in composing his letters, 'prizes' were offered for the most humorous, the most vindictive and the most intellectually stimulating. They were given ten minutes to write them in their reading journals. There were letters to teachers, College administrators, politicians, sports heroes, public citizens, the historically eminent, relatives and neighbours. Here are two.


Dear Hannibal,

I was ever so sorry to hear of your eventual defeat by those bastards the Romans. I mean it's a sorry day when skill and tactical brilliance are defeated by superior numbers. I expect it is difficult, in your position, to be critical of the Roman tactics — I mean, you lost, didn't you. With the benefit of hindsight I can see that, all considerations undertaken, you were extremely unlucky to lose. Those pompous, imperialistic and quite often imbecile Romans had no answer to your skill and unfortunately you had no answer to the stupidity of the Carthaginian government. Any third rate politician could have seen the consequences of your unequalled victories in Italy and sent you more troops and revitalised the navy. I can sympathise with you. Your politicians were most probably private school boys who practically inherited their positions too. One small criticism of your attack would be that of the failure to besiege Rome after the superb victory at Cannae. To be blunt, the Romans were klutzes; they couldn't defend their own virginity. You'll be glad to know the Romans stuffed up their empire anyway. You should have seen the decadence — not even modern movie directors can recreate the perversion, bestiality, bastardry, homosexuality, torture and sadism, all the fun of the fair. I often wonder what would have happened if you'd eventually won. Maybe the mafia would have turned out to be good men. Maybe Australia would be run by women and maybe I could have turned out to be a woman — come to think of it, thank God you didn't win. My regards to the elephants.'

The influence of history on contemporary society is one of the themes of Herzog's massive output of unsent letters. Another is the problem of double-standards and the integrity of public figures.

'Dear Julius Sumner Miller,

Years ago when you performed scientific experiments on television, my little sister thought you were good , and she watched your programme with fascination each week. I thought she also learned from you what the word "disinterested" meant in a scientific context as opposed to uninterested or just plain bored. Now I see you are on the box again, espousing the health value of Cadbury's milk chocolate. My sister wants to know this: if the best thing in Cadbury's milk chocolate is the 1½ glasses of milk, why don't you advise people to buy the milk rather than the chocolate, as the milk is cheaper and not mixed with gunk food like sugar and cocoa powder.'

Reading and discussion of all the letters proved highly productive as a point of imaginative entry into the world of the novel. From that experience the students began to understand Herzog from the inside as well as gaining some insight into Bellow's purposes and methods.

Guidelines and purposes for keeping a reading journal should be made explicit to, and negotiated with, students. Here are the specifications/suggestions for the journal for students taking first year English in the Communications degree course at Mitchell College of Advanced Education in Bathurst. They offer an example of a framework within which students can reflect in writing on what they have read and on their own readng and learning processes in conditions of psychological freedom and security. The keeping of a journal is the first requirement of a literature course which aims to empower students by helping them to produce, take responsibility for, reflexively understand and act upon their own ideas.

## The reading journal

The purpose of the Journal is to document your progress and responses week by week through the course. For this I think you will find a small exercise book more satisfactory than any loose-leaf folder system.

I suggest that you keep the Journal like a diary, responding to the texts of the unit in turn and writing the date above each entry. You can use the Journal for notes made in preparation for class discussion of the texts and for sorting out your interpretations of other written assignments.

I want you to use the Journal primarily to make sense for yourself of your reading and the associated activities of the course. That means that your writing in the Journal will be marked by considerable informality of style. As the first and most important audience is yourself, the Journal will reflect your individuality and your personal needs as well as your way of making things clear to yourself. Much of the writing might be in the form of notes. It may include jottings, doodling, drawings, graffiti, poems and specific questions you want to have discussed in class. Most importantly, perhaps, it will present not only your ideas about your reading and activities, but your feelings and attitudes to them.

The amount of writing you do is up to you. However, the intention is not that you write hundreds of pages. For *one* novel I expect a detailed set of responses written *during* the process of your reading. Here are some questions (offered as a guide but not a strait-jacket) to help you reflect on the novel and on your own strategies in reading it.

1. Predicting or Generating Expectations: At various stages of your reading of the text — What sorts of things could happen in the short and long term? How might the story develop? Has what has just happened altered your interpretations of past events in any way?
2. Puzzles: What puzzles or problems are you formulating at various reading moments? What specific questions are you asking of the text?
3. Filling in the Gaps: What gaps are you filling in in the text? What connections between events are you making? What is the point of each event? Why was a particular character included in the novel?

4. The Repertoire of Personal and Literary Experience: What connections are you making between events in your own experience and events in the novel? Does the book remind you of any other books you have read?

5. Mental Images: What mental images are you forming of people, places and events in the novel? Consider the nature of these mental images and where they come from. For example, are they purely pictorial or are they more significantly 'feelings about' things?

6. The Implied Author: What impression is the book giving you of the kind of person who wrote it? Do you find it difficult to sympathise with his/her view of the world?

7. The Implied Reader: What kind of reader do you think the author had in mind as his audience for this book? Are you having any difficulty suspending your own values, prejudices, world views sufficiently to enable the book to work on you?

8. Ideology: there is no such thing as an ideologically neutral text. What is the ideology of:
   (a) this text?
   (b) the society that saw fit to regard it as a great work of art?

9. Reflexiveness/Self-Understanding: From considering questions like 1 to 8, what are you learning about:
   (a) yourself as a person?
   (b) your own strengths and weaknesses as a reader? What are your really productive reading strategies?
   (c) for example, when you come to "boring" bits, think about what boredom means to you, and what you are learning about yourself from being bored.

10. If you regard some or all of these questions as 'non literary' or 'extra literary' considerations as the old but so-called 'New Critics' do, ask yourself about your criteria for making such judgements and what ideology influenced you to develop such criteria.

NB. The 'New Critics' are in unfettered control of the Higher School Certificate English Courses throughout Australia. They choose the texts and they set the examination papers.

Because you are the only person who can decide what is most relevant to you, no subject or attitude is taboo in the Journal.

Writing Style: The kind of informal, comfortable writing that I suggest is appropriate for the Journal is like written-down speech, and reflects the ebb and flow of the writer's thoughts *and* feelings.

It is the kind of exploratory language most of us use when we are tentatively grappling with new ideas for the first time and are not yet ready to produce the fully coherent and logically ordered interpretations that we make at a later stage in writing essays or stories.

So, get to it and have a go at wrapping your own language around your own thinking.

### Extracts from a student's journal

Here are some snippets from the ongoing responses of an 18-year-old student to a novel being read. Writing about Albert Camus's *The Plague*, Alison articulates her puzzles, relates events to her own cultural and experiential repertoire and anticipates what lies ahead at the same time as she tries to sort out the connections between characters and events.

The selected brief extracts from Alison's comments are just a few of the threads she traces concerning the characters Cottard and Tarrou, as well as her attempts to interpret to herself the significance of Paneloux's death and of Rambert's desire to leave followed by his decision to stay in Oran.

#### '3rd September

I've started *The Plague*. The one thing that really puzzles me so far is this bloke Cottard. The book is, so far, about the rats and probably bubonic plague and the way the population reacts, and copes with such a crisis. What could this man who just tried to hang himself possibly have to do with the story? . . . Another strange character is Tarrou. This one, however, seems much more intriguing to me. He's a bit of an enigma. What does he do all day apart from watch people (even if his observations are perceptive)? His presence in Oran is a mystery. He is almost certainly a good guy. . . .

#### '4th September

Cottard again. Is he the murderer mentioned (on page 49) by the woman in the tobacconist's shop, the man who fled to Oran from Algiers? Is that why he's being friendly to the people and trying to cultivate character witnesses? Is that why he tried to kill himself? Why does he lure the doctor into talking about the epidemic in front of the children? . . .

Just a thought — the absurdity of Chapter Two — Cottard, a man who wants to kill himself, is saved and M. Michel, a man who wants to go on living, cannot be saved. . . .

### '6th September

Tarrou is still a mystery. He sees the failure of the official authorities to cope with the plague and takes over. Why? . . . Cottard again. This time he's helping Rambert in his attempts to escape the town. If he does get out what would happen? How did Cottard find out about this way out? He's involved in crime, everything points to it . . .

### '8th September

Rambert's on his way to getting out of the town, but what I don't understand is why Tarrou and Rieux don't try to stop him. I understand about self-reponsibility but if he might be endangering millions of others surely they should do something . . .

### '9th September

Part Four. It looks very much like Rambert's going to make it . . . The old Spanish lady is right about Rambert. She sees that the meaning of his life is his relationship with his girl friend. Without her he's got nothing, is nothing, has no purpose in his life. I still think he shouldn't leave. Whatever he does he can't leave, he simply can't! . . .

### '10th September

Rambert's changed his mind! He's staying. I'm glad. I think it works better this way than if he'd taken off. He cannot live without her, but he cannot live with himself knowing he had turned his back on everyone else's suffering. My own personal philosophy — if you can change one little corner of the world for the better then your life has been worth-while . . .
Paneloux — he's come to an understanding of his own faith after the young boy dies. To have complete faith he must also have complete acceptance of God's will even if that includes what he can't understand, like innocent suffering. Now he sees that there *is* such a thing as innocent suffering. For a priest to call a doctor to tend him is for him to defy God — when he thinks God has caused the illness for His own purposes which are beyond human understanding. It shows a lack of faith and lack of accepting His

will as almighty. Paneloux will not renounce his faith, even in the face of death. Does this make Paneloux a sort of existential hero? . . .

Othon has changed. What does Tarrou mean by:

"Poor M Othon! One would like to do something to help him. But how can you help a judge?"

? To be a judge goes against Tarrou's beliefs—that each is responsible for his own actions and therefore cannot be accountable to anyone else??

## '13th September

Now I think I understand why Tarrou could not object to Rambert trying to leave, apart from the fact that he refuses to interfere with the freedom and freedom of choice of others. To do so he may indirectly cause his death. If Rambert chooses to leave and dies, it is his own decision which decides life or death, not Tarrou's. Also his interest in Cottard. His friendship with Rieux is based on their common struggle against death. Also another reason he says "how can one help a judge?" about Othon—as a judge he has had a hand in condemning people.

## '14th September

Part Five. Cottard's shaking in his boots. p. 227. He resents the return to normal life with the disappearance of the plague. While the plague was going everyone in Oran was in his position of being threatened with death, but now the plague is over he is on his own. Everyone else alive is saved, but he will be hunted by the police . . .

Tarrou is dead! Why? He can't die! I'm still old-fashioned enough to expect that the good guys just don't die in books and movies, even if it is appropriate or significant. Everyone has the chance to make a fresh start—Rieux with his wife, Grand with his book and his job and his attempt to find his wife, everyone but Tarrou had done what he set out to do or came to a new understanding of himself like Paneloux . . .

But Rieux's wife has died too! He can't make a fresh start with her. He must start again on his own, knowing that he messed that relationship up . . .

Rambert hasn't come through unscathed either. He realises that he has been changed by the ordeal and his girl might have changed too. The double irony of this is that when Rambert realises that his love might have become an "abstraction" directed towards an "abstraction" of the woman he thought he knew and who now may have changed, he was the one who at the beginning described Rieux's work as a doctor saving lives as too detached and "abstract". It's easier to love mankind as an "abstraction" than real people.'

## TEACHING THE STRATEGIES

Alison said in discussion after completing her journal entries about *The Plague* how much more competent she felt herself to be as a reader. She found the guidelines for the writing to be valuable in helping her to think about the texts and her own reading strategies, and thus to gain some power and control over her own meaning-making/interpreting activity. You will have recognised that the ten groups of questions offered as a guide to students for the ongoing journal responses to a chosen novel are derived from the reader response theories considered in Chapter Three — particularly Iser's phenomenology, but also structuralism and psychoanalytical and political criticism.

One of the best ways to develop students' reflexive understanding of their identities and reading processes would seem to be to encourage them to read back over their own journals and 'to monitor their own engagement with the text'[26], as Brian Johnston so neatly puts it. The following are extracts from the journals of three 18 to 19-year-old students who are reviewing their own progress at the end of a semester's literature course.

'This semester I feel I've suddenly learned how to read in a way I never could before. I've done it by writing and talking honestly about what I've read, and that includes asking the real questions I want to ask about poems, novels and plays, or bits of them that perplex me. In a way I've learned to read by writing and talking about reading, just as I've learned to write better about my own experience by reading literature. It's got a lot to do with being open with myself — and others — and using my own language for my own thinking.'

'In re-reading the imaginative writing I did this semester I can see the influence of the literature I read in the course — the ideas I took up from writers and the methods of writing—the narrative viewpoints and styles I experimented with. Reading over my essays and stories and poems, and most of all this journal, I have also learnt something about myself as a person as well as how I read and learn. This has been of great help in coming to terms with myself, in finding out who I am and in recognising my own strengths and weaknesses. It has made me feel more capable as a human being and as a student.'

'Since I've been writing my own "literature" I've been reading the literature in the course from the writer's point of view. I figure out how they approach a topic, what their problems were. You can see things that don't work, too, where the writing's gone wrong. When you can't see connections, you know that the author has gone wrong or you, as the reader, have gone wrong by not making the connections the writer has implied. I used to lose interest when this happened to me, but now when it happens I go back and forward through the book checking details, tracing events and characters and trying to find the points of connection.'

Students can be taught to interrogate literary texts and fill in their gaps if they understand the point, and experience the rewards, of doing so. David Jackson says that the key issue in teaching students to read better is 'setting up a question and answer pattern of thinking about what you read that can take you further and further into the poem and, perhaps, might later be internalised as a habitual mental approach'.[27] For example, we need to train students to consider, in the act of reading, not just what might happen ahead in the short and long term, but also the different significance and implications of the alternative outcomes they predict. Speculations about events and outcomes should be discussed and justified. If students learn to predict alternative possibilities and to discriminate between them, as well as to weigh the alternatives suggested by other class members, they are drawn deeper into the text and into themselves. When small groups are set the task of asking questions about the text that they don't know the answers to, and feel they need to know the answers to, they not only find out something about the text—by discovering some of the answers in the act of formulating the questions—but they also discover something about reading and learning processes. Therefore, I would add to Jackson's emphasis on reflecting on and questioning the text, the importance of reflecting on both your personal reaction to the text and your own way of reading it, and examining these for their significance.

Here are two examples of teachers teaching reading strategies in such ways as to make their students more conscious of their own activities as readers.


**Example 1.**

Jane Ogborn began a unit of work on Henry James' novel, *Washington Square*, with her sixth form at Crown Woods School in London, by inviting the students to pool their expectations of the first chapter of any novel they might read. Her motive was to make the students conscious of the fact that their past experience of reading novels made them better equipped to read new novels – that ways of reading literature are transferable. She wanted the students to make explicit to themselves the expectations they brought to the reading of *Washington Square* from their existing literary repertoires, so that they would recognise that they already had some understanding of the way novels work from their experience of reading them.

> I decided to say nothing at all by way of preliminaries about Henry James, about New York in the 1830s, or about the kind of novel *Washington Square* is. Instead I asked the group to draw on their own reading of fiction so far and to think about what they expect the opening chapter(s) of a novel to do for them. They volunteered: (1) set the scene; (2) introduce main characters; (3) start the plot; (4) tell you what sort of novel it's going to be; (5) introduce you to the "style" of the book; and (6) Be Interesting! In the light of this list – and particularly points 4 and 5 – I then read aloud the first chapter of *Washington Square*. I don't usually read aloud to 6th formers – largely through fear of being accused of ego-tripping – but in this case I was anxious for them to tune in quickly to the shades of James' irony, and flattered myself I would be able to help them do this through my reading. At the end of Chapter 1, we considered our list and discussed how far, and how well, they felt James had fulfilled it. I was then asked to read Chapter 2, which brings the novel to the point where the action begins, and which therefore gave the group a good incentive to read on for themselves.[28]

**Example 2.**

Barbara Say, Head of English at Bathurst High School, took over the bottom-stream Year 11 class in second term and soon realised that most of them hadn't read the class novel, *The Catcher in the Rye*, that they'd had for some time. She asked them to write down why they hadn't read it and what was difficult about it or, if they had read it all, just what they really thought of it and what they liked and didn't like about it.

The main complaint was that 'nothing happened'; there was too much of Holden talking and 'just airing his opinions'. As novels are made of language, you could say this about all of them, and no doubt many of these students did. 'Novels *are* all talk, somebody's talk', as Barbara so rightly put it. When Barbara discussed their criticisms openly with them, it emerged that what the students meant was that as their minds weren't actively involved in the reading, questions like what might happen next or how Holden might end up didn't engage their interest, so they found the book boring. They needed to experience the pleasures of reading and to learn some of the productive strategies.

*The Catcher in the Rye* was set aside, temporarily, and Barbara read to the students (who didn't have copies) Shirley Jackson's short story, 'The Lottery', stopping at various stages asking them what they thought was going on, what puzzled them and what they thought might eventually happen. The idea that anyone should ask these sorts of speculative questions in the process of reading a book stunned them. They thought that these were the concerns of the writer alone, that the reader's job was to remember the details of events so they could summarise the plot later. (So much for their experience of literature in school!) Interrogating the text was a strange new idea. The students confessed that in being asked such questions, before they could know what the right answers were, they felt vulnerable. They felt that their answers would most likely be wrong and if they were, they would be seen as incompetent by their teacher. It was a 'no-win' situation, they believed, one that would merely reinforce their sense of inadequacy. However, they *did* like the story and were shocked by the ending, when the whole population of a village takes to throwing stones at the winner of its lottery, and by the realisation that the victim will be stoned to death.

After the reading, in discussion of the story and their ways of processing it, the students recognised that the power of the story's impact depended on the reader's *not* anticipating that an apparently co-operative and harmonious community would calmly and deliberately murder one of its respected citizens. The realisation that this was an annual event led them to discuss the significance of the lottery as ritual. They considered the story's relevance to their own community and discovered parallel scapegoating rituals in their own experience. Above all, they were excited by the new and powerful knowledge they had that it was not only legitimate to make wrong hypotheses about outcomes of stories, but that experiencing the impact of some stories — like 'The Lottery' — depended on your being wrong. In this case, you not only could, but should, be mistaken in your expectations to 'read well'. The most important discovery was that you had to generate expectations, question the text and fill in its gaps. In other words, the students began to understand what being an active reader involved them doing.

As the next stage in the class's development, Barbara Say found an unfinished novel (*Come Along with Me*) by Shirley Jackson and asked the students to work in groups to discuss alternative possible endings, to justify them to one another in terms of the logic of the text (as they interpreted it), and to consider the different interpretations each ending would create for the text as a whole. After the discussion, the students were asked to write the rest of the novel. The fact that none of them could be shown to have written the 'wrong' ending was a compelling attraction. In work like this, students not only learn how to read and enjoy literature better, but they develop a sense of their own competence as meaning-makers.

From the reader-response literary theories and the research on response levels and processes, we have some idea of what good readers do and what poor readers don't do. However, it is crucial that we keep in mind that our aim in teaching reading is to actively help all young readers to adopt, habitually, the strategies of better and more experienced readers, as means to ends and not as ends in themselves. There is the danger that reading strategies can be taught rigidly as mechanical, routine exercises. This has happened with the strategies of reading developed from the work of I.A. Richards and the New Critics, and could just as easily happen with those developing from reader-response theories. The skills of reading and the methods of teaching them are valuable when they illuminate textual understanding and enjoyment; they are successfully employed when they enhance response and personal growth. The strategies must be taught in contexts of reading complete texts and exploring students' personal meanings rather than through programmes that isolate discrete skills which are drilled as ends in themselves divorced from meaning.

Students will soon become bored if we don't use a variety of approaches in our teaching. There are warning signs that potentially liberating reader-response ideas are being reductively processed into mindless teaching routines. Teachers are already talking about 'prediction exercises' which are rapidly becoming a new methodological orthodoxy. The back-to-basics and behaviourist camps in contemporary education are always ready to defuse enlightened new ideas and incorporate what is left of them into their own systems. Instead of asking students what might happen next all the time while they are reading, we can ask them to discuss or jot down what is happening in their heads as they read a specific part of a text; or to consider what they would do if they were in a particular character's predicament, and then to compare their reaction with what the character does, and then to reflect on the significance of the difference for what it reveals of them and of the novelist's purposes, and so on. We must ring the changes in our methods and in the activities we ask students to participate in. We must never let our teaching take on a mechanical, stimulus→response pattern. If our minds, as teachers, are not engaged on what we are doing, then neither will our pupils' minds be engaged on what they are doing.

## LEARNING IN SMALL GROUPS

Small group discussion of literature is another important classroom activity facilitating the formation and development of personal response. It helps students to engage with texts, to sort out, clarify and extend their understanding of them, and to reflect on what they have learned, in collaborative social settings that do not threaten. It is in the security of the non-judgmental small group that students are most likely to use the expressive, exploratory, thinking-aloud kind of informal language so productive of learning. They will use it for expressing honest feeling, for making connections between their real and fictional worlds, and for the consideration of other people's viewpoints that might expand their individual perspectives. Reading, which is initially a private activity, can become far more enjoyable and profitable when responses are shared so that a community of readers is established in the classroom, a situation which is itself conducive for the further dissemination of the reading habit.

What has to be avoided in small group organisation is the formality that can arise from too much structure imposed by the teacher in the attempt to guide students' responses. Guidance can so easily become direction, as it does when groups are routinely given five closed questions on every chapter of a novel to test their understanding. Barry Cooper, Head of English at Woolooware High School in Sydney, emphasises that students should see group discussion as a time for exploration, and explains why they should be encouraged to gossip about texts, play the role of characters with whom they have empathised, and chat about them as if they were real: 'Then can they better assimilate the world of the book to their own. Then can they accommodate its experience to affect their own feelings about the world and their behaviour in it.'[29]

This does not mean that teachers should never set questions for small groups to work on. For students who have had no experience of working in groups, it may well be necessary for the teacher to set specific questions, at least initially, until they become consciously aware of the benefits of this form of organisation. As pupils become more experienced, and more prepared and able to take more initiative for themselves, the amount of guidance the teacher offers can be gradually reduced. David Moss, Head of English at Ingleburn High School in Sydney, suggests that when teachers do set questions for small groups the questions should be open ones:

> those which encourage the cognitive skills of speculation, inference, hypothesis, antithesis and synthesis, and those which encourage the exercise of the imagination, particularly in ways that allow students to relate the poem to personal experiences.[30]

David Moss emphasises the importance of training students in groups to take corporate responsibility for their progress, to summarise and synthesise the contributions of members, to ask themselves frequently, 'Where have we got so far?' He provides every encouragement to students to reflectively evaluate their learning and their own learning processes so they make them conscious to themselves:

> When I ask students what they learned in a small group session they begin by telling me what they *learned to know*, whereas I am even more interested in what they *learned to do*. They think

they learned something about a particular poem; I try to get them to see that they learned something about themselves, their feelings, their ideas and about processes they can use to come to understandings about other people and themselves. It's a sort of auto-voyeurism![31]

A useful way to develop this 'auto-voyeurism' is to get groups to tape record their discussions and then to listen to them to sort out what they think they have learned and how they think they have done so. Such discussion is often usefully followed by encouraging students to write in their journals reports of what they have found out about their own learning processes and the implications of these findings for their future behaviour as learners.

## A small group in action

Cliff Smith, Head of English at St Stanislaus College in Bathurst,[32] set groups in his new Year 11 class, which had just finished a 'reading/acting' of Act One of *Death of a Salesman*, the following task:

'Imagine yourself at the theatre, seeing *Death of a Salesman*. It's Intermission. With reference to the play, what would you talk about with your friends? You might consider two general questions:
(a) What have you learned so far?
(b) What are your expectations for Act Two?'

After 'roaming around' listening for five minutes, Cliff joined one of the groups which had a tape recorder. Cliff's analysis of the transcript of the group's discussion before he joined it includes the following points:
- The group listened intently to one another and regularly supported one another's hypotheses with evidence.
- One of the students regularly used questions as a learning technique. Several of his questions used the words of a previous speaker; his intention seems to have been to clarify his own ideas, but the result was that the previous speaker also had to clarify and support *his* contention.
- Other students achieved similar learning outcomes, not by asking direct questions, but by articulating ideas in such ways as to invite

commentary and further exploration. For example, two utterances — 'I like Ben. I think Ben's an interesting guy, unusual . . . ' and 'That bit with the tubing behind the heater . . . took me a while to work it out . . . It's funny . . . like suicide . . . ' — not only revived the discussion, but actually triggered animated and lengthy interchanges.

- The students formulated the questions they wanted the rest of the play to answer, and articulated their problems.
- The discussion indicated that: the students had a grasp of the general movement of the play; they could envisage developing conflicts within and between characters; at least two of them were conscious of the relevance of stage directions, lighting, etc.; and they were finding the play interesting.

Here is a section of the transcript of the group at work from the time Cliff joined in.

| *Small Group With the Teacher* | *Teacher's Comments* |
|---|---|
| *Teacher:* What've you come up with so far? | Information seeking. |
| *M:* Oh, we've come up with . . . Willy's cracked. There's something wrong with him. . . | Putting forward an idea — reporting group findings. |
| *J:* How the setting's like . . . the double time sort of thing . . . trying to follow two different people at one time . . . where they've got Willy in his bedroom and Biff wandering down to have a cigarette . . . it's sort of confusing trying to watch both sides. | Supporting, reporting, summarising. |
| *P:* When Willy's talking about the football game, this great star, and all of a sudden you see the great star picking up a cigarette. That's not a great star . . . | |

*J:* Not somebody you'd want to idolise.

Supportive of each other.

*P:* No, a degenerate sort of person.

*J:* And, umm, how Biff at the end of Act One, he's bathed in a golden light . . .

*M:* We can't work out exactly why Willy wants to commit suicide, because he gives the impression to everyone that he's successful, and Charley and Linda know that he's a fake . . . at this stage. So we're not exactly sure why . . . which I suppose is good to this point, Act One.

Putting forward a query.

To this point, M and J are summarising. Out of this summary, M suggests a tentative hypothesis.

*Teacher:* Why?

Seeking further explanation.

*M:* Because as I said, it leaves us expecting something.

*J:* Yeah. Probably because he's worth more dead than he is alive.

Supportive of M.

*P:* We don't know whether he actually believes what . . . his lies . . . or . . .

*Tim:* Yeah, back here . . . (flicking through book)

*M:* Leaves us up in the air.

*Tim:* Linda questioned him about how much he's sold in Boston and Providence . . .

*P:* . . . gets out the pencil . . .

*Tim:* And he had to correct himself . . .

M: Linda *knows*, doesn't she?

Making an assertion, as much as seeking support.

. . .

P: And we also came up with Happy was pretty well put down by Willy and Linda, because Linda disregards his "I'm gonna get married".

J and P, in supporting each other, develop their ideas about Happy.

J: He's not, not part of the family.

P: Something like that is pretty important.

J: He's more the American type, you see . . .
womanising, on the grog all the time, got his own apartment . . .

P: He plays the system . . .

Teacher: Can we summarise the situation so far by imagining yourself in the foyer of the theatre. Act One has just finished. How do you *feel*? Are you looking forward to Act Two, or are you feeling that you've wasted your money and you might as well go across to M<sup>c</sup>Donald's over the road?

Asking for comment/suggestions. Steering the discussion away from summarising the first question to focusing on the second (suggested) question.

J: I think I'd like to see Act Two.

D: Depends how much I know about the play. If I know it's a tragedy, then I'd be, sort of . . .

P: . . . expecting.

*D:* . . . umm, something terrible's going to happen. And everything's gone pretty well so far.

*M:* I'd be interested because I could tell by this stage that Willy's not the full quid, and you wouldn't know *exactly* what to expect. It's just not the normal. It doesn't feel normal, like, umm, Shakespeare or something where you can foresee everything upon him. umm . . .

M begins to talk himself towards a point of clarity.

*Teacher:* What are you saying, Mike? That . . .

Asking for clarification.

*M:* I'm saying that, *yes*, I *would* stay around, for sure, because there's the suicide bit with the pipe . . . And Willy's not all there . . .

M is now quite definite in his own mind.

*D:* And the situation with Bill Oliver, see how that ends up.

Extra ideas supporting M.

*P:* And what about Howard?

*D:* Yes, Howard.

*Teacher:* OK. You seem to be saying that the interest lies with what happens with Willy.

*Several:* Yeah.

*Teacher:* Any other characters? . .

Asking for information.

*J:* Yeah, Biff, how he comes good at the end, or he falls down and out, further than what he is.

Speculation.

*P:* Whether he finds himself.

. . .

| | |
|---|---|
| *M:* And we were just talking about how the dreams let us in to so many things, like all the past history though it really gave us the insight into everything, and it's given us a few reasons for this and that . . . And we were just saying that if *we were seeing* this we'd be a bit . . . I dunno . . . depressed or perplexed about what was said and how people walked through doors . . . | Summarising *and* hypothesising. |
| *Teacher:* Did you have any issues that you didn't agree on? | Asking for comment. |
| *P:* We had . . . with Willy . . . some people didn't . . . I thought he was the typical American and some didn't think that. | Summarising. |
| *J:* Yeah . . . you know how most Americans are . . . idolise lots of money, the great American dream . . . Willy doesn't seem that at all; he hasn't really made anything with his life. | Evidence in support of 'some didn't think that'. |
| *P:* He's tried to . . . | |
| *J:* He's tried to but he hasn't succeeded . . . | |
| *P:* He's got the American dreams, but . . . | |
| *Tim:* But not everybody's obsessed with them! | Questioning the assertion. |

(general discussion)

| | |
|---|---|
| Yeah, that's right. 'Cause he's obsessed with the idea that he should have made it. That's why he wants to tell everyone he has . . . | Tim is clarifying, reshaping his original misgiving. |
| *P:* He tries to make out that he's a typical American, but deep down he isn't . . . he's really been a failure. | Supporting, clarifying. Changing from initial opinion. |

Cliff's analysis includes the following points.

1. Initially the teacher changed the role of the group members from exploring meaning to reporting findings.
2. The teacher's questions fell into two broad categories:
   • Information extracting: 'What have you come up with so far?' and 'Did you have any issues that you couldn't agree on?'
   • Seeking clarification: 'How do you feel (at the end of Act One)?' and 'What are you saying?'
   In both cases the group acted as a unit, offering summaries of earlier discussion and supporting one another.
3. The teacher (possibly conscious of the tape recorder or wary due to his professional reading about stifling student initiative in small group situations) acted as a participant rather than an evaluator, but even so, he was obviously guiding the discussion. The first half of the discussion was devoted to the students feeding back information from their earlier discussion. The second half focussed on speculating on what would happen after intermission. *All* group members involved themselves and there is some evidence of a return to some more tentative language, e.g.: 'Death of a Salesman . . . I don't know. It's not just the normal. It just doesn't feel normal, like, umm, Shakespeare or something where you can foresee everything upon him . . . umm . . . ' Such a contribution encouraged other students to speculate, e.g.: 'And the situation with Bill Oliver, see how that ends up . . . ' or 'And what about Howard and that?'
4. Towards the end of the discussion, a previously mentioned point of contention — which character is the typical American — resurfaced. The students at this stage seemed genuinely interested in the issue to the extent that the focus shifted from the teacher

to within the group. The student who initially suggested that Willy was the typical American ended up by saying, 'He *tries* to make out that he's the typical American, but deep down he isn't . . .' He has changed his opinion through discussion which at no stage rejected his opinion as wrong or stupid.

The presence of the teacher did not significantly alter the informality of the language used or the relaxed supportive relationships. However, it did ensure that the group would approach the 'reading/acting' of Act Two with some definite ideas to be tested and verified. In focussing the students' attention on their expectations, Cliff foreshadowed to them that their activities as readers, as well as the dramatists' methods, would be on the classroom agenda in the near future. I think this short extract shows how the trusted-adult teacher's intervention in small group discussion can be very valuable without stifling exploration.

## NOTE-MAKING

The Higher School Certificate English course is primarily a course in writing, and the mode of writing most demanded is the formal literary critical essay. In Years 11 and 12 the quality of the final draft essay depends to a large extent on the quality of the talk and the more informal writing that precedes it. Too often students are expected to write critical essays with no other preparation than a first reading of a text and some discussion in class. Their problems are considerably exacerbated if the only kind of expository writing they have experienced in Years 7 to 10 is narrative re-telling in its worst form of mindless plot summarising.

What we are really looking for, then, in a course in writing in response to literature for senior students, is ways of helping them to develop and refine their interpretative skills. We need to encourage and legitimise simpler forms of writing in which, as John Dixon puts it, 'reflective commentary has a steady opportunity to emerge without creating [the] structural problems'[33] that the critical essay creates. If, as James Britton says, active response involves 'an unspoken monologue of responses — a fabric of comment, speculation, relevant autobiography'[34], then we need not only ways of developing this active response in students, but also transitional forms of writing in which 'commentary, speculation and relevant autobiography' are combined to facilitate the development of the analytical written skills needed to express and communicate that response with some precision. What is needed is an informal kind of note-making which stays close to the text and helps students interpret the significance of events, and which, like journal writing, is seen by them as a medium for personal reflection and discovery, an aid to the development and articulation of response rather than as an impediment to these processes.

## Column notes

Lola Brown suggests that a class keep two running commentaries as they read a novel, with the left-hand page used for recording what happens and the right-hand page used for 'commentary, speculation, relevant autobiography', the formulation of possible connections and personal significances.[35] Jane Ogborn encourages her London sixth form students to keep a 'chapter chart' during their reading of an A-Level set text. The columns for the note-making are headed 'Chapter Number, When, Where, Who, What Events and Why'. These columns, filled in as briefly as possible, 'form a source of reference when finding specific incidents later to illustrate points in essays and discussion'.[36] Jane Ogborn says that for novels which have a complex time sequence this kind of chart 'can alert students to aspects of structure in a focused way'. Students can become more perceptive about characterisation, too, by listing or summarising each main character's actions in one column, indicating the interpreted motives and predicted consequences of them in a second and third column, and drawing conclusions about the character's role and significance in a fourth column.

John Dixon shows how students encouraged to adopt forms of writing which 'interweave commentary and text' can be helped to sort out the sense of a poem, to see the poem as a construction of a poet's feeling and intent, and to move towards personal judgments.[37] He also says that the column form of note-making can be useful in developing response to drama texts by helping students to visualise the action on the stage and, at the same time, to reflect on its progressive significance. The left-hand column summarises in narrative form the stage movements and events, and the right-hand column consists of commentary, headed 'Reasons for stage directions and interpretation of lines'. As Dixon says, 'Even to detach the "comment" from the effective narrative of the play (the left-hand column) is a steady reminder to the student of the value of both sides'.[38]

Such forms of note-making provide an excellent basis for class discussion and for moving into continuous prose of a more sustained, coherent and analytical kind. They are designed to assist students to develop their language, thought and feeling in response. They can lead to both greater insight into texts and more carefully structured critical writing that is appropriately detached without any loss of the personal elements of response. The aim in introducing such note-making methods is always to help students become more aware of the significance of events, character, situation and setting, and of the ways these things are ordered in texts; and, further, to be able to make interpretative generalisations about them.

### Diagrams

Another form of note-making transitional between the narrative summary and the shaped essay is the diagrammatic representation which helps students, as David Jackson puts it, to begin 'systematizing their fragmentary response into patterns of meaning'[39]. The advantage of the diagram over linear notes is that in constructing it, students are guided towards making a coherent representation of the work as a whole. For example, a student

Table 3: Structural Pattern of *Free Fall*

| D present | → | ABC past | → | E present |
|---|---|---|---|---|
| first part of Chapter 1 | → | memory: Chapters 1 to 12 | → | Chapters 13 and 14: visit to Beatrice in mental hospital and to Nick Shales and Rowena Pringle |
| what I am like now | → | search into past to find when/how I became as I am now | → | consequences of what I have become and where I can go from here |

working from a 'chapter chart' he had kept on William Golding's novel *Free Fall* produced the following diagram of the novel's structural pattern. It compares the chronological order of events with Golding's complex restructuring of them as they occur in the memory of the protagonist, Sammy Mountjoy, who is searching for a pattern that explains his own life. In subjecting his own past life to intense scrutiny, Sammy is looking particularly for the time/event/decision in his life that lost him his freedom and turned him into the automaton, or freely falling object in spatial vacuum, he believes he has become.

However, this is an oversimplification because it does not indicate that the selected episodes from Sammy's past life are not recalled in chronological order. A more detailed diagram is needed to show the narrative structure accurately. There are 14 chapters, but in Chapter One we have two parts — Sammy at the present moment and his reminiscences of early childhood — so we need 15 letters, A to O, for 14 chapters, with alphabetical order representing the chronological order of events.

## Table 4: Structural Pattern of *Free Fall* in detail

| Chapter | | Chronological | | Event |
|---|---|---|---|---|
| | 1 (pp.5-9) | M | | Sammy in the *present* — self-reflecting |
| | 1 (pp.9-35) | A | | early childhood |
| Pre-Fall | 2 | B | | primary school |
| | 3 | C | | young boyhood — adventures |
| | 4 | F | F | Beatrice — Communist Party — young manhood |
| | 5 | G | l a | seduction of Beatrice |
| | 6 | H | s | marries Taffy, joins army and war |
| Post-Fall | 7 | I | h | prisoner — interview with Halde |
| | 8 | J | b | reflections on Halde and Watts-Watt |
| | 9 | K | a | confinement in cell |
| | 10 | L | c k | release |
| | 11 | D | | secondary school — Nick Shales (Science) and Rowena Pringle (Religion) |
| Fall | 12 | E | | secondary school — to leaving |
| | 13 | N | | visit to Beatrice |
| | 14 | O | | visit to Nick and Rowena final reflections — no bridge between worlds of flesh and spirit, science and religion |

Greg's diagram helps him to recognise that the logic that governs the narrative order of events is non-chronological, and it gives him a framework for beginning to decipher that logic. It also helps him to realise that behind Sammy Mountjoy's selection and re-ordering of the events of his past as they occur in memory according to their apparent importance to his enquiry, there is Golding's purpose as author. He has, therefore, a framework for exploring and interpreting the structural significance of the novel in relation to its themes.

A further example of the use of diagrams to help senior students to find coherence and patterns of meaning in texts comes from the work of a Year 11 class at Kelso High School (in Bathurst) working with the Head of Department, John Payne. After reading and discussing four poems of John Keats ('Ode to a Nightingale', 'To Autumn', 'Ode on a Grecian Urn' and 'Ode on Melancholy'), the students were asked to summarise what they saw as Keats' major concerns in any form they liked, using key words to define the main concepts, but not writing in continuous prose. Payne wanted the students 'to crystallise Keats' concerns clearly and eye-catchingly, to identify commonalities and differences in the poems strikingly'. The diagram in Figure 1 represents a flawed but productive attempt to realise the abstractions of the poems. The student, Liz, is taking the first steps towards formulating Keats' paradoxical notions about the relationship between the truth and beauty of art and the truth and beauty of life — that beauty is truth, but not achievable in life, and that life is truth but, being ephemeral, is not permanently beautiful. The organisational power conferred by this form of note-making enables students like Liz to make sense for themselves of complex concepts in literature.

Another student in the class drew a diagram in the form of a spider's web stretched between poles of life and death on one dimension and of permanence and impermanence on the other. This brought out to the student the binary oppositions and paradoxes of sickness/health, mortality/immortality, acceptance/rejection, reality/escapism, humanity/inhumanity, sadness/happiness, and an understanding of Keats' theme of the limitation of the reconciliation of these oppositions achieved in art. Getting ideas down on paper in diagrammatic form helps the student to formulate and connect the generalisations, and then see at a glance their global structure of relationships. It is the instant self-evaluation that the diagram makes possible that enables students to see the repetitions, contradictions and vaguenesses in their conceptualisations and to

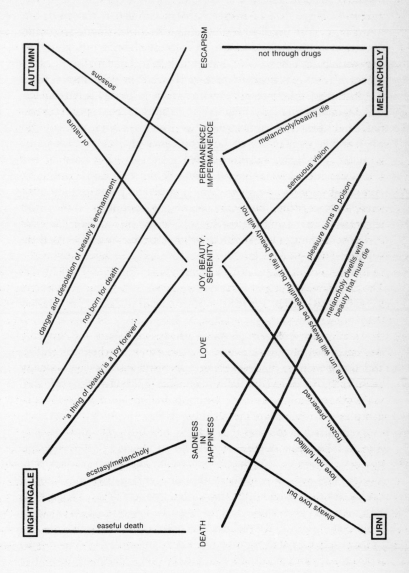

Figure 1: Diagrammatic description of four Keats poems

amend them. The diagrams can also be discussed in small groups in which each student has the opportunity to justify his or her representation and be challenged and questioned by others.

After the work on diagramming the odes, John Payne asked the class to write a sustained first-draft essay in class on a Keats poem they hadn't discussed: 'To what extent is the poem "Bright Star" typical of the Keats poems you have studied? In your answer refer to at least three other poems.' The students were told to avoid making comments they were not prepared to explore, such as pointing out that 'Bright Star' is a sonnet while the others are odes, unless some substantial statement about the significance of these forms was to be made. The essays written varied in quality, but most of the students produced something that was better than would normally have been expected of them. The important point is that their perceptions were their own, and personally formulated, rather than being taken over from the teacher or a crib, and so they gave the teacher something to work with in helping to develop and refine their responses.

## EXTENDED GROUP WORK

In organising work in English that emphasises coherence, connectedness, integration and continuity in reading, listening, talking and writing, the teacher needs to provide frameworks which are sufficiently ordered to offer students guidance, support and understanding of purposes without being strait-jackets, and sufficiently flexible to encourage them to take the initiative without being confused as to what they are expected or entitled to do and why. As John Dixon said in *Growth Through English*, 'What we want is something less specific than a curriculum and more ordered than chaos.'[40] This section consists mainly of a unit of work based on a literary text organised by David Moss with a Year 10 class at Cabramatta High School. It illustrates the 'negotiated curriculum' in practice, with the teacher's purposes and rationale for his framework being made perfectly explicit to students who were invited to develop their own initiatives in groups and to take responsibility for their own learning. An understanding of students' processes of literary response and of the role of language in learning informs David Moss's planning and classroom methods.

David's unit of work is based on a shared class text, with the class divided into groups each of which considers a different aspect of the text. There are many other ways of organising units of work involving literature. There are the various forms of thematic organisation, for example:

- *the multiple sources approach*, which draws on a number of related verse and prose extracts, film, photograph and song, chosen from a variety of sources such as short story, novel, non-fiction, newspapers, magazines, television and records. Beginning with personal experience and/or reading, pupils move into talking, dramatic improvisation, writing, co-operative presentations and wider related reading.
- *the multiple text approach*, which uses a number of texts linked by a shared theme. This involves, amongst other activities, comparing the different responses and attitudes of writers to similar topics, and/or the different methods they use to dramatise similar themes. Sometimes, five or six different groups in a class might be given different novels on the same general topic. For example, on the topic of war, six groups in a Year 8 class might each explore one of the following novels and then report back to the rest of the class in a plenary session where comparisons and contrasts are drawn: *The Silver Sword* (Seraillier), *Carrie's War* (Bawden), *Fireweed* (Walsh), *Friedrich* (Richter), *I Am David* (Holm) and *The Machine Gunners* (Westall).

Units of work might sometimes be based on texts with similar themes and distinctively different narrative methods in order to enable the students to focus on narrative techniques and their different effects. On another occasion, texts might be selected on the basis of having similar narrative methods and quite different themes to help students to explore the range of effects that a narrative mode can achieve. Genre studies and author studies are other forms of unit organisation, the former enabling students to explore specific characteristics of science fiction or the sonnet, for example; and the latter involving students in considering texts as human constructs rather than as awe-inspiring artefacts to be admired from a distance.

Apart from the range of forms of writing that students might produce individually in response to literature (see pp.295–336), there are many co-operative group performative activities that can take them deeper into texts and into themselves. These include preparing readings to present to others, sometimes live and sometimes on tape, with or without sound effects and musical backing; role playing the author or a character and being interviewed by others (at a press conference, for example); debating issues raised by a novel; rewriting and re-presenting in another medium (for example, turning a short story into a radio play on tape, writing newspaper reports of events in novels); making film or video versions of episodes from texts or improvisations of them; mock trials of appropriate characters; making board games from novels structured as quests or escapes (for example, *The Hobbit*); and conducting television, radio and newspaper advertising campaigns for a book to promote it to readers of the same age group. There are variations within all of these activities, too. For example, in recreating a text through film or video, there is a range of possibilities, all important in helping students to see the constructed nature of literature through engaging in processes of construction themselves. One group might take from a story the same characters, the same events and the same setting but change the time and the social values; another might keep everything else constant except the setting, and so on. Students involved in this kind of imaginative recreation come to recognise that they are the creators of new texts, that their improvisations vary the meanings of original texts in ways that are consciously understood and controlled by them.

Ultimately, most important of all, the active involvement and performance must be followed by reflective (and reflexive) evaluation so that students are given the time and opportunity to make explicit to themselves and to others what they have learned from their activity about literature, about themselves as people, and about their productive and not-so-productive ways of learning. Here are some of the sorts of questions that need to be discussed as part of the final, evaluative stage of a unit of work involving performance.

- What were the problems?
- How did you solve them?
- Were there any not solved?
- Would you go about it any differently if you were starting again now?
- What was the effect on your working of knowing that you had to produce a finished product?
- How valuable was it as a way of exploring literature?
- What did you learn about the text? the world? yourself?
- What did you learn about your ways of learning?
- Consider the kinds of language you used throughout the unit in

talking and writing. What would you say about your competence in language? What can you do well? What do you do not so well? What kinds of things do you need to do to keep on improving?

At all stages of work in English, students must see themselves as part-owners of the game and not as the teacher's puppets.


## *A UNIT OF WORK ON* TO KILL A MOCKINGBIRD *WITH A YEAR 10 CLASS*

by David Moss, Head of English at
Ingleburn High School (formerly
Head of English at Cabramatta High
School).

The approach was developed because:

- I was sick of handing down interpretations to students intelligent enough to have their own;
- I wanted students to tell me what they thought was worth study in a particular novel;
- I wanted a dramatic increase in the active participation of my students;
- I wanted lots of writing of different sorts;
- I wanted student talk ranging from informal to formal and public to be the basis of the unit; and
- I wanted the chance to observe students' performances in a range of different activities.

**The aim of the unit** was not just to teach a novel because of the value I thought it had; there were other issues I regarded as more important:

- improving social interaction in the class;
- reducing competitiveness and increasing cooperation;
- encouraging genuine thinking, hypothesising, speculation and use of the imagination;
- relating literature to their own lives, since this novel touches so much on issues alive and well in Cabramatta; and
- allowing me to get to know a new class and its pupils much more quickly and intimately than a classroom normally allows.

**My evaluation of the unit:** The level of talk in both small groups and full class left me reeling and I'll let the quality of their study guides testify to that. Students reached degrees of hypothesising and synthesising I have often seen since but not before.


### *To Kill A Mockingbird* by Harper Lee

This unit of work was developed by 10E1 in 1981 as a result of group discussion and panel-conducted classroom lessons. The following procedure was adopted.
1. One week was spent by students in reading the novel. There was no formal classwork at this stage.
2. Two periods were spent in full-class session to negotiate the topics of major importance and interest. Suggestions were made and discussed by class members and collated into the lists of aims and guidelines following.
3. Two weeks were spent in groups of five or six as students discussed and prepared their study guide on the topic they had selected.
4. One week was spent in class discussions in which each group acted as a panel to lead work on its particular study guide.
5. Each group set an assignment as a result of its particular lesson. These assignments were handed to Mr Moss for marking when the unit was completed.
6. Each group was assessed according to the following criteria:
   • cooperation, initiative, relevance, organisation in small groups;
   • the written product (study-guide) of the group's work; and
   • the quality of the lesson the group gave.
7. Individuals were assessed according to these criteria:
   • contribution to group work;
   • role in his/her panel;
   • participation in full-class discussion; and
   • quality of written work on five assignments.


### Aims for 10E1's Unit on *To Kill a Mockingbird*

These aims were negotiated by the whole class in collaboration with the teacher.

1. **To examine closely the courtroom scene in order to:**
   - show how racial discrimination interferes with better judgment;
   - show Atticus's skill as an attorney; and
   - discuss town's reaction to a verdict of not guilty.

2. **To examine the effects of children's curiosity:**
   - Jem's dare to touch the Radley house;
   - Night time adventure to Radley house;
   - the hole in the tree and the wheel incident;
   - play scenes;
   - fire/blanket; and
   - children question Atticus.

3. **To examine the changes in the Jem/Scout relationship:**
   - Scout goes to school and disowns Jem;
   - Jem and Dill ignore Scout;
   - closeness between Scout and Jem early in the novel and together in crisis at end;
   - the way Jem and Scout mature during the novel; and
   - the effects on them of these people: Aunty Alexandra, Mrs Dubose, Calpurnia, Maudie Atkinson, Tom Robinson, Dill, Heck Tate, Boo Radley.

4. **To discover if Maycomb is a typical town, and what the characteristics of its people are:**
   - religious attitudes of townsfolk;
   - attitudes of townsfolk to negroes;
   - isolation of Maycomb;
   - attitudes to education;
   - attitudes to each other; and
   - the social ladder.

5. **To examine the character of Atticus:**
   - mad dog incident;
   - background;
   - relationship with younger brother;
   - human sympathy;
   - sense of pride and responsibility;
   - the gaol scene;

- Atticus as a father, and a brother; and
- his seriousness.

6. **To examine racial prejudice as a general human characteristic:**
   - short stories and poems; and
   - our own prejudices.

7. **To examine changes in the classroom or educational system:**
   - relevant sections of *To Kill a Mockingbird*; and
   - extracts from other novels or short stories.

8. **To examine the novel's language:**
   - regional variation; and
   - style.

Five groups formed to explore topics 1 to 5 with topics 6 to 8 left for discussion in the full-class situation.

**Guidelines for group work 10E1 March 23 to March 27**
(NB: Absolute deadline Friday March 27)

To Kill A Mockingbird, Harper Lee

1. Appoint a recorder to take notes on everything done. No one else is to write during discussion.
2. Discuss the stated aim for your group (1 to 5).
3. Write out your aims in more detail stating what you wish to achieve or discover.
4. List exactly all the scenes from the novel that your group is examining, e.g. p. 75-76 "sometimes we heard . . . orange centre".
5. Explain why you think each of the above scenes should be included in your aim.
6. Read, re-read and discuss each scene carefully.
7. Prepare a list of questions on each scene which can later be discussed in class.
8. Set a small assignment for the class to do on your particular theme:
   - a *brief* composition;
   - a letter, essay, report;
   - a series of questions; or

- a statement of opinion.

But it should be brief enough to do in one night.

9. Write out all the above material on stencils to be given to the class.
10. Your group will form a panel to run a lesson on your topic (so decide who is to do what). Your stencil will form the basis of this lesson.

**Marks will be awarded to each group on the basis of:**

(a) quality of the work on the stencil; and
(b) the lesson you give.

Here is one group's preparation for panel presentation to the rest of the class.

**Group 2: Children's curiosity**

The purpose of group 2 is to examine the effects of Dill's, Jem's and Scout's curiosity, as well as children's curiosity in general. We have discovered that a child's weird explanations of things he/she doesn't understand is usually just an excuse or reason for what they believe in. The children's questioning of Atticus became more like a habit. If Jem and Scout wanted to find out about something they didn't understand, they knew only to ask Atticus for a truthful answer. Maybe they only asked Atticus for a truthful answer because they knew he would answer them to the best of his knowledge, which he had a lot of, and also he left a lot of things up to their imagination.

Each individual from our group will discuss each scene and will look upon you to give us your opinion on each scene.

**Jem's dare to touch Radley house** (pp. 19, 20, 21)

The first incident backs up our conclusion about their overpowering imagination and curiosity. This simply came about with Jem's description of Boo Radley (who they have never seen in real life) stated on p. 19. Boo was supposedly about 6½ feet tall, judging from his tracks; he dines on raw squirrels and any cats he could catch. There was a long jagged scar that ran across his face. What teeth he had were yellow and rotten; his eyes popped, and he drooled most of the time.

Dill suggested that they try to make him come out to see what he looks like thus discovering if he met Jem's description.

Jem at first was against even placing a toe in the Radley property. He stated, if Dill wants to get himself killed, all he had to do was to go up and knock on the front door. This unrealistic point of view was shared by the three kids.

In all Jem's life he had never declined a dare, therefore Dill was satisfied. Jem agreed only to touch the house and he did so, and he never stopped running till he got home. To them the house still looked the same — droopy and sick looking, and with their imagination they thought they saw a shutter move.

The kids' curiosity was more of a guessing game. They believed the legends (and accusations) they had heard from other people. *Question:* Do you think Jem took this dare on to prove himself not scared or to solve his own curious feelings?

### The Playscenes (pp. 44-45)

The kids like playing "The Radleys" for many reasons. Maybe because they have no real explanation for what the Radleys are really like. The only explanations they have is what they get from gossip or neighbourhood legend, or what they make up themselves.

Once they gathered their information they acted out the parts of the Radley family. Scout was Mrs Radley, who only came out to sweep the porch. They had probably seen Mrs Radley doing this so they exaggerated.

Dill was old Mr Radley: the only thing he had to do was walk up and down the footpath and cough everytime someone spoke to him.

And of course Jem was Boo: naturally being the oldest and bravest (as Dill and Scout considered him to be).

Most of their information came from Stephanie Crawford who said more about the Radleys than anyone. Going from what they had portrayed, Boo was something evil and stupid.

All Jem had to do was sit and cut up newspapers and jab a pair of scissors into Dill's leg. Dill was considered the villain's villain. Dill had to do mean things to everyone, such as cram Jem under the porch and hit him with the broom now and again, whenever Boo let out a shriek or howl.

Scout had the quiet part, Mrs Radley. They didn't know much

about her but from what they were told she was a beautiful lady until she married Nathan Radley. They also thought she had lost her forefinger when Boo bit it off when he couldn't find cats or squirrels to eat.

They played the scenes as they thought they should be played. Each day adding a piece of dialogue until they had come up with a small play of the Radley family. They played these scenes to give them some sort of explanation. Even if they weren't true, they still gave them satisfaction and pride.

*Question:* Why do you think that the kids act the way they do? Is it because they are trying to hide the truth about the Radleys or is it because they are just kids who are growing up too quickly? And why are they always asking Atticus the explanation of everything? Are they too curious for their ages?

## The night time excursion (pp. 57-60)

The whole purpose of the night time excursion to the Radley house was to satisfy curiosity. "Dill and Jem were simply going to peep in the window with the loose shutter to see if they could get a look at Boo Radley." (p. 57)

As the children were sneaking through the Radleys' back yard just the sight of it made them scared. This boosted the children's curiosity even higher. Even though the children had a terrifying experience it didn't stop them from trying to lure Boo out, later on.

Jem's pants were caught in the fence, and he was scared to go back to get them, there was a very high chance that he would be caught by someone or perhaps even shot by Nathan Radley. But he was determined to go back there to get his pants no matter how Scout tried to talk him out of it.

I think that the shock of Jem finding his pants roughly sewn scared Jem more than when Nathan took a shot at him. He had a feeling deep inside of him that kept on telling him that it had been Boo who had repaired his pants but he couldn't face it in reality, because it was "like somebody was readin' my mind . . ."

*Question:* Was it something the children were trying to prove to each other or themselves that caused them to venture into the Radley house?

292

### The fire incident (p. 75-78)

This started when Miss Maudie Atkinson's house was on fire. The children were told to stand in front of the Radley house and they did. When the fire was under control they went home and had hot chocolate. Scout found a blanket had been placed around her. Thinking it was Miss Maudie's blanket, Scout thanked her. Miss Maudie said that it wasn't hers. Then, Atticus said that Boo put the blanket around her. Their stomachs turned. The thought of Boo Radley putting a blanket around them scared them but also aroused their curiosity as to what kind of a person Boo is.

Whether Boo is a kind enough person to put the blanket around them or whether he is a psychopath and he was going to strangle them with the blanket, but his plans were foiled. That was what was probably going on in their heads. They're probably trying to remember unknown faces at the fire in the hope of identifying Boo.

Jem did a portrayal of Boo putting on the blanket. He slouched and dragged his feet, portraying Boo as a monster.

Question: Do you think this incident would urge on Scout and Jem in their quest to find out who or what Boo Radley is?

### The hole in the tree incident (pp. 41, 65)

It all began when Scout ran past the Radley house after school and some tin foil, which reflected in the sun, caught her attention. The tin foil was hanging from a hole in a tree which was in front of the Radley house.

It was Scout's curiosity which made her approach the tree. She stood in front of the Radley house, not even scared, as if she did not realise she was standing there. I think the reason she didn't notice she was standing there was that she wasn't influenced by Dill and Jem.

Scout took the foil and ran home. Again her curiosity made her unwrap the foil. Jem's and Scout's curiosity led them to the hole but each time they found an object, they both tried to convince themselves that Boo did not put it there, that someone else did. But in both their minds they knew it was Boo.

Impulse made them approach the tree once more to find two dolls, a girl which resembled Scout and a boy which resembled Jem. This time there was no explanation for them to make up. They knew it was Boo who put them there.

The next day Jem and Scout found the tree-hole was filled with cement. Mr Nathan told them the tree was dying, but Atticus said it was perfectly all right.

Questions:
    1. Did Scout notice she was standing in front of the Radley House?
    2. Why was each object wrapped in tin foil?
    3. Why were Jem and Scout trying to hide the fact that Boo put the objects in the hole?
    4. Why did Mr Nathan lie about the tree?

## The wheel incident (pp. 43-44)

The curiosity of the children leads them to hear and believe things that are likely to be untrue.

The wheel incident is a good example of this. The wheel incident was when Jem accidentally pushed Scout into the Radley house right up to the front steps.

Scout had mentioned that apart from all the excitement and shouting she had heard a low laugh that could not have been heard if she were further away. The issue here is whether Scout had really heard it or was it in her imagination.

Was she so curious to know what Boo looked like, how he talked etc., that she had heard the sort of laugh that she thought Boo would utter.

Also, when Jem had gone back to the Radley house to get the tyre, why did he walk in like he was treading water. Why was he scared? Boo wasn't out to get him. It was just that the children imagined Boo to be some maniac.

Questions:
    1. Do you think Scout really heard a laugh from inside the Radley house?
    2. Do you think Jem and Dill would have believed her if she had told them? Would they say it was her imagination because girls also imagine things?

## *To Kill a Mockingbird:* Group-set assignments

### Group 1: The relationship of Jem and Scout

In your opinion what was the major incident causing the reconciliation of Jem and Scout? Give your reasons for believing that this particular incident helped them get back together more than any other event.

*20 marks*

**Group 2: Children's curiosity**

Is the curiosity displayed by Jem and Scout normal for children of that age or are they excessively curious?

Does their curiosity stem from the isolation of the town or is it more the result of their upbringing?

Give reasons for your opinions.

*20 marks*

**Group 3: The character of Atticus**

1. Do you think that when Atticus said "Don't waste time, Heck, go on," he meant to compete with Heck in his skill or hand over his responsibility due to remorse or some other reason?
2. Did Atticus shoot an escapee in the past? Is this a reasonable inference? Was Atticus reliving *some* past incident involving a gun? Does this help to explain his dilemma?
3. The neighbours seem to praise his one shot talent regarding the mad dog. Would Atticus have been a hero in the early days? How would this praise have affected Atticus? Why is this the sort of father Jem would want instead of Atticus as he was?

*20 marks*

**Group 4: The courtroom scene**

Imagine you are Tom Robinson in prison awaiting execution. Write a letter to your wife telling her how you feel and describing the things that have been happening to you.

*20 marks*

**Group 5**

Can you see any similarities in social and racial attitudes between the people of Maycomb county and the people of Cabramatta? If so, what are they?

*20 marks*

*Note:* This is your major term 1 assessment; it should be presented bound in a foolscap folder with each section 1 to 5 clearly defined and separated from the others.

The Group 4 assignment must have *one rough copy included*.

# DEEPENING RESPONSE THROUGH WRITING

## *STARTING POINT: THE LONDON UNIVERSITY AND SCHOOLS COUNCIL RESEARCH ON FUNCTION AND AUDIENCE CATEGORIES OF WRITING*

In the 1970s, James Britton and his colleagues of the London University and Schools Council 'Writing Across the Curriculum' research team showed that writing, like talking, can be an instrument of learning; that not only do we learn to write by writing but we can learn by writing.[41] Because we can work on writing until we are satisfied with it, the shaping process in writing can be more sustained and rigorous than it is in talking. Writing offers a better opportunity for more searching private engagement with experiences, ideas and feelings than talk does.

The London research team examined over 2000 pieces of writing from a representative sample of students aged 11 to 18, and categorised each piece according to the predominant function it served and the sense of audience the writer took up with the reader. They classified writings 'according to the nature of the task and the nature of the demands made upon the writer'[42], hoping by this classification to shed light on the writing process itself. They considered the traditional categories used by teachers — narration, description, exposition and argument, emanating from classical rhetoric — to be inadequate as a 'conceptual framework for the study of writing'[43]. The hypotheses and theoretical positions behind the Britton model, the starting positions of the research, were that language is functional; that writing is a reflective activity, related to cognitive and affective processes; that the writer's sense of audience influences the way she or he writes; and that children's early writing is likely to be expressive — the expressive being the 'relatively undifferentiated matrix from which differentiated forms of writing are developed'[44].

### Britton's function model

On this broad theoretical framework, and including the concept of spectator and participant roles in writing, Britton constructed a function model showing that the purposes of writing might be plotted along a dimension divided into three main sections: Transactional, Expressive, and Poetic (Figure 2). The Transactional function in the

## Figure 2: Function model of the purposes of writing

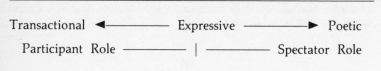

Transactional ◄——————— Expressive ——————► Poetic

Participant Role ——————— | ——————— Spectator Role

participant role lies at one end of the dimension; the Poetic function in the spectator role lies at the other end; and the Expressive function occupies the middle section.

### The expressive function

The notion of the expressive function derives from Edward Sapir's belief that 'ordinary speech is directly expressive'[45]. Expressive language reveals at least as much about the writer (or speaker) as it does about what he is saying. It is informal, intimate language, and the person addressed is regarded as being in a position of trust. Expressive language, then, has an important role in learning, offering the pupil the opportunity to make sense of his own and others' experiences, information and ideas, on his own terms, as well as allowing him to relate the new experience, information and ideas to his existing understanding. Expressive writing, in its relatively unstructured, relaxed expression of a pupil's own feelings and responses to experience in a sympathetic and supportive school environment, is an essential preparation for the more tightly structured situations that will ultimately need transactional and poetic formulation. Britton explains the central importance of the expressive, as follows:

> It appears to be the means by which the new is tentatively explored, thoughts are half-uttered, attitudes half-expressed, the rest being left to be picked up by the listener, or reader, who is willing to take the unexpected on trust. Its use is not, of course always exploratory, but exploratory situations seem to call for it.[46]

### The transactional and poetic functions

Expressive writing, at the centre of the function dimensions, shuttles between participant and spectator roles very easily. The shift from the expressive into the transactional takes place by the elimination of the uniquely personal elements that are inessential to the information we wish to convey. The shift from the expressive to the poetic takes place by a heightening of the feelings, and the latter find expression and take shape in structured patterns. The process is similar to that of writing a poem or a short story, where the structured pattern of feeling is significant for its own sake in creating the total impact of what is, in effect, a verbal artefact.

As expressive writing changes to meet the requirements of transactional writing — recording, reporting, informing, persuading and so on — it becomes more explicit. It has no personal context to depend on so that it needs to provide a context. It needs specific references to give the reader his bearings, and it needs the kind of formal organisation of language most appropriate to the task. It eliminates, therefore, the feelings and individual tones that characterise expressive writing.

The basic model, when placed over the range of writing activities occurring in schools, does provide a useful instrument of classificiation, and indicates the central importance of the expressive function in facilitating the development of a pupil's thinking and the process of incubation of an idea to allow it to grow into something which can be realised in the transactional or the poetic.

## The audience categories

Another dimension to the model, that of audience, was developed as Britton's research team found that the sense of audience the writer has in mind exercises a powerful influence on his writing. The four main audience categories are writing for self, teacher, wider-known audience and unknown audience. The most interesting to this investigation is the second category, obviously because a great deal of students' writing in school is, in one way or another, written with the teacher ultimately in mind. The important aspect of the teacher as an audience category is the role he takes up in the eyes of his pupil.

For a pupil to feel free to write in the expressive mode it would appear that he would need to see his teacher as a trusted adult; whereas the pupil's feeling constrained to write for the teacher-examiner would turn his writing into occasions for testing rather than occasions for learning.

## The research findings

By far the greatest bulk of the writing in all subjects and all years was transactional, and of that, the vast majority was to give information, either in the form of a report or in generalisation. The absence of speculation and hypothesis in the pupils' writing, even among sixth-formers, was noticeable. The strong impression was gained that the unbroken diet of transactional writing had led pupils to believe that their own thinking and their own feelings were deemed to be irrelevant; that what was required of them was the regurgitation of someone else's thinking in someone else's language. Further, as pupils moved up through the secondary school, the increasingly dominant audience was that of the teacher in his most authoritarian role: that of examiner. It would appear that early in the secondary school many teachers set demands on, and audience relationships with, their pupils that tighten the framework for writing tasks, shut out the expressive, and move them increasingly towards transactional writing as a task for assessment. The options available to pupils become increasingly reduced as they moved up in the secondary school.

In the subject English, the main form of writing was the literary critical essay, set and marked as a test of pupils' understanding of their reading and of their mastery of the conventions of formal writing. The predominance of the critical essay in the Higher School Certificate examinations in Australia ensures that the classroom situation here is little different from that in England. The emphasis is on writing as finished product rather than on writing as a process of facilitating pupils' development as readers, writers and people.

In this section, Britton's function model is used as the point of departure for examining some of the kinds of writing that can be encouraged in the classroom to help students to explore and deepen their responses to literature and, simultaneously, to develop their competences in writing in the transactional and poetic modes. The value of Britton's model lies in its clear delineation of the range of purposes writing is used for. In clearly identifying the varied functions of writing in a more coherent and logical way than traditional classification systems, it serves as a guide and check to the teacher that his or her writing programme should encompass the whole range of functions along both arms of the continuum so as to extend students' writing repertoires and to develop their proficiency in all the modes.

## LEVELS OF THE EXPRESSIVE

Britton's notion of the expressive function is a brilliantly productive one. If writing is to be an instrument of learning in the classroom, there must be considerable emphasis on the expressive. Students will write expressively only when they are able to explore a topic in their own way so they become interested in it, and thus, responsible for their own learning, and when they feel secure with their audience. Unless the teacher becomes a trusted adult audience, there will be no expressive writing in the school. However, where Britton sees the expressive as a 'seed bed' for more 'mature' forms of writing like stories and poems (poetic) and critical essays (transactional), I believe that it is more than a mere transitional form: it has its own range of levels along a scale of increasing abstraction, just as the more formal transactional has its levels from recording and reporting to generalising, speculating and theorising. Or, to put it another way, I disagree with Britton when he says that as writing becomes more transactional it sheds its informal and personal elements. Why should it?

At its highest level, expressive writing can be an academically respectable, publishable finished product which is as conceptually powerful as the highest level of the transactional while still retaining its own characteristic informality. Or, to put it another way, the highest level of the transactional is far more effective as communication if it retains its expressive elements. Writing that is relaxed, personal, anecdotal and affective is not necessarily less explicit and/or conceptually weaker than writing which sheds these elements.

The origin of what later becomes high level expressive writing (or transactional writing that retains its expressive elements) might be a spoken comment in class or a tentative jotting in a student's journal. For example, take the following remark of a student in a class of apprentices in response to Shakespeare's 'Sonnet 116' ('Let me not to the marriage of true minds admit impediments'), as reported by David Mallick:

> 'I had a mate and he took his bird on the back of his bike and they had an accident and her face was all cut up and he never went out with her again. That wasn't love, do you reckon, was it?'[47]

Beginning in anecdotal oral responses like this, the expressive develops by relating personal experience and observation to the world of the text and expressing the connections. For example, the next stage might look something like the following, written by Rosemary aged 14, in response to Robert Hayden's poem, 'Those Winter Sundays', after about half an hour's discussion in class.

'THOSE WINTER SUNDAYS

'This poem was really good because it could reach people. It was describing real life and real feelings. The situation written about in the poem involves all of us sometime or other and this is why it was received and analysed so well. Everyone abuses their parents' love at least once, whether in a small or large degree. Everyone has probably intentionally or unintentionally hurt their parents. When we realise we have hurt them we feel guilty. This poem reminds me of times when I have not confided in my parents when they could have wished me to, of times when I have been selfish and said things aimed to hurt. All these and many more I remember. I also remember of how when I was hurt, they comforted me, when I was lonely they befriended me, when I could not help myself, they helped me and when I needed love they loved me.

'I felt guilty about the goodness they have shown which I have not returned. I realised all the little things I hadn't noticed and how, before attending to themselves, they attended to me.

'I feel that no matter how much I show my love for them I will always feel guilty and that I did not show it enough. I will often wonder if they know I love them, even when I am angry at them and I will always think "Am I showing my love the right way?" So, no matter how much we love them and show our love for them we will always feel guilty, for who of us could match the love of our parents?'[48]

In the discussion which preceded the writing, Rosemary had said to her teacher: 'Of course, you know my old man well. Him and I squabble a bit, and he's a bit of a tyrant and he picks on us. You can really hate them sometimes.'

The value of the writing is clearly the greater self-knowledge Rosemary achieves by standing back and looking at herself and her relationships by way of the poem. The poem enlightens her understanding of herself which she clarifies by making explicit in writing. She could now, if she wished, go on to write at a higher level, but still expressively, by exploring the poem more deeply by way of her own personal experiences. In writing this piece, Rosemary is 'thinking aloud' for herself and for her teacher. This not only helps her but it helps the teacher to understand her and the way she responds to literature. Thinking aloud in writing needs to be legitimised as a necessary part of learning. It gives the student an active learning role and a sense of her own competence as a meaning-maker.

Whatever we call this informal kind of writing which progresses through a range of levels as well as varieties, it leaves room for discoveries to be made in the act of writing. It can become a ruminative essay, or a narrative retelling of a story or poem with commentary, or a philosophic reflection. In all its forms and at each level, it is a way of helping students to explore the text as experience. In Rosemary's class, the range of written responses to 'Those Winter Sundays' included poems, narratives based on personal and imagined experience (these along the expressive to poetic arm of Britton's function continuum), journal entries (expressive, in both participant and spectator roles), critical reflection in the form of notes of analysis interweaving text and commentary (ranging along the expressive to transactional arm of the continuum), and ruminative essays with penetrating insights about self and poem (at various levels of the expressive and transactional).

In this next piece, 13-year-old Jane reflects on her process of responding to Tolkien's *Lord of the Rings*.

'I just couldn't stop. It was addictive. The characters were so real. I was absolutely dissolved, transported to a different world.

'It was a book of fantasy—gnomes, goblins, hobbits, elves, dwarves. I was there with them—thinking, looking, seeing what they did. I wanted to read more and more. It was on my mind all the time . . . It was like I was asleep to the world around me, but alive in my thoughts to theirs. I would mentally scream at them not to do this or that but they couldn't hear me. I would never talk to them but just keep silent and follow. It was really great. I didn't want it to stop. I felt very sad at the end, and sometimes through the book I would cry out of pity and sorrow.'[40]

In their writing both Jane and Rosemary are savouring and

clarifying experience at the same time as they are informing their teachers of their responses. While both pieces are predominantly in the spectator role, it is important to note that it is only when the teacher is perceived as a trusted adult audience that pupils can genuinely adopt the spectator role in their writing. When the teacher is perceived as an examiner audience, the transaction with him or her, with its emphasis on performance rather than on learning, inhibits pupils from adopting the spectator role as well as from writing expressively. They feel too vulnerable to express deeply felt matters. The writing of Rosemary and Jane combines reflection on personal feelings and values with communication of information to trusted others. The participant role is evident but it is less pronounced than the spectator role.

Expressive writing could, then, be considered as lying along a continuum from tentative comments, through brief journal entries and responses like Rosemary's and Jane's, to increasingly higher levels. In the section of Chapter Four illustrating level 6 of the developmental model (pp. 213), there are examples of students going further than Jane in making their own reading processes explicit to themselves and to their trusted teachers. At a still higher level of the expressive is the journal writing of Alison, which we looked at in an earlier section of this chapter. Alison traces some of the complex themes in a novel in a more sustained way, and explores them more deeply, than the younger writers whose work is illustrated above.

At the highest level of all — in finished product, publishable form — is the highly explicit expressive 'essay' below, written by David Moss, Head of English at Ingleburn High School. David wrote this analysis of some poems and a short story of Ted Hughes for his Year 12 students and himself. Through demonstration, such as this piece of writing, and continually in his teaching, David encourages students to create personal contexts for interpreting literature.

'When was the last time you lay down on your back and looked at the stars, marvelling at the size of it all? When did you last really look at a tree? Have you ever felt like screaming loud and actually done it? When was the last time you ran naked along a beach in pelting rain? (Remember these questions are rhetorical!) When did you last succumb to some urge you could not name?

'Most of our behaviour in a civilised society is very conventional and according to a formula. There are certain things that are acceptable and some that are not. There are written laws to follow but also a whole host of unwritten customs and traditions we dare not break. In *Huckleberry Finn* we have seen one boy's attempts to escape "civilisation" to a natural freedom: "it's lovely to live on a raft". In Bruce Dawe's poetry we've seen what he sees to be the effects of institutions on individuals. In *The Club* we're going to see the effects of power and institutions on personal relationships.

'Ted Hughes, like these others, believes we have become civilised at great cost. Civilisation has cost us our once close contact with our environment. Once our connection with the earth was basic to our survival. Now we divorce ourselves from our origins. From four feet we have gone to two feet, from two feet we have taken to the air. We control our climate by air conditioning and we control our food by refining it.

'The word "refining" is an interesting one when we look at Hughes' poetry. Normally we regard it as a compliment to call someone "refined" — it means, among other things, educated, well-mannered, charming, sophisticated and above all, civilised. Would Hughes necessarily regard "refinement" as a good quality? It might be helpful here to think of another use of the word "refined". Is it good for your health to eat only heavily refined food? Dieticians are starting to associate our civilised emphasis on refined foods with the civilised disease called cancer. When food is refined we lose much of its original goodness. To Hughes the refined man has lost much of his original quality too — his connection with the power of nature, with his environment. You'll remember that the hawk doesn't think much of the benefits of civilisation such as sophistication when he says:
    "There is no sophistry in my body."
Clearly Hughes does not think much of sophistication when it's compared to the power of a creature such as the hawk.

'In "The Rain Horse" the horse itself is a symbol for all that power and wildness, all those urges, which civilisation has removed. The narrator is reminded that in 12 years he has lost the connections he once had with his land. The Camel regards him as an outcast and the horse serves as a reminder. He does not feel safe until he returns to the civilised farm, but it's important that the story finishes with the man feeling "as if some important part had been cut out of his brain". This man has been "refined". What has been cut out is his connection with this world, the earth, nature. He is now more concerned with his suit, a sign of his civilised life style.

'In the poem called "The Thought-fox" Hughes shows us the power of the poetic imagination in restoring a man's links with the environment. Hughes is actually so close to nature here that his own thought processes are likened to the movement of a fox. It's important that Hughes wrote this poem spontaneously, without effort or organising, as if the very power of nature inspired him. This is not the typical image of the poet who forces his ideas into a literary conventional form. Hughes' poem takes its own shape. As he says himself, it actually captures an animal.

'Of course animals don't always escape the influence of civilisation. The jaguar is forced into the civilised surroundings of a zoo. Many of the zoo's animals succumb, are prostituted and exploited, reduced to nursery wall images only. The jaguar is an animal whose spirit refused to be confined. This is the sort of power and dynamism we have denied ourselves by imprisoning ourselves within an artificial environment.

'Hawk Roosting' is Hughes' ultimate statement about the power which resides in nature. Here is an animal with no rationalisations, falsifying dreams, arguments, manners or sophistry. Its arrogance asserts not only nature's power but man's ultimate inability to totally destroy nature. Because nature will ultimately triumph, man must come to terms with it, regain his connections with it, tap its awesome power.

'All of these animals are symbols. Hughes is not just saying that it's too late for mankind because he has lost his origins. These animals symbolise human characteristics and potential that we have repressed under civilised niceties. But the fact that these primal and elemental urges lurk in our mind like the pike in Hughes' pond mean that we are always dissatisfied, always yearning, longing, seeking something in our lives which is just out of reach. Hughes thinks we need to acknowledge and use these primitive drives, not squash them under a load of civilised rules and roles.

'As I write this essay I can look to my left and see logs burning, embers glowing, flames licking up the chimney. Why is it we all love to stare into an open fire, can do it for hours, are fascinated and mesmerised by fire? Is it a legacy from the campfires of our primitive ancestors, the campfires they, and therefore we, needed so desperately for survival? And yet even this one lingering trace of our origins can be submerged under more artificial attempts to control our environments . . . oil heaters, space heaters, air conditioning . . .'

You will note the fluid movement between expressive, poetic and transactional modes in a piece of writing whose predominant function is transactional but whose expressive elements, far from being a barrier to communication, make it a far more interesting and compelling piece of reading. The range of felt and thought response is conveyed with exactness because of David's use of a range of writing modes. In matching his own world views with those of Ted Hughes (as dramatised in the poems and story), in consciously considering his relationship with the author and in making explicit elements of textual ideology, David reaches the highest levels of literary response specified in the developmental model outlined in Chapter Four (p. 179). Also, in terms of Britton's model of writing functions, this piece reaches the highest level of the transactional informative function ('tautologic' or theorising) in that 'generalisation is the subject of the discourse' and 'meaning is carried by an interconnected web of generalisations, serving to advance a theory'.[50]

You don't get students in Year 12 producing writing of this outstanding quality unless they have been encouraged to talk and write expressively along the way. It is the frequent opportunity to write and talk as Rosemary and Jane have written and talked that leads, eventually, to writing such as David's. David's essay combines the most effective features of the expressive and transactional functions. It has the coherence and logic of organisation, the explicitness and depth of analysis characteristic of the highest levels of the transactional informative, and it retains the informal, personal and affective elements of the expressive.

## TRANSACTIONAL WRITING: FORM AND FUNCTION

David Moss's essay on Ted Hughes shows how, at the highest levels of critical writing, expressive modes can be used to fulfil transactional purposes and that they can be more comfortable for the writer and more effective for the reader than the traditional transactional forms. For learners, the conventional literary critical essay favoured in scholarly publications and public examinations is merely an inhibiting form, having no value in helping students to order their own responses or to communicate them clearly to others. It is a form of writing that creates apprehension and fear among many students who, in feeling compelled to imitate its stylistic superficialities, shift their focus of attention from what they are ostensibly thinking and writing about to the instrument they are using.

Here are the comments of two final-year Teacher Education students about their experiences of writing transactionally in a tertiary institution. Both students graduated with distinguished records, so their disgruntlement is not caused by failure or a sense of personal inadequacy.

'If more expressive writing was permitted in this College — people writing from their own experience in relation to *whatever* subject they are writing about, rather than writing neat paraphrases from the works of educational gurus as demanded by lecturers — then this institution might become a place of real learning rather than a diploma factory.'

'All we write is formal essays in which any trace of honest thinking or feeling gets penalised. Look, if this was not my last semester, what I'd like to do for my next Education assignment is to hand in a sheet full of references and write on the bottom, "This is what you want → the experts' opinions, read it yourself". After 12 months at this institution I found out that lecturers don't want to know what I feel or think. They just want to know that we know what the experts think. Any assignment with four or more quotations (properly footnoted) wins an A. The fewer quotations, the lower the mark. In other words, they don't believe we could possibly have the brains to offer anything worthwhile . . . I want to learn, but I don't just want to know. I want information to register in my brain as something I understand. If the authorities could let you write more personally and express your real feelings and honest evaluations of the ideas you read about, rather than just summarise and coldly analyse them alone, we might learn (and want to learn) a bit more.'

These students find the forms of the transactional more of a straitjacket than a helpful framework. The features of the transactional essay that they criticise most, and which are demanded by many of the lecturers in their tertiary course and by the Higher

School Certificate English examiners, include:

1. the elimination of the subjective 'I' and the active voice in favour of the impersonal 'it' and the passive voice, to create a spurious impression of objectivity;

2. the adoption of specialist subject terminology, much of which is unnecessarily pretentious and seems to be demanded because it gives an appearance of expertise and scholarship;

3. the suppression of personal, committed and emotional response in favour of the calm, aloof, objective statement; and

4. associated with all of the above, an implied approval of assertive dogmatism because of the impression students have picked up that tentativeness, or awareness of alternative interpretations, might be taken by examiners (and by teachers as examiners) as evidence of a lack of understanding.

It is clear that there is a real need for the acceptance of high level expressive writing (or of transactional writing which retains its expressive elements) in educational circles. In schools, the expressive forms should be acceptable at all levels of students' development and in all stages of the writing process, from tentative first thoughts to final draft essays. In the public examinations, there should be a similar acceptance of the expressive, particularly in the present form of assessment which requires first drafts as finished products in conditions of limited time and considerable stress. (It would be far more meaningful if the final examination were to be replaced by the assessment of a selection of each student's writing completed over the final two years of schooling and covering the whole range of writing functions.) The problems of students in the public examinations, as they are presently constituted, are exacerbated by the forms of the questions that are set. In researching the effects of the questions on students' ways of writing about literature in public examinations in England, John Dixon and Leslie Stratta have shown how the wording inhibits students' real responses by structuring the way they are expected to write. They explain how specific words and phrases in questions on literature ('describe . . . showing how', 'discuss the ways . . .', 'explain why . . .', etc.) 'set up and control the student writer's strategy — shaping the student's authorial position or role, determining the level of generalisation for the main structure, and shutting out certain kinds of understanding'.[51]

As we have already seen (in the section of Chapter Three on Psycho-analytical Criticism, pp. 129–136), both Hugh Crago and Norman Holland argue that it is more honest, and more useful to students, to encourage them to write in more personal and informal ways, acknowledging that their feelings in response to literature, and their evaluations of it, are subjective. Holland sees most literary critics as dishonest in the way they give the impression that they are 'just passively reporting what is "objectively" there' in the text when they are, in fact, subjectively making meanings from text in accordance with their own identities.[52] When students are encouraged to ape such criticism they are being manipulated into being false to themselves because they present interpretations that are not their own. They are also being misled about the processes of literary interpretation: they think all the meaning is in the words on the page. Writing that is transactional in function but which retains its personal, emotional, expressive forms is more likely to help students to develop what John Dixon calls 'interpretative abstractions' that are 'personal and exploratory' rather than 'dogmatic and unanalysed'.[53]

## IMAGINATIVE RECREATION OF LITERATURE

This section offers just one example of the wide range of expressive to poetic writing that involves students in interpreting and exploring texts by recreating all or parts of them in different forms or media and through different character viewpoints or narrative modes. In writing of this kind, students might be asked to script and present a radio version of a short story or an incident from a novel; to write a newspaper report of an event in a novel or play; to write a letter from one fictional character to another, expressing a viewpoint and/or explaining the motives for some aspect of behaviour; to write about an event from the point of view of a character whose viewpoint is not presented; to write in interior monologue to present a character's intimate thoughts and feelings that are not presented in the original text; and so on.

It is suggested that writing such as this should supplement rather than replace the various forms of analytical, critical writing in response to literature. The important point about such imaginative writing is that it is not only a creative response but also an interpretative and evaluative one. As Leslie Stratta, John Dixon and Andrew Wilkinson say in *Patterns of Language*, such work involves the writer in 'interpretation by re-creation and re-creation by interpretation'[54]. Most of the arguments advanced to support recreative writing focus on the way it helps students to get inside the text and imaginatively experience what it might feel like to be in a character's predicament. However, this empathy with characters, although crucial, is only half of the experience of being the detached evaluative onlooker or spectator. With emotional involvement, there is also cool detachment. In adding a new imaginative dimension to a novel they have read, students are constrained in their creation to ensure that it is psychologically consistent with, as well as illuminating of, character relationships and motivations already presented in the text. Further, in being explicitly invited to choose a viewpoint and form, they are unavoidably involved in conscious explorations of those aspects of literary rhetoric they have to use. Therefore, in exploring literature imaginatively in writing, students are very likely to reach deeper understandings of textual meanings and of the ways they are constructed and communicated. Other, more profound, evaluations are more likely to ensue too, but, before considering those, here is an example to work with.

It is by an 18-year-old tertiary student. Lynette's piece is an imaginative extension of Saul Bellow's novel, *Herzog*. She writes from the point of view of Ramona, Moses Herzog's young-middle-aged sex-kitten and hopefully prospective wife. At the end of the novel, Herzog, having apparently overcome the neuroses occasioned by divorce from his second wife (Mady), the breakdown of relationships with his former best friend, and the disorders of his intellectual and professional life, is waiting for Ramona to arrive for dinner at his broken-down remote country house in New England. Lynette's writing, an addition to the novel, is Ramona's interior monologue as she is driving to Herzog's Ludeyville house.

'Dear old Moses you funny, balding man, what are you cooking for your famished Ramona? As long as it's not undercooked. Moses was a dear but a godawful cook. Men, what was it with them? They could spend half their lives absorbed in papers, abstract theories, haggling over dead men's ideas and yet when it came to things that *mattered*! Oh well, Moses was slowly learning, and to give credit where credit's due Ramona ole girl you are a good teacher . . . mmm.

'Hey! Watch it! Yeah yeah you sit on that horn of yours as if it was ya Christmas present. These hicks, damn country rubes, they take one look at a good car and WHAMMO! they have to prove something. It doesn't help that it's a woman driving a Mercedes.

One time on a highway . . . long long time before I met Moses, even before George (poor, pathetic, jelly-fish George, funny in the old days . . . the knight dying with unrequited love, it was all the rage, but now — no, lady, no thinking about George, not on a day like today. Not when Moses is so near and so close to committing himself.) Now where . . . umm . . . oh yes, the accident, that terrible time in Jersey, at night and it was so cold and so wet and that man so goddam arrogant! He nearly wiped me out. A toad of a man all red in the face and all full of beer. What was it he said — "Lady if y-ya c-c-can't shlook after that b-big f-fancy car of yoursh then give it to ya ole m-mansh." God what a hide! Men, ah men, the mystery. They could never seem to reconcile the woman who was a success in the world and the woman, *this* woman, me, the me who needs a lover. Expecting me to be some kind of schizophrenic ball-tearer. Even Moses, he's a good man but he's only seeing the parts of me he wants to see.

'The parts! Ho ho Ramona, that's a good one, he's got the biggest tit fixation I've ever known. Must be the mother fixation. Mummy! Mummy! Cuddle me, hold me, kiss it better! That's cruel, lady, and an extreme, and besides you dress to be seen don't you. Why wear a plunging neckline tonight?

'Oh hell, was it left or right here? Left, um, yeah, left. Ah princess Merc you've got the best turning circle, the best. You old lump of classy nuts and bolts, you're my obedient steed. Men come and go but we are a team. A two bit Chicago florist and a reconditioned bargain Merc. The . . . the . . . princess (sure sure) and her white charger. Never mind Ramona, your prince Moses is coming, coming around.

'Almost there, steady girl, steady. God, a thumping heart! After all this time you should be a little blase about this game. You're the expert, remember. The all-knowing, all-understanding sex-goddess, Ramona. Lives with an old relic of Tsarist Russia, Aunty Tamara. A florist with a jungle seduction room.

'Moses you're a funny old guy. Heh, who are you kidding, you're no spring chicken yourself. So now's the time to start creeping, ready to pounce. Moses needs you, you need him, and he's quieter now, those titanic struggles with wives and children, ah my funny Herzog they've all taken something from you, but it's okay baby, Ramona's gonna make it work. Just let go a little my sweet and we'll exorcise Mady and her peg-leg puppet.

'There it is. That house! And here he is, the man of the house
. . . One more embrace, Moses, and let's go eat.'


Lynette's writing shows she has a deep and sensitive understanding
of Bellow's purposes and methods in this novel. She said that what
she enjoyed most about *Herzog* was Bellow's sense of humour,and
her interior monologue shows how successfully she has analysed the
elements that create and communicate that quality of humour, and
used them herself. She perfectly captures Ramona's understanding
of Herzog's vanity, whimsicality and eccentric romanticism, as well
as Ramona's own capacity to laugh at her own motives and
affectations. Her sensitivity as a reader is sufficiently developed for
her to recognise the pathos as well as humour in Ramona's cheerfully
self-conscious attempts to impress Herzog. Lynette's whole piece
elaborates the sense of Ramona that Herzog himself expresses in one
of his most lucid insights: 'She had a good heart and she had on black
lace underpants.' Bellow's skill in creating sympathetic characters
whom we laugh at and with at the same time is demonstrated by
his admirer and imitator. It was in writing this that Lynette achieved
a deeper understanding of how the language of literature texts works
to initiate the reader's creation of meaning. She has developed a
sophisticated control of Bellow's tone of writing in sections of the
novel. She learned something about herself as a reader and about
the processes of writing and reading literature. She said that it was
having to write in this form that made her explore the textual
methods that created the effects she had enjoyed so much, and that
having tried them out for herself she became more aware of the
constructedness of literature which, in turn, opened up new avenues
of pleasure to her as a reader.

Whereas the New Critics condemn the practice of considering what
happens to characters outside the boundaries of the text as the
misleading importation of irrelevant meanings, I believe that
imaginative writing of this kind helps students to test their values
against those of authors and to debate with them. Engaging in a
creative process similar to that of an author enables students to better
understand the author's meanings and the ways they are constructed.
Writing fictions logically related to and continuous with the fictions
of published authors is a way of helping students to become aware
that fiction is an artefact or, as Harding puts it, 'a social convention,

an institutionalised technique of discussion'[55]. And, as Harding goes on to say,

> The more we have this awareness of an author who is offering his own values and preconceptions for acceptance or rejection the more defences we can muster against being emotionally bullied — harrowed, horrified, disgusted, frightened, distressed, in a way that fails to carry its own justification and acceptability.[56]

## Imitation and creativity

The piece of writing reproduced below was written by an eleven-year-old primary school boy during some work on Aboriginal legends organised by two student teachers on practice teaching. The student teachers had read and discussed some legends with the class and they asked the pupils to write and illustrate some of their own legends, using those they had read as a model. After the stories had been written they were read in groups and then taped with appropriate corroboree music as background. The pupils' illustrative paintings were photographed, made into slides and used in conjunction with the tape as a synchronised tape-slide presentation. Here is one of the stories. (Unfortunately I cannot reproduce the paintings which go with it, they are beautifully stylised in the form of Aboriginal cave paintings and rock carvings.)

### How the Apes turned into Man

Way off in the Dreamtime when man looked like monkeys and apes, an ape had a tremendous fight with a kangaroo. The kangaroo went hopping half over the country with the ape close at his heels. Soon, nearly all the apes and monkeys were in pursuit of the kangaroo. When evening came they were sitting around making plans among themselves. The kangaroo, meanwhile, was getting tired of the chase, so he made up nasty plans to get rid of his enemies. Excited by his plans, he led his enemies to a giant hole with trees growing on the sides. The kangaroo took one big leap across the hole, while the apes in pursuit were unable to stop and piled into the hole. By instinct, the apes and monkeys tried to grab the trees as they fell, but the apes, being too heavy, broke the branches and rolled further on down. As they rolled, sharp rocks tore at their hair, leaving it only on the top of their heads. The monkeys, being lighter, were able to hold on to the branches without breaking them. That's why monkeys today remain the same, and only a few apes live with hair, as the rest have turned into men.[57]

You will recognise how different these sentences are from the everyday language of eleven-year-olds. They are literary structures the writer has internalised from his reading of the Aboriginal legends. Savouring the language of literature you have read is an advanced level response, and imitating the structures of writing you have admired, in creating your own literature, seems to me to be a most effective way of expressing that response. I doubt whether the invitation to write a discursive analysis of the style of the originals would have appealed to the pupil very much or resulted in such linguistic empowering as the piece he wrote did. Ian Reid gives a very clear explanation of the value of such imitative creations in his book, *The Making of Literature:*

> It can test the precision of one's understanding of the original text, and it can open a possibility of recreating the power of that text, giving its conventions a new lease of life . . . Structural patterning, rhythmical and lexical quirks, thematic or imagistic preoccupations — these things need to be observed closely for an imitation to work at all. So the student has a motive for careful study of the text, and simultaneously there is a refinement of writing skills, especially through growing intimacy with literary conventions — a very particular *inside* knowledge of ways in which written forms are made and remade.[58]

The two poems below were written in her English journal by a girl in Year 11 at Casino High School. Gary Whale, her English teacher, says about Michelle's improvised versions of the two frequently anthologised poems, 'Naming of Parts' and 'The Tiger': 'I think they show an appreciation and understanding of the poems better than any lit. crit. could ever do.'

### 'Lessons of Flowers: Naming of Parts

"Today we have naming of parts. Yesterday we had classification and tomorrow morning we shall have the floral formula."

Honeysuckle sweetly wanders its way through the open classroom window and tickles my nostrils with the fragrance of Spring, but, today we have naming of parts.

"As you all know the flower is simply a specialized reproductive shoot. It consists of an axis which, I'll thank you to remember, is called receptacle. On this receptacle are inserted four different sorts of organs."

Next to me sits a girl, she has long golden hair, and inserted in the wisps and curls is a single flower still with tiny sparkling dew drop diamonds sprinkled by the early morning sunshine.

"Outermost are the sepals, usually green and leaflike known as the calyx. Next we have the petals. Now, the petals you will be recognizing by their usually conspicuous brightly coloured . . . er . . . parts which you will be referring to as the corolla. These parts are not really necessary to study, as they are not directly concerned with reproduction. They are, in fact, accessory parts."

I gaze entranced at the delicately sculptured petals wavering in rosy cheeks and ivory skin like a child's lips quivering tearfully under cruel, taunting words.

"Within these accessory parts are the *stamens* and the *carpels* which I have no time to explain now. Go home tonight and read the first 100 pages of your text book which tells in detail their function. Tomorrow you will be tested on your knowledge of these essential parts of the flower or as YOU will learn — 'the reproductive shoot of the plant.' Do not bother about the accessory parts of the reproductive shoot as, *for those who weren't listening*, they are not our immediate concern."

The small ray of sunshine within our darkened classroom curls in sorrow to cradle and comfort its injured beauty. The Lesson is over. Outside, out of earshot the honeysuckle provides its perfume with wings to fly and follow the springtime, while on a lonely desk is strewn the remains of a withered and torn single ray of dying light.

For today we had naming of parts.'

### 'In Response To The Tiger

Tiger, Tiger Burning bright
In the forests of the night,
Slinking low, a snake of gold,
Treasure rare yet heart so cold.

A mind of terror, blackness, fear
I wonder what your business here.
From the fiery eye you fell?
Or cast out from the depths of hell?

What your maker? Was it He
Who plucked you from the light that be?
What your root, from whence you came?
Perhaps the black of ash we blame.

Coat of flame, the glory, power,
Is fashioned from the heaven flower,
Heart of serpent, eyes of fire
Tell the devil is thy sire.

Who else has a heart of stone?
What else dare defy your throne?
Of light and darkness you are King,
Alone you crouch, alone you spring.'

In imitating other voices, in trying them on herself as it were, Michelle is on the way to finding her own voice.

Terry Ryan, Head of English at Brisbane Grammar School, regularly involves his students in imaginative recreation of poetry. Here are several versions of 'The Lord's Prayer' written by his Year 9 students, the first in contemporary 'hippie' style and the second in 'ocker' idiom.

'Hey Old Man, way up there in the Big "H",
Your name in lights,
make this joint your scene
like it is in the blue beyond.
Spare me a crust for I am hungry.
Forgive the mistakes we make,
as I forgive the "burke" next door for being noisy.
Don't give us any crazy notions, and get us out
of trouble if we leave this straight and narrow
After all, You run this circus,
and You've got top billing.
The writing on the posters won't ever fade.
Stay cool.'

'G'day Mate, how are ya'?
All of us down 'ere think you're a real top bloke
I hope what we're doin' down 'ere is something
like you'd want it.
Make sure I get a bit of tucker and some other stuff
I might need.
Don't worry about the crook things I done,
Just like I'll not worry about the crook things
the other blokes done on me.
Don't let me be sucked in to anything stupid.
And don't let anything bad happen to me.
Thanks a lot, see ya later.'

As Terry Ryan says, to handle this kind of parody effectively, 'students must fully understand the concepts inherent in the original prayer and sharpen their understanding of different language registers'.

In another improvisation activity with poetry, Terry presented Ted Hughes' poem 'Wodwo' to his Year 9 class and set them to work in groups to answer the question, 'Who or what is Wodwo?' Here are the opening lines of Hughes' poem, followed by one of the poems written by a group of students as an answer to Terry's question.

### 'Wodwo   Ted Hughes
What am I? Nosing here, turning leaves over
following a faint stain on the air to the river's edge
I enter water. What am I to split
the grassy grain of water looking upward I see the bed
of the river above me upside down very clear
What am I doing here in mid-air? . . .'

### 'Who Or What Is Wodwo?
Wodwo, Wodwo
Where are you going?
Where are you from?
What are you doing so high?
You have no roots and aren't tied down.
How and why do you enter water?
What are you Wodwo?
What is your aim?
What will you be when you grow up?
Or don't you grow?
Is your life long or is it short?
Or do you live your life in cycles?
What can you be Wodwo?
What can you be?
Rain,
rain,
that's what you are.
We know you can go anywhere you want
You have the freedom that we don't have,
Freedom in this world.
We can imagine you following a faint stain on the air,
to the river's edge.
We even see you enter water.
You enter water so often, Wodwo
Just to please us.
To let us swim in your rivers
to give us water to drink
to help our plants to grow.
We thank you Wodwo.

We know you are only in mid-air
for a very short time,
Rain comes down from the clouds
into mid-air, and down to earth.
We know you don't mean to pick
bits of bark off rotten stumps.
It gives us no pleasure either.
Rain is sometimes separate from the ground
Rain drops casually out of clouds
We understand how you feel, Wodwo
But now you don't need to worry.
You know what you are.'

Terry Ryan's comments on this support the argument of this subsection about the value of imaginative recreation in writing:

'The above poem indicates that the original poem by Hughes has been fully analysed. It acknowledges the mystery of the original poem, yet at the same time indicates a solution to the mystery. This response also stands on its own as a poem, and would adequately fit alongside Hughes' poem in an anthology. A point that needs to be made is that the Year 9 students who wrote these poems had no prompting from me, and arrived at their conclusions and responses by themselves. There was no need here for the question and answer comprehension exercise to see if the students understood the poem. They successfully demonstrated an excellent knowledge of the poem, and as a bonus, created something of their own.'

## TELLING AND WRITING STORIES

'I enjoy the way a book is written because I write too. I notice how when a character gets excited and then calms down the way the writer expresses the emotions without telling you what they are, so that you have some sense of those feelings yourself.'
(Year 8 Bathurst girl)

Research and contemporary literary theory emphasise that reading and writing are both active, creative processes. They are both taught best when they are taught as complementary to and interactive with one another. You can become a much more perceptive reader of literature if you are regularly creating something like literature of your own, and you can become a much more successful writer of poetry and stories from personal and imagined experience if you have done enough enjoyable reading of literature for it to produce internalised after-effects. As we have seen above, sometimes the most appropriate response to someone else's poem or story might be to write a poem or story of your own.

In explaining this concept of the role of the onlooker (or spectator), D.W. Harding makes it clear that gossip and fiction both serve the same purposes, the main difference between them being the greater sophistication of form that literature has from its more careful shaping and patterning in the processes of construction.

> The ends achieved by fiction and drama are not fundamentally different from those of a great deal of gossip and everyday narrative. Between true narrative and fiction there exist, in fact, transitional techniques such as the traveller's tale and the funny anecdote in which the audience's tacit permission is assumed for embellishments that enhance the effectiveness of the story. True or fictional, all these forms of narrative invite us to be onlookers joining in the evaluation of some possibility of experience.[59]

In this brief outline of the function and range of spectator role storying, Harding gives us the clue for a programme of helping our students to progress from spoken anecdote to written fictional story. We have already considered (at the beginning of Chapter Three) how important storying is in students' psychological, social, intellectual and emotional growth. Through storying, in talk and writing, we can organise the potential chaos of experience.

Peter Moss of Adelaide University has been collecting oral stories on tape for some years to show 'that in us all there is a drama capable of being told, with power and sympathy, providing that there is the prior condition that others will encourage and listen'.[60] It is not difficult to meet this condition in the classroom. If the teacher understands the value of this work, she or he will certainly 'encourage' by organising contexts in which students can share with others their anecdotes from personal experience and oral stories they have heard, and by being a trusted adult audience. Students enjoy this sharing of stories, and the teacher's first task is merely to legitimise in the classroom the kind of storytelling that occurs naturally when people meet to gossip.

An encouragement to pupils to tell their own stories and anecdotes in their own voice — personal experiences of school, home, peer group and society, together with the more fictitious tall stories and yarns they tell one another — leads logically into the writing of stories. After all, written anecdotes differ from true experiences told orally in two ways: they are embellished, and they are more consciously shaped in a literary way to meet the demands of an audience not immediately present. Short stories represent the outcomes of the same process of conscious literary shaping taken much further: not only is there embellishment, modification, addition and deletion of events and details, but also there is the need to move from an egocentric viewpoint to experimentation with a range of narrative perspectives; to stand back from one's own personal feelings and make conscious decisions about the ordering of events, and about such matters as tone and style. The stages of progression from spoken anecdote to written fictional short story could be something like the following, although this sequence is not offered as an inflexible routine:

1. sharing personal experiences, yarns, tall stories in small groups;
2. taping monologues, after the details have been rehearsed and worked out in the more informal small group situation;
3. studying the language characteristics of the monologues;
4. writing versions of the spoken stories; and,
5. occasionally, going on to the writing of short stories.

I have found, in practice, that where stage 1 is easily accomplished and enjoyed tremendously by students, stage 2 often causes some self-consciousness. While some students are happy to tape their yarn in private, some need a trusted friend to tell it to while the tape is running. Stage 3 is something that can be introduced occasionally to make students more conscious of the artistic decisions they have made and have to make. Stage 4 always produces surprises for students, and considerable discussion, as they find that a literal transcript of their oral story is not as effective as literature as the spoken story. In the discussion that follows this discovery, there needs to be a close comparison between spoken and written versions so that students are able to discover for themselves and articulate quite explicitly the differences between these two forms of story and the different expectations of audiences of them. Keith Garvey's Australian bush yarns, *Tales of My Uncle Harry*[61], available in both spoken and written form can be introduced into the discussion at this stage to show that the discoveries students have made about their own creations apply equally to the works of published authors. Garvey's stories work far more effectively heard on tape than they do read from written transcripts because they are constructed as oral tales, not written ones. Stage 5, the processes of literary shaping, requires a series of drafts, each of which needs to be discussed with peers in small groups (class editorial committees), and with the teacher along the lines recommended by Donald Graves in his accounts of pupils 'conferencing' with the teacher during the writing process.[62]

In shaping their own stories, students learn more about the way professional writers work, and thus become better readers, as well as writers of literature. They certainly understand the constructedness of literature and, thus, can be more easily taught the higher level reading (and writing) strategies. If they experience this kind of work right through their years of secondary schooling, they are also more likely to do well in the public examination at the end of them.

Obviously it is not desirable that the whole five stage sequence from anecdote to short story be followed every time the oral story-telling takes place in the classroom. Sometimes the sequence will end at stage 2 with the taping of some of the stories and anecdotes after they have been shared in groups; sometimes it will end at stage 3 as part of work on literary analysis; and sometimes it will end at stage 4 as it might, for example, when the teacher involves a class in exploring the linguistic and structural differences between a published short story read in class and a story that works most effectively as a spoken yarn.

The following short story, written by an 18-year-old student, began as a few anecdotes about school days told to a small group in class. The shooting expedition of the finished story is an invention. Its seeds were in Paul's feeling of envy for kids who always seemed to have all the most fashionable personal equipment like clothes and sporting gear, and the confidence and social ease that goes with such possessions. During the writing of the story and the conferencing with his teacher over several stages of drafting, Paul was encouraged to reflect on his own writing processes. He said that his original anecdotes in the small group were about unconnected humorous escapades and that it was not until later when he thought about the events of that time in his life that he realised how envious he had felt of more advantaged fellow students and their casual acceptance of their privileges. After completing his story, Paul had this to say about his invention of the hunting expedition:

'Something like that could have happened to me a few years ago. I was a bit jealous of the kids who had guns and fishing rods and fancy bicycles and swimming gear and all that, and the kind of confidence they had. They sort of assumed the world was theirs to use. I knew a few kids like Neil and I liked them. I was always pleased when they let me in on what they were doing. While I was thinking about the story, and trying to write it at the beginning, I was trying to express the idea of having my boring life livened up a bit by these sorts of kids, but at the back of my mind there was this feeling that they took things too much for granted. They got things so easily they never thought about why they used the gear they had—they just used it. And then when I thought of the idea of the hunting trip it came to me that they were really exploiters of the earth, the environment. It's not that they were nasty in any way. They were just irresponsible, because the idea of responsibility never occurred to them, and it would take something pretty dramatic to make it occur to them.

'AN ADVENTURE

Part 1

"Paul! Come on, get out of bed. It's time for school!" Mum yelled. It was her third attempt at 'dislodging' me from my daze and I felt I'd better get up before hell-fire broke loose.

"Orright, I'm comin!" I replied, as I began donning my basic greys. The same old routine. Get up, have breakfast, catch the bus, put up with old Flutesnoot, come home, do my homework. School is such a worry, wasting all that valuable time. We could be surfing, fishing or playing soccer. Anything would be better than school, and three days to go!

"Your cereal is on the table, son. Hurry up!" Mum interrupted my thoughts with another loud bellow. "And comb your hair!"

"Orright, give us a go," I answered crankily.

I finally reached the kitchen table, after having considerable trouble with a broken shoelace. It took me five minutes, at least, to repair the broken lace and if Mum could have only heard my cursing, I would be having a stand-up breakfast.

"Don't forget to pick up the papers on your way home will you, Paul. And don't slop your milk!" Mum ordered.

"Nah, it'll be sweet!" I said, with a final quick 'sluurrp', in retaliation against Mum's orders. "Well, I best be off, or I'll be late. See ya."

"Yes, now, you be good, won't you. Fourth form is an important year, you know. Life's not all surfing, son. Here's your dinner and make sure you eat your apple. Goodbye now, and don't forget the papers." Her voice trailed off.

Mothers are such worriers, I thought, as I boarded the schoolbus on the corner. "Eat my apple, indeed." It should be up to me whether I eat it or not.

It only took about ten minutes on the bus today as the traffic on the bridge was unusually light. I spent the whole time thinking about my basic existence in which surfing was my main release from the drudgery. Even that had suffered this past fortnight, as some natural phenomena had flattened out the swells. It was now hardly worth going up to the beach, and as for fishing and soccer, well, I was pretty sick of those, too. Same old routine, day in day out, I just wish something different would happen along.

I entered my classroom feeling very dejected, head hung low. I sat down quietly with hardly a glance around me. Old Flutesnoot, Mr Fairweather, that is, my humble teacher, placed the homework sheet in front of me, to be completed by the morrow.

"You look sad today, Paul. Anything the matter?" he queried.

"No Flute . . . I mean, Mr Fairweather. I'm okay, just tired, I guess," I answered. Why does everyone have to worry, I wondered.

"Well, then, all right," he said, and proceeded to go out to his desk and conduct our geography lesson.

"Well, good people, as you know, we have a new boy in our midst . . ." Mr Fairweather commented. A new boy!! Where? I looked around me and saw him. A new uniform in our midst, the mystery of it all.

"Neil Langford is his name and his father is taking up business here. I know it is a big thrill having a new face here but could you please keep your chattering until recess. Thankyou. Now, about the wheat/sheep belt of NSW. What is the . . ."

Mr Fairweather's voice slowly trailed off and I was wondering where Neil was from, what sports did he play? All sorts of questions were going through my head and I couldn't wait until recess to find out all about him. It may not be such a dreary day, after all.

Well, it wasn't long before all the questions were answered, and the stories Neil could tell were seemingly never-ending. He told of his shooting and camping treks around Warren, his home-town, amid wild pigs and snakes. The kangaroo chase and the excitement involved as they pursued them along the dry, barren "westland".

My friends and I were fascinated by Neil's tales, but especially me, who had never even handled a rifle, a mysterious killing machine.

"What! Never even shot a rabbit or bird, Paul?" he said in astonishment. "We'll have to do something 'bout that, eh?"

The bell told us that recess was over, but I could just about put up with Flutesnoot now. My mind was on other things, the thrill of the chase and the boom of the gun.

By the end of the day, it was arranged that we were to go on a camping and shooting weekend, this very Saturday, along Dorawank Creek. A pretty place, renowned for its abundance of wildlife. I thought of it all the way home.

Mum wasn't too happy, at first, thinking this type of activity far too dangerous, but my father changed her mind.

"He's got to experience it some day, dear, and I feel he's old enough now," he said. "It'll do the boy good."

I could tell she still wasn't too happy about it, but I knew she would listen to Dad.

*Part 2*

It was a beautiful Saturday morning, the sun shining brilliantly and a cool breeze gently blowing. Spring is such a beautiful season, and early morning is a beautiful part of the day.

I was to be picked up by Neil and his father at about eight o'clock, another 20 minutes. The butterflies of excitement were playing havoc in my stomach, as I peered at all my gear. The tinned food, my sleeping bag, my old jeans, pen knife and other various knick-knacks, arranged neatly on the footpath.

I looked at the corner in anticipation, hoping to see their car come around the bend.

"Oh, hurry up!" I said to myself loudly. "I hope they haven't got lost or something."

A car came around the corner. Was it them?

No, it continued on past me, the butterflies in my stomach really fluttering now. Another car came around the corner. I peered at my watch.

"Hmmm," I mused, "five ta eight, this must be them." And, sure enough . . .

The car grinded to a halt and I felt like shrieking out in enjoyment. The beginning of my first shoot. I was the proudest person alive.

It only took several minutes to stow everything in the boot. I noticed Neil's tent, his sleeping bag, and primus. Beneath them, the rifle cases! To think I would be using one of them. The boot was suddenly shut on my daydreams and we 'piled' into the front seat, next to the smiling Mr Langford. The trek had begun.

It was a beautiful day. No clouds in the sky and hardly a breeze to bustle the leaves. The only sound we could hear was 'Mr Whiffles', Neil's faithful dog. He was one of the family and could fetch sticks, but most importantly, I thought, was his ability to smell out game for us to shoot.

The car slowed down and turned left into a dirt road. The car suddenly stopped, we were there! It was hard to stop myself from screaming out in pleasure. Mr Whiffles was scurrying and yapping around our feet as we began to unpack.

"Should be a good day for shooters, Paul," Neil said. "Eh, Whiffles, stop that!!!" Mr Whiffles was chasing a flock of zebra finches along the bank.

"Stupid dog," he said. "Yeah, a good day for shooters."

"Yeah, I can't wait. I just can't wait," I replied excitedly.

I picked up the rifle case from the boot and stood holding it. It felt so light. I undid the zipper and the gun slid out. It was so simple a machine, sleek and strangely lethal. I couldn't wait to . . .

"Well boys, there you are. I'll be back tomorrow night to pick you up. This very place, boys. Okay now, you be careful." Mr Langford's gruff voice interrupted my daydreams.

"Sure, Dad, see ya then," Neil said.

"Yeah, thanks, Mr Langford. See ya tomorrow!" I answered.

We watched the car fade into the corner. We were alone.

"Well, that's it then, Paul. We'd better get our camp set up, eh? What about over there near that rock?"

"Yeah, looks orright to me, mate. What do you reckon, Whiffles?"

The little fox terrier yapped and barked as though he understood me. He had so much energy.

It was only several hundred metres to the proposed campsite and only took five minutes or so to transfer our gear.

In half an hour our camp was set up. We were ready to begin our adventure. My first shoot, how exciting.

"I think now's a good time to show ya how one of these things works, Paul. Here." Neil handed me one of the rifles. "That was my first rifle. Not a bad gun, either."

It was older than Neil's shiny and decorative Winchester, but that didn't worry me.

He then showed me how to squeeze the trigger and not jerk it, how to aim steadily and how to load up. I couldn't believe it was so easy to shoot.

"Well, let's go," he said, "and bag us some dinner."

"Beauty, let's go!" I answered.

The gun felt strange in my arms, as we plodded along. We disturbed a flock of pelicans on the wide creek and they squawked into the air. Mr Whiffles yapped at the surge of movement.

It was a pretty place all right. The cool, wide, clear creek slowly moved seaward. The tide must be going out. The bank, in which we were walking, was lush and green, palm trees and eucalypts standing proudly in our path. To our left was a grass plain, a perfect site for rabbits. I thought I saw a pair of ears, a kangaroo, perhaps. Wildflowers were everywhere, slowly wavering in the air.

"It sure is a beauti . . ."

"Ssshhhh!!!" Neil interrupted. "I can see me a shot." Even Mr Whiffles was bewildered. There was seemingly nothing in sight.

Neil was concentrating on the "hidden" target. His mouth was firmly set, his eyes unblinking. The suspense was overwhelming. Oh, hurry, hurry!

"Beearhowwbeerkow" the gun bellowed. Echoing, shattering the tranquility. Out of a nearby tree dropped an osprey, the sea eagle, one of the most beautiful of sea birds. It now seemed belittled as it hit the ground with a dull thud.

"Not a bad shot, eh, mate?" Neil said proudly.

"But I didn't know ya could eat ospreys, Neil," I replied.

"Ya can't, it's just the fun of it. Don't worry, you'll get a shot," he said, as he kicked the dead bird into the creek. Mr Whiffles barked at Neil, seemingly telling him how good a shot it was.

I wonder how many more cases of senseless slaughter Mr Whiffles had witnessed Neil carrying out.

"Yeah — I'll get a shot," I said half-heartedly. "But don't ya think that killing that osprey was a bit stupid and senseless?"

"Nah, those eagles are pests anyhow, just like magpies," he replied.

I had several chances of shooting rabbits as the day progressed. Mr Whiffles would smell them out and bark at their presence. He was well trained. I shot to miss though, unbeknown to Neil, and pretended it was just my inexperience that caused my bad shooting.

"Don't worry," he said, "you should get plenty of easy shots back at the camp. Maggies and that, ya know."

"Yeah, great," I replied, feeling very disillusioned with shooting. I cast a glance over at the two dead rabbits around Neil's belt, bouncing hideously from side to side in time with his gait. There was no skill in this type of sport; targets would serve the same purpose and take more skill.

Those two poor rabbits. We'd only come a mile or so from the camp and were still following the slow moving creek. The going had got a little tougher, the flat grasslands now changing into small foothills. We could catch a glimpse of the sea sometimes when the trees allowed us to.

Mr Whiffles would run suddenly forward and almost without fail, a rabbit would appear. It was only a matter of waiting for the rabbit to stop and then attempting to kill it. Mr Whiffles, in the meantime, was seeking out more game, in logs, burrows and bushes.

This sequence of events went on about nine times, Neil and I shooting alternatively. Of course, I shot to miss, but Neil blamed his inaccuracy on the sheer distance of the shots.

One of his targets was not killed instantly by the shattering bullet. It jumped up in the air, hit, and mortally wounded, trying desperately to seek cover.

"Hadn't ya better put it out of its misery," I said, looking at the "pleading" rabbit.

"What, and waste a bullet. It'll be dead soon," he answered gruffly.

I shot the rabbit before Neil could stop me. I thought it better to end its suffering. Neil just shrugged his shoulders, looking at me as though I were stupid.

"Berrkower." My thoughts were shattered by the thundering gun.

"Got him!" Neil said. "Come on, it's over there by the stump, in that briar." He was so proud.

I followed Neil the one hundred metres to the bush and found him kneeling over his "reward". The afternoon sun cast long shadows about us, the air was still, interrupted by the occasional squawk of a bird. We couldn't see the creek from the briar, but we could hear the "whoosh" of its movement.

Neil picked up Mr Whiffles, a bloody mess forming on his hand and shirt front. The bullet had caught the dog in the stomach, and the poor thing was still alive, but apparently paralysed.

I felt sorry for Neil, as I felt sick in the stomach, and I imagined his feelings. The gun lay at his feet, looking like the lethal machine that it was.

The only life that could be seen in the dog was through his eyes, looking pleadingly at his master. "Do something, do something."

Neil lay Mr Whiffles down gently, took the rifle, and shot the dog through the head, ending his suffering, I couldn't look and turned to the sun.

He unbuckled his belt and let the two dead rabbits slide off next to the terrier. All was silent. He glanced at the bloody heap and then back at the rifle, back to the heap and then back to the rifle. The dilemma he must have been going through.

Neil then picked up the rifle, threw it as hard as he could and knelt down and cried, sobbing openly. I put my arm around his shoulder, consoling him and tried to ease his grief.

He was all right after several minutes and together we buried the "heap". The look in his eyes showed that he would never forget today.

I had to carry his rifle back for him, as he said he would never touch one again.

I didn't know what to say to him, so I kept my words. A flock of pelicans landed on the river, skating along the glassy surface. I wondered if they were the same flock that Mr Whiffles yapped at earlier in the day.

I think Neil thought the same thoughts. I would be glad to get back to my worrisome mother.'


In including this story here I am not suggesting that it warrants a place in an anthology of literature. The important point about it is not its literary merit as measured against the published stories of others, but its immeasurable value to its writer's reading and writing development. While Paul's narrative mode (subjective narration) is not unusual or unexpected for an autobiographical kind of story, it was deliberately chosen after he had experimented with it and with anonymous narration from single and dual character points of view. His other literary choices — selection of details, ordering of events, dialogue, creation of tone, and so on — while not revolutionary, were made fully consciously.

## WRITING LITERATURE AS PART OF THE CURRICULUM

At Galston High School in Sydney, the English Department (in 1984) required that all Year 10 students present a major literary work as part of the year's assessment.[63] While the scheme began partly as a necessary supplement to the Year 10 public 'reference tests' (requiring first draft finished products, and implicitly but clearly communicating the message to teachers and students that writing doesn't need to be re-drafted and polished), its success suggested that it would outlast that highly suspect public examination. The specifications of the work, the aims, the kinds of issues discussed with pupils in individual writing conferencing sessions, the kind of written communication between student and teacher, and the scope of students' achievements are outlined below by Helen Esmond, one of the organisers of the project.

### Instructions to students

The following letter was given to every Year 10 student:

Dear Student
    As a Year 10 English student you are required not only to study literature written by other people, but to write a literary work of your own.
    While it is hoped you will take care with presentation, *the work will be judged on its literary content*, so drawings, pictures and elaborate presentation will not win extra marks.
    Your English teacher will act as your consultant and will read and respond to your drafts. He/she will be able to make suggestions for improving/expanding/editing/eliminating technical errors/elaborating on certain aspects and so on.
    Your teacher is your collaborator, not your judge.
    The works will be marked by two other Year 10 English teachers using a common standard across the whole of Year 10 with marks ranging from 0 to 100.
    The major work will make up 15 per cent of your final mark for Year 10 English.

It is hoped that a varied selection of works will be published.
Length: As a general guideline aim for 1200-1500 words.
Consult your teacher if you have any queries about this.

You are free to choose any *topic, theme* or *idea.* Your class teacher will be required to give her/his approval.

Some possible forms: Short stories/TV, radio or stage scripts/ poems/autobiography/a gallery of portraits/essays on any topic/ reviews of films, books or records/a short novel/travelogue/ material suitable for newspaper or magazine publication etc.

*Aims:* We worked on the assumption that a sustained piece of writing on a topic chosen by the writer encourages personal involvement, commitment and real achievement.

We wanted students to:

- develop initiative, independence and self-confidence;
- experiment;
- reflect on, assess, and if necessary re-think their work;
- become aware of and deliberately manipulate such things as structure, form, pace, tone, atmosphere, point of view, symbolism in order to achieve their own purposes — i.e., learn to write by writing;
- see the writing of others, its strengths and weaknesses, more clearly;
- regard their teachers as useful allies who would help them define objectives and difficulties, make suggestions and give practical assistance; and
- feel successful with good reason.

Judging by teachers' observations, the writing produced and students' written comments, all those aims were to some extent achieved.

## What happened in conferencing sessions

Students had to explain to me their idea, their purpose, their feelings about what they'd done or wanted to do. They wanted reassurance and help. They made sure I understood what they were saying and also that they understood what I was saying because they felt they needed to get the full benefit. This conferencing was a good exercise in communicating.

Some students just needed reassurance that their idea was "OK" and not "dumb". Some said that they'd got to a certain point and didn't know how to proceed. Sometimes a very broad statement was enough to jog the process: e.g., "You need to make this central character *do* something — you'll have to decide what her motives are and make her act on them, and it'll have to affect the character whose eyes you're telling the story through." It seemed that definition of the problem got students part of the way towards solving it. I found it was not hard to give advice having read the work students had already done: e.g., Frances needed to be told to create an *earlier* incident in her story to establish for the reader that character X was a spoiled brat and Granpa's favourite.

At other times I suggested to students which parts of their material I thought held the most interest for readers. Nerida wrote about living in a remote part of Central Australia and about the Aboriginal people she knew and learnt about there. I encouraged her to include her own emotional reactions to her experiences. A lot of students seemed to feel that "proper" writing cuts out the personal, eliminates it as a kind of indecency or evidence of indiscipline.

During my discussions with students, these were some writing issues that came up.

- Plot construction
- Establishment of character
- Selection of material — elimination of 'flat' draft sections
- Ordering of material
- Increasing subtlety of writer's communication with reader
- Emphasising some things in anticipation of readers' needs
- Supplying convincing material to support assertions
- Allowing the writer's feelings or views to be apparent
- Increasing sensory detail in descriptions
- Deciding aptness of details
- Deciding aptness of effects created by rhyme
- Elimination of weak repetition
- Correction of spelling and paragraphing
                          sentence punctuation
                          dialogue punctuation

I felt that because students were writing for purposes they had devised freely themselves, they were more likely to want to learn about these issues to improve their skills in the craft of writing.

## Written communication between teacher and student

Helen Esmond discussed with students and wrote to them her ongoing responses to written drafts during the process of her reading of them rather than after she had finished, as she says she

'wanted to emphasise that writers must take into account the processes that go on in a reader's mind as s/he moves through a text — to emphasise that writers must be expert at deciding how much to tell their readers and when and in what way'.

Here is her final two and a half paragraphs of three pages of comments on the first draft of a student's story called 'Full Circle' and, following it, the student's reply to the comments. At all stages, Helen is making students reflexive about what they are learning:

Maybe you should get another student to do the same as I did for you and compare the responses! I'd be very interested to see what another student wrote! Or maybe a *couple* of others! But *don't* show them what I said first — get completely individual responses — I'd like copies of those too!

If you feel a bit shy about doing that now, wait until you've done your final version to your utmost satisfaction so you don't feel so vulnerable. *But* I am hoping our class will build up trust of one another to form a kind of "community of writers" as some people have called it — where people share their writing.

Another thing I'd be grateful if you'd do — could you *write down* your responses to the comments that I've made? Not necessarily *every one* — but some that you have a reaction to one way or the other? Be completely honest. I'd like you to do this *as well as* doing any re-working of your actual draft.

Thanks.

H. Esmond 23/5/84

First draft of 'Full Circle' — Reply to comments.

Thank you for your detailed response to my writing. It helped me enormously. It is very useful to get someone else's opinion. Quiet often, you overlook things in your own writing, inconsistencies and such. It also particularly useful for me, because my spelling is not what I would like it to be, and someone else reading it usually finds many mistakes.

I must admit, I got quite a shock when I saw the length of points you handed me. At most, I only expected verbal comments and help. But most of the things you commented on were certainly in need of work. I think I acted on just about all of them. Some of them prompted me to re-write and extend portions of the story. In fact I ran out of memory space on my computer, and was forced to split the story into 2 separate files. But I did try to keep as close to my original ideas as possible. Many of your points made me rethink some of the story but I tried to keep the thought the same.

The one point that made me sit back and study my story, was the one about my quote "I exist as long as you do . . ." This opened fresh channels of ideas, and I restructured the end of my story as a springboard for my new ending, which hopefully completes the "Full Circle", if you'll pardon the pun. I had been toying with the idea of originally having the narrator die because of his actions, but when you said "I wondered whether he might kill the tree and die himself!" everything fell into place. I had the tree haunt him, and took out anything that told the reader that it was his imagination, when he realised the tree was imagined. In the end, he does kill himself, but it is more subtle than the usual bullet in the head etc. He in-advertantly (sic) slashes his wrists, and then decides to bleed to death. Symbolically, he ends up in the love seat under the scortched (sic) tree.

I was not offended by your question as to whether I was dabbling in plagiarism and getting my ideas from other works. In answer, I don't usually write stories like this one. But as it happened, one day, as I was listening to my favourite group on tape, I was in a rather mellow and, for lack of another word, soppy, mood. I decided to write a love story. (The group is Dire Straits, and their music is rather passive and moody, or as Jason M likes to say "tediously boring".) When I listened to them it put me in the mood for writing this particular brand of story, and this was the only source of outside inspiration that I used. I am, normally, very critical of such stories, and, to my memory have never read, nor watched one.

Only one other person has read any part of the story aside from you or I, and that is my mother. I don't think that I would like anyone else that I knew to read it, as it would bring me a great deal of embarrassment, no matter what state it was in. Not that

I think it is bad or anything, but this particular work stems from personal thoughts and such like, the kind that you normally keep totally private. To be honest, when I finally finished it I seriously considered writing a completely different story and submitting that instead, so I don't think that I would be able to contribute my story to be read by our "community of writers". Sorry about that, but until I change my mind, (which is always possible), I would like it just to be read by teachers etc. not friends. I hope you understand.

Once again, thank you for your detailed analysis of my writing. I am sure that your efforts have improved my writing style and ideas markedly.

R.P.

## The variety of the forms and approaches

The writing included autobiographies, biographies of parents and relations, experiments in prose-poetry, stories for children, plays, historical fiction, reviews of writers' works (single author studies), detective stories, fantasy stories, science fiction, as well as more conventional short stories based on personal experience.

Jason's main character was an Australian fighting in the Vietnam War. Sandy's story was about a plane passenger who had drugs planted on him by another. David told the story of a character who, we realised gradually, was in the grip of mental illness. Michael used his character's thoughts to show the frustration of adolescence when freedom is blocked by dependence.

Margaret in 10E4 wrote a play about the end of the world, to be presented on a stage divided into three – the U.S. leader's office, the Russian leader's office, and a suburban family home. The same sort of thinking in each of the leaders' minds leads to needless panic with ominous results for the helpless citizens. Another boy from the same class did a series of reports on a helicopter accident on an oil rig. The different writers – doctor, engineer, rig worker – had different styles reflecting their different backgrounds and involvements.

Robert in 10E2 did a history of the world with each section introduced by a few lines of verse with a decidedly Biblical flavour that suited his theme of man's reckless treatment of the earth. Several of the works I read revelled in styles reminiscent of *Star*

*Wars* and *The Hobbit* combined. One of the earliest comments made by a teacher in reaction to the students' writing for the works was that it was amazing how students could establish and sustain a certain tone and style . . .

Quite a few students found history a source of inspiration for their works. Janine in 10E8 wrote a fictional biography based on her interviews with two different people on World War II's effects on children and on Jewish people . . .

Kristina in 10E8 wrote a work titled "On the Goldfields": "Many petitions have been sent to the N.S.W. Legislative Assembly against the Chinese. Ever since the Chinese have arrived they have been harassed and ridiculed. The anti-Chinese feeling was widespread on the diggings, but of course there are some whites who show some sympathy towards them. In fact after some of the riots that broke out, some of the injured Chinese were assisted by whites and they suffered beatings by the other whites for their efforts. You wouldn't catch me getting a beating just to help them." There are some problems with establishing point of view and language style and tense consistency in this excerpt, but it is an interesting synthesising of different elements that is going on . . .

Other students looked into their own families' histories. Adam in 10E3 wrote about his Aboriginal grandfather; another girl wrote about one of her forebears who was an "exile" — sent out from England not as a convict, but not allowed to return to England for a specified period either! Heidi in 10E10 wrote about her grandfather who was an inventor.

## PROMOTING REFLECTION ON TEXT AND SELF

'I had a choice . . . Because of what you had given me I had a choice.'
Susan, Open University student of English Literature,
to her course tutor, Frank, in the film *Educating Rita*,
based on Willy Russell's novel of the same name.

In the film, *Educating Rita*, the young working-class woman, Susan, develops not just an understanding of literature and the ability to write about it in an institutionally sanctioned (critical) way, but also an understanding of her world and an ability to act in it through her control of language. Susan's motives in enrolling in her Open

University Course may have involved the romantic hope of living a more glamorous life by becoming part of a culturally superior elite of academically qualified readers of socially approved 'good' books. However, after trying out a name (Rita) and styles of clothing that she sees as being intrinsic to the life style she aspires to, Susan eventually discovers herself and becomes a decision-making human being with control over her own learning and life. In accepting her own name and in settling for clothes that are comfortable for her to wear, she progresses beyond her tutor, Frank, in self-understanding and wisdom. Frank continues to call her Rita long after she has dropped the affectation, and in telling her that in taking the course in literature she has found only 'a different song to sing' rather than the better one she was looking for, he fails to recognise that Susan has learned a great deal more than the 'load of quotes and empty phrases' that he cynically believes constitutes learning in university literature courses. He fails to recognise that finding 'a different song to sing' at least involves the realisation that there are different songs, or alternative life styles, and that such realisation offers to those who have it the liberating power of choice. He fails to recognise that she is able to use her literary knowledge and language power as means of understanding herself and her world, whereas he is imprisoned by his knowledge because he doesn't use it for any purposes beyond itself.

In Susan's education, reading literature and talking and writing about it are the means, not the ends, of learning. Unfortunately, as Peter Medway points out, in many schools literature and language are seen as ends in themselves rather than the means to knowledge. 'The possibility of a language used heuristically as a means of interpreting and understanding, of making the world available to thought, does not seem to be allowed for in the prevailing implicit model of language.'[64]

In this short section, the emphasis is on ways of empowering students to understand themselves and their world through deconstructing texts and exploring their reactions to them. All students are entitled to an education in English that offers them choices. As English teachers, we can help students to shape their own lives by, first of all, making our purposes and procedures explicit to them, and then by giving them the knowledge and power to make conscious choices and to take responsibility for them.

## DECONSTRUCTING TEXTS

Deconstructing literary texts, as well as media texts and other forms of non-literary discourse (and, indeed, all artefacts of cultural production), is valuable to students if it is organised to help them to understand the ideologies of the texts and the processes of their own cultural shaping, and to use for their own purposes the rhetorics they have uncovered. There are facts they should know about literature and its language, and there are certain powers they can be helped to develop from knowing these facts. They should be taught that language structures reality; that literature is artificial — a construct of words; that literature is historically and culturally produced — and, therefore, ideological. With this knowledge, students can explore how the language of any literary text (or any structure of cultural transmission) works to produce its meanings and to communicate its ideology. An understanding of the rhetoric of literature not only gives students the power of being in conscious control of other people's literature but it can be used by them to make their own literature. Further, as Richard Exton says, 'Through a knowledge of the relationship between texts and the societies which produced them and the societies in which they are read' students can be made 'aware of the workings of those societies'.[65]

In his articles 'The Post-Structuralist Always Reads Twice' and 'The Language of Literature',[66] Exton shows how the insights of structuralism and post-structuralism can be used in the classroom to empower pupils. For example, here is his account of some work with a 'low ability' second-year class on Graham Greene's short story, 'I Spy'.

Drawing upon the idea of all narrative being the movement from one state of equilibrium through a disruption to another modified state of equilibrium — a concept deriving from the French structuralist, Todorov — I asked the pupils in pairs (so that ideas and hunches could be tested and shared), to note down a list of facts from the beginning and ending of the story which remained unchanged and another list of things that had changed. What was revealed was most illuminating. As well as making accessible to thirty "less able" 13-year-olds the central theme of the boy's feelings towards his father, the exercise also drew attention to the way that the mother in the story is totally marginalised: she is asleep in bed throughout! A whole range of issues could have been pursued with the class at this point, but the one I chose to concentrate on was the construction of the characters of father and son, using Barthes' notion of the semic code — the narrative code which operates as the organising principle for character. The class were asked to list similarities and differences between Charlie and his father, and through this exercise they developed deeper insights into the story, its language, form and structure. They noted what is made obvious in the story, the tugging at the collar and the use of proverbs, but they also explored more fully that other explicit similarity, the "doing things in the dark which frightened [them]". They were able to speculate most fruitfully upon the title of the story in relation to all this.[67]

In another example, Exton gave a mixed ability class of 15 to 16-year-olds the opening chapter of John Steinbeck's novel *Of Mice and Men*:

They were asked for their general impression of the characters of George and Lenny, and replied that Lenny was "soft" and that George was "hard". They were then asked to underline all the adverbs ending in -ly in the chapter, to list them according to whether they were attached to George or Lenny, and to divide them according to whether they felt the adverbs to be "soft" or "hard". What resulted was a confirmation of Lenny's softness but a discovery that George was as much "soft" as "hard".[68]

In this kind of work, Exton says, class groups were able to see that 'there is nothing "natural" about character, but that all character is constructed in language held in common by writer and reader, and that the language carries with it the assumptions of the society which generates it'.[69]

Examples of other activities that might involve students in understanding the constructedness, rhetorical methods and ideologies of texts include the following:
• comparing the openings of different novels by the same author to discover any general stylistic characteristics in setting scene and introducing characters;
• reading a number of novels by the same author to see if there are thematic preoccupations which indicate an embedded ideology and/or unconscious sub-text revealing the author's individual psychology;

- identifying the linguistic means by which different authors communicate mood, emotion and atmosphere in specific passages, and going on to rewrite some of the passages, changing the mood or emotion to its opposite (e.g. from impending disaster to expected happiness), or using the same methods to communicate similar feelings about personal experiences in the lives of the students themselves;

- exploring and comparing the narrative methods of different stories and novels and experimenting with such narrative viewpoints in writing about personal experience — for example, writing about the same event from a number of different viewpoints;

- presenting to students the lines of a poem or the paragraphs of a short story one at a time and asking them, at each stage, to explain how they think the poem or story will develop, and how each new line or paragraph confirms, modifies or alters their previous expectations and interpretations;

- showing students several drafts of professional writers' poems and stories, and discussing the effects of, and possible motives for, specific revisions;

- mixing into a poem a section from another poem, or prose piece, and asking students to identify the part that doesn't fit and to explain their decision. As Paul Ashton and David Marigold say, when students start 'to articulate what the differences are, they find themselves discussing line-length, tone and vocabulary, as well as the context of the poem' and thus begin to understand how poems work;[70] and

- passing on to students some of the 'secrets' of literary structuring by introducing, for discussion and experimental use, a formula for writing a story or novel, such as the one offered by L.M. Hannan and W. Hannan.[71] In one of the folios for teachers included in the kit accompanying their publication *English Part Three*, Hannan and Hannan illustrate their formula $C + P + T + I + X = NOVEL$ (where C is character, P is place, T is time, I is incident and X is climax), by offering a range of alternatives for each item. In their example, the character can be villain, coward, fool or cheat, etc., and child, old man, heiress, journalist, taxidriver or clergyman, etc. The place can be a city street, country house, in a political meeting or in a restaurant, etc. The time can be now, 1990 or war time, etc. The main incident can be two girls have their eyes on the same man, or several people are in a ridiculous accident, or one person is trying to use another's prestige and influence for his or her own ends, etc. And the climax can be a swindle, a double cross, a romance or a loss, etc. The invitation to students is to 'substitute in these formulas (or make up your own) and express the result as a whole novel'.

In activities like these, the important thing the English teacher is emphasising is not that students understand the meanings and methods of a particular work of literature, but that, as Richard Exton puts it, 'they can read any poem (or story or novel or play), have insight into how it works and how its meanings are produced, and also have a model for their own writing'.[72] Formal analysis of this kind is a means to an end of helping students to understand how social values are constructed and communicated in literary (and other) texts so they can interpret their ideological assumptions and implications.

Ian Reid gives examples of other empowering activities that are appropriate for classrooms that operate as 'literature studios' but which are spurned as being 'political' by teachers who see themselves as curators of 'literature galleries'. (As if there is any literary activity that is not political!) Reid suggests that students might be invited to explore the processes by which certain texts and authors are privileged over others in our society so that they come to understand how society's dominant ideologies are constructed and passed on. Such activities might help to demystify both literature and society for students.

> Even fairly young children could be given some research tasks: they could ask a librarian to explain how books get chosen for purchase. A letter might be sent from a class to the literary editor of a newspaper, inquiring into reasons for selecting this book or that reviewer . . . Senior students sitting public examinations might be keen to find out who determined their syllabus, and according to what criteria. At the upper levels of school it would also be appropriate to carry out a larger case study of the classicising of an individual author. How have the writings of Patrick White, for example, been institutionalised for us as "great literature"? When did they begin to enter school reading lists? . . .[73]

Other investigations of this kind that relate to issues raised earlier in this book include exploring the reasons for, and the effects of, radio's saturation level promotion of popular music compared with its almost total neglect of the Australian oral story, and trying to find out from universities, colleges and examination boards why such Australian writers as Brian Penton, Ruth Park, Dymphna Cusack, Vance Palmer, Eleanor Dark, Judah Waten, Frank Hardy, Gavin Casey and Dorothy Hewett never appear on their lists for study.

## EXPLORING SELF

Many of the classroom activities outlined in this chapter are designed to make students more conscious of their own identities and reading processes. Reflexive exploration of their own reactions to texts and of their own strategies for making sense of them is essential for the development of self-understanding and reading power. It is only by testing their initial responses to literature against the responses of others (as can happen in small groups) that students become aware of a range of possible alternative responses, and it is this awareness of possible alternatives that can lead them to see their own reactions as personal and to subject them to closer scrutiny.

The teacher's role in the development of students' reflexive understanding is crucial. Louise Rosenblatt gives the example of first-year female college students who rejected Shakespeare's *Antony and Cleopatra* because of their strong dislike of Cleopatra.

> The students were challenged to consider the basis for their antipathy. It finally became obvious that theirs was the point of view of the average woman to whose marital peace a person like Cleopatra would be a decided menace.[74]

When the teacher invited the students to consider what their reactions showed them about themselves, they came to recognise aspects of their values, beliefs and emotions that they had hitherto not been consciously aware were influencing their judgments. Louise Rosenblatt reports the reactions of a psychologist to the girls' initial responses:

> The students' reaction to Cleopatra was as much in terms of their present adolescent relationships as of any future adult situations. We tend to forget . . . that adolescents in their boy and girl relationships are already engaged in an intense emotional life

parallel to adult experiences. They are already, for instance, experiencing the disillusionments and triumphs of sex rivalry.[75]

It is important that students become aware that their reactions to specific texts say as much about themselves as they do about the texts, and that reflexively examining these reactions — too often seen as an embarrassment — can lead to deeper understanding of both self and text.

As we have already seen in Chapter Four, varying degrees of reflexive understanding can be taught at all developmental stages of response. In the interviews there are many examples of students becoming aware of aspects of their own values and identities in the act of talking about their responses to texts, as well as many examples of them making their own reading processes explicit to themselves. This reflexive understanding can be developed through the reading journal, if teachers actively encourage students to use it for these purposes, as well as through small group discussion. Occasionally it is valuable for students to write expressively about what happens in their heads while they are reading a book, as the following examples show.

Cliff Smith, Head of English at St Stanislaus College, Bathurst, asked students in his English classes to 'think of the best book you've ever read and write about what went on in your head while, and after, you read it'.[76] Before they wrote, Cliff explained to the students his purposes in setting the exercise and what he saw as its possible value to them. The first account is by Cliff himself. He chose to write about George Johnston's *My Brother Jack* trilogy and Katherine Paterson's *Bridge to Terabithia*.

Fascinated by my own choices and by my inability to separate them, I turned to my journals to find the following quotes:
(a) "Without her you could never have taken the road.
Ithaca had given you the beautiful voyage
But she has nothing more to give you.

And if you find her poor
Ithaca has not defrauded you.
With all the great wisdom you have gained.

With so much experience
You must surely have understood by then
What Ithaca means."

*Clean Straw for Nothing*

(b) "Jesse had come to value Leslie as his other, more exciting self — his way to Terabithia and all the worlds beyond . . . Leslie had failed him. She went and died when he needed her most. She went and left him . . . She had made him leave his old self behind and come into her world, and then before he was really at home in it but too late to go back, she had left him stranded there — Alone."

*Bridge to Terabithia*

Why did I find both reading experiences compelling? Subconsciously I must have known–the Ithaca-Terabithia symbol is what was working on me so powerfully. These novels did act as an "ice-axe to break the sea frozen inside us". I could "give myself" to the books. The re-created worlds of the novel were relevant. I could empathise so definitely with David Meredith and Jesse Aarons. I'd experienced similar traumas to those that they experienced, and I needed to see how *they* would cope, how they would act, and how they could change.

In their realism they offered positive reflection — hope. No fairytale ending. Aloneness is real and can be painful, but these novels show how it is necessary and valuable.

Reflections on David Meredith's experiences in the triology led me to adjust my attitude to some of my own reactions and values, and they led me to write (significantly, in the spectator role) of other possibilities, viz.:

"Ithaca has given me the voyage
but not the rhyme
Ithaca has given me the chance to fly,
to savour time.

Ithaca has offered butterfly days
whose memory now stays
and stirs within
let the butterfly flit, again." (Nov. '77)

One such change in personal attitudes was so connected with the notion of self-worth and integrity that it helped lead me to opting out of routine for a year: to "flit" in Europe. I'm quite sure that my attitudes to teaching were also altered irrevocably as a result.

I never wanted to *be* David Meredith or Jesse Aarons; I never wanted to *change* the story; I remained a detached observer in that sense, but I was compelled to share their feelings and to observe their actions, and then to compare them with my own in similar situations.

The next two pieces are extracts from more extensive comments by Year 9 students.

'I have not read all that many novels but the ones I have read have ranged from one extreem to another. But the novel that I liked the most, so far, is Arthur Clark's *2001, a Space Oddessy*.

'But why is it a "best book"? I regarded *2001* as my best book because it was more than just another shoot-em up, good guy always wins, science fiction story. It had a message behind it and was well thought out and written.

'The story began at the beginning of time when man was just evolving from the apes and went right through until about the year 2001.

'I thought it was a good book because of the somewhat unusual story line, because of the fact that you couldn't put it down in case you missed something, and because it had a message.

'So in summary, for a plain old novel to be a good one for *me* it has to be a little bit unusual, have a message behind it and be a science fiction story (sometimes).'

'When I read a good novel I subconsciously seem to put myself in the place of the main character/s in the book. So, in a sence, I have to keep on reading to find out what happens to me. It is like I am reading something that greatly concerns my livelyhood or something similar to that. I get so wound up about it I just can't wait to find out what happens next . . .

'Reading gives me a sort of enjoyement that I can't explain. It is as if I float off into another world where only the book and what is happening in it seem to matter. To me reading is a form of enjoyment, of relaxation. It makes the rest of the world seem far away and unreal.'

Here is the full report by a Year 11 student of his reaction to A.B. Facey's autobiography, *A Fortunate Life*.

'This novel is the best I've ever read for many reasons. It is written in simple language, but is at the same time very descriptive — it is easy to picture the settings scattered over

Western Australia. The book is deeply emotional, showing the incredible hard life that the autobiographer, A.B. Facey experienced. Moreover, it describes his ability to overcome any hardship.

'A.B. Facey's life is one of continual heartbreak – his father died when he was about 2, his mother left Victoria for Western Australia when he was 4, and then got remarried, making her own sons pay board when they came back. Facey went to work at other people's properties in W.A. at the age of 6, and was once whipped so hard that he was given life-long scars. Later on things seemed to look up a bit as Bert (Facey's name) came to work with tank-sinkers, drovers and such other men. This was short lived as he was sent to Gallipoli where he lost his brother and caught a large piece of schrapnel in his back, where it stayed for about 10 years. Then he got married, but after working hard to get a farm of his own, he lost it in the Depression. Bert survived all this – the continual rejection, the physical and mental pain of the slaughter at Anzac Cove, the loss of loved ones and his property he cherished. Bert beat all the odds and it is not surprising that he finds it impossible to believe in any God.

'I can relate very easily to the setting and the happenings, much of which was in the bush which I love – the pioneering of a distant corner of Australia. There is also much Australian history enclosed up in the novel, especially the historic battle at Gallipoli. One must sympathise with Bert because nothing every seemed to go right for him, yet he was not at all bitter about it, as can be seen from the title. One would expect the result of such hardship to be a cranky, pessimistic man, but Bert remained as good a bloke as ever, friendly and obliging; I really admire him for that and I suppose I began to look up to his character.

'The book was written only because of much encouragement from his family, and there is not once a hint of pride in his words, only the plain truth as it was seen through his honest eyes. Many a heroic deed was performed by Bert, but he wrote the book with a humility which would be hard to beat.

'Overall, I loved the book, I wish more like that were written. Not because Bert Facey, ex-soldier, ex-farmer, ex-labourer is a great novelist, using all the devices of English, but simply because it is an honestly written book, set in a great place and enhancing some of Australia's great history and man's ability to overcome the harsh conditions often presented to him in this timeless continent.'

In all of these responses the writers are shown in the act of becoming more conscious of their own values in making explicit the qualities they most admire in other people and in fiction. Such writing is, however, not the end, but rather the beginning of self-understanding. Having begun the process of reflective self-exploration in writing, students are then able to read over what they have written and reflect further on the implications of what they have said, perhaps going on to formulate more questions about themselves and their reading processes for deeper consideration. In this process of self-exploration, writing and talking are aids to reflection. The English novelist, E.M. Forster, expressed this idea exactly when he said, 'How do I know what I feel until I see what I say'.

Those students who are not sure what their reaction is to a book they have read, beyond making the vaguest of generalisations such as 'boring' or 'great', can be helped by being provided with copies of conflicting reviews of it and asked to mark with a tick the passages of each review which they agree with, and with a cross those passages they disagree with. In looking over what they have ticked and crossed, such students become much clearer about their own judgments of the book, and are thus better prepared to express and reflexively explore their own interpretations.

## A CLASSROOM EXAMPLE: USING THE ORAL STORY TO PROMOTE REFLECTION ON TEXT AND SELF

There are ways of slowing down the reading process so that readers can become conscious of the strategies they are using to make personal sense of literary texts. This conscious awareness of what they are doing when they read gives readers greater control over their reading and the power to reach higher levels of response. One of these ways of slowing down the reading process to develop readers' reflexive understanding of what they are doing is to teach a poem or short story by revealing its text line by line or sentence by sentence. (This has already been mentioned in Deconstructing Texts, p. 338, as one of the ways of helping students to understand the constructedness of literature.) A variation of this is to use the technique (adopted in the Bathurst interviews) of reading the opening paragraph of a short story or novel and inviting students to discuss their expectations, mental images, gap-filling activities and so on. One of the most productive and unanticipated results of the interviews was the way students developed a reflexive understanding of their own reading processes. However, the approach outlined here, as illustration, is that of using oral stories on tape and slowing down students' reading/responding processes by stopping the tape at appropriate stages of the story to invite them to consider the ways they are making meaning.

The use of taped oral stories to investigate and teach literary awareness was pioneered in Australia by Peter Moss of Adelaide University.[77] Working with 13 to 17-year-old secondary students, Moss found that all of them, including the least able ones, were 'capable of making mature judgements':

> The evidence from my investigation suggests that students are able to make much more acute judgements than we have assumed they were capable of. The oral tales used may not be as demanding as a Shakespeare play but that fact does not explain the levels of response. I make a two-fold speculative explanation. Firstly, the material is immediately assimilable because of the familiar voice patterns. This is not the same as "ease-of-assimilation" because a frequent complaint was that hard concentration was necessary. Secondly, no adult critical language was foisted upon the students. They were allowed to make judgements in their own language and no expectations were made upon them.[78]

As I have suggested earlier in this chapter, students' development in reading literature, in talking and writing about the literature they have read, and in telling and writing their own literature are all intimately interrelated and mutually supportive activities. We have already seen how the oral story is useful in the classroom as a form facilitating students' own creation of literature. Here, I want to explain how the oral story can be used as a text for literary analysis, along the lines of Moss's work, and to show how it can, at the same time, be used to help students to understand their own responding processes. It is a way of helping students to find what Margaret Spencer calls that 'list of secret things that all accomplished readers know yet never talk about'.[79]

The text below is the transcript of an oral tale collected by Moss.

The numbers in parentheses, (1) to (9), indicate the stages at which it is appropriate to stop the tape to invite students to consider 'what is happening in their heads'.

### The Death of Johnny Ah Kee
Outside Dalton up near the Carnarvon Ranges there, in the 1920s, there were two characters had selections there. One was an Aussie-born German descendent called Otto Schneider and half-way between his selection and Dalton, a Chinese, or half-Chinese bloke called Johnny Ah Kee, also had a selection.(1) So Otto Schneider's habit was to ride into Dalton once a month and pick up hard rations. He'd stay there for three days and get blind drunk, and then ride back. On the way in, he'd call in at Johnny Ah Kee's place, at his hut and they'd have a billy of tea and a bit of damper, and real old rough stuff, have a bit of a yarn and Otto would ride into Dalton.(2)

So on this particular occasion something went wrong and, at about just on dark at the police station at Dalton, Otto sings out, "Are you there sergeant?" And the sergeant comes out and looks around, and drooped across the withers of Otto Schneider's horse is a body, and it's the body of Johnny Ah Kee.(3) So the sergeant is quite upset and he says, "Yeh, we'll get him off." So they take the body off and put it in the lock up — or somewhere. He said, "Well you better tell me the story." "Well," he said, "I come through there today and I usually have a billy of tea with Johnny." He said, "When I got there he was lying flat on his back outside the hut, dead." "Jesus" he said, "And you brought him in fifteen miles on a horse?" "Yeh", he said. "But Jesus", he said, "He'd weigh about fourteen stone."(4) "Yeh," he said "I knew that of course. I had to gut him first."(5)

So the sergeant suddenly realises he's got a bit of a problem on his hands. He said, "Now what are you going to do Otto?" He said, "I'm going around the pub. I'll put me horse in the stables and I'll just box on today and tomorrow." So the sergeant gets a bit upset, a bit worried and he rings up the inspector in Toowoomba, and tells him what his problem is, that he's got a corpse on his hands and the corpse has been disembowelled and so and so. So the inspector blows his top. He says, "Do you realise what you've got on your hands? You've got an unsolved crime on your hands." He says, "Somebody brings in a body", blah, blah,

blah. He says, "You've got to go out — tell this bloke Otto Schneider," he said, "to go out and get the contents of his stomach where he disembowelled him."(6) So the sergeant goes round to the pub and Otto is boozing on. So he puts it to him and he says, "No, you got to go Otto." And he gets a canvas bag from the PMG Department or somewhere, some water-tight bag. He said, "Otto you've just go to do it. First thing tomorrow morning go out. This is an unsolved crime." He said, "We're in trouble, I'm in trouble. You're in trouble. The police inspector is in trouble, everybody's in trouble."(7) So Otto, much against his will, rides off at daybreak on the Saturday morning. Rides out fifteen miles. So he's back about four o'clock in the afternoon and there's the PMG mail bag tied on the dees of his saddle. Nothing in it. And the sergeant said, "Didn't you get it?"(8) "No," he said, "it's all fixed." He said, "All fixed". He said, "clear case of poisoning". He said, "When I got there, there was no guts left, but there were four dead dingoes."(9)

Fictitious names are used in this transcript.[80]

The kinds of questions that can be used for discussion at each of the 'stops' and at the end of the story, are set out below. Each of these questions can be asked and discussed at a range of levels, according to the audience. I have formulated the questions in language that would be familiar only to those who have some acquaintance with contemporary 'reader-response' literary theory (such as readers of this book).

## 1. Mental images

Q: What *mental images* are you forming while reading/listening? Are they pictorially sharp? Semantically sharp? Both? What is your impression of Dalton and the surrounding countryside? What meanings and feelings are associated with it? What experience (first and second order) can you draw on to form these mental images?

Q: What are your *mental images* (pictorial and semantic) of Otto Schneider, Johnny Ah Kee and the police sergeant?

Apart from drawing on their cultural knowledge and personal experience (see 3. below) to fill in the gaps (see 4. below) to form these mental images, students become aware of their own cultural stereotypes of German and Chinese people, so that, at stop (4) on the tape, the information that Johnny Ah Kee weighed 14 stone produces shocked laughter.

## 2. Forming expectations

Q: What are your *expectations* about the way the story will develop at each stage of reading/listening? How will it end? What do you expect will be the tone of the ending? Will you be laughing or crying or . . .?

Good readers generate expectations about the possible developments of a story, and look ahead for the kind of information that will help them to solve the puzzles they have formulated. They also reinterpret past story events in the light of what they are discovering at the present reading moment. The complex possibilities of the action and the shifts of tone in this story keep readers continually guessing, and searching for clues as to the appropriate reactions to the events. Sometimes expectations are raised only to be dashed!

Predicting what might be ahead, and modifying, correcting and extending impressions formed are active, moment-by-moment activities that can be developed by teaching.

## 3. The repertoire

Q: What cultural understanding and experiences from your own life do you bring to your understanding and interpretation of the story?

Personal experience and knowledge is not an intrusive irrelevance to textual understanding, but essential to it. Forming connections between personal experience and text through anecdote should be encouraged. English and American listeners, for example, would probably have difficulties with the term 'selection', which would be familiar to many Australians.

Q: What structures and conventions of literature have you mastered that enable you to understand the story and the way it works?

The more books we have read, the better readers we are likely to become as we learn to understand and internalise the conventions and structures. Most Australian listeners to this story would be familiar with the outback yarn as a genre of fiction.

## 4. Filling in the gaps or blanks in the text

Q: What semantic *gaps* or *blanks* are you filling in while reading/listening? What connections between events are you making?

Gaps or indeterminancies create puzzles for the reader, challenging her/him to participate in making meaning of the text, to become a collaborator or co-author. Establishing connections between events, details, characters, etc. leads to the formulation of meaning. Meaning is formulated by the reader, not by the text. Students can be helped to actively question and argue with the text by being encouraged to formulate their own questions arising from their own puzzlement rather than being directed to answer the questions set by the teacher. (For example, see the questions listed on p. 126.)

## 5. Matching representations of the world with the author

Q: Does the story confirm, extend, modify or change the impression you (previously) held of:
   (a) Australia, Australians and the Australian way of life?
   (b) The Australian short story?

Q: Do you see the narrator as an educated man? Uncouth? Barbaric? What do you think of his use of language? Is he a good yarn spinner or not?

The literary work can teach us new ways of understanding, so we can recognise the limitations of our routine habits of perception.

## 6. Reflexiveness

Q: What are you learning about yourself from:
   (a) Your ongoing responses to, and final interpretation of, this story?
   (b) Your answers to question 5 above?

Examine your criteria of evaluation. We can learn to understand ourselves by analysing our own responses to literature. Psychoanalytical critics like Norman Holland claim we recreate works of literature in terms of our own identity and according to our characteristic patterns of adaptation and defence in the world — i.e. we will find in a work the kind of thing we characteristically fear or wish most.

Students can be given more control of their own reading processes by knowing about them. They can also be made aware of how authors influence and interest them. Such kinds of self-knowledge are forms of personal power.

## 7. The relationship between the implied author and the implied reader

Q: Who is the implied author in the tale? What kind of person does the text suggest s/he is?

The young reader needs to find in the story an implied author 'whom he can befriend and thus be wooed into the book'.[81]

Q: Who is the implied reader/listener, the one addressed by the author and constructed by the text?

The reader has to become, at least temporarily, the implied reader the text demands.

Q: How does the author establish his tone — his relationship with his implied reader/listener? What techniques does the author use to draw the reader/listener into the text in such a way that the reader/listener accepts the role offered (of implied reader) and enters into the demands of the work?

These questions invite readers/listeners to deconstruct the text and make explicit its rhetorical methods.

## 8 Textual and critical ideology

*Textual Ideology*
Q: How does the author invite us to feel about outback characters like Otto Schneider? Are we expected to feel any differently about the police? What is the author's ideology in portraying outback people and their lives the way s/he does?

*Critical Ideology*
Q: What theoretical or ideological predilections mediate between you and the text? Do you automatically respond to it as Coleridge or Leavis or Richards or Eliot or the American New Critics or the Structuralists would?

Have you, therefore, internalised one particular critical theory which you regard as the best or the only or the most natural one?

Our perceptual strategies are socially/historically influenced, conditioned, determined(?). Every critical theory is ideological. Knowing this is a form of power, which enables us to recognise the processes of our own cultural shaping.

If you don't agree with this statement ask yourself what are your criteria for distinguishing between 'literary' and 'extra-literary' judgments about literature. Are there any judgments about literature that could be said to be 'non-literary'? Who says so? Why?

In using an approach like this to slow down the reading process so that readers become aware of their own and, perhaps, other, more productive processes of meaning-making, it is important to remember that methods are means to ends and not ends in themselves. Work such as this could so easily degenerate into a pointless exercise if it became a mere regular routine in the classroom. Teachers must always have clearly understood purposes in doing what they do, and these should be made explicit to students. Oral stories can be used productively as literary texts to teach students how to read more deeply. However, they should not be used in this way regularly or routinely. Often they will be best played straight through and enjoyed with or without discussion following. Methods and activities in the classroom should be varied.

Novels, printed stories and poems can also be used in much the same way as the taped oral stories in a slowing down of the reading process to make students more conscious of literary structures and to teach them to read more effectively. An excellent example of a novel that does just this in the way it is written, and without any necessary help from the teacher by way of presentation, is Aidan Chambers' *Breaktime* which specifically addresses its implied readers as 'new adults' on the dust-jacket and title page, and teaches its readers the kind of active reading it requires. As Terry Eagleton points out,

> We read a scribbled note from a friend without paying much attention to its narrative structure, but if a story breaks off and begins again, switches constantly from one narrative level to another and delays its climax to keep us in suspense, we become freshly conscious of how it is constructed at the same time as our engagement with it may be intensified.[82]

In *Breaktime*, the many shifts in narrative viewpoint and the varied methods of construction are deliberately made obvious without any weakening of interest in the story itself, so that in reading an enjoyable novel, young readers are made entertainingly and consciously aware of the author's construction processes and their own reading processes. Further, students might well be interested in trying to find out why such an outstanding novel for teenagers as *Breaktime* was not, until 1985, available in paperback when it was first published in 1978. Questions such as this arise in the English class only when the traditional definitions of 'literary' and 'non-literary' are challenged. Why do 'literature', 'commerce' and 'politics' have to be mutually exclusive categories? When the restrictive boundaries of old categories are broken down, there is a greater space created for new thinking, and it is in that more open territory that we want our students to be.

And approach to the meaning restores the experience
In a different form.

T.S. Eliot, 'The Dry Salvages'
*Four Quartets*


## REFERENCES

1. Harold Rosen, 'Narratology and the Teacher', in Harold Rosen, *Stories and Meanings*, NATE Papers in Education, National Association for the Teaching of English, Sheffield, 1983.
2. Lola Brown, 'Do We Teach the Way We Read?', *English in Australia*, no. 62, October 1982.
3. Ibid., p. 34.
4. Loc. cit.
5. Peter Medway, 'Doing Teaching English', in Margaret Meek and Jane Miller (eds), *Changing English: Essays for Harold Rosen*, Heinemann Educational Books, London, 1984, pp. 135-6.
6. Ibid., p. 141
7. Garth Boomer, 'The Politics of Drama Teaching', in Meek and Miller (eds), *Changing English: Essays for Harold Rosen*, p. 114.
8. Ibid., p. 152.
9. Loc. cit.
10. Garth Boomer, 'Negotiation Revisited', *Interpretations*, vol. 16, no. 2, November 1982, p. 5.
11. John Dixon, 'Imaginative Encounters with Life', *English in Australia*, no. 47, March 1979.

12. John Carroll, 'Language, the Role of the Teacher and Drama in Education', *English in Australia*, no. 53, September 1980.
13. Ibid., p. 35.
14. Ibid., p. 40.
15. Loc. cit.
16. Ibid., p. 41.
17. Loc. cit.
18. Harold Rosen, 'Narratology and the Teacher', in Harold Rosen, *Stories and Meanings*, p. 24.
19. Margaret Meek, 'How Do They Know Its Worth It?', in Roslyn Arnold (ed.), *Timely Voices: English Teaching in the 1980s*, OUP, Melbourne, 1983, p. 152.
20. Margaret Early, 'Stages in the Growth of Literary Appreciation', *The English Journal*, vol. XLIX, March 1960.
21. Clark McKowen, 'English for Everyone', *The English Journal*, November 1963, National Council of Teachers of English, Champaign, Illinois.
22. This is an edited version of Gary Whale and Ken Patino's article of the same title submitted to *The Secondary Journal*, NSW Department of Education.
23. in Jane Miller (ed.), *Eccentric Propositions: Essays on Literature and the Curriculum*, Routledge and Kegan Paul, London, 1984.
24. James Britton *et al.*, *The Development of Writing Abilities (11-18)*, Macmillan, The Schools Council, 1975; Douglas Barnes, James Britton and Harold Rosen, *Language, the Learner and the School*, Penguin, Educational, 1971.
25. David Jackson, *Continuity in Secondary English*, Methuen, London, 1982, p. 210.
26. Brian Johnston, *Assessing English*, St. Clair Press, Sydney, 1983, p. 99.
27. Jackson, *Continuity in Secondary English*, p. 106.
28. Jane Ogborn, 'Teaching A Level: A Two Year Plan', *The English Magazine*, no. 12, Spring 1984, Inner London Education Authority English Centre, p. 18.
29. Barry Cooper, 'Response to Literature and Implications for the Classroom', in a limited circulation journal of the post-graduate Language in Education course, Mitchell College of Advanced Education, Bathurst, Autumn Semester, 1983.
30. David Moss, 'The Role of Small Group Discussion in the Teaching of Poetry', in a limited circulation journal of the post-

graduate Language in Education course, Mitchell College of Advanced Education, Autumn Semester, 1983.

31. Ibid.

32. Cliff Smith, 'Small Group Work in the Classroom', in a limited circulation journal of the post-graduate Language in Education course, Mitchell College of Advanced Education, Spring Semester, 1984.

33. John Dixon, 'English Literature – a course in writing', in Arnold (ed.), *Timely Voices*, p. 57.

34. Quoted in Brown, 'Do We Teach the Way We Read', *English in Australia*, p. 34.

35. Ibid., p. 35.

36. Jane Ogborn, 'Teaching A Level: A Two Year Plan', *The English Magazine*, p. 18.

37. John Dixon, 'English Literature – a course in writing'.

38. Ibid., p. 60.

39. David Jackson, *Encounters With Books: Teaching Fiction 11-16*, Methuen, London, 1983, p. 173.

40. John Dixon, *Growth Through English*, NATE, Oxford University Press, Second Edition 1969, p. 91.

41. Britton *et al.*, *The Development of Writing Abilities (11-18)*.

42. Ibid., p. 3.

43. Ibid., p. 4.

44. Ibid., p. 83.

45. Quoted in James Britton, *Language and Learning*, Pelican, Harmondsworth, 1972, p. 166.

46. Britton *et. al.*, *The Development of Writing Abilities (11-18)*, p. 11.

47. David Mallick, 'Text and Reader', in David Mallick, Peter Moss, Ian Hansen (eds), *New Essays in the Teaching of Literature*, Proceedings of the Literature Commission, Third International Conference on the Teaching of English, Sydney, 1980, p. 211.

48. I am indebted to Gary Whale, Head of English at Casino High School, for this piece of writing.

49. I am indebted to Barry Cooper, Head of English at Woolooware High School, for this piece of writing.

50. Britton *et. al.*, *The Development of Writing Abilities (11-18)*, p. 158.

51. John Dixon and Leslie Stratta, Literature Seminar, 'What do we want out of character studies?' unpublished paper, October 1984.

52. Norman Holland, *Poems in Persons*, Horton, New York, 1973, p. 3.
53. John Dixon, 'Taking Too Much for Granted? A Level Literature and Its Assessment', *The English Magazine*, no. 12, Spring 1984, p. 30.
54. Leslie Stratta, John Dixon and Andrew Wilkinson, *Patterns of Language*, Heinemann, London, 1973, p. 87.
55. D. W. Harding, 'Considered Experience: The Invitation of the Novel', *English in Education*, vol. 2, no. 1, Summer 1967, p. 13.
56. Ibid., p. 14.
57. I am indebted to Roberta Baker and Robyn Balderstone for providing this piece of writing by a Year 5 pupil.
58. Ian Reid, *The Making of Literature: Texts, Contexts and Classroom Practices*, Australian Association for the Teaching of English, 1984, pp. 28-9.
59. D.W. Harding, 'Psychological Processes in the Reading of Fiction', *British Journal of Aesthetics*, 2, 1962, p. 138.
60. Peter Moss, 'Oral Stories and Literary Awareness', *English in Australia*, no. 46, November 1978, p. 25; see also *Telling Tales: Australian Voices*, Australian Studies in Language in Education, Curriculum Development Centre, Canberra, 1977, in which Moss gives an account of his work and includes transcripts of a range of Australian oral stories.
61. Keith Garvey, *Tales of My Uncle Harry*, Australian Broadcasting Commission, in association with Hodder and Stoughton, Sydney, 1978, text and cassette tape.
62. Donald H. Graves, *Writing: Teachers and Children At Work*, Heinemann, Exeter, New Hampshire, 1983.
63. Helen Esmond, 'Major Works in Year 10 English Assessment, Galston High School, 1984', an unpublished dissertation for the postgraduate Language in Education course, Mitchell College of Advanced Education, Bathurst.
64. Peter Medway, 'Doing Teaching English', in Meek and Miller (eds), *Essays for Harold Rosen*, p. 139.
65. Richard Exton, 'The Post-Structuralist Always Reads Twice', *The English Magazine*, no. 10, 1983, p. 18.
66. Richard Exton, 'The Language of Literature', in Jane Miller (ed.), *Eccentric Propositions: Essays on Literature and the Curriculum*, Routledge and Kegan Paul, London, 1984.
67. Ibid., p. 73.
68. Exton, 'The Post-Structuralist Always Reads Twice', p. 18.

69. Loc. cit.
70. Paul Ashton and David Marigold, 'Poetry in the First Three Years of Secondary School', in Miller (ed.), *Eccentric Propositions*, p. 119.
71. L.M. Hannan and W. Hannan, *English Part Three*, Teachers Folio, Cheshire, Melbourne, 1971.
72. Exton, 'The Language of Literature', in Miller (ed.), *Eccentric Propositions*, p. 77.
73. Ian Reid, 'Literature in the Making', in Bill Green (ed.), *Life in Literature/Literature in Life*, Proceedings of a Joint Conference of the English Teachers' Association of Western Australia, Library Association of Australia School Libraries Section (WA Group), Reading Association of Western Australia, December 1983, p. 13.
74. Louise M. Rosenblatt, *Literature As Exploration*, Noble and Noble, New York, 1968, p. 231.
75. Loc. cit.
76. Cliff Smith, Assignment Activity 4, 'Response to Literature and Implications for the Classroom', in the unit New Developments in the Teaching of English, post-graduate Language in Education Course, Mitchell College of Advanced Education, Bathurst, Autumn Semester 1985.
77. Moss, *Telling Tales: Australian Voices*, and 'Oral Stories and Literary Awareness'.
78. Moss, 'Oral Stories and Literary Awareness', p. 35.
79. Margaret Spencer, 'Children's Literature: Mainstream Text or Optional Extra?' in R.D. Eagleson (ed.), *English in the Eighties*, Australian Association for the Teaching of English, Adelaide, 1982, p. 126.
80. Moss, *Telling Tales: Australian Voices*, pp. 26-7.
81. Aidan Chambers, 'The Reader in the Book', *Signal*, no. 23, 1977.
82. Terry Eagleton, *Literary Theory: An Introduction*, Basil Blackwell, Oxford, 1983, p. 4.

# Response to Literature

| Process Stages: Kinds of Satisfaction | Degree of Intensity of Interest | |
| --- | --- | --- |
| (Requirements for satisfaction at all stages: enjoyment and elementary understanding) | Weak Passive | Strong Active |
| 1. Unreflective interest in action | ←——————→ | |
| 2. Empathising | ←——————→ | |
| 3. Analogising | ←——————→ | |
| 4. Reflecting on the significance of events (theme) and behaviour (distanced evaluation of characters) | ←——————→ | |
| 5. Reviewing the whole work as the author's creation | ←——————→ | |
| 6. Consciously considered relationship with the author, recognition of textual ideology, and understanding of self (identity theme) and of one's own reading processes | ←——————→ | |

# A Developmental Model

| Degree of Sophistication of Response | | Process Strategies |
|---|---|---|
| ple Rudi- ary | Developed and Subtle | |
| → | | (a) Rudimentary mental images (stereotypes from film and television) <br> (b) Predicting what might happen next in the short term |
| → | | (c) Mental images of affect <br> (d) Expectations about characters |
| → | | (e) Drawing on the repertoire of personal experiences, making connections between characters and one's own life |
| → | | (f) Generating expectations about alternative possible long-term outcomes <br> (g) Interrogating the text, filling in gaps, <br> (h) Formulating puzzles, enigmas, accepting hermeneutic challenges |
| → | | (i) Drawing on literary and cultural repertoires <br> (j) Interrogating the text to match the author's representation with one's own <br> (k) Recognition of implied author |
| → | | (l) Recognition of implied reader in the text, and the relationship between implied reader <br> (m) Reflexiveness, leading to understanding of textual ideology, personal identity and one's own reading processes |

362

SELECTED BIBLIOIGRAPHY: BOOKS AND ARTICLES

Roslyn Arnold (ed.), *Timely Voices: English Teaching in the Eighties*, OUP, Melbourne, 1983.
Roland Barthes, *S/Z*, translated by Richard Miller, Hill and Wang, New York, 1974.
Jean Blunt, 'Response to Reading: How some young readers describe the process', *English in Education*, vol. 11, no. 3, Autumn 1977, pp. 34-47.
Garth Boomer, *Negotiating the Curriculum*, Ashton Scholastic, Sydney, 1982.
Garth Boomer, 'Negotiation Re-visited', *Interpretations*, vol. 16, no. 2, November, 1982.
James Britton, Tony Burgess, Nancy Martin, Alex McLeod and Harold Rosen, *The Development of Writing Abilities (11-18)*, The Schools Council, Macmillan, 1975.
Rhonda Bunbury, Ern Finnis, Geoff Williams, 'Teachers Talk About Their Teaching of Fiction, A Preliminary Report of the National Reading Project, Children's Choice', *English in Australia*, no. 64, June 1983, pp. 3-15.
Aidan Chambers, 'The Reader in The Book', *Signal*, no. 23, May 1977.
Jonathan Culler, *Structuralist Poetics: Structuralism, Linguistics and the Study of Literature*, Routledge and Kegan Paul, London, 1975.
Jonathan Culler, *The Pursuit of Signs: Semiotics, Literature, Deconstruction*, Routledge and Kegan Paul, London, 1981.
Jonathan Culler, *On Deconstruction: Theory and Criticism After Structuralism*, Routledge and Kegan Paul, London, 1983.
Pat D'Arcy, *Reading for Meaning*, Volume 2: *The Reader's Response*, The Schools Council, Hutchinson, London, 1973.
John Docker, *In A Critical Condition: Reading Australian Literature*, Penguin, Ringwood, Victoria, 1984.
Terry Eagleton, *Literary Theory: An Introduction*, Basil Blackwell, Oxford, 1983.
D.W. Harding, 'The Role of the Onlooker', in *Scrutiny*, vol. 6, no. 3, 1937, pp. 247-258, reprinted in Asher Cashdan (ed.), *Language in Education: A Source Book*, Routledge and Kegan Paul and The Open University Press, London, 1972, pp. 240-244.
D.W. Harding, 'Psychological Processes in The Reading of Fiction', *British Journal of Aesthetics*, 2, 1962, pp. 133-147.

D.W. Harding, 'Considered Experience: The Invitation of the Novel', *English in Education*, vol. 2, No. 1, Summer 1967.

D.W. Harding, 'The Bond with the Author', *The Use of English*, vol. 22, no. 4, Summer 1971.

Wolfgang Iser, *The Act of Reading: A Theory of Aesthetic Response*, Routledge and Kegan Paul, London, 1978.

David Jackson, *Continuity in Secondary English*, Methuen, London, 1982.

David Jackson, *Encounters with Books: Teaching Fiction 11-16*, Methuen, London, 1983.

Brian Johnston, *Assessing English: Helping Students to reflect on their work*, St. Clair Press, Sydney, 1983.

David Mallick, Peter Moss, Ian Hansen (eds), *New Essays in the Teaching of Literature*, Proceedings of the Literature Commission, Third International Conference on the Teaching of English, Sydney, 1980.

Margaret Meek, Aidan Warlow and Griselda Barton (eds), *The Cool Web: The Pattern of Children's Reading*, The Bodley Head, London, 1977.

Margaret Meek, with Stephen Armstrong, Vicky Austerfield, Judith Graham, Elizabeth Plackett, *Achieving Literacy: Longitudinal Studies of Adolescents Learning to Read*, Routledge and Kegan Paul, London, 1983.

Margaret Meek and Jane Miller (eds), *Changing English: Essays for Harold Rosen*, Heinemann, London, 1984.

Jane Miller (ed.), *Eccentric Propositions: Essays on Literature and The Curriculum*, Routledge and Kegan Paul, London, 1984.

Peter Moss, *Telling Tales: Australian Voices*, Australian Studies in Language in Education, Curriculum Development Centre, Canberra, 1977.

Elaine Pascoe and Margaret Gilchrist, 'A Study of Reluctant Readers, Children Who Least Enjoy Literature', in Stuart Lee (ed.), *Issues 1984*, Primary English Teaching Association, Sydney, 1984.

Robert Protherough, *Developing Response to Fiction*, Open University Press, Milton Keynes, 1983.

Ian Reid, *The Making of Literature: Texts, Contexts and Classroom Practices*, Australian Association for the Teaching of English, 1984.

Harold Rosen, *Stories and Meanings*, NATE Papers in Education, National Association for the Teaching of English, London, 1983.

Louise M. Rosenblatt, *Literature As Exploration*, Noble and Noble, New York, 1968.

Leslie Stratta, John Dixon and Andrew Wilkinson, *Patterns of Language: Explorations in the Teaching of English*, Heinemann, London, 1973.

Jack Thomson, 'Response to Reading: The Process as Described by one Fourteen-year-old', *English in Education*, vol. 13, no. 3, Autumn 1979.

Jane P. Tompkins (ed.), *Reader-Response Criticism: From Formalism to Post-Structuralism*, John Hopkins, University Press, Baltimore, 1980.

Kevin Tindall, David Reid and Neville Goodwin, *Television's Children*, Sydney Teachers' College Audio-Visual Research Centre, 1975.

Kevin Tindall, David Reid, and Neville Goodwin, *Television: 20th Century Cyclops*, Sydney Teachers' College Audio-Visual Research Centre, 1977.

R.D. Walshe, Dot Jensen and Tony Moore (eds), *Teaching Literature*, Primary English Teaching Association, and English Teachers' Association of N.S.W., Sydney, 1983.

Ken Watson, 'The Reading Habits of Secondary School Pupils in N.S.W.', in *English in Australia*, no. 46, November 1978, pp. 68-77.

Ken Watson (ed.), *Reading Is Response*, St. Clair Press, Sydney, 1980.

Frank Whitehead, A.C. Capey, Wendy Maddren and Alan Wellings, *Children and Their Books*, The Schools Council, Macmillan, 1977.

W.K. Wimsatt and Monroe Beardsley, 'The Affective Fallacy' in W.K. Wimsatt, *The Verbal Icon: Studies in the Meaning of Poetry*, Lexington, Kentucky, 1954, reprinted in David Lodge (ed.), *20th Century Literary Criticism: A Reader*, Longman, Harlow, 1972, pp. 345-358.

# Index